AIR WARFARE IN THE MISSILE AGE

Lon O. Nordeen, Jr.

SMITHSONIAN INSTITUTION PRESS
Washington, D.C.

Library of Congress Cataloging in Publication Data

Nordeen, Lon O., 1953-
  Air warfare in the missile age.

  Bibliography: p.
  Includes index.
  1. Air warfare—History. 2. Military history, Modern—
20th century. I. Title.
UG630.N564   1985   358.4′009′04   85-600029
ISBN 0-87474-680-9 (alk. paper)

Printed in the United States of America

The paper in this book meets the guidelines for permanence
and durability of the Committee on Production Guidelines
for Book Longevity of the Council on Library Resources.

Design: Ernest McIver / McIver Art

Contents

Acknowledgments

The author is indebted to a large number of individuals for their assistance in preparing the manuscript for publication and the collection of photographs: Dana Bell; Jerry Broening; Glenn Connor; Lt. Comdr. Randy Cunningham, USN; Julian and Lillian Farren; Bruce Frisch; William Green; Jerrey Gray; Bob Hanes; Dottie Hombach; David Isby; Shirley King; J. Margulies; Tim McGovern; John Memmolo; Michael O'Connor; R. Schall; Gp. Capt. A. Shah, Pakistan Air Force; Air Com. M. I. Singh, Indian Air Force; Col. A. Shoemaker; Capt. M. Steadman, USAF; Lt. Col. B. Watts, USAF; Jim Stevenson; Major B. Williams, USAF.

Trudy E. Bell made significant editorial contributions to the manuscript.

David L. Parsons deserves special mention for his assistance. His efforts have been substantial and are gratefully acknowledged.

Suzy and Brad deserve special thanks for their patience and understanding.

Introduction

The major aim of air warfare is to help ground and naval forces gain control over desired territory or sea lanes for tactical and strategic purposes. In so doing, the key is to avoid or eliminate threats to one's own aircraft, ground forces, or ships while exacting maximum damage to the enemy. Although an essential element of warfare, air power has never won a war on its own.

Air warfare can be offensive or defensive, and has several components usually operating in concert. Most frequently, the goal of offensive air warfare is the *destruction of enemy aircraft, men, or material*. One major component is interdiction: bombers or attack aircraft flown against important enemy targets—usually factories, supply routes, ports, railroads, bridges, and the like—to disrupt the enemy's industrial base and transportation network supplying battlefields. For example, the U.S. military's bombing of North Vietnamese transportation routes to stem the flow of supplies to Viet Cong insurgents in the South. Interdiction has played a role in most air wars.

A second component of air warfare is *air superiority:* Shooting down enemy planes to allow friendly planes to dominate the air. Air superiority is the task of fighters, which also escort and protect bombers en route to targets. It is in the air-superiority role that fighters engage in aerial combat. This can be interceptor-type combat beyond visual range detection and attack with missiles or air-to-air dogfighting at close visual range.

The United States attempted to gain air superiority over North Vietnam in the 1960s and early 1970s, to protect bombers interdicting supply routes and attacking industrial targets.

A third component of air warfare is *offensive counter-air:* attacking an enemy's airfields to prevent aerial threats. The potency of offensive counter-air attacks was demonstrated in 1967's Six-Day War when waves of Israeli aircraft in surprise attacks against Arab airfields destroyed more than 300 planes on the ground in less than two days. This surgical effort virtually destroyed a numerically superior force. Offensive counter-air was also successfully employed in 1971 by the Indian Air Force in the Indo-Pakistan War.

A fourth component of air warfare is tactical bombing or *close air support* to support troops either engaged with enemy units or in close proximity. During the Vietnam conflict, the United States relied heavily on close air support against Viet Cong or North Vietnamese forces.

Air warfare must be viewed in the context of a conflict's greater military and political aims. The advent of air-to-air and surface-to-air missiles altered the technology and tactics of modern air warfare; the political environment not only created conflicts but often altered the face of the conflict. For example, the rules of engagement that governed U.S. air power in North Vietnam or the decision by Israel on the eve of the Yom Kippur War not to launch a preemptive first strike in self-defense.

The book is a general history and overview of the role played by military aviation in the wars of the past two decades. This period saw the widespread introduction of tactical air-to-air, surface-to-air, and air-to-surface missiles. The book is based on openly available unclassified sources.

The historical and political background of each conflict is reviewed, followed by a chronicle of events. The summary includes a discussion of how aircraft, weapons, tactics, training, political aspects, and other factors influenced the outcome of battle. The final chapters of the book discuss past and present generation tactical aircraft, weapons, and equipment.

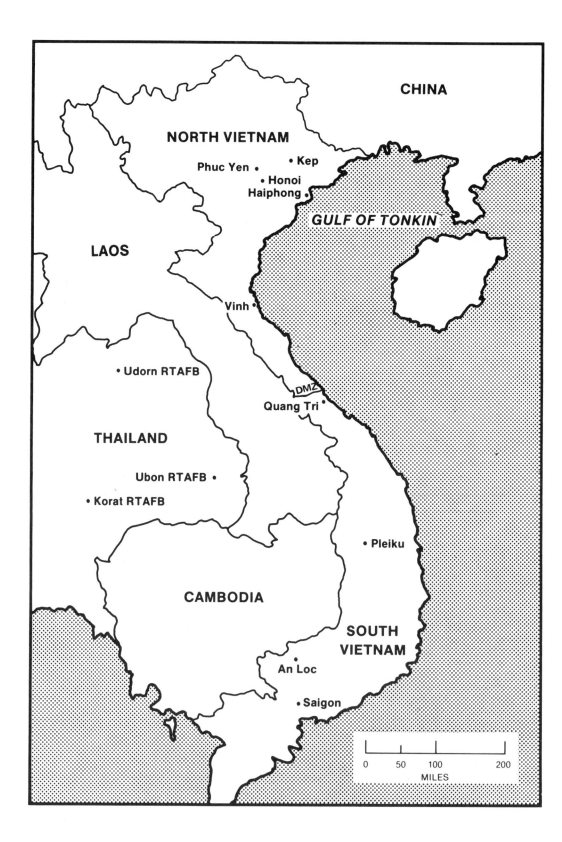

CHAPTER I

Rolling Thunder:
North Vietnam, 1964-1968

Introductory Overview

In the very beginning of August 1964, North Vietnamese torpedo boats opened fire on the American destroyer U.S.S. *Maddox*, which was on surveillance patrol in international waters. As a result, the U.S. Joint Chiefs of Staff approved punitive air strikes against North Vietnamese naval bases. The Congress of the United States passed the Gulf of Tonkin Resolution, giving President Lyndon B. Johnson blanket authority to commit U.S. military units to Southeast Asia.

By 1965 it was evident that, under Soviet sponsorship, North Vietnamese defenses were extensively building up.

Not only did the North Vietnamese Air Force flex its muscles for the first time in that year, but the occasional conflicts also saw extensive use of the then-new Soviet built SA-2 surface-to-air missile. Vietnam soon became the proving ground for United States and USSR technology and tactical concepts. The Hanoi regime relied on the Soviet pattern of ground-controlled interceptors, radar-directed antiaircraft artillery, smaller caliber visually-sighted automatic weapons, and surface-to-air missiles—all of which were tied into an integrated air-defense network that relied on a great number of radar stations for early warning and tracking of approaching U.S. aircraft. With each passing month, the United States faced an increasingly sophisticated and heavily concentrated air defense network. The United States quickly found it necessary to modify both its tactics and its technology to cope with the triple threat of surface-to-air missiles, antiaircraft artillery, and MiG interceptors flown by increasingly skilled pilots.

Gulf of Tonkin Incident 1964

Following the withdrawal of the French from Southeast Asia in 1954, U.S. efforts to support the non-Communist regime in South Vietnam had gradually increased. Up to 1964, U.S. involvement was limited to financial aid and military advisers. However, in 1964 the South Vietnamese government's inability to hold the line against the Viet Cong insurgency became obvious.

U.S. political and military leaders were handicapped by the lack of accurate information on the extent of the Viet Cong insurgency. On July 31, 1964, the U.S. Joint Chiefs of Staff approved a naval patrol to gather further intelligence off the coast of North Vietnam.[1] The U.S.S. *Maddox*, a destroyer equipped with special electronic intelligence gear, began such a patrol.

On August 2, three North Vietnamese torpedo boats closed on the *Maddox* at high speed.

Against torpedoes and machine-gun fire, the *Maddox* opened fire and assisted by aircraft from the U.S.S. *Ticonderoga* sank one of the boats and heavily damaged the others.[2]

The U.S. Department of State protested strongly to the Hanoi government, warning of "grave consequences"[3] of any further unprovoked action against U.S. forces. Another destroyer, the U.S.S. *Turner Joy*, joined the *Maddox* to provide increased security and the aircraft carriers *Constellation* and *Kearsarge* were ordered to the Gulf of Tonkin to join *Ticonderoga*.[4]

On August 3, the *Maddox* and *Turner Joy* resumed patrol, venturing no closer than 11 nautical miles off the coast of North Vietnam, according to official reports. At sundown of August 4 the ships picked up radar contacts some 36 miles distant. The contacts, assessed to be the type of torpedo boats in the earlier attacks, were taken under fire as they closed to within 6,000 yards. In fighting that continued until midnight, two of the North Vietnamese boats were sunk and two more damaged. The U.S. vessels were untouched.[5]

To retaliate for the attacks against the U.S. ships in the Gulf of Tonkin, the Joint Chiefs of Staff approved immediate air strikes against North Vietnamese naval bases.[6] On the afternoon of August 5, aircraft from *Constellation* and *Ticonderoga* bombed five North Vietnamese patrol boat bases and the oil storage depot at Vinh—one of the most important transshipment centers in North Vietnam. Eight torpedo boats were destroyed, 21 more damaged, and the oil storage tanks virtually demolished. The United States did not retaliate unscathed: two aircraft were downed by unexpectedly heavy antiaircraft artillery (AAA) defenses.[7]

U.S. Navy fighter squadrons VF-142 and VF-143 were the first units to fly combat missions with the F-4 Phantom II. Operating from the U.S.S. *Constellation*, squadron aircraft attacked North Vietnamese naval installations and torpedo boats on August 5, 1964. (McDonnell Douglas)

Two days after these first U.S. air strikes against North Vietnam, the first Soviet-built Mikoyan/Gurevich fighters appeared. A mix of 30 MiG-15s or MiG-17s (from similarity of appearance it was not clear how many of which) supplied by Communist China were spotted at Phuc Yen airfield. These maneuverable aircraft comprised the kernel of the North Vietnamese Air Force, which had previously consisted of four helicopters, 30 trainer aircraft, and 50 transports.

On August 7, the U.S. posture toward involvement in Southeast Asia changed drastically when the Congress passed the Gulf of Tonkin Resolution empowering the President to "take all necessary steps, including the use of armed force."[8] Immediately two squadrons of B-57 bombers were deployed to Bien Hoa in South Vietnam and several squadrons of F-100 and F-102 fighters to Da Nang. Other F-105 fighters were assigned to the Royal Thai Air Force Base (RTAFB) at Takhli.[9]

Flaming Dart

By the end of 1964, it was estimated that the Viet Cong controlled between two-thirds and three-quarters of South Vietnam. In 1965 the Viet Cong increased its attacks against both U.S. and South Vietnamese forces. On February 7, a Viet Cong mortar attack at Pleiku killed eight Americans and wounded 126. Nine helicopters were destroyed along with a transport plane; nine more helicopters and six light observation aircraft were damaged.[10]

President Lyndon B. Johnson, infuriated by the attack, immediately ordered retaliatory strikes, stating he wanted them to be "joint," "prompt," and "appropriate." That afternoon, under the code name Flaming Dart I, U.S. and South Vietnamese Air Force aircraft hit the Chap Le barracks in North Vietnam. In addition, a joint U.S. and South Vietnamese force of A-1Es, F-100s, and aircraft from the U.S.S. *Ranger* bombed Vinh the next day. The Viet Cong struck back against U.S. facilities at Qui Nhon, provoking the South Vietnamese Air Force, U.S. Navy, and U.S. Air Force to bomb Vinh again on February 11 as part of Flaming Dart II.

Viet Cong activity continued to escalate and the political and military situation in South Vietnam remained unstable. This led the Joint Chiefs of Staff to recommend a longer and harder-hitting series of air strikes against North Vietnam.

Rolling Thunder 1965

President Johnson's approval for the air strikes—dubbed Operation Rolling Thunder—came on February 13. On March 2, 130 U.S. and South Vietnamese Air Force aircraft bombed the naval base at Quang Khe and the ammunition depot at Xom Bang. Nineteen A-1H Skyraider aircraft attacked Quang Khe while 44 F-105s, 40 F-100s, and 20 U.S. Air Force B-57 bombers raked the ammunition depot. Four aircraft were lost to antiaircraft fire, prompting the United States to reevaluate strike tactics.

To minimize aircraft exposure to ground fire, the aircraft were then ordered to fly only one pass over subsequent targets. The bombing runs were also shifted from low-level, high-speed approaches to medium altitudes of between 10,000 and 15,000 feet; at that altitude, aircraft flew above the murderous small arms and antiaircraft artillery, most effective up to about 4,000 feet.

Initially, the Rolling Thunder campaign was limited to targets south of the 20th parallel. Only targets on a list prepared by the Joint Chiefs of Staff and approved by the Secretary of Defense and the President could be hit. A revised list was released each day, informing local commanders in Vietnam exactly when, how, and where to attack. U.S. bombers were restricted from attacking ports and industrial plants, and concentrated on such targets supporting logistical

North Vietnamese MiG-17s at Phuc Yen airfield. The MiG-17, along with the similar MiG-15, were the first modern jets to equip the North Vietnamese Air Force in 1964. (U.S. Air Force)

flow of supplies to the south as bridges, storage areas, barracks, ammunition depots, railroad lines, and choke points.

In the middle of March restrictions were loosened. Washington still had control over lists of permissible targets but these were now released weekly, allowing for more flexibility by theater commanders.[11]

The bombing runs on March 19 as part of Rolling Thunder VII marked the beginning of sustained U.S. air strikes against North Vietnam. The objectives of these strikes were to:

- raise the morale of the South Vietnamese by showing U.S. support and protection for the South Vietnamese government;
- impose penalty on Hanoi for its support of Viet Cong aggression in the south;
- reduce the flow of men and supplies to the south.[12]

As Rolling Thunder progressed through March, the target lists began to include radar sites, an important element of the North Vietnamese air-defense system.[13]

In the first week of April, U.S. forces felt the effectiveness of the integrated air-defense system as MiGs clashed with U.S. aircraft for the first time. On April 3, as Navy planes bombed the Thanh Hoa Rail and Highway Bridge, MiG-17s tangled with Navy F-8 Crusader fighters flying escort for the A-4 Skyhawks. Neither side lost aircraft,[14] but the Navy issued a warning to be on the lookout for MiGs.

First Blood: Phase One of the Battle for Air Superiority

The next day MiGs appeared again and the first blood of air contests was drawn. U.S. Air Force F-105 fighter-bombers from Korat RTAFB in Thailand, escorted by F-100s, were again sent to bomb the bridge at Thanh Hoa. Out of the haze in a classic ground-controlled intercept attack, two MiG-17s closed on a flight of four F-105s orbiting 10 miles south of the bridge.

Sliding in behind two of the F-105s, the MiGs made a perfect hit-and-run attack, closing to some 3,000 or 4,000 feet before being discovered by the second pair (element) of the flight. Despite warnings from the second pair, the first element of F-105s did not respond; the MiGs closed to 1,500 feet and opened fire, downing both the F-105s and escaping before the F-100 escort could come to the rescue.[15]

Analysis of the surprise attack brought several things to light:

1) Strike aircraft were at a serious disadvantage when laden with bombs, and thus should utilize tactics that took into account the possibility of being attacked by MiGs.

2) Strike aircraft needed sufficient warning of an impending MiG attack. (In this case MiG warnings went unheeded by the F-105s.) But sometimes MiGs were not detected until too late, because the U.S. lacked ground-based radar coverage over North Vietnam.

3) The slow orbit speed of the escorting F-100s rendered them incapable of accelerating quickly enough to thwart the MiG-17s' hit-and-run attack.

The results of the surprise attack underscored the effectiveness of a properly-executed, ground-controlled hit-and-run intercept as well as the inadequacy of U.S. strike tactics. Immediately thereafter, the F-100s were replaced as strike escorts by F-4s, which not only were faster, longer-range, and more maneuverable, but also could carry the AIM-7 Sparrow radar-guided air-to-air missile. Realizing now that North Vietnam was not the semi-permissive environment that U.S. aircraft enjoyed south of the 17th parallel, the United States began re-evaluating North Vietnam's weaponry and American capabilities.

Antiaircraft Artillery (AAA)

North Vietnam's antiaircraft artillery was by far the most dangerous and most numerous threat to U.S. strike aircraft, claiming at least two-thirds to three-quarters of all American aircraft downed. Typically, the antiaircraft fire was heaviest up to 4,500 feet where aircraft ran into a barrage of steel ranging from rifles to 37-mm cannon. Between 5,000 and 10,000 feet, 57-mm and 85-mm cannon were a threat and 100-mm shells could reach as high as 20,000 feet, all aimed by radar control.[16] By the end of 1965, North Vietnam had emplaced more than 2,000 of these heavy radar-controlled guns.[17]

By mid-1965 antiaircraft artillery had downed 50 U.S. aircraft.[18] To avoid all losses to antiaircraft artillery would mean flying at an altitude of at least 25,000 feet. But above 5,000 to 7,000 feet the accuracy of targeting bombs was degraded. To avoid the worst of the smaller-caliber antiaircraft artillery, the U.S. Air Force and Navy directed that bombing take place from between 4,000 and 5,000 feet.

Against the radar-directed antiaircraft artillery, however, a strike aircraft's only defense was mild "jinking"—abrupt change in direction, speed, and altitude of the aircraft just as the antiaircraft gun fired. Once the radar again showed the aircraft on its new heading, the aircraft would "jink" again. Such sporadic maneuvering was fine, however, until the pilot had to stabilize the aircraft's path over the target to make an accurate attack. Once the aircraft released its bombs, the pilot would immediately "jink" hard to throw off any tracking radar.

Aircrews learned very early that multiple passes over the heavily-defended targets were not healthy, and they limited bombing runs to one pass—when possible, criss-crossing in differing directions as closely timed as possible to confuse and confound tracking by antiaircraft artillery. Even so, many of the targets were so densely protected that the North Vietnamese resorted to barrage-firing—aiming their guns for the points where they estimated the bombers would release their ordnance—to create a solid curtain of steel through which aircraft had to fly.

The quad-mounted 14.5-mm heavy machine gun—four mounted on a mobile vehicle—was frequently encountered in North and South Vietnam. Developed during World War II, the robust Soviet weapon could fire a tremendous number of projectiles and constituted a great danger to low-flying aircraft. Optically guided, the quad 14.5 was most effective at an altitude up to 2,000 feet. Antiaircraft fire accounted for about three-quarters of the U.S. losses over North Vietnam. (U.S. Army)

In late 1965, to lessen the effectiveness of the heavy radar-controlled guns, EB-66C "Brown Cradle" aircraft were deployed to Vietnam to jam the antiaircraft guns' fire-control radars by radiating high-powered electronic noise on the radar's own frequency. The radar receiving antenna picked up the noise, which showed up on the operator's radar screen. This "snow" overwhelmed the returning signal from the radar pulses reflected from the attacking aircraft.

The EB-66C aircraft were used in two roles, either to escort the bombers all the way to the target, or to stand off a safe distance from the target area and jam the radars.[19]

Surface-to-Air Missiles (SAMs)

On April 5, 1965, photographs taken over North Vietnam by U.S. Air Force U-2 and Navy RF-8 reconnaissance aircraft confirmed what long had been anticipated: construction of surface-to-air missile (SAM) sites. Completing the second leg of the integrated air defense system, the Soviet-built SA-2 missile (NATO code-named Guideline) extended the ground-based air defense envelope around any target to a slant range of 24 miles.

Although the missile sites clearly represented a serious threat to U.S. aircraft, they were ruled off limits as targets because of the fear of killing Soviet technicians helping to build them and train the North Vietnamese in their use.[20]

The SA-2 batteries launched a telephone-pole-size missile that was guided to its target by radar control and detonated by a proximity fuse. A normal firing battery consisted of six launchers arranged around a central guidance radar. The SA-2's guidance-control radar, NATO code-named Fan Song, was effective in guiding the missile to altitudes of between 3,000 and 60,000 feet.

On July 24, 1965, the United States began to learn the hard way how well a surface-to-air missile could work. An SA-2 missile fired from 40 miles northwest of Hanoi hit aircraft of a

Soviet-supplied SA-2 Guideline surface-to-air missile shown here on its launcher. The SA-2 missile could hit a target at a slant range greater than 23 miles and at altitude above 60,000 feet. If seen in time, the missile could usually be out-maneuvered. It was a considerable technological surprise and forced changes in U.S. tactics and technology to counter it. (U.S. Army)

U.S. Air Force F-4C flight; one F-4C was lost and the remaining three heavily damaged as a result of their close proximity.[21]

The appearance of SA-2 necessitated a dramatic change in U.S. strike tactics. After the loss of the F-4C in July, strike aircraft attacking targets within the range of a missile site began flying at only several hundred feet above ground level, thus remaining below the 3,000-foot effective altitude of the SA-2 missile system. Aircraft would pop up short of the target just long enough to acquire the target and release the bombs.

This temporary solution was less than ideal, because it placed the aircraft back within the range of the deadliest antiaircraft artillery. Nonetheless, zooming in at high speed and very low altitude plus "jinking" gave the antiaircraft gunners the least amount of time to react, and complicated their tracking solution.[22] Meanwhile, the United States embarked on a crash program to provide tactical aircraft with passive and active electronic equipment that could counter the threat of North Vietnamese SA-2 missiles, radar-directed antiaircraft artillery, and acquisition radars.

In November 1965 the U.S. Air Force deployed specially modified F-100Fs to Korat RTAFB in Thailand.[23] Labeled "Wild Weasel I," two-seat aircraft were equipped with sensitive radar homing and warning (RHAW) receivers. The RHAW gear allowed the Wild Weasel to detect and locate the S-band Fan Song fire-control radar of the SA-2 missile and also to warn the pilot of the radar's changes to the L-band guidance emissions when a missile was about to be fired.

In addition, the RHAW gear could detect and locate the C-band radar of antiaircraft guns and the X-band radar of interceptor aircraft.[24] This RHAW equipment was fitted to an increasing number of U.S. Air Force, Navy, and Marine Corps fighters and attack aircraft.

With this RHAW gear, strike aircraft were able once again to penetrate missile-protected areas at more than 4,500 feet, putting them up out of range of the deadliest antiaircraft artillery while remaining at an altitude low enough to frustrate the optimum performance of the SA-2. With adequate warning from an aircraft's own RHAW gear or from the standoff EB-66C surveillance aircraft, pilots of the strike aircraft had a good chance at 4,500 to 15,000 feet of visually spotting a rising SA-2 missile and evading it by diving in a steep spiral. Once the Fan Song radar corrected the SA-2 missile for the aircraft's diving maneuver, the aircraft would abruptly pull up, timing it so the missile would be unable to turn in time to remain locked on the plane. The missile's speed would make it fly wide.

Mikoyan/Gurevich Aircraft (MiG)

The North Vietnamese force of MiG-15s and MiG-17s proved to be a match for the best of the U.S. fighters. The MiG-17s could turn faster and tighter in the horizontal than any of the 1965 period U.S. planes—the classic measure of a fighter's maneuverability. The United States realized that its tendency to build multi-role aircraft or interceptor-oriented fighters had sacrificed pure air-to-air capability.

While long-range missile fire could reduce the likelihood of a dogfight, if the rules of engagement required visual identification or the missile failed to kill the target, the attacking aircraft would be forced to run or engage in close-in combat. Moreover, the sporadic air-to-air fighting in 1965 made it painfully clear that close-in dogfighting was not a thing of the past, and that the long-range missiles-only design philosophy that had spawned the gunless F-4 had left it with a serious close-in fighting liability. And anyone who thought the 10-year-old MiG-17 was an obsolete aircraft with no capability against the modern U.S. fighting machines was sadly mistaken. Many a pilot was heard to cry, "Oh, for an F-86!" While the foundations of fighter design were being shaken, the United States pressed on in North Vietnam with what aircraft it had on hand.

North Vietnam's Air Defense Network

The combination of antiaircraft artillery, surface-to-air missiles, and MiG fighters in North Vietnam was integrated into a tight network by early-warning radars and visual observers all in communication. This network was able to bring any intruding aircraft under attack. While antiaircraft artillery constituted the most effective element of the defense network, its effectiveness decreased with altitude. With increasing altitude, however, the potency of surface-to-air missiles increased because the missile accelerated to its maximum speed.

The MiG fighters posed a threat at any altitude and often enhanced the effectiveness of the other elements of the air defense network by baiting U.S. fighters into surface-to-air missile traps or antiaircraft artillery "flak" traps,[25] or by chasing off EB-66C jammers and Wild Weasels. By the end of 1965, the combination of air defense elements in North Vietnam's new air defense network had downed 80 U.S. aircraft.[26]

Rolling Thunder II and III, 1965–1966

Between May 12 and 17, 1965, U.S. air strikes were suspended to allow American and North Vietnamese diplomats to negotiate. In less than a week, however, the talks broke down and U.S. aircraft resumed bombing on May 18. The renewed bombing was known as Rolling Thunder II; along with a new name came new targets north of the 20th parallel.

Dogfighting With MiGs

In June 1965 the Navy downed its first MiG. F-4Bs from U.S. Navy Fighter Squadron 21 (VF-21) off the U.S.S. *Midway* picked off two MiG-17s with a pair of AIM-7 Sparrow air-to-air missiles in a head-on pass. This engagement was most unusual because the radar-guided AIM-7 Sparrow—then the only missile that could be fired toward the target's forward quarter as well as to the side or to the rear—was a medium-range weapon.

Yet the U.S. rules of engagement in air combat over North Vietnam required that a pilot could not simply fire at a target aircraft after picking it up on a radar scope, but first must visually identify it. By the time a pilot closed in near enough to see the target aircraft, he was generally inside the Sparrow's range. At that point, if the target aircraft were approaching head on it was momentarily immune until the attacking pilot could maneuver to a new position to fire a heat-seeking Sidewinder missile toward the target's hot engine in its rear quarter.

U.S. Navy, Marine Corps, and Air Force F-4 Phantoms could not attack close-in targets because their missiles were ineffective at less than 2,000 feet and because they lacked a cannon.

In the June 17 engagement, however, the F-4's radar allowed the crews—Comdr. Louis C. Page, his backseater Lt. John C. Smith, and Lt. Jack E. D. Batson and his backseat radar intercept officer—to set up for an AIM-7 shot before entering within range of the MiG-17s' weapons. The key was that Commander Page was able to visually confirm the identity of the radar bogeys as MiG-17s before they closed inside the minimum range of the AIM-7.

As the U.S. air strikes against North Vietnam continued, the number of MiGs encountered increased. During the summer of 1965, the North Vietnamese Air Force lost five MiGs. However, new aircraft arriving from the Soviet Union brought North Vietnam's MiG strength up to 70 by the end of the year. Nonetheless, after their recent losses—which amounted to about 10 percent of their fledgling air force—they flew ground-controlled intercepts only to break off before reaching an attack position. This pattern of standing down from combat in order to retrain pilots and perhaps reevaluate tactics was to be repeated by the North Vietnamese Air Force several times during the war.

SAM-Hunters: *Wild Weasel, Shrike,* and *Ironhand*

After losing the first F-4C to an SA-2 missile in July 1965, several of the surface-to-air missile sites—previously off limits to attack—were targeted for United States air strikes. On July 27, F-105s bombed two missile sites 40 miles northwest of Hanoi, inflicting heavy damage. However, antiaircraft artillery shot down three aircraft and two more were subsequently lost when one of the damaged aircraft collided with another as they returned to base.[27] Rolling Thunder missions continued to be flown against North Vietnamese targets including radar and missile sites.

All bombing came to a halt on Christmas Day of 1965 to allow diplomats to have another go at the negotiating table. The pause continued through January 30, again with no diplomatic solution coming.[28] Thereafter, the United States initiated Rolling Thunder III.

The North Vietnamese had made good use of the pause, repairing bomb damage to ground installations and expanding the coverage of both antiaircraft guns and surface-to-air missiles. In the space of a month's time, the fledgling air-defense network grew considerably. In addition to 22 surface-to-air missile sites, North Vietnam had also dug in more than 400 antiaircraft guns.[29]

Moreover, numerous new dummy missile sites added to the difficulty of pinpointing the real batteries. As noted by Adm. U.S. Grant Sharp, "It soon became clear that the SAM sites were being moved around quite frequently, but we were forbidden to hit them until we had analyzed photographs of suspected sites. By the time the photographs were analyzed, of course, the SAM sites had been moved elsewhere . . . and so the hunt was on again."[30]

The growth of the surface-to-air system began in the Hanoi area, taking advantage of the U.S. restriction against bombing within a 30-mile radius. From there additional sites were constructed covering the major railway links to China along which supplies came from both Russia and China.

SA-2 sites were also sheltered within a 10-mile radius of Haiphong, airspace through which U.S. pilots were even prohibited to fly. Bombing missile sites and the targets they protected exacted a heavy toll of U.S. planes. After the Wild Weasels were deployed, one of them teamed with three F-105 fighter-bombers with conventional weapons. The four aircraft together formed what became known as an Ironhand flight, and flew ahead of the main strike group.

The Wild Weasel would seek out any radar emissions from SA-2 sites, and its F-105 escorts would release bombs and fire rockets to try to destroy the missile site before the main strike group arrived to attack the primary target. If the Ironhand flight was successful, the main strike group was able to approach the target at medium altitude, free from the missile site's threat and above the worst of the antiaircraft fire.

The first four Wild Weasels were augmented by three more in February 1966. By that spring, the U.S. Air Force had modified the F-100F Wild Weasel to carry its own weapon: the AGM-45 Shrike air-to-ground anti-radiation missile (ARM) developed by the Navy. When launched, the Shrike missile homed on the SA-2's Fan Song radar emissions.[31] This gave the radar operator two options: shutting down or risking the site's destruction. Shutting down the radar meant that no SA-2 missile could be fired. The cessation of the radar emissions, the source of guidance for the Shrike, would also cause the missile to go "dumb" and thus negate its chances of destroying the radar.

Although it was preferable to destroy the radar site altogether, for short-term tactical purposes it was just as effective to suppress the radar by causing it to shut down.[32]

Ironhand SAM-suppression flights became standard for major strikes in North Vietnam. In addition, to suppress antiaircraft artillery "flak" the Air Force used its Wild Weasel aircraft in conjunction with F-105Ds configured with bombs and 2.75-inch unguided air-to-ground rockets. The Navy defense suppression counterparts were A-4 and A-6 bombers equipped with Shrike missiles and bombs.

Later in 1966, both services introduced a specialized bomb that was especially effective against personnel manning antiaircraft artillery sites. Known as a cluster bomb unit (CBU), it consisted of many bomblets within a larger canister. After the canister was released, it split in half to scatter the bomblets in a large pattern sufficient to pepper an antiaircraft artillery site with hundreds of live explosive submunitions like a rain of mortar shells. These made short work of any personnel not under cover.

Flak-suppression flights would enter the target area first and drop their cluster bombs or other wares on antiaircraft positions just as the strike aircraft started their bomb-runs. If timed properly, the antiaircraft gunners would be suppressed (that is, forced under cover away from their guns) long enough for the strikers to complete their runs and escape.

While the flak-suppression flights held off antiaircraft, the Shrike-carrying Ironhand flights stood off ready to greet any active SA-2 radar operators with a Shrike missile. As in tactics of SAM suppression—even though the artillery sites might not be physically destroyed—if the guns were shut down long enough to permit the strike aircraft safe passage to the prime target, the defense-suppression mission was considered a success.[33]

Introduction of the MiG-21

The MiG-21 entered the NVAF's inventory in late 1965, qualitatively improving the interceptor element of the air defense network. Like the earlier MiG-15, MiG-17, and MiG-19 designs, the MiG-21 Fishbed was a point-defense interceptor. While the MiG-21's payload capability and endurance were less than those of western aircraft design, its air-to-air

A North Vietnamese pilot climbs into the cockpit of a Soviet-built MiG-21 interceptor. The North Vietnamese Air Force began receiving MiG-21 Fishbed fighters late in 1965. The Mach-2 fighter could make fast hit-and-run attacks and proved to be a tougher opponent than the subsonic MiG-17. (M. O'Connor)

performance was excellent. At high altitude, it could out turn both the F-4 Phantom fighter and the F-105 Thunderchief fighter-bomber. The North Vietnamese initially flew the MiG-21F Fishbed C model armed with an internal 30-mm cannon, and two AA-2 Atoll infrared-guided air-to-air missiles. Owing to its simple avionics, the MiG could operate only during the day and in clear weather, possessing a simple range-only radar that had no capacity to search out targets. Those limitations, however, did not detract from its effectiveness in its role as a clear-weather interceptor.

Rolling Thunder IV, 1966

The monsoon weather in February and March 1966 limited both ground and air activity. April saw gradual clearing of weather; with it came Phase IV of Rolling Thunder, which for the first time authorized air operations over the whole of North Vietnam excluding only the Chinese border zone and restricted areas around Hanoi and Haiphong. For the first time, petroleum-oil-lubricant (POL) storage areas could now be hit.

With improved weather in mid-April, aircraft from *Kitty Hawk* and *Ticonderoga* conducted strikes farther northward. Railroad yards, a water pumping station, coal treatment plant, the Cam Pha power plant near the Chinese border, and the Uong Bi thermal power plant near Haiphong were all struck in rapid succession.[34] As new targets were authorized, a new target assignment system was developed.

The U.S. Air Force and the Navy divided North Vietnam into six target areas or route packages; previously the services rotated where strikes would take place to alternate their pilots' exposure to more and less dangerous areas. Now the U.S. Air Force took the western and Hanoi route packages closer to its Thai and South Vietnam bases while the Navy took the Haiphong and coastal route packages near its aircraft carriers.

With this new system, the area in which each service assigned targets was halved, allowing crews to become more familiar with the terrain and the defenses.[35] The new division had a telling improvement on losses. Once familiar with an area, crews could plan better attack routes to minimize exposure to enemy defenses.

Technology also allowed the Air Force and the Navy to begin to interdict supply routes in North Vietnam throughout the entire year regardless of weather. During the monsoon season until 1966, many Navy strikes were cancelled in the northern route packages, thus allowing the North Vietnamese to move freely under cloud cover. The Air Force was able to fly despite bad weather because its Skyspot radar bombing system allowed F-105s to hit targets via radar bombing. A ground radar station, Lima Site 85 in Laos, tracked the aircraft and signalled when to drop ordnance.[36] After July 1965, the Navy introduced its A-6 Intruder all-weather bomber with a radar system sophisticated enough to allow it to operate both in bad weather and at night.

Second Phase of the Battle for Air Superiority

After the infrequent engagements in the first five months of 1966, U.S. Air Force and Navy strikes moving farther northward brought these aircraft within the operational radius of the MiGs. Subsequently, engagements with MiGs rose sharply.

The first dogfight of 1966 occurred between a flight of U.S. Air Force F-4Cs from the 555th Tactical Fighter Squadron, Eighth Tactical Fighter Wing, which was providing escort for an F-105 strike against the Bac Giang bridge about 25 miles northeast of Hanoi. The flight of Phantoms detected by radar a similar number of MiG-17s approaching them head-on. During the first pass, the Phantoms fired Sparrows and Sidewinders with no hits and a swirling

Maj. Paul F. Gilmore (left) and Lt. William T. Smith pose for pictures after returning from a mission during which they shot down a North Vietnamese MiG-21, the first MiG-21 downed by U.S. forces in the Vietnam conflict. (U.S. Air Force)

dogfight ensued. Both sides traded fire: MiG-17s employing cannon and F-4s missiles. It was the Phantoms' missiles, however, which finally struck home, destroying two MiG-17s. A Sparrow accounted for one and a Sidewinder the other.

Three days later an F-4C escorting an EB-66C engaged in a dogfight with several MiG-21s. The F-4C, piloted by Maj. Paul Gilmore and Lt. William Smith, destroyed one MiG-21 after several attacks with Sidewinders. This was the first MiG-21 destroyed in the Vietnam War. During the next several weeks, U.S. Air Force F-4Cs also scored several victories against MiG-17s.[37]

The Navy drew its first blood of 1966 when F-8E Crusader fighters escorting A-4 Skyhawk bombers tangled with four MiG-17s north of Haiphong and downed one with an AIM-9 Sidewinder air-to-air missile at an altitude of 50 feet—a difficult feat because of ground interference with infrared signatures. Comdr. Harold L. Marr, commanding officer of VF-211, became the first F-8 pilot to score an aerial victory above North Vietnam.[38]

As of the end of June 1966, the Navy had downed five MiG-17s against no losses, while the Air Force had scored 10 kills and lost two. While at first glance those ratios seemed to demonstrate a clear U.S. edge in air superiority, two factors emerged from the first year of air-to-air encounters: first, the main purpose—and effect—of the MiG attacks was to force U.S. aircraft to jettison their ordnance, thus neutralizing the strikes. In fact, many times the MiG would intercept right up to the point of attack and then abruptly break off. When executed properly, the MiG achieved its goal of thwarting the strike while only briefly exposing itself to fire from U.S. fighter escorts.

The second factor was more serious: the rapidly growing experience of the North Vietnamese pilots. Barely in existence two years, the North Vietnamese Air Force was intensely motivated to defend its homeland. While the United States had a large population from which to draw pilots, that of North Vietnam was much smaller and the technological level lagged far behind. Most North Vietnamese Air Force pilot candidates had not even driven a car, let alone a Mach-2 interceptor.[39] Nonetheless, through 1966 the fledgling air force grew in maturity and aggressiveness, honing its tactics and rising continually throughout the summer to engage U.S. aircraft.

AAA: The Surest Killer

During the summer of 1966, North Vietnam continued to add to its formidable air defense network. It was estimated that the North Vietnamese possessed 5,000 antiaircraft guns, half around Hanoi and Haiphong.[40] According to John M. Van Dyke in *North Vietnam's Strategy for Survival*, a correspondent visiting Hanoi in 1966 reported "antiaircraft batteries on the roof of every tall building, including the hotels, the ministries, and the opera house."[41] Antiaircraft artillery was by far the major killer by 1966. Out of 455 aircraft lost over North Vietnam since the beginning of the bombing two years earlier, fully 85 percent fell to antiaircraft fire.[42]

Aside from the fixed antiaircraft batteries covering Hanoi and Haiphong, mobile batteries continually moved as U.S. targeting changed.

The North Vietnamese carefully studied U.S. strike tactics to concentrate maximum fire. The North Vietnamese also set up fake artillery sites that aircraft would avoid, only to fly over nearby real camouflaged sites waiting for aircraft to take the bait.[43]

F-105 Wild Weasel: The Definitive SAM Hunter

The summer of 1966 also saw introduction of the U.S.'s definitive SAM-hunter, the F-105F Wild Weasel. As the second operational SAM-hunter aircraft deployed to Southeast Asia, the F-105F was even more aptly suited to seek out and destroy missile sites than its F-100F predecessor. The F-105F could fly faster than the F-100F, had greater range, and could thus keep up more readily with the strike groups of F-105 fighter-bombers. By the summer of 1966, 13 F-105F Wild Weasels had been delivered, followed by 10 more in the next three months.

Wild Weasel F-105F/G fighter-bombers were deployed by the U.S. Air Force to detect and destroy SA-2 missile sites. The specially-modified aircraft struck at SA-2 sites with Shrike missiles that homed in on a SAM site's radar, operating in conjunction with Ironhand F-105Ds armed with conventional bombs and rockets. (U.S. Air Force)

Surface-to-air missile operators began to modify their tactics in an attempt both to reduce their vulnerability to Shrikes and to increase the effectiveness of the SA-2 missile, which so far had downed few aircraft. The surface-to-air missile radar operators learned to radiate only during a minimum time needed to acquire targets and launch missiles. It was here that the redundancy of the Soviet-style air defense network demonstrated its inherent flexibility.

Although each missile operator preferred his own acquisition radar to locate and track invading aircraft, the advent of Shrike meant a sure alert to an active missile site. To avoid alerting Ironhand aircraft, the long-range early warning/ground-controlled intercept radars assumed the search role.

Using preliminary information from the early-warning radars, each missile operator could stand by with his radar machinery warmed up in ''dummy load'' ready to track the target aircraft once external sources indicated they were within range. During the attack, the missile site would radiate long enough only to lock onto its target and guide the SA-2 missile home.

If the operator could not pick up the target and begin tracking within moments of being informed that aircraft were in range, the site would shut down again.

Since the Shrike required continuous radar emissions to home on, the missile operators' tactic was quite effective. The SAM operators also used other techniques to evade the SAM hunters. For example, if Shrike-equipped Ironhand aircraft were presumed to be nearby (they were usually discernable by their medium altitude at the flanks of a strike group) then the missile operators would launch the SA-2 missile along a simple ballistic trajectory and keep the radar silent in dummy load until the last possible moment.

When the SA-2 missile began to near the target, the operator would switch on the radar to finally guide it home. Because the SA-2 missile travels faster than the Shrike, the SA-2 operator had the edge: The Ironhand aircraft could launch a Shrike, but if the missile operator shut off the Fan Song radar as soon as the SA-2 either hit or missed its target then the chances were good that the Shrike would not hit the radar site.

This pattern of tactical move/countermove was to continue and grow in complexity as the hostilities wore on.

Blinding the Enemy: Radar Jammers

In September 1966, individual radar-jamming pods were introduced and fitted to F-105Ds, for the first time freeing individual aircraft from the necessity of being accompanied by a jammer escort. The first pod, initially known as the QRC-160 and later designated ALQ-71, was 10 feet long and installed on the wing pylons that normally carried bombs. Each pod contained three pairs of noise jammers, which radiated in the L, S, and C radio-frequency bands to counter the acquisition-and-guidance radars of the long-range antiaircraft guns and surface-to-air missiles. At bottom of the pod were three pairs of antennas, so that each jammer radiated both vertically and horizontally polarized signals.

For maximum mutual protection, each flight of F-105Ds flew a stepped up 'V' formation at a 30-degree angle, in which the planes in the rear flew several hundred feet higher than those in the lead. At first, the pods were available only in small numbers and so initially were fitted only to the two F-105s comprising each flight's wings. These aircraft were more exposed than the planes in the center.

The EB-66C standoff-jammer aircraft continued the role of degrading the effectiveness of the radar-dependent early warning/ground controlled intercept network to supplement the F-105 jamming. In addition, the EB-66C electronic intelligence gear monitored the area's electromagnetic activity, which was subsequently evaluated to determine proper frequency settings for the jammer pods on the individual F-105s.

Determining the frequency settings became increasingly important as the North Vietnamese began to alter their radars to lessen jammer disruption. The EB-66C's electronic intelligence also allowed U.S. forces to keep tabs on the moving missile batteries—an activity that required constant monitoring on the part of both the EB-66C and photo-reconnaissance aircraft. The missile batteries could be dismantled in about four hours, moved to a new site, and be operating again within another six hours.

The QRC-160 pod on the F-105D was first tested in combat in early October 1966. F-105Ds of the Air Force's 388th Tactical Fighter Wing flew more than 100 sorties (a sortie being one excursion by one aircraft) to assess the pod's effectiveness. The flights of F-105Ds flew at altitudes between 10,000 and 17,000 feet where aircraft normally could expect shells from 37-mm, 57-mm, and 100-mm guns as well as SA-2 missiles.

On an October 7 mission, 10 antiaircraft guidance radar signals and 12 Fan Song radar signals were detected without a single gun or missile battery being fired. The pods' effectiveness was more graphically illustrated the next day. The pod-free aircraft in one flight dodged 37-mm, 57-mm, and 85-mm shells and one missile. The flight's other two aircraft, equipped with the pods, encountered only relatively inaccurate visually-sighted barrage firing from 37-mm guns.[44]

With the advent of the jamming pod, F-105D flights could once again penetrate at medium altitude between 12,000 and 15,000 feet where airspeed, range, and maneuverability were all good—above the range of the murderous automatic weapons and without fear of the higher-altitude radar-directed antiaircraft artillery and surface-to-air missiles.

While U.S. Air Force fighter-bombers employed such active jammers as the QRC-160, the U.S. Navy concentrated on equipping its tactical aircraft with such internally-mounted deception jammer/repeaters as the AN/ALQ-100. This equipment deceived the radars of surface-to-air missiles and antiaircraft guns and forced them to break the lock-on required for accurate fire control. The Navy also began fitting many of its aircraft with chaff dispensers such as the AN/ALE-29, which fired out bundles of aluminum foil chaff to create false images on radar scopes as it floated to earth.[45] Standoff jammers (the Air Force's EB-66C, the Navy's EA-1F and EKA-3, and the Marine Corps' EF-10B) further added to the survival rate of aircraft by creating ingress and egress corridors with their jamming strobes.

The immediate result of the electronic countermeasures' degradation of the North Vietnamese radar system was an increase in engagements with MiGs.

Operation Bolo: Baiting the Trap, 1967

While the U.S. had introduced passive and active equipment and tactics to reduce the effectiveness of both radar-directed antiaircraft artillery and surface-to-air missiles, its posture against the rising MiG threat was defensive. Although bombing North Vietnamese airfields would have been the most effective means of curtailing MiG activity, airfields were still on the list of restricted targets. Therefore, the only way to contend with the MiG force was to take it on in the air.

Although 23 MiGs had fallen to U.S. Air Force and Navy aircrews,[46] in virtually all the engagements the MiGs had had the initial advantage through being vectored to intercept the U.S. flights by their ground controllers. Mostly when U.S. pilots bested MiGs it was either because they had used poor tactics, or MiG pilots had failed to make certain they were not being tailed when fixating on a target.

In either case, eager U.S. aircrews had to wait for the MiGs to intercept them before they could do battle, and this opportunity did not come often. With this frustratingly unpredictable situation in mind, the U.S. Air Force went to work on a plan to deliberately lure the elusive MiGs into an air-to-air confrontation.

The plan, laid out on December 22 at Seventh Air Force Headquarters, was to be tested under the direction of Col. Robin Olds, Commander of the 8th Tactical Fighter Wing equipped with F-4Cs.[47] Code named Operation Bolo, the scheme was designed to take advantage of what the North Vietnamese had begun to take for granted. They relied on their extensive early warning/ground-controlled intercept radar network as their eyes to see strike groups well before they arrived over the target area.

By now the almost-daily strikes all flew standard formations, refueling in the air from KC-135 tanker aircraft, virtually telegraphing via radar that a strike was in the offering. The different types of planes in the standard strike groups met with their respective tankers at different specified locations, the bomb-laden F-105s refueling at a lower altitude than the lighter, faster F-4 Phantom escorts.

The North Vietnamese carefully analyzed these formations, deducing from the respective position and movement of aircraft on the radar screen the aircraft types and missions. On the basis of their radar information and analysis, the North Vietnamese vectored their MiG interceptors towards what they then knew were either bomb-laden aircraft or such aircraft as the EB-66C or the Wild Weasel that were degrading their radar defenses. U.S. intelligence further revealed that the North Vietnamese also monitored aircraft communications to glean any information on specific targets or tactics.

Operation Bolo counted on the North Vietnamese following these by-now standard procedures. What the North Vietnamese would not be able to discern from their radar scopes was that the main strike group, instead of being bomb-laden F-105s, would be F-4 air combat fighters armed with air-to-air missiles.

The Phantoms would fly in the standard F-105 formations, mimick their lower-altitude refueling behavior, carry the F-105 radar jamming pods, and go through the F-105 standard communications.

The ruse would be perpetuated until the MiGs rose to intercept the strike force, whereupon they would face an unpleasant surprise: instead of meeting bomb-heavy F-105s, the MiGs would suddenly be embroiled in aerial combat with 14 flights of missile-ready F-4C Phantoms.

The remainder of the Bolo mission comprised six flights of F-105 Ironhand fighter-bombers with their radar-"sniffing" Shrike-equipped Wild Weasels and four flights of F-104 fighters escorting the supporting flights of the EB-66C standoff jammers, EC-121 long-range airborne radar surveillance aircraft, and KC-135 tanker aircraft.

Each of the 14 flights of F-4C Phantoms was separated from the one behind by five minutes, to provide for 55 minutes of continuous F-4C air coverage over the "target" area. The 55 minutes of on-station time was estimated to be sufficient to exhaust the endurance of the North Vietnamese MiG-21s. Once the MiGs were engaged, the U.S. Air Force did not plan to lose the opportunity to inflict further losses by making them fight until they ran out of fuel.

Absolute secrecy was essential to ensure the deception. The F-4 Phantoms had to be secretly modified to carry the QRC-160 radar jamming pods that so far only the F-105 carried. The F-4 pilots also had to use standard F-105 communications and operating procedures.

The fighters were divided into an East and West Force. The East Force, comprising of F-4Cs from the 366th Tactical Fighter Wing, was assigned to cover Kep airfield and Cat Bai airfield while forming a BARCAP (Barrier Combat Air Patrol) to the north to block the MiGs' sanctuary at airfields in China.

The West Force was the bogus F-105 strike group, made up of Colonel Olds's 8th Tactical Fighter Wing F-4Cs using the F-105 "tanker anchors, refueling altitudes, approach routes, approach altitudes, airspeeds, and radio call signs and communications" to perpetuate the hoax. After they succeeded in bringing the MiGs up to do battle, the F-4Cs would cover Phuc

Yen airfield and Gia Lam airfield, waiting above the cloud cover to attack MiGs as they rose off the ground.[48]

The date was set for January 2, 1967, as all the machinery of strategy fell into place. Poor weather over North Vietnam delayed takeoff one hour. Olds himself led the first flight into the target area at 3:00 p.m., initially flying to the southeast of Phuc Yen airfield in an unmolested pass before turning to the northeast and returning.[49] Somewhat more belatedly than expected, the North Vietnamese took the bait.

Colonel Olds reported the following:

"At the onset of this battle, the MiGs popped up out of the clouds. Unfortunately, the first one to pop through came up at my 6 o'clock position. I think this was more by chance than design. As it turned out, within the next few moments, many others popped out of the clouds in varying positions around the clock."

Olds broke left to defeat the MiG's advantage and fired two AIM-7E sparrows at a second MiG at his 11 o'clock. The second MiG disappeared into the clouds with the Sparrows failing to guide. Olds then turned his attention to the other MiG-21s in the area.

"I'd seen another pop out in my 10 o'clock position, going from my right to my left; in other words, just about across the circle from me. When the first MiG I fired at disappeared, I slammed full afterburner and pulled in hard to gain position on this second MiG. I pulled the nose up high about 45 degrees, inside his circle. Mind you, he was turning around to the left so I pulled the nose up high and rolled to the right. This is known as a vector roll. I got up on top of him and half upside down, hung there, and waited for him to complete more of his turn and timed it so that as I continued to roll down behind him, I'll be about 20 degrees angle off and about 4,500 to 5,000 feet behind him. That's exactly what happened. Frankly, I am not sure he ever saw me. When I got down low and behind, and he was outlined by the sun against a brilliant blue sky, I let him have two Sidewinders, one of which hit and blew his right wing off."[50]

Olds's hit brought the score to three MiG-21s against no U.S. losses. Aircraft 4 of Olds's flight had, with an AIM-9 Sidewinder, downed a MiG attempting to track Olds's wingman (Olds 2). Simultaneously, Olds 2 was chasing another MiG-21 attempting to slip behind the other three F-4 Phantoms. Olds himself launched two AIM-9 Sidewinders whose infrared sensors misguided on the sun's reflection on the overcast. Olds 2 locked his radar on boresight (straight ahead of his plane) and launched two AIM-7E Sparrows; the second Sparrow guided unerringly a mile and a half to two miles, exploding just forward of the MiG's stabilizer and enveloping the aircraft in a fireball. The MiG tumbled end over end and plunged through the overcast in a flat spin, trailing black smoke.

Despite these early losses, MiG-21s continued to pop through the clouds, obviously intercepting the flights under ground control. The MiGs were coordinating their attacks from the U.S. planes' forward and rearward quadrants, trying to lure the F-4s to turn into their rearward threat and thus placing the original forward MiGs, which arrived slightly later, in a favorable 6 o'clock position.

Olds's original vertical vector roll negated such a tactic. After the three kills, however, Olds's flight was low on fuel and so headed for home, just as the flight dubbed "Ford" entered the arena.

Ford flight, led by Col. "Chappie" James, Jr., arrived at 3:05 p.m. and was attacked in the same fashion as Olds's flight: two MiG-21s from 10 o'clock and a third from 6 o'clock low. In testimony both to the effectiveness of such a tactic and to the advantage of having a two-seat aircraft, Colonel James initially turned into the two MiGs at his 10 o'clock unaware of the MiG-21 slipping into firing position at his tail. The MiG-21 had actually come within range to

This North Vietnamese MiG-21 fighter was photographed during a dogfight near Hanoi. The MiG-21 proved to be a tough adversary when its pilots employed hit-and-run tactics acting on information from radar ground controllers. (U.S. Air Force)

fire its Atoll missiles at Ford 3 and Ford 4 before James's backseater spotted the attacker and urgently called for a defensive break.

The next flight, five minutes later, was "Rambler" led by Capt. John B. Stone. Stone himself entered chasing the two lead MiG-21s when another MiG zoomed past with guns blazing. While evasively maneuvering, Stone lost his wingman, who mistakenly joined on Rambler 4. Stone continued to pursue the two MiG-21s, firing three AIM-7E Sparrow missiles. Not sure of a boresight lock, Stone tracked the MiG with his gunsight pipper, which guided the second Sparrow into the wing root at the fuselage; the MiG erupted into flames and its pilot bailed out, parachuting through the clouds.

With the score now at six of the elusive MiG-21 "Blue Bandits," Rambler flight continued to pursue MiGs in the plane-filled sky. Rambler 3 locked his missile guidance radar onto one MiG and salvoed two AIM-7E Sparrows; the first did not guide and the second followed its MiG into the clouds, barring any observation of the outcome.

Stone then picked up more MiGs being vectored in: three at his 1 or 2 o'clock position 12 miles away and another two only three miles away at his 10 or 11 o'clock. As he turned to engage the MiGs on his left, Rambler 3 reported another MiG on Stone's tail. As Stone turned to check his six o'clock position, he saw a MiG-21 shooting past only 700 feet behind his tail, muzzle flashes coming from its 30-mm cannon.

As Stone broke hard into the MiG to defeat the attack, Rambler 2 and 4 engaged the other two MiGs. Responding to the attack the MiGs split, one down to the left and one up to the right. Stone's wingman, Rambler 2, launched two AIM-7E Sparrows, one of which scored— bringing the day's talley to seven.

Rambler 4, pursuing the other MiG-21, fired two AIM-7E Sparrows unsuccessfully. Switching the position of his stick to HEAT, he loosed two AIM-9B infrared-guided Sidewinders, both near misses. He fired again but was forced to break hard right to elude a MiG attack on himself, and could not observe the missiles' course.

Rambler 3 launched a Sparrow as another MiG spiraled downward to safety. The tables then turned on Rambler 3 as a MiG-21 fired a barrage of rockets and 30-mm cannon his way, but Rambler 3 turned left and escaped.

An F-4C from the U.S. Air Force 8th Tactical Fighter Wing taxies in after Operation Bolo. Several squadrons of Phantoms flew a profile that simulated an F-105 strike force. When the North Vietnamese MiGs attacked the formation they met Phantoms armed with air-to-air missiles and not the heavily laden F-105s they were expecting. During a series of dogfights, USAF Phantoms destroyed seven MiG-21s without a loss.

Poor weather prevented the East Force from entering the target area from its Gulf of Tonkin position, and it was thus unable to engage any MiGs. The day's score stood at seven MiG-21s confirmed destroyed—almost half of the estimated North Vietnamese MiG-21s. Intelligence had indicated the North Vietnamese Air Force had approximately 15 MiG-21s operating at the end of 1966 with additional MiG-21s stored in crates.

Operation Bolo demonstrated that, given equal opportunity, U.S. aircrews could take on the strengthening North Vietnamese Air Force and defeat it. Operation Bolo was the first aerial encounter over North Vietnam in which the United States so clearly reigned supreme.

The North Vietnamese Sting: "Things That Don't Kill You Outright . . ."

The North Vietnamese had been dealt a stunning blow but did not stand down as previously. Instead, like angry bees swarming from a hive, the next morning the MiGs began harassing the regular weather/reconnaissance RF-4Cs flying over North Vietnam. Such flights were necessary for planning strikes, as they monitored both weather and ground activity around potential targets.

MiG attacks on both January 3 and 4—the two days immediately following Operation Bolo—turned back such reconnaissance missions. It was decided to counteract this MiG threat with a ruse similiar to Bolo, to take advantage of the MiGs' repeated harassment and hopefully hand out another surprise.

On January 6, much in the fashion of Bolo but on a much smaller scale, two real fighter F-4Cs took the place of the routine RF-4Cs. Flying a tight formation to give the impression to radar observers of being a single RF-4C, the two F-4Cs flew the weather/reconnaissance route in an attempt to draw MiGs. As before, the North Vietnamese responded by vectoring in four MiGs to intercept the interlopers. The two F-4Cs engaged them, downing two and further depleting the MiG-21 inventory.

". . . Make You Stronger"

The solid overcast, heavy rain, and poor visibility of the monsoon season curtailed further action over North Vietnam in late January and early February, except for brief spells of clear weather when large-scale strikes could be coordinated. While the torrential downpours also

In April 1967, the U.S. for the first time began attacking North Vietnamese airfields to reduce the MiG threat. Hoa Lac airfield was bombed by several flights of F-105s and put out of action. (U.S. Air Force)

made it difficult for troops to move on the ground, the constant flow of men and supplies from North Vietnam to strengthen the insurgency in South Vietnam did not let up. Low clouds were perfect for moving barges and trucks without fear of marauding strike aircraft that in clear weather patrolled the roadways and waterways.

When the weather began to break in March, the U.S. forces found that the number of antiaircraft guns had increased from the estimated 5,000 in 1966 to 7,000—1,200 being radar-directed. Sixty percent of the new antiaircraft artillery was the highly effective 37-mm and 57-mm guns.[51] In concert with these growing numbers, the SA-2 batteries were estimated at about 30, each battery comprised of six launchers.

Moreover, by April 1967, the North Vietnamese Air Force was estimated to possess 97 aircraft, the highest number to date. Comprising the aircraft were a small number of MiG-15s, 75 MiG-17s, 16 MiG-21s, and six Il-28 medium-range bombers. Along with the high inventory of aircraft, more pilots than ever were available to the MiG force.

In April, the first month of good weather in 1967, U.S. aircraft clashed with MiGs some 50 times, shooting down nine MiGs but losing seven aircraft—testimony to the maturing skill of the North Vietnamese pilots. As many as 16 MiGs flew to intercept U.S. strikes. In response, for the first time the U.S. Joint Chiefs of Staff authorized the bombing of MiG airfields at Hoa Lac and Kep. By May, 26 MiGs had been destroyed on the ground.[52]

U.S. aircrews continued to engage MiGs each day through May, the tide turning now to favor U.S. aircraft. By June, the United States had achieved a 5:1 ratio over the NVAF. One by one, more MiG fields were listed for strikes as the NVAF continued to send MiGs to aerial battle. After losing three MiGs on June 5 alone, however, the North Vietnamese stood down. At this point, 54 MiGs had been destroyed in the air in addition to those on the ground, while the United States had lost only 11 aircraft to MiGs.

In June, many of the MiGs were moved to airfields in China to prevent them from being destroyed on the ground, and U.S. aircrews subsequently did not see MiGs in the air except on rare occasions.

New U.S. Weaponry, 1967

F-4D Phantom II

In 1967, the U.S. Air Force began flying the F-4D Phantom II in Vietnam. The D model F-4 had an improved bombing computer and gunsight. The new gunsight was a stabilized radar-ranging lead-computing type for air-to-air combat; it automatically calculated the trajectories of both the aircraft and the target and indicated to the pilot where he needed to fly and point the nose of his plane in order to fire his boresight Vulcan cannon true.

On June 2, 1967, the F-4D Phantom entered combat and the aircraft scored its first combat victory three days later. The first F-4Ds to achieve a victory were from the Air Force's 555th "Triple Nickel" Tactical Fighter Squadron.

Vulcan Cannon

In May 1967, the U.S. Air Force introduced a new air-to-air cannon, the SUU-16: an M-61A1 20-mm Vulcan cannon retrofitted to a pod and carried on the centerline of the F-4. The F-4 Phantom originally had been designed to carry only air-to-air missiles, under the assumption that with the new technology of guided long-range air-to-air missiles, the close-in dogfight was a relic of the past.

The new Vulcan cannon filled the short-range gap when missiles proved to be ineffective. In testimony to the cannon's effectiveness, F-4s scored three MiG kills the first month it was installed, and downed seven more MiGs with it before the bombing halt of April 1, 1968.

Walleye Glide Bomb

The Navy first introduced the AGM-62 Walleye glide bomb in the Southeast Asia theater in March 1967.

The Walleye glide bomb, about 11 feet long and a foot in diameter with stabilizing fins to allow it to glide accurately, homed in on its target by means of a television guidance system. First the pilot locked the bomb's guidance system onto a particular light-dark contrast point on his modified radar-television screen in his cockpit. This action locked the guidance camera in the nose of the Walleye glide bomb to that point on the ground, allowing the aircraft to launch the bomb from a stand-off altitude and then leave, minimizing the aircraft's exposure to antiaircraft fire.

The pilot then continued to receive the television picture from the bomb's guidance camera right up to the moment of impact, giving him the capability to correct the bomb's trajectory if needed. Not only did the Walleye glide bomb increase a bomber's survivability, but its accuracy as well—meaning that fewer aircraft were needed for success for any given mission.

On May 19, during a Walleye glide bomb attack mission the Navy's largest air-to-air engagement thus far in the war took place. The huge dogfight resulted from an "Alpha" (maximum-effort) air strike staged from two aircraft carriers—the *Bon Homme Richard* and the *Kitty Hawk*—against the Hanoi thermal power plant.

Two A-4 Skyhawks were assigned to deposit the Walleyes literally through the windows of the power plant—the heavily-guarded target's most vulnerable spots. To suppress antiaircraft fire, six F-8E fighters from VF-24 preceded the A-4 Skyhawks into the target area. In addition, aircraft from *Kitty Hawk* staged a diversionary strike against a nearby truck park to further distract the North Vietnamese's attention and to saturate the defenses.

MiG-17s intercepted the main strike group as it penetrated, only to lose an aircraft to the F-8 of Lt. Phil Wood. Tobogganing down in altitude to increase speed and out-distance the MiGs, the A-4s dropped to the deck for the final 10 miles. Intense antiaircraft fire and SA-2 missiles filled the sky, downing two of the F-8 escorts. The A-4s, however, successfully popped up and delivered the Walleyes on target. The F-8s from VF-24 and VF-211 intercepted as many as 10 MiG-17s attempting to pursue the escaping A-4s, engaging the MiGs in a swirling dogfight from "treetop level up to 4,000 feet." Comdr. Paul Speer latched onto one MiG-17, dispatching it quickly; his wingman, Lt. J. G. Bob Lee, downed another MiG-17 as the strike group of A-4s successfully flew across the mountains and back out to sea.[53]

EC-121 Radar Surveillance Aircraft

In August 1967, an improved EC-121 Airborne Early Warning (AEW) radar surveillance aircraft with a superior radar system became operational. With the initial EC-121 introduced right after the first F-105s were shot down in April 1965, U.S. radar surveillance from the air was able to compete with the NVAF radar coverage from the ground-controlled intercept (GCI) radars on the ground. While the integrated defense radar network had given the North Vietnamese an important initial advantage, EC-121 aircraft orbiting over Laos and over the Gulf of Tonkin, in addition to electronic intelligence gathered from Navy PIRAZ (Position Identification Recognition Alert Zone) "picket" ships, allowed the United States to monitor much of the airborne traffic over North Vietnam.

While this capability was good at high altitudes, the lower altitudes were generally masked to radar coverage due to the clutter of spurious radar signals returned from the ground. Yet much of the critical air combat occurred between the deck of vegetation up to a few thousand feet—exactly where radar was generally its poorest, especially at long standoff ranges.

The improved EC-121, called the EC-121M Rivet Top, had the new ability to indicate the position of MiGs even when the radar couldn't see the aircraft due to clutter. The capability was derived from the EC-121M's advanced IFF (Identification Friend or Foe) capability.[54]

The MiGs Rise Again: Third Phase of the Battle for Air Superiority

Through June and July 1967, the MiGs virtually disappeared, leaving the antiaircraft guns and surface-to-air missiles to deal with the "Yankee Pirates." What MiGs did venture into the North Vietnamese skies kept a healthy distance from U.S. strike groups, limiting their activity to "training and to practice intercepts." The U.S. continued to move closer to Hanoi as its bombing of North Vietnam intensified.

MiGs became briefly active in late July, tangling with U.S. Navy F-8s from the *Bon Homme Richard*. Three F-8Cs from VF-24 and an F-8E from VF-211 downed four MiG-17s on July 21, doubling the MiG tally of the carrier's air wing.[55]

The air battle heated up again in August, the MiGs returning in force to challenge the U.S. for air superiority, with a new tactic that took full advantage of the vulnerability of the F-4 escorts. The NVAF began to vector its MiG-21s at low altitude on the deck, where they remained hidden behind ridges to the search radars of the EC-121Ms, Navy picket ships, and F-4 MiGCAPS until they had reached a position well abreast and slightly behind the intended targets. Once a MiG-21 was to the rear of the strike group, the GCI controller would call for it to climb at maximum rate to an attack position.

Properly executed, the U.S. aircraft had little or no warning as the MiG made a single high-speed pass. With an initial climb rate of approximately 30,000 feet per minute, the MiG-21 could climb to attack position in 30 seconds or less. That would give the rotodome radar of the EC-121M or picket ship only a few "paints" of the fast-moving MiG before its Atoll air-to-air missiles came off the rails.

Even with a warning, the MiG's small size made it tough to spot—and just seeing the MiG was crucial to any pilot trying to evade it, not to mention surviving its attacks. After making his firing pass, the MiG pilot would dive away again before any escort fighter could get on his tail.

On August 23, the U.S. Air Force got its first taste of the new tactic against a mission sent to bomb the railyard at Yen Vien. Two MiG-21s materialized from below a 25,000-foot overcast, each firing an Atoll missile at the MiGCAP flight. Capt. Nyugen Van Coc of the Second Co. led the element of two MiG-21s.

According to Michael O'Connor writing in "Aces of the Yellow Star" in *Air Combat:* "The MiGs went low to pick up speed and energy. GCI, feeding the MiGs continuous updates on the bandits, brought the North Vietnamese into position behind the Americans. The MiGs cut in their afterburners and climbed to 25,000 feet. Diving through the overcast the MiGs bounced a flight of F-4Ds from the 8th TFW's "Triple-Nickel" Squadron. Coc and his wingman both fired single Atolls, one at the lead F-4 and the other at Number 4. Ford 04, crewed by Capt. Larry Carrigan and Lt. Charles Lane took a hit in the tailpipe and blew up. Shortly thereafter Ford 01, manned by Maj. Charles Tyler and Capt. Ronald Sittner, exploded in a fireball. Three chutes were observed descending to the ground."[56]

Each Atoll missile had found its mark before the MiGs had even been spotted and the two "Blue Bandits" were long gone before anyone could react.

The strike force, now minus two of the MiGCAP F-4s, encountered still more MiGs as it attacked the Yen Vien railroad yards. The sky soon became a swirling mass of MiG-17s, MiG-21s, F-4s, and F-105s. One of the F-4s fired a pair of AIM-7 Sparrows at what turned out to be an F-4, not a MiG as the pilot had supposed. Discovering this to his horror as the missile

This F-105 was struck by a North Vietnamese-launched AA-2 Atoll infrared-guided, air-to-air missile. Despite extensive damage, the F-105 was able to return to its base in Thailand with the missile embedded in its rear fuselage. The missile's tail is visible to the left of the hand-held ruler. (Fairchild Republic)

homed true, the pilot had his backseater Weapons System Officer (WSO) break lock, causing the two missiles to go ballistic.

Meanwhile, MiG-17s latched onto the tails of several of the F-105s completing their bombing runs, damaging one with gunfire. Another MiG-17 intent on pursuing a F-105 found himself the target of the angry 20-mm Vulcan cannon of Lt. David B. Waldrop III. At the end of his bombing run, Waldrop was pulling off target in his F-105 when he spotted the fellow F-105 in trouble. Firing his afterburner to close distance with the MiG, he opened fire. In his words:

"Shortly afterwards, some fire shot out from his wingtips and about midway across the wing he started a slow roll over to the right. I backed off and fired again. He continued rolling right on in and blew up when he hit the ground."

As later described by Colonel Olds, who had witnessed the engagement: "It was beautiful. The MiG-17 was diving toward the ground with flames coming out of his tailpipe. It wasn't the afterburner, he was on fire. There was that great, great huge Thud (F-105) right behind him with fire coming out of his nose. It looked like a shark chasing a minnow."[57]

Waldrop, however, was not through for the day; he slid up behind two more MiG-17s and opened fire nearly broadside—85-degree angle off—and 3,000 feet distant, scoring hits with his 20-mm shells before losing sight of the MiGs in some clouds. Rolling inverted as he reemerged on the other side, he regained the object of his pursuit, only to find that the attitude gyros of his gunsight had tumbled during the maneuver and his gunsight was no longer functioning. Waldrop fired without it, striking from the canopy back and causing the MiG to explode.

The day ended with the two original MiGCAP F-4Ds lost to MiGs and one F-105 heavily damaged from cannon fire. The NVAF had lost two MiG-17s with another damaged.

To reduce losses of MiGs on the ground that had been mounting as U.S. forces continued to strike MiG airfields, the North Vietnamese Air Force moved all but about 20 of its MiGs to bases in the prohibited zone of South China where they were immune from attack. Each day the MiGs were flown to bases in North Vietnam, using the Vietnamese bases as staging areas for interceptions, and retiring the MiGs to South China right after attacks to prevent any of them from being caught on the ground. The sanctuary also allowed the NVAF unmolested airspace in which to retrain pilots and polish tactics without interference from U.S. aircraft.

In late August, President Johnson ordered a ban on the bombing of the restricted area around Hanoi. The respite was ordered for 10 days beginning August 24, giving the North Vietnamese time to respond to U.S. peace initiatives. The ban was extended when Hanoi did not respond by the deadline initially set forth. During the ban, air-to-air encounters between MiGs and U.S. aircraft slackened, and no victories were scored by either the U.S. Navy or the Air Force.

When negotiations broke down, 10 new targets were added to the list. Nine of the new targets were inside the prohibited areas of Hanoi and Haiphong.[58]

In late October, approval finally came to hit Phuc Yen airfield—the NVAF's heavily-defended main field and the central hub for ground-controlled intercept operations. On October 25, the first strike was scheduled against this primary MiG field often overflown but never attacked.[59]

U.S. Navy and Air Force aircraft coordinated their attacks to suppress the heavy defenses around Phuc Yen. The first strike succeeded in destroying on the ground four MiG-21s, four MiG-17s, and possibly damaging a MiG-15; moreover, a MiG-21 was downed in aerial combat. This MiG was first damaged by an AIM-7 Sparrow from an F-4 piloted by Maj. William L. Kirk, and finished off with the same F-4's 20-mm Vulcan cannon.

Even after the attack on Phuc Yen, MiGs remained active, losing four on October 26: three to U.S. Air Force Phantoms and one to a Navy F-4.

Fall 1967: No Holds Barred

As the U.S. resumed its bombing of North Vietnam, MiGs continually engaged strike forces in renewed aerial combat. The U.S. military now had permission from the Joint Chiefs to strike all the MiG bases except Gia Lam International Airport, and the MiGs fought to protect them.

In addition to dogged opposition from the MiGs, U.S. aircraft began feeling pressure from the other legs of North Vietnam's integrated air defense network, encountering unprecedented numbers of surface-to-air missiles protecting those targets at the heart of the Iron Triangle (the triangular area defined by Thai Nguyen, Hanoi, and Haiphong encompassing the heart of North Vietnam's industry).

Defeating the surface-to-air missiles was getting tougher. The North Vietnamese began receiving the latest version of the SA-2 tracking radar, the Fan Song F, which had electro-optical tracking capability. These trackers were being rushed to North Vietnam to compensate for the radar jamming by U.S. aircraft.

The electro-optical capability of the Fan Song F system allowed the operator to fire the SA-2 missile even when radar jamming was intense; furthermore, the passive optical mode prevented the lethal Wild Weasel from picking up any Fan Song radar emissions and firing a Shrike missile. The electro-optical device could also permit the SA-2 to be fired at targets below 3,000 feet where radar clutter had interfered with previous versions. With the introduction of the latest Fan Song radar, U.S. pilots were once again at a tactical disadvantage.

A U.S. Air Force weather/reconnaissance RF-4C is shot down by an SA-2 missile—graphic evidence of the missile warhead's effectiveness. Both crew members successfully ejected, but only one was released with other prisoners of war following the peace treaty that ended the Vietnam War.

MiG Tactics: Evening the Score

By the end of 1967 U.S. pilots scored eight more victories against the MiG interceptor force. Through August 1967, the United States clearly had the edge: the NVAF lost 24 MiG-21s compared to the U.S. forces' loss of six aircraft. But the NVAF began to even the score; more than one MiG pilot now claimed several kills and some reportedly reached the status of ace with five kills or more. In the next six months from August 1967 to February 1968, the United States lost 18 aircraft and killed only five MiG-21s.

Nonetheless, over the same six months the United States did wage heavy attrition on the MiG-17s, scoring 17 victories.

On a December 19 mission to bomb the railroad yards at Viet Tri and Tien Cuong, the United States discovered that the MiGs had evolved a new tactic. MiG-21s and MiG-17s were now coordinating their attacks on strike groups by approaching in multiple passes from different directions.

Their varying direction and altitude compounded the MiGCAP aircrafts' protective mission by making detection and continued observation difficult. The MiGs' new tactic was so effective that all the aircraft in one of the mission's two strike groups were forced to jettison ordnance in order to defend themselves against the well-timed attacks.

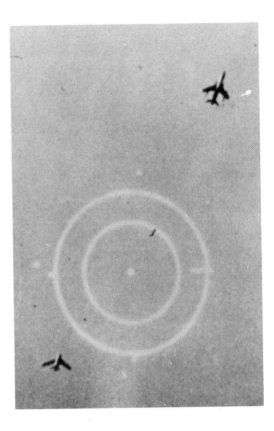

A North Vietnamese MiG-17 makes a firing pass at an F-105 in a dogfight northwest of Hanoi on December 19, 1967. The action was filmed by the gunsight camera of another F-105. North Vietnamese MiGs became very aggressive through the end of 1967 and early in 1968. (U.S. Air Force)

It became clear that the MiGs were coordinating their attacks more skillfully with other elements of the integrated air-defense network—evidence not only of increased proficiency of the pilots but also of the growing ability of the air-defense controller to choreograph such attacks.

The proportional share of U.S. losses to MiGs alone compared to losses to MiGs, antiaircraft fire, and surface-to-air missiles combined rose from eight percent in 1967 to 22 percent in the first three months of 1968.

Quite often MiGs would attack in sets of two pairs—one pair trailing the other—to try to sandwich between them any U.S. aircraft that went after the first pair, which acted as bait. As the dogfight developed, the MiG-17s would take advantage of their superior turning ability to go into a wagon-wheel orbit, usually near the U.S. strike group's primary target. Often the wagon-wheel orbits carried them near antiaircraft artillery batteries, which would ambush any U.S. fighters going after the MiG-17s.

The North Vietnamese expanded the number of SA-2 sites protecting targets and began firing unprecedented numbers of missiles to compensate for their degraded radar. U.S. pilots were dodging as many as 60 missiles a day. Nonetheless, the effectiveness of the U.S. electronic countermeasures showed as North Vietnamese SA-2 kills dropped from 2.8 percent in 1966 to 1.75 percent in 1967 despite the fact that almost three times as many missiles were fired.[60]

On January 14, 1968, two MiG-21s downed an EB-66C. With this loss, and in the face of increased resistance, the orbits of the EB-66C jammers were moved well away from the Iron Triangle into safer areas over Laos and in the Gulf of Tonkin.[61]

Although the more-distant orbits were safer from MiG attack, their distance considerably reduced the power and effect of jamming. By using the MiGs to counter a threat to the other elements of the integrated defense network, the NVAF won this round, degrading the effectiveness of the EB-66C support jamming.

One of the first air-to-air kills of 1968 was certainly one of the most unusual engagements of the war. It occurred above the ground-based radar station in Laos known as Lima Site 85 between a helicopter and three piston-engine light transports. Lima Site 85 was attacked by three Russian-made AN-2 Colt biplanes that attempted to strafe and bomb the base.

A U.S. helicopter responded, the crews of both the helicopter and the biplanes firing handheld weapons at each other. The helicopter downed one Colt in this duel, and another attempting to bomb the site. The third fled and was pursued by the helicopter, which inflicted such heavy damage that the Colt crashed 18 miles from the site.

Frustrated by the abortive aerial attack, the North Vietnamese later sent ground units to capture the site, crucial to guiding U.S. bombers to their targets especially during the monsoon season.

On March 10, after savage hand-to-hand combat with 100 Meo tribesmen tasked to guard the site, the North Vietnamese troops succeeded in overrunning the facility.[62]

On January 30, U.S. and South Vietnamese troops were shocked into confronting an all-out ground offensive that struck every major population center in South Vietnam including Saigon. During the first three days, an estimated 70,000 determined shock troops attacked 36 of the 44 provincial capitals, five out of the six autonomous cities, 64 of the 242 district capitals, 50 hamlets, and almost all airfields.

The widespread fighting raged throughout February, the worst combat centering in Saigon and Hue with bitter street fighting. However, the offensive never fulfilled North Vietnam's expectations, nor did the South Vietnamese crumple as expected; they acquitted themselves well and thereby renewed their own faith in themselves and that of the public.

The Tet offensive was a tactical disaster for the North Vietnamese. It was estimated that more than half of the attacking Viet Cong and North Vietnamese had been killed while failing to capture and hold any major territory. NVA's Gen. Nguyen Vo Giap had failed to achieve any of his stated objectives save one: the offensive, although a tactical loss, had indeed inflicted major political wounds on the U.S. resolve.

President Johnson, faced with an election in a country disillusioned with war, announced that the United States would cease all bombing north of the 20th parallel on March 31, inviting the North Vietnamese to the conference table. Hanoi, now wounded and anxious to relieve any pressure in order to lick its wounds, desperately needed time.

For the first time the North Vietnamese government reversed its hardline stance against negotiation. A few days later, the prohibition was extended 70 miles farther south to the 19th parallel.

Losses in 1967 exceeded the capability of the North Vietnamese to supply replacements and the Tet offensive further killed an estimated 100,000 North Vietnamese troops. The North Vietnamese had far more to gain than the United States by agreeing to negotiate. The immediate gain was the cessation of the bombing up north; the long-term gain was to buy time to infiltrate men and train cadre in the south.

In the long months that followed the bombing halt of 1968, the United States reevaluated its position while talks continued in Paris. With the new U.S. President, Richard M. Nixon, came the concept of Vietnamization: letting the Vietnamese take the forefront in their war against the Communists by increasing the South Vietnamese ranks, strengthening their military capabilities, and creating a strong infrastructure in the country under the title of pacification to resist the Communist subversion in the countryside.

Washington began reequipping the South Vietnamese with M-16 rifles, M-60 machine guns, M-79 grenade launchers, mortars, howitzers, armor, helicopters, and jets. The United States also began a massive training program to retrain South Vietnam troops and to train others in specialties that they had relied on the United States to provide.

In December 1967, the Navy introduced a new strike aircraft into the battle zone: the A-7A Corsair II. A-7s of VA-147 flying off the *Ranger* saw action on December 4 during a strike against bridges and highways near Vinh.

Superficially similar to the F-8 fighter, the subsonic A-7 was designed to carry a large weapons load over a long distance. Compared to its A-4 predecessor, the A-7 could carry twice the payload of bombs or range twice as far with a similar weapons load.[63]

In mid-March 1968, the U.S. Air Force deployed to Takhli RTAFB an aircraft that could fly missions under all weather conditions and at night: the F-111. Developed as a high-performance fighter-bomber, the 46,172 pound (empty) F-111A could accommodate up to 30,000 pounds of weapons and fuel tanks on eight underwing stores stations and in a small internal weapons bay. The large swing-wing attack aircraft could carry three times the combat load of an F-4 or F-105, penetrate at high speeds and low altitudes, and strike targets at long range.

Under a program entitled Combat Lancer, the F-111As flew 55 missions during March and April against well-defended targets in North Vietnam. During the attacks, three of the aircraft were lost, two in March and one in April. Maintenance problems, systems failures, and bad publicity due to the losses resulted in the F-111As being withdrawn from combat operations in April 1968.[64]

MiG encounters and air combat were greatly reduced during 1968. Air Force F-4Ds fought with MiGs several times, destroying three MiG-21s and five MiG-17s during January and February. However, the North Vietnamese also shot down a number of U.S. Air Force aircraft and the kill-to-loss ratio of both sides was running parallel.

Analysis

Although this chapter has concentrated on the air warfare over North Vietnam, it must not be forgotten that the main conflict was being fought on the ground in the south.

While the introduction of aircraft to the close support role in South Vietnam provided devastating destructive power, in practice its effectiveness was lessened by the nature of the war in the South. The North Vietnamese Army and Viet Cong rarely committed themselves to battle in the open where air power could readily deal with them. Massive numbers of sophisticated command-and-control sensors and weapons were used to pinpoint the elusive North Vietnamese Army and Viet Cong aggressors. The lush jungle from which they attacked rendered virtually all activity beneath the fronds invisible to airborne surveillance.

The same impediments to turning the tide of battle in the close support role hampered the interdiction effort waged against the extensive supply caravans that wove through the rugged foliage-shrouded hills of Laos and Cambodia. Specialized aircraft were designed to deal with the complex interdiction mission. An entire series of gunships culminating in the AC-130 Spectre proved to be very effective in detecting movement of men and destroying materiel coming down the Ho Chi Minh Trail. These relied on low-light electro-optical sensors and infrared tracking devices to pinpoint trucks moving southward at night.

In many cases, large areas were bombed in an effort to block such choke points as the Mu Gia pass, the main portal out of North Vietnam into Laos and Cambodia. Cells of B-52 bombers destroyed acres of terrain in an effort to knock out supply caches and suspected locations of North Vietnamese troops. Despite the periodic bombing halts called for several weeks at a time in North Vietnam, the bombing of the Ho Chi Minh Trail in Laos, Cambodia, and South Vietnam was continuous throughout the war.

During the massive Tet offensive in the spring of 1968, air power provided the margin of victory. Offered the opportunity to hit the North Vietnamese and Viet Cong units in fixed positions, U.S. air might was able to greatly attrit the Tet invaders. The effectiveness of the bombing of North Vietnam must be looked at in light of the self-imposed restrictions on the employment of U.S. air power. The restrictions were applied primarily to prevent direct Soviet or Chinese intervention that could have turned the limited war into a direct confrontation between superpowers. As a result, U.S. airmen were forced to fight a war following tight rules of engagement and restrictions. The net result was to dilute the potency of the air campaign, turning it into a war of attrition against the North Vietnamese.

The growth of the North Vietnamese air defense network was undoubtedly aided by the gradualness of the U.S. bombing campaign—allowing the air defense network to grow largely unhindered into an extensive system that extracted a heavy toll of U.S. aircraft. In the three years of bombing, the United States lost more than 900 aircraft to the North Vietnamese defenses. Antiaircraft artillery accounted for more than 700 aircraft, the SA-2 Guideline surface-to-air missile downed about 100 aircraft, and MiGs claimed more than 50 aircraft.[65] These statistics are all the more impressive when it is considered that before the August 1964 Gulf of Tonkin incident the North Vietnamese possessed an air-defense network comprising only a handful of radars and antiaircraft artillery pieces.

The United States had declared SA-2 sites under construction off limits to avoid killing any Soviet advisers. This ban, along with restricted areas around the important cities of Hanoi and Haiphong and a buffer zone along the Chinese border, gave the North Vietnamese a sanctuary for supplies and air defense positions.

Moreover, the U.S. practice of pauses to try to bring North Vietnam to negotiations gave North Vietnam further opportunity to rebuild and improve its defenses. The determination of the North Vietnamese and U.S. restrictions and pauses tended to offset the U.S. military, technological, and economic edge, allowing North Vietnam to sustain the war in the face of heavy air attacks.

Air Warfare Tactics and Technology

Over the course of the Vietnam conflict the tactics and technology of aerial warfare evolved, as they have in all wars since the first dogfights in World War I. Radar, the invisible ally that provided a decisive edge in its first use during the Battle of Britain in 1940, played a major role in air war over North Vietnam.

The entire air defense system of North Vietnam was predicated on many radar sites to provide long-range early warning of approaching U.S. aircraft, to guide the SA-2 missile, to aim and fire the larger antiaircraft artillery pieces, and to be the eyes for the ground-controlled intercept network that vectored MiG interceptors into firing positions. The value of this interlocking, redundant radar system cannot be overestimated.

An early lesson of the Vietnam conflict was that antiaircraft artillery was indeed very effective despite the increased speeds of modern jet fighter aircraft. In fact, flying at altitudes below 3,500 feet was virtual suicide. By 1968, U.S. aircraft minimized their exposure to the everpresent antiaircraft artillery fire by flying above the heaviest concentrations at lower altitudes, and by using the then-available electronic countermeasures to negate the radar fire-control of the heavier-caliber antiaircraft artillery that was able to reach the usual flying altitudes of between 10,000 and 15,000 feet.

Mild jinking in heading and altitude also threw off the aim of visually-sighted antiaircraft artillery. These tactics, although improving the odds of survival, still did not render aircraft immune from the antiaircraft artillery, which in 1968 still caused the lion's share of U.S. losses.

These statistics forced defense planners around the world to reconsider antiaircraft artillery as a viable part of their air defense systems and not as an old-fashioned weapon that would be rendered obsolete by guided missile defenses.

On the other hand, the SA-2 Guideline surface-to-air missile, making its combat debut in North Vietnam, proved to be somewhat of a disappointment. When it was first introduced in July 1965, it did create technological shock in the United States and forced a change in tactics until electronic countermeasures could be devised to defeat it. Initially, U.S. aircraft went back to low-altitude flying, below the 3,000-foot minimum operational envelope of the SA-2—a move that made them vulnerable to the deadliest antiaircraft artillery. Within a year, however, U.S. aircraft were equipped with radar homing-and-warning (RHAW) equipment that alerted them to nearby SA-2 radar activity.

That radar warning, coupled with evasive maneuvering upon sighting a missile launch, allowed U.S. pilots to shake off a pursuing SA-2. The advent of RHAW gear let U.S. aircraft return to the preferred higher altitudes where the effectiveness of antiaircraft artillery was less and where aircraft fuel consumption and tactical coordination were better.

In order to better jam the SA-2, antiaircraft artillery, and acquisition radars, the U.S. Air Force introduced the standoff EB-66 aircraft, and supplemented it with a whole series of jamming pods: ALQ-71, ALQ-87, ALQ-101, and others. ALQ-72 pods were used to jam hostile airborne fire-control systems such as the MiG-21's Spin Scan radar.[66]

The F-100F and subsequently the F-105F/G two-seat aircraft were deployed with special radar-detection devices to track enemy radars. Once those radars were detected, these aircraft and others attacked the radar sites with Shrike anti-radiation missiles and other ordnance.

The Navy reacted to the threat of the SA-2, antiaircraft artillery, and MiG threat with its own electronic countermeasures effort: In addition to RHAW equipment, Navy aircraft were fitted with chaff dispensers and internally mounted deception/repeater electronic countermeasures equipment. Such standoff detection and jamming aircraft as the EA-6A, EA-3, EA-1F, and Marine EF-10B added electronic noise to suppress or deceive North Vietnamese radars and jam ground-controlled intercept communications.

Ironhand flights—tactical aircraft armed with Shrike and conventional weapons—provided the Navy with the ability to suppress defenses just prior to an air strike.[67]

The battle against the SA-2 developed into an evolving move/countermove situation during which both sides introduced newer technology and tactics to better those of the other. While the SA-2's effectiveness lessened over time as U.S. countermeasures improved, the missile did force the United States to devote considerable numbers of aircraft to defeat it, such as Wild Weasel and Ironhand aircraft. In many cases, the SA-2 forced aircraft to jettison ordnance in order to evade it, which in effect negated an aircraft's mission while exposing it to the other elements of the North Vietnamese air defense system. In any case, the fearsome sight of the telephone-pole-sized missile hurtling skyward belching flame from its tail never failed to rivet the attention of U.S. aircrews.

The Air Superiority Battle

North Vietnam's MiGs were the leg of the air defense system that improved most dramatically during the three years of the Rolling Thunder bombing campaign. Tied closely to the extensive ground-controlled intercept network, the MiGs proved to be very flexible; by the end of 1966, barely one year after the NVAF's first aerial encounters, the MiGs had become a serious impediment to the U.S. bombing campaign. Taking advantage of superiority in radar coverage, the MiGs were vectored into the rear quarter of U.S. flights, giving them the advantages of initial surprise, favorable firing position, and the option of disengaging if conditions were unfavorable.

The MiG-17 and MiG-21 were the mainstays of the NVAF's interceptor force. The subsonic MiG-17 flew primarily at lower altitudes, usually as a point-defense interceptor at the strike force's target. The MiG-17 usually attacked just before the bombing run, in an attempt to force jettison of bombloads.

Strike aircraft were particularly vulnerable just before reaching the target, as they had to fly a predictable flight path while acquiring the target and making the attack run. If the MiGs couldn't force the strike aircraft to jettison ordnance before reaching the target, they held off while the strike force flew over the actual target, letting the antiaircraft artillery and the SA-2 batteries have a shot; more MiG-17s waited on the other side of the target, ready to pay particular attention to any battle-crippled aircraft.

The Mach-2 MiG-21 proved to be North Vietnam's most effective interceptor. The MiG-21's high-speed attacks were very difficult to detect and counter. North Vietnamese GCI controllers were well aware of the U.S. radar limitations and would vector the MiG-21 around the flanks of the strike groups below the coverage of U.S. radar. Once in position at the rear, the controller would instruct the MiG pilot to climb fast and fire his Atoll missiles—giving standoff radar platforms almost no time to detect the attack and warn the strike force. Fighter escorts were also hard-pressed to visually spot the small high-speed MiGs closing fast from their rear.

Moreover, as the Vietnam conflict progressed, the MiG attacks became more numerous and coordinated, approaching from several directions simultaneously and flying baiting maneuvers to draw off fighter escorts from the more vulnerable strike aircraft. By the time of the bombing halt of 1968, there was no doubt in anyone's mind that the MiGs were a force to be reckoned with.

Between 1965 and 1968, U.S. aircraft downed 120 MiGs in dogfights while suffering 55 losses. The following chart shows a breakdown of these air combat kills and losses by U.S. service and aircraft. (The "half" kill for both the Phantoms and the Thunderchiefs comes from one dogfight in which an F-105 damaged a MiG and an F-4 finished it off.)

The air superiority battle over North Vietnam went through a number of phases:

Southeast Asia Air-to-Air Combat 1965–1968

	Victories	Losses
U.S. Air Force	86	41
U.S. Navy	34	14
U.S. Air Force	(aircraft type and number of victories)	
F-4C/D		58½
F-105D/F		27½
U.S. Navy		
F-8C/E/J		18
F-4B/J		14
A-1E		1
A-4C		1

Data compiled from: *Aces and Aerial Victories, MiG Master, Armed Forces Journal,* May 1974, and *Combat Losses to MiG Aircraft in Southeast Asia 1965-1972,* Center for Naval Analysis Paper 78-0397.

I April 1965–March 1966

The initial period began with the loss of two U.S. Air Force F-105Ds to MiG-17s. The primary North Vietnamese interceptor was the MiG-17 while the U.S. Air Force and Navy employed F-4 Phantoms and F-8 Crusaders. The North Vietnamese had few experienced pilots and they generally refrained from attacking. Most U.S. Air Force and Navy strike missions during this period were flown against targets in the southern or western areas of North Vietnam, away from the MiG bases. North Vietnam relied primarily on its SA-2 and antiaircraft batteries to challenge American aircraft. As a result, there were few air combat engagements and kills or losses on either side during this period.

II April 1966–July 1967

During the spring of 1966, MiG sniping became very aggressive against U.S. strike formations in an attempt to force them to jettison their bombs. The MiG-21, phased into service during this period, introduced a high-performance missile threat to U.S. aircraft. The United States, on the other hand, using medium-altitude penetration tactics, radar warning, and electronic countermeasures equipment reduced the effectiveness of the North Vietnamese SA-2 and antiaircraft defenses, forcing heavy reliance on interceptors. While a number of U.S. aircraft were shot down, the MiGs took a beating: In June 1967, the exchange ratio was 3.77 MiGs for each U.S. aircraft.[68]

III August 1967–October 1968

During the summer of 1967 the North Vietnamese perfected the integration of their ground-controlled intercept network with new MiG attack tactics to counter U.S. strike formations and escorting fighters. MiG-21s, for example, accurately vectored by GCI controllers made slashing supersonic attacks against U.S. strike groups. Between June and December 1967, MiG-21s downed six opponents with no losses. These tactics combined with MiG-17 low-altitude engagements were highly effective between July 1967 until March 1968; the United States lost 24 aircraft while downing only 27 MiGs.

Although the U.S. military increased escort forces, and employed new formations, the kill-to-loss ratio remained only slightly in its favor until the cessation of operations over North Vietnam on October 31, 1968.

U.S. Navy Air-to-Air Performance

From the totals the F-4 Phantom emerges as the overall leader with 71½ kills. In Navy kills, however, the F-4 was edged out by its predecessor, the F-8 Crusader. The F-8 also ranked highest in kills per engagement (0.7).

Often referred to as ''the last of the gunfighters,'' the F-8 was armed with four internal 20-mm cannon and four Sidewinder missiles. There was intense competition between the Navy's older F-8 squadrons and their successor missile-only F-4 squadrons. Most F-8 pilots believed the larger F-4 was more suited to intercepts than to the close-in dogfighting role. The F-8 scored its first MiG kill in June 1966, almost a year after the first MiG kills of the war made by Navy F-4s. The F-8 proved its worth and garnered an impressive share of MiG kills while losing few.

The F-8 was the only U.S. fighter able to take on the MiG-21 and MiG-17 in a horizontal-turning fight. Moreover, the preponderance of F-8 training centered around air combat maneuvering, which gave F-8 pilots considerable experience. The value of this was

The U.S. Navy F-8 Crusader proved to be an excellent air superiority fighter. U.S. Navy Crusader pilots scored 18 victories against North Vietnamese MiGs between 1965 and 1968. (Lou Drendel)

demonstrated by the exchange rate. The training of F-4 pilots was divided between air combat maneuvering and intercept missions.

Although the F-8 possessed a lower wingloading and greater capability for instantaneous high-g accelerations with which to take on the MiGs on their own terms, the F-4 crews discovered that the Phantom's greater thrust-to-weight ratio and sustained-g capability allowed it to fight in the vertical dimension of air combat and to take on the MiGs (and even F-8s in mock combat) and emerge victorious.

Over North Vietnam, the F-4 proved itself a potent adversary, possessing the longer-range, radar-guided Sparrow missile and advanced all-weather fire-control system that enhanced its lethality over the F-8 and its MiG opponents. This longer-range capability was not always exploited to its full potential, however, because of the U.S. rules of engagement.

The backseater and operator of the F-4's fire-control system and radar, known as the radar intercept officer (RIO), proved his worth as an extra set of eyes in the close-in, maneuvering dogfight. While the crew concept of the two-seat F-4 sparked a controversy over single-seat vs. two-seat aircraft, there is no doubt that many F-4s survived dogfights because of alert backseaters.

One severe F-4 deficiency noted after the early engagements was the lack of a gun for close-in fighting. Another was the less-than-optimum performance of the Sidewinder and Sparrow missiles. The missiles were not originally designed to engage small, highly-maneuverable targets, and the engagement envelopes were limited in a confusing array of restrictions in the ratio of altitude to speed, angle-off, and look-down (clutter: AIM-7, heat return: AIM-9). These combinations precluded their use in some situations and resulted in out-of-the-envelope firings in others. As a result, the missiles had to be modified and crews trained to greater familiarity with the envelopes.

A-1 and A-4 attack aircraft victories against the MiG-17 are also worthy of note as they demonstrate the effectiveness of aggressiveness and tactics. Although neither of those aircraft, particularly the A-1, were designed for air combat, they turned the tables on the MiG-17 through their pilots' superb airmanship, application of sound tactics, and marksmanship.

Following the bombing halt of 1968, the Navy initiated a detailed study to examine its air-to-air performance. The study, known as the Ault Report, concluded that the experience over

North Vietnam had shown that air-to-air missiles were not sufficient by themselves, and that the United States needed to devote renewed emphasis to the close-in air combat arena. Such air combat training should include pitting aircrews against dissimilar aircraft, and operating missiles in a dogfight environment. These recommendations led the Navy in 1969 to establish its Top Gun Fighter Weapons School.

The Ault Report also recommended that the technology of the next generation of fighters recognize the demands of the dogfight, and reinstate such features excluded from the Phantom's design as cannon, superior-visibility canopies, and smokeless engines.

U.S. Air Force Air-to-Air Performance

The U.S. Air Force's leading MiG killer was the F-4 Phantom, in service barely a year before its first MiG encounters in the summer of 1965. Originally a Navy aircraft, the Phantom was ordered by the Air Force as its primary air superiority fighter when the Department of Defense called for commonality between the services.

In contrast to Navy practice, the Air Force manned its F-4s with two pilots (the backseat pilot known as the weapons system officer or WSO) instead of a pilot and radar intercept operator. In 1968, with 58½ kills, the Air Force Phantom crews emerged as the top MiG-killing combination of both services.

The Air Force soon realized the close-in deficiency of the Phantom and in May 1967 began equipping some F-4s with external 20-mm gunpods; it also specified an internal cannon installation for its forthcoming F-4E version. The externally mounted gunpod was only a short-

An F-4D from the 555th "Triple Nickel" Tactical Fighter Squadron of the 12th Tactical Fighter Wing at a rendezvous with a KC-135 tanker to refuel. U.S. Air Force F-4s were tasked with MiGCAP and strike escort missions and, as a result, scored the majority of MiG kills during the Vietnam War. (U.S. Air Force)

term fix because the gunpod's drag increased fuel consumption and decreased maneuverability. However, from 1965 through 1968 gunpod-equipped F-4Cs and F-4Ds accounted for 10 MiGs.

Air Force crews found that a horizontal turning fight was to be avoided against the tighter-turning MiG-17s and MiG-21s; instead the crews utilized the superior acceleration and vertical-climbing capability of the F-4 to turn the tables on their North Vietnamese adversaries.

In all cases, a slow fight was to be avoided especially against the spry darting MiG-17 but F-4 pilots would gladly fight their machines at low altitude where the thick air gave them the best engine response and turn performance.

The F-4's high thrust-to-weight ratio, two-man crew, superior radar, and longer-range missiles offset its large size and visibly smoking engines. Its aggressive crews gave the F-4 the margin against the MiGs in the end.

The F-105 Thunderchief was thrust into the role of MiG-killer not by design but as a matter of pure survival. The bomb-laden "Thuds" (as they were nicknamed) were MiG's prime target, and more often than not F-105s were forced to shoot their way out of the target area. Designed originally as a high-speed, low-level tactical nuclear bomber, the Thud was modified for the Vietnam strike role by adding external bomb racks. The two Thailand-based F-105 wings bore the brunt of 75 percent of all strike missions flown by the Air Force into North Vietnam.

Luckily for the F-105, its design included an internally-mounted 20-mm Vulcan cannon that gave it its lethal sting against the MiGs. The F-105's small slim wings provided no turning ability to speak of, but did contribute to its unmatched speed at low altitude. Once rid of its cumbersome bomb load, there was nothing on the face of the earth that was going to catch a Thud on the deck.

The F-105 assumed the duties of primary strike aircraft and of Ironhand or Wild Weasel defense-suppression aircraft; it was never assigned an air superiority mission. It is thus to the Thud's credit that it succeeded in downing 27½ MiGs, ranking it as the second-highest MiG-killer. When MiGs became highly active in late 1966, Thuds began carrying the AIM-9 Sidewinder heatseeking missile to augment self-defense. It scored 2½ kills with the Sidewinder, the rest with the 20-mm cannon.

The difficulty of bringing the MiGs to battle was as frustrating to the U.S. aircrews as was the attempt to lure the Viet Cong and North Vietnamese Army out of their jungle lairs.

This guerrilla-style fighting both on the ground and in the air was characteristic of the entire Vietnam conflict, and conventional-style warfare was waged only when conditions favored the Communists.

A number of significant factors contributed to the 2.18-to-1 kill-to-loss ratio U.S. forces achieved during the Vietnam air superiority campaign between 1965 and 1968.

Air-to-Air Missile Effectiveness

During the period 1965 to March 1, 1968, U.S. Air Force aircraft fired 442 missiles to achieve 52 MiG kills or an 11.7 percent effectiveness ratio. While this *raw* listing of data does not examine missiles deliberately fired out of their envelope, reliability failures, or other influencing factors, the results do show that air-to-air missiles did not perform as well as expected.[69]

The U.S. Air Force F-4C, F-4D, and U.S. Navy F-4B and F-4J Phantoms were armed with the radar-guided AIM-7 Sparrrow. The F-4, like the F-8, could carry infrared-homing AIM-9 Sidewinder missiles; in addition, the F-4D could carry the AIM-4D Falcon air-to-air missile. All three of these missiles were designed as defensive weapons to be used against non-maneuvering bomber targets. The missiles and their associated fire-control systems and equipment were complex, sensitive, and demanding with respect to handling and maintenance.

The AIM-7D/E Sparrow is very maneuverable and its lethal radius is large due to the missiles' sizable warhead and proximity fuse; this Sparrow also has the ability to detect and track targets at all aspects and at long range. In a stern attack, the missile has a range of 5,000 feet to three nautical miles; attacking head-on, it is effective between 12,000 feet and 13 nautical miles.[70]

The missile has a number of drawbacks, however, that reduced its effectiveness in Vietnam. A Sparrow attack required a high degree of crew coordination, and numerous cockpit control functions made it difficult to fire the missile accurately under the stress and high-g conditions of a dogfight. Because the Sparrow is a semi-active radar homing missile, the Phantom crew had to keep the radar illuminating the target from lock-on until the moment the missile struck home. If the pilot of a small, highly-maneuverable target aircraft is aware of the attack, the entire procedure of tracking, lock-on, and continued illumination is extremely difficult.

In addition, the Sparrow could not easily detect low-flying targets because its guidance system frequently shifted track from the target to a strong radar return from the ground. As a result, the AIM-7D/E's low-altitude performance was limited.

During the period 1965 to March 1, 1968, U.S. Air Force Phantoms fired 224 AIM-7D/E Sparrows to achieve 20 kills, a kill-probability ratio of 8.9 percent.[71]

The AIM-9B Sidewinder air-to-air missile homes on infrared emissions from a target's engine and airframe. The missile is simple, lightweight, and relatively cheap. To fire it, the pilot arms the weapon and listens for an audio tone in his headset indicating that the missile's seeker has detected the target.

Once sure of lock-on he punches the firing button and the missile is launched toward the target. The pilot can then break off and attack another target since he does not need to supply further information to the missile for guidance. The AIM-9B has a minimum range of 2,000-plus feet and a maximum range of between 4,000 feet and 2.6 nautical miles, depending upon altitude.

In spite of its ease of operation, the AIM-9B demonstrated a number of shortcomings. The missile had to be fired in a pursuit course within a very narrow degree of the target's tail. The AIM-9B seeker is limited to a three and a half degree field of view and +/−25-degree look angle.[72] If fired in the heart of the envelope against a target unaware of the attack, the missile has a reasonably good probability of a hit. The success of the MiG-21 with its Sidewinder-like Atoll can be attributed to ground-controlled intercept-vectored surprise attacks against U.S. aircraft. The limited look angle of the AIM-9B and the similar Atoll can be easily exceeded by an aircraft pulling several g's. This made it difficult for a pilot to set up a firing position against a maneuvering target.

The AIM-9B's uncooled lead sulfide seeker reacts to shortwave infrared energy. The missile's guidance seeker is very susceptible to transferring its lock to infrared sources of higher intensity than the target such as the sun, cloud reflections, hot spots on the ground, or reflections of the sun off water.

Another AIM-9B limitation is g launch restrictions. To fire a Sidewinder accurately the pilot could not pull more than two g's because the infrared seeker would fail to track the target.

Despite all these limitations, the AIM-9B was the preferred air combat weapon because of simplicity of operation, reliability, and fire and target capability. U.S. Air Force aircraft from February 1965 to March 1968 fired 175 AIM-9B Sidewinders to achieve 28 victories, a kill probability rate of 16.0 percent.[73]

U.S. Air Force F-4D Phantoms were equipped with the AIM-4D Falcon infrared homing air-to-air missile in 1966. The missile's operational procedure is similar to the AIM-9B with the exception that it incorporates a cooled, more sensitive seeker, is more maneuverable, and can be launched under higher g limitations. The missile has a minimum range of approximately

2,500 feet and a maximum range of 1.2 to three nautical miles depending upon altitude. Its drawbacks are a two-minute limit on seeker cooling and the ability to destroy the target only if the missile actually hits it. In Southeast Asia from 1965 to March 1, 1968, 43 AIM-4D firings scored four victories for a kill probability of 10.7 percent.[74]

Complexity, reliability factors, environmental constraints, and inherent missile/weapons system deficiencies combined to make the weapons employed in 1965 to 1968 relatively ineffective against small, highly-maneuverable fighter-sized targets.

Rules of Engagement

A medium-range AIM-7 Sparrow missile could have been employed more effectively in the mid-range, look-up environment that it was designed for had the rules of engagement not required that a target be visually identified. In negating most long-range Sparrow shots, the visual identification requirement minimized the element of surprise that contributed greatly to an air-combat kill.

Political Factors

Until April 1967, U.S. aircraft were forbidden to attack North Vietnamese MiGs on the ground, which allowed the North Vietnamese either to choose the time and place to engage or refrain from combat unless conditions were favorable. Once the United States chose to go directly against MiG airfields, the North Vietnamese were forced on the defensive. As a result, they lost a significant number of aircraft on the ground and in the air, and reacted by dispersing aircraft to China and remote airfields. The dispersal reduced the threat of MiG attack on U.S. aircraft.

Multi-Role Aircraft

U.S. forces were compelled to fly a majority of their air-combat missions with an aircraft designed for fleet air-defense and multi-purpose roles, not one optimized solely for the air-superiority mission. The F-4B, F-4C, F-4D, and F-4J Phantoms in service with the U.S. Air Force, Navy, and Marine Corps did a creditable job as fighters and fighter-bombers. However, their anti-bomber-oriented missile systems, lack of a close-in gun system, and limited maneuverability hampered overall performance.

According to a report by Maj. Robert D. Goertz: "It is clear that the MiG-21 enjoys an enormous instantaneous maneuvering advantage in terms of energy rate and g throughout most of the supersonic portion of the flight envelope. Subsonically, at both maximum and military power, the MiG-21 has a sustained maneuvering advantage in the upper portions of the envelope that spreads to the lower portions as g increases. On the other hand, the F-4C has a sustained maneuvering advantage in terms of efficiency throughout the entire subsonic portion of the envelope extending through most of the supersonic envelope. Only in range and first shot capability does the F-4C enjoy a substantial advantage over the MiG-21 throughout the envelope."[75]

To counter these performance differences, F-4 pilots utilized hit-and-run tactics that took advantage of the high-energy potential and varied weapons suite.

U.S. Air Force Strike Operations

U.S. Air Force interdiction operations over North Vietnam began on February 8, 1965, when South Vietnamese Air Force and U.S. Air Force A-1 Skyraiders and F-100 Super Sabres attacked the North Vietnamese barracks at Chap Le. U.S. Air Force aircraft involved in

Rolling Thunder included the A-1 Skyraider, the F-100 Super Sabre, the F-104 Starfighter, the B-57 light bomber, the F-105 Thunderchief, the F-4 Phantom, the F-111A, and B-52 Stratofortress.

Aircraft such as the A-1, the B-57, the F-100 and—later for a brief period the F-104—flew missions over North Vietnam but were subsequently withdrawn because of the increasingly effective air defense. The principal strike aircraft during Rolling Thunder was the F-105D Thunderchief. Originally designed to deliver tactical nuclear weapons, the Thud was one of the biggest single-seat, single-engine fighter-bombers ever built.

Despite its size, the Thud was capable of Mach-2 performance at high altitude and was one of the fastest aircraft in the world at low altitude. The aircraft was armed with an internal 20-mm M-61 Vulcan cannon and could carry up to 8,000 pounds of ordnance on five external stores stations or in its internal weapons bay. On a typical long-range Rolling Thunder mission, the Thud carried an internal fuel tank in one weapons bay, two 450-gallon external fuel tanks, six 750-pound bombs, and two jamming pods.

The other U.S. Air Force tactical aircraft widely used was the F-4 Phantom. The two-seat, twin-engine Phantoms initially employed in combat in the air patrol role began flying strike or dual-role strike/escort missions in mid-1965. The F-4 could carry a maximum load of up to eight tons of weapons and/or external fuel tanks. The F-4C was later augmented in Southeast Asia by the F-4D, which incorporated an improved weapons-delivery system and a gyro-stabilized lead-computing gunsight.

The U.S. Air Force introduced the sophisticated F-111A to Southeast Asia in March 1968. The aircraft underwent a brief combat evaluation, ultimately being withdrawn as a result of technical shortcomings, technical maintenance problems, and adverse publicity.

B-52 Stratofortress strategic bombers were also involved in Rolling Thunder. The eight-engine heavy bombers flew several thousand missions against targets in North Vietnam's southern panhandle from April 1966 to 1968. Picking areas well away from the SA-2 and MiG threats that were concentrated in the Hanoi/Haiphong area, B-52s plastered targets such as transportation networks with between 28 and 30 tons of high-explosive bombs per aircraft.[76]

U.S. Air Force tactics changed as ground-to-air threats grew more deadly. Initially, the basic tactic was to penetrate at medium altitude until near the enemy area and then fly a high-speed, low-level profile to the target. Once close in, the pilot would pop up and make a quick diving attack, and then exit at high speed and low altitude. This procedure was successful initially but as the North Vietnamese increased the number of their antiaircraft guns and developed ways to determine the approach of attacking aircraft losses began to mount.

Tactics were changed to medium-and-high altitude penetration to put aircraft above the threat of light and medium antiaircraft guns. EB-66C jamming aircraft coupled with jinking tactics helped to elude the worst of the radar-directed guns. With this combination, the only time penetrating fighter-bombers were in danger from light and medium antiaircraft artillery was during a small segment of the dive-bomb attack.

With the introduction of the SA-2 in July 1965, the North Vietnamese threatened aircraft penetrating at medium to high altitudes. At least 13 SA-2 missiles were fired at U.S. Air Force strike groups, downing three planes and damaging several others. The SA-2 was a serious threat and tactics again shifted to low altitude to evade this new weapons system.

As losses to antiaircraft artillery began to mount, however, penetration altitudes were shifted between 6,000 and 12,000 feet. With increasing experience, pilots discovered that given adequate warning the SA-2 could be evaded. Radar homing-and-warning (RHAW) sensors fitted to U.S. Air Force strike and MiGCAP aircraft improved the aircrews' chance of detecting the SA-2 missile. EB-66C jammers and Wild Weasels were also employed to degrade or destroy SA-2 batteries during strike missions.

Beginning October 1966, U.S. Air Force strike aircraft were equipped with electronic countermeasures jamming pods. Aircraft were grouped in pod formations of four aircraft that formed part of a larger strike group. The mutually supporting pods jammed SA-2 radars and fire-control radars that direct the gun, allowing aircraft to again penetrate at medium altitude between 15,000 to 20,000 feet above most of the antiaircraft artillery threat.

To protect the strike formations against MiGs and further degrade ground defenses, such support forces as F-4 escorts, EB-66C standoff jammers, and Wild Weasel suppression aircraft were employed. This orchestrated effort involving several different types of aircraft remained the standard strike tactic until the bombing halt in 1968.[77]

U.S. Navy Strike Operations

When North Vietnamese torpedo boats attacked the *Maddox* on August 2, 1965, the U.S. Navy retaliated with F-8 Crusader fighters and A-4 strike aircraft. Following this incident in the Gulf of Tonkin, Navy fighter and attack aircraft were involved in attacks against North Vietnam targets until the bombing halt of October 31, 1968. Between 1964 and 1968 the Navy employed the A-1 Skyraider, the A-3 Skywarrior, A-4 Skyhawk, the A-6 Intruder, the A-7 Corsair II, and the F-4 Phantom series aircraft.

The A-1 Skyraider, a large propeller-driven attack aircraft, still served in first-line service with numerous Navy attack squadrons in the early 1960s. Initially, A-1s performed strike missions but the aircraft proved to be vulnerable to antiaircraft artillery, surface-to-air missiles, and MiGs. Removed from strike operations against heavily defended targets, the aircraft served as an escort for search-and-rescue operations.

By 1968, however, the A-1 was totally phased out of service in favor of newer aircraft. Early in the war, A-3 Skywarrior light bombers were sent north to attack targets, but because it was large, relatively slow, and vulnerable to ground defenses and MiGs, the A-3 was transferred to tanker, reconnaissance, and electronic countermeasures missions.

Because the diminutive A-4 Skyhawk was the primary Navy light attack aircraft, it logged the most strike missions over North Vietnam. Toting bombs, rockets, and Shrike anti-radiation missiles, A-4s were employed in strike, armed reconnaissance, and Ironhand antiaircraft defense-suppression missions. Several squadrons of Marine A-4s provided close support in the South but did not participate in the North over areas of high threat.

The A-7A Corsair II was introduced into service in December 1967. A light attack bomber operating in daylight with good visibility, it could carry twice the payload of the A-4 Skyhawk and was a welcome newcomer to the battle zone.

In July 1965, A-6As of the VA-75 Squadron of the *Independence* began combat operations. With its advanced avionics system and large payload and range capability, the Intruder could strike at targets in bad weather and at night. U.S. Marine Corps A-6As operated against targets in North Vietnam below the 20th parallel and flew close support missions in the South.

The U.S. Navy used the F-4 Phantom, which served with both Navy and Marine Corps fighter squadrons, primarily for combat air patrol, although these aircraft also flew numerous flack suppression and attack missions. Marine Phantoms, on the other hand, flew most of their sorties in the attack role, providing close air support for allied forces in South Vietnam and striking at targets above the DMZ in the southern part of North Vietnam.

Aircraft carriers in the South China Sea and the Gulf of Tonkin operated on station for a period of several weeks to a month and then rotated for rest and resupply. Ships sending aircraft to the North orbited off the northern coast of South Vietnam in what was called Yankee Station.

Navy strike tactics generally evolved as previously described for Air Force attack aircraft. Initially, aircraft flew low-level profiles but shifted tactics to reduce losses to the extensive antiaircraft gun threat. The minimum altitude was raised to 3,500 feet and by coordinating attacks to saturate defenses, simultaneously sending in multiple attacks with only one pass for each aircraft, exposure time was reduced. Support aircraft, such as EA-1E and EDA-3B jammers and flack suppression aircraft employing rockets or cluster bomb units (CBUs), accompanied the strike force.

With the introduction of the SA-2 in mid-1965, the Navy withdrew the A-1 from areas of high threat, began deploying radar homing-and-warning systems, and fitted individual aircraft with defensive electronic countermeasures equipment. A-6A strike aircraft were sent in at night or in bad weather against heavily defended targets to reduce their exposure to MiGs and guard defenses. Bullpup and Walleye standoff guided missiles were employed to reduce aircraft exposure.

The Navy, like the Air Force, found that individual aircraft electronic countermeasures, jammers, standoff jammers, flack and surface-to-air missile suppression were required to reduce losses and accomplish the bombing mission. Accordingly, quick reaction electronic countermeasures programs, coupled with experience that demonstrated the SA-2 could be outmaneuvered, and the Ironhand surface-to-air missile suppression reduced aircraft losses by ground threats.

On March 31, 1968, U.S. air attacks against North Vietnamese targets above the 20th parallel ended and the restriction was shortly extended south to the 19th parallel. During the summer and early fall, U.S. aircraft continued to strike at targets south of the 19th parallel. Since North Vietnamese MiGs were based in the North, there was no air-to-air combat, but antiaircraft defenses continued to take their toll.

On October 31, 1968, three years and nine months after the Rolling Thunder operation began over North Vietnam, the bombing was suspended. The U.S. Air Force, Navy, and Marine Corps had flown approximately 304,000 tactical and 2,300 B-52 sorties and delivered 643,000 tons of ordnance against targets in North Vietnam.[79]

CHAPTER II

Linebacker I and II:
Vietnam Conflict, 1971-1973

Introductory Overview

After the bombing halt of March 1968, and the U.S. cessation of all but reconnaissance flights over North Vietnam, the United States began withdrawing troops from South Vietnam; by late 1971, the South Vietnamese had assumed the responsibility for their own ground defense. In 1971, U.S. aerial reconnaissance of North Vietnam revealed a renewed logistical buildup even larger than the one that preluded the Tet offensive of 1968. However as uneventful months passed, the allies gradually relaxed their alert. Suddenly, on March 29 the North Vietnamese Army rolled across the Demilitarized Zone (DMZ) with massive artillery and tanks in the lead.

The low cloud ceilings kept what U.S. air power that remained in Southeast Asia from launching any close support or interdiction strikes against the massive formations pushing back the defending South Vietnamese. Outnumbered and without the benefit of air power, the South Vietnamese were forced to fall back. Pressure increased in April as North Vietnamese forces invaded along three additional fronts: across the Cambodian border in Binh Long province, in the Central Highlands, and in the coastal provinces of Binh Dinh and Quang Ngai.

On April 6, President Richard M. Nixon authorized U.S. aircraft to begin bombing north of the DMZ for 25 miles. This region was extended to the 19th parallel and later to the 20th parallel. By May 8, all North Vietnam was cleared for attack except for the buffer zone along the Chinese border and the restricted areas around Hanoi and Haiphong. President Nixon also ordered the mining of North Vietnamese harbors and a blockade of the coastline.

Unlike the creeping gradualism of the 1964–1968 Rolling Thunder bombing campaign, the 1972 bombing campaign—christened Linebacker—began with a roar. The United States, in the process of disengaging from Vietnam, began redeploying airpower elements of its Air Force, Navy, and Marine Corps to blunt the four-front invasion and to prevent the fall of South Vietnam.

The majority of all air-to-air combat was fought between May and October 1972, during Linebacker I. Nearly all air combat victories in 1972 were scored by F-4 aircraft.

The NVAF used basically the same hit-and-run and wagon-wheel tactics with the MiG-17 and MiG-21 as were evolved during Rolling Thunder. Two new MiGs had been introduced into the inventory: the Chinese-built F-6 (MiG-19) and the MiG-21MF Fishbed J.

The combination of better training, precision-guided weapons, improved electronic countermeasures, and flexibility in strike planning and tactics enabled U.S. aircraft to hit and destroy targets in the North even in the face of the dense and sophisticated North Vietnamese air defense network. The invasion was eventually repulsed in the South and the North

Vietnamese Army began suffering supply shortages resulting from the bombing and mining the harbors. North Vietnam turned to negotiation to end the conflict.

When the first attempt at negotiation failed, the United States boldly initiated Linebacker II—an intense 11-day bombing campaign lasting through Christmas 1972. The B-52 long-range bomber was the primary tool, and waves of strategic bombing proved to be the answer: a negotiated peace was signed and became effective on January 29, 1973.

Building Tension 1968–1971

The Tet offensive in 1968 had severely hurt the North Vietnamese and Viet Cong. The North Vietnamese who had failed on the battlefield to achieve their objective of overthrowing the South Vietnamese government were willing to accept a temporary cessation of hostilities, to allow their forces to rebuild and equip.

Under the terms set by President Johnson on November 1, 1968, and continued by President Nixon over the next three years, the number of U.S. troops in South Vietnam steadily decreased until by 1971 no major ground combat forces remained. Under "Vietnamization," the South Vietnamese had taken over the responsibility for their own defense on the ground.

By late 1971, reconnaissance and intelligence began picking up signs of a widespread logistical buildup in North Vietnam and along the sanctuaries in Laos and Cambodia. Among the obvious signs of an invasion was the ominous presence of Soviet-supplied T-34, T-54, and PT-76 tanks and unprecedented numbers of 130-mm field artillery pieces.

To better monitor the logistical buildup in North Vietnam, the United States stepped up the number of reconnaissance flights heading north.[1] The number of "limited duration protective reaction" (reconnaissance flights with armed escorts) strikes also escalated in 1971—until "reconnaissance" flights were hitting storage areas and concentrations of artillery north of the DMZ.

The public was still quite averse to any escalation of the U.S. role in Vietnam, particularly bombing. Troops were still being withdrawn, and despite graphic evidence of an impending North Vietnamese invasion, it was obvious that nothing short of a "bloody nose" to the South would receive public support for intensification of America's role.

The Bloody Nose: January, 1972

By 1972, U.S. manpower had been steadily reduced to less than a quarter of what it had been at its peak three years previously—from 543,000 in 1969 to 95,000, of whom virtually none were ground troops.[2]

The resumption of bombing over North Vietnam in early 1972 brought a renewal of air-to-air combat. Navy Lt. Randy "Duke" Cunningham scored the first victory heralding a new phase of the war and his first in a string of five that would make him and his radar intercept officer (RIO), Lt. J. G. Willie Driscoll, the first U.S. aces of the Vietnam conflict.

On January 19, 1972, "Duke" Cunningham was flying one of two F-4 MiGCAP aircraft escorting a "protective reaction" strike against the MiG airfield at Quang Lang. While the strike aircraft rolled in on target, the F-4s were kept busy by several surface-to-air missile sites that fired 18 SA-2 missiles at the two F-4s. Coming out of an evasive maneuver with the last pair of SA-2 missiles, Cunningham spotted what he thought were A-7s heading out of the target area:

"Coming through about 15,000 feet, I looked out ahead of me and saw two airplanes in afterburner . . . I just saw two glows, I could just tell they were dots . . . I couldn't tell they were MiGs or anything . . . no one had seen MiGs for two years. You think about MiGs all the time, but the odds of you seeing a MiG are so slight. You say, "Naw, that's not a MiG.""

U.S. Navy F-4 Phantom from VF-96 displays a MiG-21 kill marking on the forward edge of its vertical stabilizer. The first U.S. kill of 1972 was scored by Lt. Randy ''Duke'' Cunningham and Lt. J.G. Willie Driscoll on January 19, 1972—the first of five kills scored by this team that year. The victories made them the first U.S. aces of the conflict. (U.S. Navy)

I said to Willie, ''I've got two A-7s exiting the target.'' The light went on in my head. The two airplanes I had seen had their afterburners lit, and A-7s don't have afterburners! I heard the other F-4s over on target, they had just wiped out one of the SAM sites at our 9 o'clock. This mental giant said the F-4s were over there and they're the only other afterburner aircraft in the area. I looked back and still saw the glows. But still, two days earlier our sister squadron, VF-21, had called MiGs, MiGs, MiGs, arm 'em up and it turned out to be an RA-5—so there wasn't any way I was going to yell out 'cause we gave them all sorts of gas for arming up on our own RA-5.

''Suspicious of their identity, I closed on them and still couldn't tell what they were. I got about 600 knots on the airplane and they never came out of burner. When we got close enough to identify them, I saw two of the prettiest delta-winged MiG-21s. The leader was about 600-700 feet above the ground in a canyon with walls on both sides of him, with his wingman in fighting wing, stepped up to his right 400-500 feet on his wing slightly aft at about 700 to 1,000 feet.

''We came down into position, behind them nose down. I started an easy climb and then went down. By this time the trees were above us. I was at about 2-2½ miles behind them, and I could barely see them. I could just see a dot. I thought, ''Boy I better start climbing back up where I can get a better view of him.

''Then he started to climb a bit and we got a radar lock. Right then Willie said, 'He's in range, SHOOT, SHOOT, SHOOT!' We were doing 600 knots, and so was he. We were hardly closing with . . . MiG-21s weren't supposed to go that fast, not that type. I had him locked, but due to my past experience with AIM-7s I reached over and hit the heat switch and fired at about a mile and a half—and he just went ''Crank.'' I know he couldn't have seen me . . . because I was dead 6 o'clock at just a slight look up. I know his wingman must have seen the missile come off and called the break because there's no way he could have.

''When he broke I expected him to do a cross turn. I picked my nose up and started to do a lag pursuit roll to his belly side. I looked over my wing at his wingman who pushed off and kept going straight, just left of his leader to fight me alone. When the MiG broke he bled all kinds of energy off and I was closing to a few thousand feet. There was a huge rock on the side of the canyon which I can still remember the shape of. I'm no Blue Angel and it scared me. My lag pursuit roll turned out to be more of a canopy roll. I was holding top rudder and just as the nose started to drop through, I leveled out into a slight turn and saw the MiG's wing tip start to drop. I still had probably 60 degrees left to go and I thought, "AHHH, he can't see me anymore," and I fired. Sure enough, he kept turning back the other way—by the time the missile hit him it was dead six o'clock. I popped over on a wing to take a look as he hit—he must have been still full of fuel 'cause it looked like napalm as he tumbled in.

"His wingman was about two miles ahead of us and I could barely see him. We locked him up on radar and then could not see him. He was doing a defensive weave to clear his six and every once in a while he would turn to give it a look and I'd say to Willie, 'Hey, I got a tally on him, Willie' and then he'd roll out. He was opening on us—our V_c (closure rate) was somewhere around 75 knots to his advantage and I was down to about 600 knots which put him around 675 knots. We tried to close with him and at that time Willie came up and said, 'Duke, what's our fuel state?' My exact words were, "Willie, don't bother me, I'm chasing a MiG.' Willie insisted and I looked down and saw we were at 6,500 pounds. I still had to go back 50 miles towards Quang Lang and inward through Laos to get to the carrier which was off the coast of South Vietnam. As it stood I had to hit a tanker or be the guest of the Air Force.

"The MiG got away—we radioed the E-2A which attempted to vector the CAP to cut him off. He apparently loaded at Bai Thuong, got fuel, and got out of there.

"I found an A-6 tanker that was heading towards Nakom Phenom RTAFB, Thailand. Two guys had plugged into the tanker and couldn't get gas out of him so I said, 'Let me try.' I was down to about 3,700 pounds (20 minutes flight time). I plugged in and the fuel came back like golden honey.

"I learned my lesson about gas that day—in my later engagements with MiGs, I was looking at my fuel gauge every two seconds. We also realized it was better to tank the fighters before going in rather than waiting till they came out. This also paid off later on May 10. We tanked on the way in and coming off target I still had gas in my center line."[3]

Cunningham's surprise as to how fast the MiG-21s were moving was explained by the fact that he was flying against the MiG-21MF Fishbed J—the most advanced flying machine the Soviets had yet supplied to North Vietnam. It was the first time any U.S. pilot had tangled with one. But the MiG-21MF Fishbed J was not the only surprise the North Vietnamese had in store.

The NVAF had grown considerably since 1968 and had introduced yet another MiG interceptor in its inventory, the twin-engine F-6. This aircraft was a copy of the Soviet MiG-19 built in the Peoples Republic of China. The MiG-19 was a predecessor to the MiG-21. The Soviets had not provided the MiG-19 to the North Vietnamese; instead, Russia had sent large numbers of highly maneuverable, subsonic MiG-17s and Mach 2 MiG-21s. F-6s were supplied by the Peoples Republic of China in 1969.

By 1972, the NVAF possessed 33 F-6s, 93 MiG-21s, and 120 MiG-15s and MiG-17s. Almost every target of strategic value in North Vietnam was covered by SA-2 missile sites, and MiGs were operating farther south than ever before and also west into Laos. The North Vietnamese began chasing U.S. aircraft operating in Laos and had several SA-2 sites on the Laotian/North Vietnamese border that had fired on U.S. aircraft in Laos.[4]

The first U.S. Air Force victory of 1972 came on the night of February 29, when MiG-21s attempted to intercept U.S. aircraft over Laos. Maj. Robert Lodge and 1st Lt. Roger C. Locher were flying a MiGCAP mission when they received warnings from Red Crown, code name for the U.S. Navy picket ship in the Gulf of Tonkin. Vectors from Red Crown positioned the F-4 into a head-on situation and Locher locked on one of the MiGs. Lodge fired an AIM-7E at 11 nautical miles and two more at eight and six nautical miles. Lodge saw the first AIM-7 detonate and then the second, which resulted in a large secondary explosion and fireball. Lodge then turned and exited the area, with two MiGs giving chase. Lodge descended and eluded the pursuers.[5]

Invasion: March 29, 1972

On March 29, three North Vietnamese divisions numbering 40,000 troops suddenly rolled across the DMZ. Bad weather was on Hanoi's side; during the first few days, U.S. and South Vietnamese aircraft were hampered by low ceilings and rain, allowing the North Vietnamese Army to push back the 3rd ARVN (Army of the Republic of Vietnam) division. The North Vietnamese Army's offensive continued unchecked until determined resistance by the ARVN held the invaders just short of the city of Quang Tri.

The predicament worsened on April 5 when a second invasion force crossed the Cambodian border in the Binh Long province driving toward An Loc and Strategic Highway 13 between Phnom Penh and Saigon.[6] North Vietnamese troops supported by tanks took Loc Ninh, laid seige to the important provincial capital of An Loc, and managed to block Highway 13 at the town of Chon Thanh 37 miles from Saigon.

Still a third front was opened almost simultaneously in the Central Highlands. Again, North Vietnamese armor was able to overwhelm the South Vietnamese defenders at Dak To and Tan Canh. Several firebases were overrun; Highways 14 and 19 were cut, isolating the cities of Pleiku and Kontum. Territory was traded back and forth as South Vietnamese and South Korean troops fought to keep the highways open.

The final front was in the coastal provinces of Binh Dinh and Quang Ngai. Communist units attacked Kontum City with tanks and occupied the coastal province of Binh Dinh.

The attack force comprised a total of 12 North Vietnamese Army divisions, numbering 150,000 men and hundreds of Soviet-supplied T-54, T-34, and PT-76 tanks. This huge force overwhelmed South Vietnamese units on all four fronts.[7]

The invasion did not take the allied U.S. and ARVN high command off guard as much as the Tet offensive had in 1968. Intelligence had done its job, predicting an invasion sometime in early 1972. However, as the Tet holiday of 1972 passed, U.S. and ARVN units somewhat relaxed. By delaying the date of the invasion for another two months, General Giap let the allies think that perhaps Hanoi had had a change of heart. He then caught them off guard with a conventional attack on a scale much larger than the allies believed possible.[8]

Despite the unequal odds, in most of the embattled areas the South Vietnamese gave a good accounting of themselves, often fighting off tanks with hand grenades and M-72 Light Antitank Weapons (LAWs) as their heaviest weapons. The margin of difference was U.S. air support, which was crucial to rolling back the armor-equipped North Vietnamese Army. President Nixon immediately ordered reinforcement of air units in Thailand, South Vietnam, and Guam, and ordered prompt attacks to blunt the invasion.[9]

Linebacker I: April–October, 1972

Hanoi had counted on anti-war sentiment in the midst of the U.S. Presidential election year to restrain the U.S. response to the invasion. President Nixon, however, committed the United States to an all-out effort to save South Vietnam and to inflict major damage on North Vietnam. On April 6, he authorized U.S. aircraft to begin bombing North Vietnam.

The U.S.S. *Midway* was one of six carriers assigned
to the Gulf of Tonkin's Task Force 77 to provide air
power to stem the North Vietnamese invasion of
South Vietnam in March 1972. (U.S. Navy)

The new bombing campaign, christened Linebacker, was of a scale and intensity matched
only by Rolling Thunder. The U.S. Air Force, in the process of disengaging from Vietnam,
had only 76 F-4s and A-37s (T-37 trainers modified for the attack role) in South Vietnam,
down from its 1968 peak of 350 aircraft. Another 300 U.S. Air Force jets were in Thailand
and the Navy had two carriers—the *Coral Sea* and *Hancock*—stationed off the coast of North
Vietnam.

In April, the United States quickly began redeploying air elements to prevent the fall of
South Vietnam. Under a series of rapid deployments known as Constant Guard, B-52s from the
United States made the transpacific journey to Guam. Beginning in April, U.S. Marine and Air
Force F-4s began arriving from Pacific and Stateside bases. The Marines sent three F-4
squadrons, two A-4 squadrons, and a contingent of EA-6A Intruders.

The Navy sent the carriers *Kitty Hawk*, *Constellation*, *Midway*, and *Saratoga* to join the
Coral Sea and *Hancock*. By April 30, four were on station (six carriers allowed four on station
while rotating two to Subic Bay in the Republic of the Philippines) providing 360 aircraft.

The Air Force, under Constant Guard I, moved one squadron of F-105G Wild Weasels, a
contingent of EB-66s, and several squadrons of F-4Ds and F-4Es to bases in Thailand. By May
1, 72 F-4Ds made their way to Takhli, Thailand.

Although no ground troops were ordered into battle, the U.S. Army rushed several UH-1B
helicopters equipped with TOW antitank weapons to South Vietnam to see their first combat
trial. The Tube-launched Optically-guided Weapon (TOW) is an optically-tracked, wire-guided
antitank missile that can be fired from ground launchers, jeeps, tracked vehicles, and
helicopters. Thousands of LAW antitank rockets, tactical aircraft, attack helicopters, and South
Vietnamese M-48 tanks were deployed to counter the 500 North Vietnamese tanks.

The setbacks of the initial weeks in April were consolidated and in May the tide began to favor the South Vietnamese. Air power demonstrated that it could destroy large numbers of tanks, vehicles, and men of the North Vietnamese Army when they operated in the open in a conventional manner.[10]

The immediate task of U.S. air power was to slow the North Vietnamese invasion. Once enough assets were on hand, aircraft began to interdict the supply and transportation networks fueling the invasion in the North. Most of the 94 targets on the original Joint Chiefs target list were released, and commanders had the freedom to choose when, where, and how frequently to hit a target. The target list was expanded to include nearly every military target in North Vietnam, and the restrictions on air strikes were lifted as President Nixon ordered:

- that all entrances to North Vietnamese ports be mined to prevent access as well as curtail North Vietnamese naval operations from them;
- that U.S. forces take appropriate measures within the internal and claimed territorial waters of North Vietnam to interdict the delivery of supplies;
- that rail and all other communications be cut to the maximum extent possible.

On May 9, Navy A-6 Intruder aircraft sowed minefields to block the ports at Haiphong, Hon Gai, Cam Pha, Thanh Hoa, Vinh, Quang Khe, and Dong Hoi, effectively sealing the North from its major means of supply. All ships had until May 11 to exit the waters—when the mines became armed.

As U.S. Navy aircraft were proceeding to Haiphong harbor the Red Crown surveillance ship detected the approach of MiG fighters. The guided missile cruiser U.S.S. *Chicago*, supporting the operation, engaged the group of MiG fighters with its long-range Talos missiles. One MiG was downed at a range of 48 miles and the remaining aircraft turned away, allowing the U.S. Navy attack aircraft to safely complete their mining operations.[11]

U.S. Navy Talos surface-to-air missile. A Talos fired from the U.S.S. *Chicago* destroyed a MiG over North Vietnam on May 9, 1972. (McDonnell Douglas)

Return to Hanoi, May 1972

At the beginning of May the weather was ideal for flying, allowing the full weight of air power to be brought against the Communist forces. Fighting in a conventional fashion, the North Vietnamese Army had "convoys of 100 or more trucks, tanks, and artillery"[12] moving in daylight under clear skies—ideal conditions for American aircrews. (In eight years of previous Southeast Asia experience, aircrews had fought an enemy that rarely risked exposure to the light of day.) Fighter-bombers hunted down convoys, flew hundreds of sorties in support

A U.S. Air Force F-4D, with the 49th Tactical Fighter Squadron out of Ubon RTAFB in Thailand, drops a 2,000-pound, laser-guided bomb. (U.S. Air Force)

A North Vietnamese bridge lies crumpled after an attack by laser-guided bombs. (Texas Instruments)

BRIDGE OFF ABUTMENT

BREAKS IN SPAN

of engaged troops, and knocked out dozens of tanks and artillery pieces. In addition, F-4s carrying the newly-introduced, highly accurate laser-guided bombs proved their worth.

The widespread use of such precision-guided munitions as laser-guided bombs and electro-optical (television) guided bombs was a key element contributing to the success of the U.S. interdiction effort in 1972. With a "smart" precision-guided weapon, the probability of hitting the target was estimated to be an unprecedented 80 to 90 percent, much higher than with previously-used "dumb" bombs. A single 3,000-pound precision-guided bomb could cut a rail line or knock down a bridge span.

One of the most widely used precision-guided weapons was the U.S. Air Force's Paveway family of laser-guided weapons. With the Pave Knife system, one standoff airplane—usually another fighter-bomber such as the F-4—orbited some distance from the target, and steadily directed a laser beam at the target designated for attack. All the planes of the bomb-laden strike force would then direct the seekers of their bombs to focus on the laser spot; one by one the bombs would be released and fly a guidance-corrected ballistic trajectory to hit within *feet* of the spot on the target designated by the laser.

Television-guided weapons did not require the target to be specially illuminated by the bomb-carrier or another aircraft. The pilot or weapon systems officer locked the electro-optical sensor on to the target, and released the bomb. Once falling, the bomb was self-guided toward the target until impact. Such electro-optical systems, however, require clear weather and a high degree of contrast between the target and the background for best results.

Television-guided and laser-guided bombs could do the job of at least 10 times the number of unguided bombs, meaning fewer aircraft had to be exposed to the extensive North Vietnamese antiaircraft defenses. During the 1972 Linebacker campaign, in a single day five bridges in North Vietnam were rendered impassable and a sixth was damaged. This was accomplished by only eight F-4s carrying 16 guided bombs.[13]

Furthermore, in the four years since 1968, the United States had improved its ability to penetrate the North Vietnamese air defense system and survive. Chaff bombers were used by the Air Force in one or two flights of four flying abreast, laying a "carpet" of chaff to shield the strike force behind from radar. U.S. aircraft had updated electronic countermeasures devices and the cumulative effect was to stymie the North Vietnamese ground-based air defense system. Consequently, the MiG force rose almost daily in greater numbers than ever before encountered, and the United States found itself in the midst of a real air-to-air contest.

On May 10, two days into Linebacker, the North Vietnamese got a taste of what the new capability meant. A U.S. Air Force strike group demonstrated the accuracy of its precision-guided bombs on the Paul Doumer bridge, important both psychologically and militarily. Located close to Hanoi, a major transportation link within sight of Gia Lam airfield, its loss would disrupt rail and vehicular traffic southward.

Two flights of F-4 chaff bombers preceded the strike groups into North Vietnam to lay a corridor of chaff, and 15 F-105G Wild Weasels suppressed antiaircraft artillery fire and surface-to-air missiles. The 16 F-4s of the main strike group were each configured to carry two precision-guided bombs. (Three flights carried laser-guided bombs and one flight electro-optical guided bombs.) The bombs were released from a medium altitude of between 14,000 feet and 20,000 feet, decreasing the planes' exposure to antiaircraft artillery and surface-to-air missiles.

Even so, the North Vietnamese strongly defended the important facility, firing 160 SA-2 missiles and dispatching 41 MiGs to engage the attackers. When the smoke cleared, one span of the bridge was destroyed and several others damaged by 12 confirmed direct hits. Not one strike aircraft was lost to ground fire in the attack. Two of the MiGCAP F-4s were lost in dogfights with the MiGs, however, while downing three MiG-21s.[14]

All three of these victories were scored by one flight of F-4s from the 555th "Triple-Nickel" Tactical Fighter Squadron. The flight lead, Major Lodge and Captain Locker, were downed during the engagement. As described by Number 3, Capt. Steve Ritchie: "Things really got confusing once the engagement started. There were missiles in the air all over the place, fireballs, smoke trails, debris, and airplanes everywhere. Lead and 2 got their kills head-on, then we converted to the six o'clock on the two remaining MiGs." Ritchie fired two AIM-7 Sparrows at 6,000 feet; the second missile exploded the MiG into a large yellow fireball.

Meanwhile Lodge and Locher had been tracking the third MiG-21. Unseen by Lodge—so common an occurance in air combat—NVAF F-6s had passed overhead and were angling down into position behind him. Despite calls for him to break, Lodge continued chasing the remaining MiG-21 as the F-6s closed to 2,000 feet and fired their 30-mm cannon.

The F-4D was hit, caught fire, and went out of control. Only the weapons system operator, Captain Locher, parachuted safely to earth, and he spent 23 days in the North Vietnamese jungle north of Hanoi before being recovered by a combat rescue team.[15]

Reportedly, NVAF Senior Lt. Le Thanh Dao was responsible for shooting down one of the two F-4s, quite possibly that of Captain Locher. It was the first of Dao's victories, which eventually totaled six.[16]

To conclusively damage the Doumer bridge so that repairs in the near term would not restore its traffic-carrying capability, the U.S. Air Force returned on the following day. This time, only one flight of four F-4s made up the strike group. Owing to a mixup of target times, the strike flight arrived without any MiGCAP or supporting escorts. The chaff, dropped earlier, had already dispersed and the escorts had gone home thinking the strike group had aborted its mission.

Capt. Thomas Messett led his single flight over Hanoi, expecting to encounter the usually formidable North Vietnamese defense; instead, he found virtually no opposition from antiaircraft artillery, surface-to-air missiles, or MiGs. With impunity, his flight dropped eight laser-guided bombs, crumpling three more of the bridge's spans and damaging another three. He later commented, "I think the North Vietnamese couldn't believe what was going on." The mixup on the U.S. Air Force's side had apparently caught the North Vietnamese off guard because they usually could count on almost clockwork attacks by large numbers of aircraft to alert their defenses to the approaching strike.[17]

Duke and Willie: First U.S. Aces

While the Air Force was striking the Paul Doumer Bridge, May 10 was also a red-letter day for the Navy: after seven years of air combat over North Vietnam, Lt. Randy "Duke" Cunningham and Lt. J.G. Willie Driscoll earned their status as aces.

The mission called for an Alpha (maximum effort) strike of about 35 airplanes from *Constellation* to bomb railroad yards near Haiphong.

Cunningham almost did not go. The squadron had assigned three F-4s and a subsonic light-attack A-7 aircraft as flak suppressors, because of lack of available F-4s. The VF-96 F-4 #100 (the airplane belonging to the air group commander) was being washed for a change-of-command ceremony the next day. Concerned that the three F-4s would be slowed by the A-7 in their group, Cunningham petitioned for the release of the F-4 for battle and had it loaded up as a flak suppressor with two AIM-7 Sparrows, four AIM-9 Sidewinders, and two triple-ejector racks full of Rockeye cluster bomb units.

A-6 Intruder medium bombers led, followed by two flights of A-7s as the primary strike force. The F-4s tailed them to protect them from MiGs engaging from the rear. As the group neared the prime target, the F-4s planned to accelerate, push ahead of the strike group, and drop their Rockeyes on the antiaircraft artillery. The aim was to suppress flak and draw off missile fire just as the strike group rolled on target.

Once over the target, according to Cunningham, "There were airplanes all over the sky, most of them MiGs." One F-4 had already been downed by fire from an 85-mm antiaircraft gun. Cunningham dropped his bombs and maneuvered through the congested sky, downing two MiG-17s and bringing his score to four. The officer describes the dogfight at the end of the mission that nearly cost him his life:

". . . I still had a full bag of gas. I didn't want to quit but I only saw two F-4s and one hell-of-a-lot of MiGs. At least, I wanted to regroup. I could hear the strike group going out on the radio but didn't know where anybody was . . .

"I saw a lone airplane coming at me about three miles away but couldn't tell what it was at that aspect. I said, 'Willie, I've got an airplane, but I can't tell if its a MiG or not.' I tried to rock and pull over to the side to get a side view and he moved, too. I finally identified him as a MiG-17 as I got a little closer.

"I remember thinking in training that I used to pass an A-4 as close as I could so I could hack him off, making him delay his move and giving me a split second advantage. I said, 'Watch this, Willie. I'm going to scare the—out of this Gomer!' and I headed right. *You fight like you train.* I never had an A-4 shoot at me in training. It was something I had not removed from a training situation and placed into real world. Just like you're *g*-limited in training, you're not *g*-limited in combat—until your airplane falls apart. You don't fight in clouds in training. There's a lot of things . . . you don't have real BBs fired at you . . . you have to translate into real world. You've got to say: this is training, and this is real world. I didn't do that and it almost cost me my—, and it was a mistake.

"I headed toward him to take him close aboard and he started shooting. As the flaming cannon shells began whizzing by my canopy, I finally realized, "He's *got* a gun in his nose and I don't.' I pulled up, thinking all the MiGs I'd ever known, if they hadn't had an advantage . . . had run. I thought, "I'm going to come back over the top and look back and Nguyen is going to be mile, mile-and-a-half away running for Hanoi. Either that or he's going to be in a horizontal turn.' You can imagine what a hemorrhaging thing it was to look back and see him canopy to canopy, not 30 feet away going vertical with me as if we were in formation. There he was, a little set of Gomer goggles, a little Gomer scarf, and a Gomer helmet, sitting there, looking right at me so close. I could pick him out of a lineup. I out-zoomed him, went over the top and he shot at me again. It hadn't dawned on me that this Nguyen was more than your average Nguyen. I had given him a predictable flight path—he shot and it scared me. I broke down into him to get out of the way of his nose—which put him right where I 'wanted' him—at my six o'clock. I had the nose going straight down, unloaded, and tried to get the knots back. I tried to work him to the horizon, coming down into a rolling scissors.

"I got about 500 knots on the airplane and went up again into the pure vertical, went over the top, and kicked the rudder. The same thing happened again, only this time he overshot on the pull up. It was one of those things where you lose sight and say: 'Did he overshoot? . . . Yeah, yeah he did!' He unloaded a little bit and came back up.

"You fight like you train. Back when I was a lieutenant J.G. at Top Gun, I fought against a guy named Dave Frost in an A-4. 'Frostie' showed me how I could use the one *g* of gravity against the A-4 if he early turned, and run out to six o'clock. When I came over the top with Nguyen, I remember thinking, 'I've been here before,' and the word 'Frostie' came to mind.

"After the second time in the vertical, Willie called up and said, 'Duke, let this one go.' I remember the rage inside me. I said to myself, 'No Gomer is going to make me go home . . . not when I got gas.' I couldn't imagine going back to the carrier and the guys saying, 'Hey,

Duke, did you get that last one?' and having to say 'No, he scared the—out of me, so I let him go.'

"So, I met him a third time. This time he leveled and started his nose up a little bit like he wanted to top out with me so he could get closer and gun me. He's got a lot more pitch authority on top, where I don't; I just kinda flail.

"I saw his nose too high and I wanted nose to tail and there's only one way I could really get it, crossing that fast. I went to idle, put out the speed brakes and reached over and put down half flaps. I would have put my arms out if I could have. He went right out in front and I was at his seven o'clock, about 2,000 feet, really close to him. I was down to 150 knots and lighted the burners to hold it. I thought, 'Don't flame out on me now, you J79s.' They held in there.

"I was sitting in almost a flat scissors with him and remember thinking, 'Duke, this is not really an advantageous placed to be.' If his wingman or anyone else showed up, I'm a grape and I don't have enough gas to stay here all day. I was all guts and no brains, and he could take it away from me.

"I really intended to disengage at that point by going to his belly side and unloading. I got my flaps up, rolled using the rudder and went to his belly side unloading. Right then he turned and departed his aircraft. This reversed the situation putting the MiG pilot in the disadvantage. I had 200 knots left on the airplane as I stood on the rudder and pushed the stick forward to follow him down. I squeezed the trigger and the missile (AIM-9) went out, found the MiG, and there was a flash. I started following him down, not sure I had hit him. I had read stories about Korea where MiGs had flown down low by the treetops making it back home . . . and he wasn't going to get away. The MiG-17 then began belching black smoke as it went straight for the deck . . . he never pulled out.

"As I spotted another MiG-17 at my two o'clock I heard a voice crack out, 'Duke, look at your seven o'clock!' When I looked back, what caught my eye was a Sparrow coming off Matt Connelly's F-4. My first thought, "He thinks I'm a MiG!" The Sparrow went right over our tail and when I reversed, I saw what he was shooting at. There were four MiG-17s back there, and they didn't want any part of that missile. They had been coming in on me just like a training command rendezvous, evenly spaced. One went up, one went down, one went sideways one way and one the other . . . like a fleur-de-lis.

"I headed out towards the Gulf of Tonkin at that point, climbing to get out of the small arms, 37-millimeter, and 57-millimeter. We heard a call, 'SAM, SAM, SAM, Nam Dinh' and as I looked out to the starboard side of the aircraft, I saw a SAM heading right for us. It went off no more than 400 feet away before I could make any evasive maneuver. Since the advertised lethal radius of an SA-2 is somewhere around 350 feet, I wasn't too concerned, we had had a lot more close misses than that in the past. Less than a minute later my aircraft went into a violent left yaw. My PC-2 hydraulic system indicated zero pressure and the PC-2 and backup hydraulic system were fluctuating. We were at 27,000 feet at the time, about 15 miles from the coast. The one thing I didn't want to do was spend the rest of the war as a guest in the Hanoi Hilton, not after bagging five MiGs."[18]

Cunningham managed to nurse the striken airplane to the coast. Just as he crossed the shoreline, the pressure in the backup hydraulic system bled to zero and the aircraft fell into a spin. Cunningham and Driscoll waited until the last possible moment to eject, and then parachuted down right into the mouth of a river. The North Vietnamese fired at the two parachutes all the way down and then headed toward them in boats. Some A-7s zoomed low, stafing the beach, and the North Vietnamese turned back. A Marine CH-46 helicopter plucked the first U.S. Vietnam aces out of the water, depositing them on the deck of *Constellation* where a jubliant crowd awaited them.

Navy Lt. Randy "Duke" Cunningham and Lt. J.G. Willie Driscoll, the first U.S. aces of the Vietnam conflict, grin from their seats in an F-4. Duke and Willie racked up five kills from January through May 1972, three in one mission. (The score of eight markings on the F-4 reflects VF-96 Squadron kills.) (U.S. Navy)

Their rise to ace status was made up of several firsts: first U.S. aces of the Vietnam conflict; first known all-missile aces; first jet dual-cockpit aces; and first F-4 aces.

Intelligence later indicated that the pilot of the MiG-17 who had fought so skillfully in the vertical was thought to be none other than a NVAF colonel with 13 kills and their leading ace. Cunningham commented that the pilot, Colonel Tomb, fought as well as any Top Gun adversary he had flown against, making very few mistakes. "I knew the guy was good; every time I tried to counter, he'd counter like Dave Frost or some of the guys at Top Gun," Cunningham reflected. "I don't think to this day that I would have gotten him if he hadn't had to run because he was low on fuel. I think it would be very difficult with a Sidewinder and no-gun airplane to knock down a well-flown MiG-17. Low altitude like that, he can just work it away from you too fast."[19]

May 13, 1974, spelled doom for the infamous Thanh Hoa bridge, nicknamed Dragon's Jaw, which had been struck repeatedly during Rolling Thunder without going down. The Air Force sent 14 F-4s loaded with nine 3,000-pound laser-guided bombs, 15 2,000-pound laser-guided bombs, and 48 500-pound "dumb" bombs. Chaff lessened the effectiveness of the radar-guided antiaircraft and surface-to-air missiles. The F-4s released their deadly load, enveloping the steel structure in clouds of dust. Post-strike analysis of the photographs gathered by RF-4C reconnaissance planes revealed that the Dragon's Jaw had finally been dropped. The steel superstructure was now bent and completely severed from the western abutment. This time, the damage could not be repaired overnight.[20]

Meanwhile, over South Vietnam some of the newly arriving aircraft such as F-4s began combat operations within 24 hours after landing. There was certainly no lack of targets; as one OV-10 spotter pilot remarked, "My God, you should see the people down here—all over the place—people, tanks, trucks, the whole nine yards—and everybody is shooting."[21]

South Vietnam was no longer the low-threat area to aircraft it once had been. The NVA units had brought with them 23-mm, 37-mm, 57-mm, and—for the first time—85-mm and 100-mm antiaircraft artillery guns. Near the DMZ, U.S. aircraft also encountered SA-2 missiles. As early as February 1972, 81 SA-2s were fired in one day, shooting down three F-4s in areas where previously only antiaircraft artillery had been found.

In addition, aircrews began encountering deadly "little black SAMs," the newly-introduced SA-7 shoulder-fired, infrared-guided surface-to-air missile. The weapon is mounted in a tube and fired from the shoulder in a manner similar to the well-known bazooka. The four-foot-long, infrared-guided missile flew faster than Mach 1.5, had a range of just under two miles, and could hit targets above 5,000 feet.

Aircraft such as the A-1, OV-10, and A-37, used to flying unmolested over South Vietnam at medium altitudes above the antiaircraft artillery, had never before countered surface-to-air missiles; pilots of these aircraft now had to learn evasive techniques to escape the numerous missiles fired at them during their multi-hour spotting missions. The lingering monsoon and its low overcasts made close support missions very dangerous in light of the SA-2/SA-7 threat because the ceiling did not give crews the margin of visibility needed to maneuver to evade the missiles. Attack and transport helicopters, AC-130 gunships (converted cargo planes loaded with air-to-ground weapons), low-speed light attack aircraft, and light observation aircraft, all of which had been operating until now in a semi-permissive environment, faced a whole new ball game. In March, two AC-130 gunships were downed over Laos by the SA-2 and another was damaged by an SA-7 over An Loc. In April, a standoff jammer EB-66 was downed by an SA-2 fired from inside South Vietnam.

In June, the SA-7 claimed an AC-130 gunship, its first large aircraft. AC-130s had begun carrying flares whose heat decoyed the infrared-guided surface-to-air missiles; on June 18, however, one SA-7 wasn't buying anything but the real thing when it detonated one engine of an AC-130 providing fire support. In the explosion, the right wing detached and the aircraft plummeted to earth.[22]

Meanwhile, May proved to be a successful month for U.S. MiG kills: 27 MiGs were downed in air-to-air combat and one more destroyed by a Talos missile fired from a U.S. Navy cruiser.

All bombing activity was curtailed in the Hanoi area from June 14 to 18 while President Alexei Kosygin of the USSR was visiting Hanoi. When the United States resumed its strikes in the Hanoi area on June 19, the NVAF MiGs began to exact a higher toll of U.S. Air Force aircraft, bitterly contesting the control of the skies over North Vietnam.[23]

The Tide Turns

Beginning June 19, the United States mounted the heaviest raids of the Linebacker campaign. More than 300 sorties were flown daily, concentrating on damaging the air defense network. On June 19, fully 76 surface-to-air missile launchers were reported destroyed, and 46 more on June 21 (six launchers per SA-2 site). By the end of June, it was clear that the number of missiles fired each day had been reduced. The renewed interdiction bombing of the transportation network was also having telling effects down south. Defenders at An Loc noted that the number of incoming artillery shells had significantly dropped from the high of 8,000 daily in April to fewer than 300 per day in June. An estimated 3,000 trucks were destroyed. Some 106 bridges were blasted, 15 of them determined to be major links in the supply routes to the south.[24]

In July, the first round of the air-to-air contest went to the North Vietnamese, who downed two F-4Es on July 5. As told from the U.S. side by one of the hapless crewmen, Capt. Don Logan:

North Vietnamese pilots scramble to their MiG-17s during an air defense alert. MiGs posed a serious threat to U.S. aircraft over North Vietnam in 1972. U.S. tactics and technology had minimized losses to antiaircraft artillery and surface-to-air missiles, triggering a determined response from the NVAF MiGs. (M. O'Connor)

"Our sharknosed F-4E was Number 4 in a flight of four escorts for twelve F-4E bombers, which were fragged on [assigned to] a target close to Kep airfield, about 30 miles east of Hanoi. As escort, it was our job to stick close to the bombers and to engage any MiG that came up to challenge them. The strike flights ingressed to the target with no problem, and as they made their dive bomb passes on the target, we continued past them and began a 180 degree turn, so that we could pick them up as they came off the target. As we were in the turn, I saw the Number 2 airplane in our flight get hit by a missile which seemed to come from below the flight. The F-4 immediately burst into flames, and I saw the two crew members eject. We had completed the turn and had just rolled out when we got a radio telling us to break hard right. As we rolled I felt a violent jar, and looked out to see the outboard portion of the left wing, past the wing fold, badly damaged. I then scanned the cockpit instruments and noted that the left engine tachometer was reading zero and right tachometer was winding down past 30 percent rpm. I looked over my right shoulder . . . and there was a North Vietnamese MiG-21 flying close formation on us! As soon as he saw me looking at him, he rolled over us and split S down behind us into a cloud deck, getting away from the rest of our flight. Both of his missile rails were empty. I later found out that he was one of a flight of two MiG-21s that had shot both of us down.[25]

Once again the hit-and-run attack from six o'clock had succeeded, and this time against aircraft with the job of hunting MiGs. The MiG pilots were indeed becoming formidable in their skill. Capt. Don Logan spent the remainder of the war as a "guest" of the North Vietnamese government in the "Hanoi Hilton."

The U.S. Air Force retaliated on July 8 by shooting down three MiG-21s; two of the kills were credited to Capts. Steve Ritchie and Charles DeBellevue, putting Ritchie one victory away from ace status.

On August 19, the Air Force downed another MiG-21. The crew of the victorious F-4E was Capts. Sam White and Frank Bettine, flying fighter escort for two flights of F-4 chaff bombers. August also saw the Air Force's kill ratio against the MiGs begin to improve. From 1968 to 1972, that ratio had actually declined to the point that in June and July planes were being exchanged almost one for one with the MiGs. After revising its air-to-air training in August

The Air Force gained its second ace on September 9, 1972, when Capt. Charles B. DeBellevue, flying backseat with Capt. John A. Madden, Jr., scored against two F-6s (MiG-19s) with AIM-9 Sidewinders. The victory made him the top U.S. scorer with six kills. (U.S. Air Force)

Capt. Steve S. Ritchie scored all his kills against MiG-21s with AIM-7 Sparrow missiles, becoming the first U.S. Air Force ace on August 28, 1972. (U.S. Air Force)

1972, and dubbing the new program Top Off the Air Force did see an increase in the kill ratio to four to one.

This improvement indicated that training had significant impact on the performance of U.S. aircraft against the MiGs. In addition to training, another reason for the improved kill ratio was the improved warning system instituted by U.S. radar platforms.

The U.S. Air Force logged its first ace on August 28 when Capt. Steve Ritchie downed his fifth MiG-21. He won the distinction of the first Air Force ace of the Vietnam conflict, and the first all MiG-21 ace.

Ritchie and his backseater, Captain DeBellevue, scored their kill while flying a MiGCAP mission southeast of the Hanoi area. Radar vectors from U.S. surveillance platforms were instrumental in setting up an intercept on several bandits at 25,000 feet. Ritchie's flight at the lower altitude of 15,000 feet was able to pick up the bandits on their on-board radars and maneuver below the MiGs and to their rear. Ritchie fired two AIM-7s up at the MiGs; the missiles, although fired out of their envelopes, were intended to force the MiGs to turn. Coming out of his turn Ritchie fired his remaining two AIM-7s at one of the MiGs. The first missile missed but the second homed true, destroying the MiG-21.[26]

Halting Negotiations

By mid-summer, the momentum of the North Vietnamese invasion was slowed with the tide turning in favor of the South Vietnamese in many areas. In June, the South staged counter-offensives to retake Quang Tri and to relieve the sieges of An Loc and Kontum.

The Paris peace talks, which had ended abruptly on May 4, resumed on July 13 with little progress. Despite an upcoming Presidential election, Nixon stood firm and the Linebacker bombing offensive did not let up. Hanoi's return to the negotiating table was a clear sign that U.S. air power and stiff resistance from the South Vietnamese Army were seriously hurting the North Vietnamese, and the bombing of the north was disrupting supply lines necessary to maintain conventional operations. Further, the air attacks up north were damaging the industrial base. North Vietnam's cities were also suffering food shortages.[27]

Heavy ground combat continued during the summer. U.S. and South Vietnamese aircraft flew large numbers of strike sorties in support of the ground war, while U.S. forces continued to bomb targets in North Vietnam.

September was a successful month for the U.S. Air Force, which scored seven victories over MiGs. The only other September MiG kill was credited to USMC's Maj. Tom Lassiter, in an F-4 with VFMA-333, embarked aboard the *America* in lieu of a Navy F-4 squadron. This kill evened the score for the Marine Corps which had lost an F-4J to MiGs on August 26.[28]

In early fall, U.S. forces were unleashed against North Vietnamese airfields to reduce the MiG threat. During the first week of October U.S. aircraft bombed the MiG fields at Phuc Yen, Yen Bai, Vinh, and Quang Lang, destroying or damaging 14 MiGs on the ground.[29]

MiGs were particularly active on October 6, engaging Air Force aircraft near Thai Nguyen. A hunter-killer team of F-105s and F-4Es was jumped by both a MiG-21 and an F-6, which had the advantage of initial position on the flight. The F-105s attempted to disengage as the F-4Es turned into the attacking MiGs.

One F-4E had an F-6 behind him and went into a dive to shake his pursuer. The F-6 matched the maneuver, opening fire with its 30-mm cannon. The other F-4E followed the F-6, with the MiG-21 on his tail. The first F-4E, crewed by Maj. Gordon Clouser and 1st Lt. Cecil Brunson, dove vertically with afterburner, weaving as they hurtled earthward. They pulled out at 300 feet—well below the peaks of surrounding mountains. The F-6 did not pull out in time. The second F-4E, flown by Capt. Charles Barton and 1st Lt. George Watson, pulled out and the MiG-21 disengaged. The claims board gave one-half credit to each of the crews.[30]

Capt. Jeffrey Feinstein was the third Air Force ace; he, like Capt. DeBellevue, was a backseat weapons system operator (WSO). Feinstein achieved ace status with his fifth kill on October 13, 1972, when he downed a MiG-21. (U.S. Air Force)

Capt. Jeffrey Feinstein, who had lost the race as the first U.S. Air Force ace in Southeast Asia to Ritchie and later DeBellevue, achieved his coveted fifth kill on October 13, making him the third Air Force ace. Feinstein was flying backseat for Lt. Col. Curtis Westphal as part of a MiGCAP flight. Using vectors from Red Crown, Feinstein locked on a possible bandit 17 miles away and Westphal closed to affirm the identity of the bogey. (Red Crown was able to confirm them as bandits but due to the large number of friendly aircraft in the vicinity, Westphal elected to close to visual range before firing.)

At two miles, Feinstein sighted the planes and confirmed them as MiG-21s. Westphal then turned and fired three AIM-7 Sparrows at one of two MiG-21s. The second missile impacted in the rear section, and the pilot ejected.[31]

Seven days later, on October 22, Linebacker I officially ended with a promise of peace at the negotiating tables. With high hopes of achieving a diplomatic solution to hostilities, President Nixon restricted the bombing to below the 20th parallel. By October 26, North Vietnam and the United States had agreed upon a nine-point peace plan, calling for withdrawal of all U.S. forces from South Vietnam and the release of U.S. prisoners held by North Vietnam and the Viet Cong within 60 days. November passed with negotiating teams hammering out details of the agreement.[32]

Secretary of State Henry Kissinger was optimistic to the point of announcing ''Peace is at hand'' at a news conference on October 26, welcoming the North Vietnamese cooperation.[33]

However, the negotiations broke down on November 23 and the optimism surrounding the Paris peace talks dissipated when the North Vietnamese delegation walked out on December 13.[34] Determined to bring about a negotiated resolution, President Nixon ordered resumption of the bombing on December 15.

Linebacker II: The Eleven-Day Campaign

The renewed bombing—Linebacker II—was a short, intensive campaign to ''bomb'' the North Vietnamese back to the negotiating table. The main tool was the B-52 long-range strategic bomber, which had never been sent against the industrial north in any great numbers.

The B-52, powered by eight jet engines, had an unrefueled range of up to 6,000 miles and could fly at speeds up to 650 miles per hour. Designed to carry nuclear weapons, it could also deliver a considerable bomb load of conventional high explosives. A typical load for the ''big-

December 15, 1972, marked the beginning of the heavy 11-day Linebacker II campaign when the B-52 Stratofortress saw action over North Vietnam in efforts to force the North Vietnamese back to the negotiating table. (U.S. Air Force)

North Vietnamese SA-2 missile is launched and rises trailing its characteristic smoke plume. Thousands of SA-2s were fired at B-52s and other U.S. aircraft during the 11-day Linebacker II campaign. (U.S. Air Force)

belly'' B-52D models was 42 750-pound M-117 bombs in the internal bay with an additional 24 500-pound Mk-82 bombs on external pylons.

The B-52G, modified for its conventional role in Southeast Asia, carried 27 750-pound bombs in its internal bomb bay.[35] The B-52G lacked the extensive electronic countermeasures gear carried by the B-52D, making it more vulnerable to attack from a surface-to-air missile. It did, however, have more efficient engines that gave better fuel consumption and more thrust, and it carried more fuel internally than the B-52D.[36]

One source of concern was the threat of the bombers by MiGs, which could out-maneuver them. All B-52s had a tail turret with four 50-caliber machine guns aimed by radar, providing a sting with which to counter a stern attack.

The surface-to-air missile threat was also of major concern. Prior to Linebacker II, the B-52s had been used exclusively in the lower route packages in North Vietnam where the missile threat was low, and in South Vietnam, Laos, and Cambodia where no missile threat existed. For years the North Vietnamese had been trying to knock down a B-52 with the SA-2, succeeding only on November 22 during a strike on a target in the heavily-defended area around Vinh. That loss was the first B-52 downed by hostile fire in the seven years of their deployment to Southeast Asia.[37]

The B-52 was especially vulnerable to both the SA-2 surface-to-air missile and the Atoll air-to-air missile, both of which had been designed specifically to hit nonmaneuverable targets such as the B-52. The B-52 would bomb from a height of 30,000 feet, putting it above most antiaircraft artillery but in the area where the SA-2 was especially effective. The B-52's large size, however, allowed it to carry an extensive set of electronic countermeasures to deceive the SA-2.

When B-52s flew in close cells of three aircraft, their electronic countermeasures equipment was most effective against the SA-2 radar system. Maneuvering turns degraded the electronic countermeasures shield so B-52 crews were instructed to maintain formation despite SA-2 firings. After several crews had attempted to dodge the surface-to-air missiles, one wing commander threatened to court-martial aircraft commanders who broke formation.[38]

On the night of December 18, 129 B-52s were scheduled to strike targets in North Vietnam in three waves. An additional force of support aircraft provided electronic countermeasures jamming, Wild Weasel SAM suppression, MiGCAP protection, preemptive strikes on MiG airfields, and protective corridors of chaff.

The first wave of B-52s hit the MiG bases at Hoa Lac, Kep, and Phuc Yen. Concurrently, F-4s directed laser-guided bombs against the Hanoi power plant, the radio station, and the railroad classification yard. A-7s and F-4s struck the Yen Bai airfield. F-111s operating along bombed airfields, surface-to-air missile sites, and marshalling yards.

The three waves were scheduled four to five hours apart. The first bombs were dropped at 7:45 p.m. Hanoi time; the second wave arrived at midnight. The last wave struck five hours later, just before dawn.[39]

The first wave, made up of nine B-52Ds and 18 B-52Gs, from Guam and 21 B-52Ds out of U-Tapao, Thailand, came in from Laos and executed a hard turn after bomb release to spend minimum time in the heavy missile-threat areas. The B-52s from Thailand were first over target at 8:01 p.m. with the last cell dropping its load at 8:18 p.m. Two cells hit Hoa Lac airfield, six hit the Kinh No complex, and the remaining three struck the Yen Vien railroad.[40] All those targets were within 30 nautical miles of Hanoi.

Massive retaliation firings of SAMs lit up the night. The lead B-52G was hit by two SA-2s before it released its bomb load, and it went down near Hanoi. Each successive wave also lost one B-52, totaling three losses, two of them B-52Gs. An estimated 200 SA-2s were fired against the bombers—some 67 missiles for each kill. A 100-knot tailwind, which had sped the bombers toward the target, had blown away the protective chaff corridor, exposing the B-52s for a longer period than hoped; in addition, the tailwind became a headwind when the cells made their post-target turns.

The major challenge to the B-52 bombers the first night was indeed the SA-2. Some antiaircraft artillery was sighted but at too low an altitude to be of serious concern. Although it was expected that MiGs might put up strong resistance, they were sighted only sporadically; one MiG that did attack one cell was destroyed by a B-52 tail stinger.[41]

SSgt. Samuel Turner, gunner aboard one of the attacked B-52s, narrates:

"As we drew nearer to the target the intensity of the SAMs picked up. They were lighting up the sky. They seemed to be everywhere. We released our bombs over the target and had just proceeded outbound from the target when we learned that there were MiG aircraft airborne near a particular reference point.

"Our navigator told us the reference point was in our area and before long we learned the enemy fighter had us on his radar. As he closed on us I also picked him up on my radar when he was a few miles from our aircraft.

"A few seconds later the fighter locked on to us. As the MiG closed in, I also locked on him. He came in low in a rapid climb. While tracking the first MiG, I picked up a second aircraft at 8 o'clock at a range of about 7½ miles. He appeared stabilized—not attacking us, obviously allowing the other fighter room to maneuver and conduct his run first.

"As the attacking MiG came into firing range, I fired a burst. There was a gigantic explosion to the rear of the aircraft. I looked out the window but was unable to see directly where the MiG would have been."[42]

Turner was subsequently credited with the first B-52 kill of a MiG-21.

The second night was a virtual repeat of the first, with the three waves facing similar numbers of SAMs. No aircraft were lost.[43]

Day three was not so lucky. Missile operators had learned the B-52s' approach pattern from the preceding two nights and knew where the B-52s would be most vulnerable. Keying on the lead cell, they pinpointed the post-target turn where the B-52s' electronic countermeasures were degraded. They then preemptively fired enormous numbers of missiles at that point in the sky. Six B-52s were downed, five while in their post-target turns. Four were the unmodified B-52G, not equipped with the same electronic countermeasures as the B-52D.[44]

The B-52Gs then received rush countermeasures modifications. It had been reported that MiG-21s were shadowing the B-52 cells and reporting precise altitudes and airspeeds to the SA-2 operators below as German aircraft had with Allied bombers during World War II. The MiGs would then break away and soon SA-2s would fill the air, striking home despite the B-52 jamming of radar transmitters.

The missiles were apparently randomly shotgunned, as the B-52s' Electronic Warfare Officers detected no uplink or downlink radar signals between missile and ground. That meant either that the SA-2s had been modified to transmit on a different frequency or that they were being launched at a precalculated area of the sky based on the positional data transmitted by the MiG-21 shadows.[45]

On the fourth night of Linebacker II, two B-52Ds were lost. One experienced radar failure and was maneuvering to the rear of its cell when an SA-2 downed it. The second was bracketed by two SAMs. That bomber, too, went down.

As a result of the losses, the attack formations were changed from being staged in several waves to 30 sorties in one wave.[46]

Two MiGCAP F-4 fighters escorting the bombers were vectored against a single MiG-21 by EC-121 and Red Crown radars, pursuing it by radar for longer than half an hour before breaking off. It was later determined that the MiG-21 crashed after running out of fuel and a kill was awarded to the lead F-4.[47]

Other changes in tactics included varying the bombers' altitudes and attack directions, and eliminating the large post-target turn. These were designed to complicate the SA-2s' task. The new tactics worked; no losses took place on days five, six, and seven.[48]

On the fifth day, aircraft approached from over the Gulf of Tonkin to bomb petroleum-oil-lubricant storage areas and railroad yards in Haiphong. The ocean approach greatly minimized the bombers' exposure to SAMs. Furthermore, the 10 cells used three different approach tracks over the Gulf, expanding to six as they closed to within 60 miles of the target. At 30 miles from the target they turned to converge almost simultaneously. This maneuver distracted the SA-2 operators and only 43 surface-to-air missiles were reported fired; the lower number was attributed to the bombers' tactics and to SAM suppression.[49]

On day six, 12 B-52Ds from Andersen AFB on Guam joined the 18 U-Tapao bombers approaching from over the Gulf. Railroad yards at Lang Dang were demolished by 24 of the bombers while six others concentrated on three SA-2 sites. There were no losses, despite the absence of the usual escorts for MiGCAP support and SAM suppression, which were late for the rendezvous.[50]

On day seven, B-52Ds from U-Tapao were augmented with 22 crews from the 43rd Strategic Wing on Guam.[51] The Thai-based bombers came in from Laos in two groups, bombing the railroad yards at Thai Nguyen and Kep. The B-52Ds flew to the northwest before heading south into their attack corridor, remaining beyond effective SAM range for as long as possible. These detours, however, brought them close to the Chinese buffer zone. After hitting targets, the bombers exited to the southeast over the Gulf of Tonkin.

Several times the bombers were attacked by MiGs to no effect. In fact, one got a burst of .50-caliber fire from A1C Albert Moore, a tailgunner aboard Ruby 3 (third bomber in the Ruby cell). Moore missed with his first two bursts but the third hit home and the destroyed MiG made the score B-52s, 2, MiGs, 0.[52]

The bombing runs were halted for 36 hours to celebrate Christmas—at least, theoretically. In reality, much of the time was spent in attack planning. On December 26, 120 aircraft flew in a single attack, the largest strike of the Linebacker campaign. Seven waves of B-52s hit nine targets simultaneously. Only B-52Ds and modified B-52Gs struck targets in high-threat areas. The first unloaded their bombs at 10:30 p.m. while the last cells came off the target by 10:45.

The waves of bombers approached their targets from different directions. Seventy-two B-52Ds bombed in the Hanoi area. Seven of the 10 targets were concentrated within a 10-mile radius of Hanoi where the heaviest SA-2 opposition was concentrated. One B-52 was downed by SA-2s over Hanoi and heavy battle damage caused the crash landing of a second at U-Tapao. The losses were suffered because one of the B-52s in their respective cells had had to abort, thus reducing their electronic countermeasures protection. In following missions no two aircraft cells would be flown. Instead, if an aircraft aborted, the remaining two would join with another cell to restore their countermeasures ''blanket.''[53]

On day nine, bombers returned to Hanoi and added the Lang Dang railroad yards. Sixty B-52s in six waves released ordnance simultaneously on seven targets. Three were SA-2 sites, one the infamous ''killer site VN 549'' with a reputation for downing aircraft with lethal accuracy. One B-52 destroyed missile site VN-243, knocking it out of commission, and in turn was hit by a missile from VN-549. The aircraft was damaged and everyone aboard wounded. The crew later bailed out over Laos safely. Another B-52 was not so lucky and took a mortal hit, the last lost during Linebacker II.[54]

On day ten, 60 B-52s attacked Hanoi and Lang Dang. Among targets were two SA-2 sites but VN-549, still in operation, was carefully avoided ''as a gesture of genuine respect.''[55] The bombers met with decreased SA-2 and antiaircraft artillery fire, indicating that the North Vietnamese had low stores of ammunition. (As part of previous attacks, SAM storage areas also had been hit, and the results were becoming evident.) In this latest attack, the B-52 force suffered no losses, and a MiG-21 fell to an AIM-7 Sparrow fired by a U.S. Air Force F-4 escort.[56]

On day 11, December 29—the last day of Linebacker II—the 60 attacking B-52s reported very few missile firings. This force again came through unscathed.

Over the 11-day span, a total of 729 B-52 sorties had been flown. Destroyed or damaged were 1,600 military-related structures, 372 railroad-related stock, 3,000,000 gallons of petroleum-oil-lubricant, and numerous industrial areas. Airfields were heavily marked with craters, as were roads, railroads, and transportation networks. The strike force had endured 1,242 SA-2 missile firings and untold antiaircraft artillery to drop 15,000 tons of ordnance. Besides severely disrupting North Vietnam's warmaking logistics, most importantly Linebacker II brought the North Vietnamese back for serious negotiations.[57]

On December 30, 1972, President Nixon announced his decision to halt all bombing north of the 20th parallel based on North Vietnam's willingness to reopen negotiations. The talks resumed on January 1, 1973, and by January 9 a cease-fire agreement had been reached. This was signed on January 23, at which time the United States ended all military operations in Vietnam, both north and south.

Analysis

Unlike the creeping gradualism of the Rolling Thunder campaign from 1965 through 1968, the Linebacker campaign was short and intense. Most of the fighting was waged from March through October 1973 and again in December. MiGs occasionally tried to interfere with U.S. strikes in Laos and southern North Vietnam; however, it was not until May when the North was being bombed regularly that air combat became common.

While extensive air combat took place during the 1972 Linebacker bombing operations, air-to-ground warfare was the element with the most impact. Following 1968's bombing halt, the U.S. Air Force, Navy, and Marine Corps primarily flew close air support in South Vietnam and interdiction missions against North Vietnamese supply and transport systems in Laos. In response to increased supply efforts in 1971 and 1972, U.S. air forces attacked the southern part of North Vietnam on several occasions to reduce the flow to South Vietnam.

Following the full-scale invasion of South Vietnam beginning on March 29, U.S. forces began daily attacks on targets in North Vietnam's southern panhandle. B-52s were sent over North Vietnam to destroy rail and petroleum targets near Thanh Hoa. While U.S. tactical aircraft bombed the north, U.S. Air Force, Navy, Marine Corps, and South Vietnamese aircraft bombd, strafed, and rocketed North Vietnamese forces in South Vietnam. Large numbers of U.S. tactical aircraft deployed to Vietnam to help check the invasion.

Shark-nosed U.S. Air Force F-4Es sport electronic countermeasures pods in the forward Sparrow missile bays. The E-model Phantom resulted from the earlier experience in Vietnam and featured an internally mounted 20-mm cannon and improved air-to-air and air-to-ground avionics and radar. (McDonnell Douglas)

In an attempt to counter U.S. air power, North Vietnam moved large numbers of antiaircraft artillery south, positioned SA-2 batteries along the DMZ, and introduced a new Soviet-produced antiaircraft missile: the SA-7. While antiaircraft artillery fire and the SA-2 were known, the shoulder-fired SA-7 was new and consequently claimed a number of kills until new tactics and countermeasures were developed. To reduce the threat of destruction by SA-7s, slow-flying attack aircraft were forced to fly above 10,000 feet and the larger gunships, such as the AC-130, were equipped with decoy flares. Such fast-moving attack aircraft as the F-4, A-4, and F-5 were rarely hit by SA-7s because they were able to outpace the missile.

Tactical aircraft using high explosive bombs, napalm, cluster bomb units, and the newly-introduced laser- and television-guided bombs destroyed dozens of tanks, hundreds of trucks, artillery pieces, and enemy troop positions, helping to blunt the invasion.

In May, U.S. aircraft returned to "northern-route packages" of North Vietnam in the first full-scale raids since 1968. On May 9, U.S. Navy A-6 Intruders dropped mines in all of North Vietnam's major harbors, to prevent resupply by sea. Air Force, Navy, and Marine Corps fighter-bombers were also given free rein to strike at major strategic targets. Delivering laser- and television-guided 2,000- and 3,000-pound bombs as well as conventional munitions, F-4 Phantoms, A-6 Intruders, and A-7 Corsair IIs destroyed several hundred bridges, cut rail lines, and blew up power plants and supply depots to disrupt the North Vietnamese war effort.

From CONUS, the F-111A was deployed to Linebacker operations on September 27, 1972. On long-range missions from Thailand, the F-111A could carry five times the weapons load of the F-4 Phantom and attack targets at night and in bad weather. The F-111A usually flew low-level night attack missions against such North Vietnamese targets as airfields, SAM sites, and supply points. F-111 aircraft flew almost 4,000 sorites between September 1972 and March 1973, losing only six aircraft—a 0.15 percent loss rate. F-111As performed much better than during their combat introduction in 1968, since many of the technical problems had been resolved in the interim.

The heavy Linebacker I attacks were a contributing factor in the return of the North Vietnamese delegation to the peace talks; as a result, the United States called a halt to the bombing on October 22, 1972. In mid-December, however, as a result of the North Vietnamese breaking off the talks, the United States resumed all-out bombing in the north—under Linebacker II. The campaign lasted through the end of 1972, and while hundreds of fighter-bomber sorties were flown day and night, night bombing by B-52s was the primary tool. Ten nights of B-52 attacks delivered 15,000 tons of bombs and destroyed or damaged 1,600 structures, cut 500 rail lines, destroyed 372 pieces of rolling stock, burned several million gallons of petroleum, and extensively damaged 10 airfields, several electrical-generating stations, and numerous warehouses.

Air Combat

The air-to-air activity accompanying the Linebacker strikes was the most intense of any period of the entire Vietnam conflict.

The majority of air-to-air combat was fought during Linebacker I from May through October 1972. Interestingly, most kills were scored by F-4 aircraft (except for two by B-52 tailgunners in December and one MiG victory credited to a Navy F-8 fighter). Although the overall kill ratio had improved only marginally from 2.3 to 2.7, the separate U.S. services had dramatically different results in the air combat arena.

Following the 1968 bombing halt, the U.S. Navy examined the reasons for its poor showing against North Vietnamese MiGs. Known as the Ault Report, the study recommended improvements in several areas: more effective and reliable missiles; increased air-combat maneuvering training for all fleet fighter units; and the development of a specialized group to study and develop air combat tactical concepts. These recommendations were followed and the Navy developed a postgraduate school kown as the U.S. Navy Graduate Course in Fighter Weapons, Tactics, and Doctrine. The school later became an independent organization nicknamed Top Gun. The increased effectiveness of Navy fighter units during Linebacker operations can to a great extent be attributed to this intensified training.[58]

1970-1973

Defense Force	Number of Victories	Losses
U.S. Navy	22	4
U.S. Air Force	51	28
Total	73	32

U.S. Navy		U.S. Air Force	
Aircraft	**Number of Kills**	**Aircraft**	**Number of Kills**
F-4	21	F-4	49
F-8	1	B-52	2 (tail guns)

Total for Entire War: 193 U.S. Kills
89 U.S. losses
2.16: 1 Kill/Loss Ratio

Data compiled from *Aces and Aerial Victories, MiG Master, Armed Forces Journal*, May 1974; *And Kill MiGs* and *Combat Losses to MiG Aircraft in Southeast Asia 1965–1972*, Center for Naval Analysis 1978 Paper #78-0397.

U.S. aircrews benefitted from improved warning of MiG activity by U.S. radar platforms. Air Force EC-121Ts, code-named "Disco," and Navy ships, code-named "Red Crown," assisted U.S. crews in detecting and shooting down MiGs. The EC-121 monitored air traffic from an orbit in Laos, warned of MiG activity and vectored fighters to intercept. Throughout the hostilities, the EC-121s gave 3,297 MiG warnings and assisted in 25 MiG kills. The U.S. Navy Red Crown ships monitored air traffic from the Gulf of Tonkin.

While the radar capability of both these platforms was limited at lower altitudes at their extreme range because of the curvature of the earth, they aided U.S. pilots in detecting and tracking MiG fighters.

U.S. Air Force EC-121 radar surveillance aircraft spotted MiGs and gave warning to U.S. aircraft. (U.S. Air Force)

The advent of precision-guided weapons reduced the number of bomb-laden aircraft exposed to North Vietnam's defenses and allowed better protection by escorts. The U.S. Air Force further enhanced effectiveness and survivability by assigning specific missions of counter-air, night attack, and bombing to designated units. The Navy did not suffer in this regard as fighter and attack missions were generally flown by different types of aircraft. By 1972, USAF F-4s had supplanted the F-105 in the strike role and was expected to perform a multitude of roles.

The survivability of strike aircraft against radar-directed SA-2 SAMs by both the Air Force and the Navy was enhanced by extensive countermeasures. The Shrike was joined by the Standard ARM (Anti-Radiation Missile) carried by the Air Force F-105G Wild Weasel and the Navy A-6B Intruder. The Standard ARM carried a larger warhead than Shrike and had longer range. The Air Force was able to provide electronic countermeasures pods for all its aircraft, many with more than one type. The Navy used angle-deception-type jamming for all tactical aircraft. The Air Force continued to use its EB-66 in a standoff role and the Navy used its counterpart, the EKA-3B TACOS or, as it was commonly referred to, the "Electric Whale."

During the Linebacker campaign, the Air Force shot down 43 MiG-21s and eight F-6s; 30 of them—or 59 percent—were downed by the AIM-7 Sparrow. Fourteen percent were downed by AIM-9 Sidewinders, and seven percent by 20-mm cannon. The Navy scored virtually all its 22 air-to-air kills with the AIM-9 Sidewinder, shooting down eight MiG-21s, two F-6s, and 12 MiG-17s.

As between 1964 and 1968, the Air Force fought MiG-21s more often, while the Navy encountered mostly the MiG-17. The MiG-21 was used to counter the higher-speed Air Force strike groups, and the MiG-17 was used over the target areas and against the slower-speed Navy strike groups. The Navy encountered MiG-17s at lower altitudes and close-in where the AIM-7 was less effective due to radar clutter, perhaps explaining the preponderance of AIM-9 kills.

The Air Force crossed a greater expanse of North Vietnam at medium altitudes and was exposed to longer periods of possible attack. Navy AIM-7s were subjected to hundreds of carrier landings in some cases, which created havoc with their delicate electronics; consequently Navy pilots preferred the AIM-9, which had fewer internal parts and was more reliable.

The AIM-9H, then the newest Navy Sidewinder, was fired infrequently because of limited supply. It demonstrated its effectiveness, however, by an impressive kill-per-engagement rate. In July 1972, the Air Force rushed a new model of the Sidwinder, the AIM-9J, to Southeast Asia. Between May 1972 and January 1973, Air Force fighters fired 321 Sidewinder and Sparrow missiles and scored 33 kills.[59]

Poor missile/fire-control system reliability, inadequate air combat training, and preemptive firing of many missiles outside their envelopes contributed to the low missile launch-to-kill ratio. The operational effectiveness of air-to-air missiles under combat conditions is difficult to project. Current estimates for the effectiveness of late-model AIM-7 Sparrow missiles is listed as 15 to 56 percent and AIM-9 Sidewinders 15 to 40 percent.[60]

Late-model Air Force F-4E Phantoms were fitted with an internal 20-mm cannon. The cannon accounted for seven MiGs in 14 firing incidents—a 50-percent kill probability, vindicating the usefulness of a cannon to supplement missiles for close-in combat.

The Air Force's 20-mm cannon accounted for seven kills. The Navy did not utilize the gun pod in an air-to-air role in its F-4 nor did it install the cannon internally as did the Air Force's F-4E. The lesson was not lost on the Navy, however; its F-14, under development, was fitted with an internally mounted 20-mm Vulcan cannon.

U.S. aircrews first encountered North Vietnamese F-6 fighters in 1972 (Chinese-built MiG-19s). While the F-6 shot down several U.S. aircraft, 10 F-6s were lost.

A North Vietnamese pilot climbs into the cockpit of MiG-21PF Fishbed fighter. The MiG-21 was the toughest North Vietnamese air combat adversary due to its speed, air-to-air missile armament, and the use of hit-and-run tactics. (M. O'Connor)

The subsonic but highly-maneuverable MiG-17 was still very much a factor during Linebacker I and II; they downed several U.S. aircraft but were badly mauled by Navy F-4s; 12 MiG-17s fell to the "Grey Phantoms." The late-model MiG-21MF Fishbed J fighters posed the most serious threat to U.S. aircraft. The J model was capable of much higher speeds at low altitude than the earlier versions used by the NVAF. The MiG-21 also had greater range as a result of its increased internal fuel capacity and its capability of carrying wing tanks on a second set of pylons.

The NVAF used basically the same tactics evolved during Rolling Thunder. The MiG-21 continually employed hit-and-run attacks from the rear of the strike groups. The extensive GCI network enabled the North Vietnamese to vector MiG-21s at low altitude around the flanks of strike groups and beneath U.S. radar coverage. Remaining hidden, the MiG-21 pilot would then effect a maximum performance climb to get behind his target for an attack run.

The MiG-21, with an initial climb rate of more than 35,000 feet per minute (clean), could climb out of the radar clutter and into position before U.S. radar operators had a chance to pick it up. Usually, the first indication the U.S. aircraft had of an attack was impact of an Atoll missile. The U.S. Air Force fighters, primary targets of these MiG attacks, increased MiGCAP flights in an attempt to stem these attacks—a tactic marginally successful. Later, improved U.S. airborne early warning platforms were introduced to greatly improve the U.S. knowledge of the MiGs' whereabouts. The U.S. success rate against the MiGs correspondingly increased. During Linebacker I and II, U.S. fighters downed more than 50 NVAF MiG-21s, most falling to USAF F-4 Phantoms.

The MiG-17 and F-6 were used at lower altitudes and often in conjunction. Having good turning performance, they utilized the wagon wheel in an attempt to "suck" in the poorer-turning F-4s. Often U.S. aircrews encountered silver MiGs sent out as bait for following camouflaged MiGs attempting to sandwich the U.S. aircraft between them.

The North Vietnamese strongly contested Linebacker I and II operations with antiaircraft artillery, SA-2 missiles, and MiG attacks. Total U.S. losses to SA-2 and antiaircraft artillery during Linebacker I and II have not been revealed. During the 729 B-52 sorties of Linebacker II, 15 B-52s were shot down and 10 more damaged—a two-percent loss rate. All B-52s were lost to the SA-2, but electronic countermeasures and tactics were effective in reducing the missile's kill ratio. During Linebacker I and II, more than 70 SA-2s were reportedly fired for each target shot down.

Medium-altitude operations and electronic countermeasures significantly reduced the effectiveness of radar-directed antiaircraft artillery fire.

The accuracy of the precision-guided weapons used in 1972 meant fewer attacks on certain targets and fewer aircraft exposed to the target defenses. A factor not to be overlooked was the release of many targeting restrictions that gave more freedom to the on-the-scene commanders, resulting in more effective tactics and fewer losses.

The Linebacker campaign was a contributing factor in returning North Vietnam to the peace table, and a treaty ending the conflict for the United States was signed on January 29, 1973.

CHAPTER III

Battle for Kashmir: Indo-Pakistan Conflict, 1965

Introductory Overview

T he roots of the 1965 Indo-Pakistan conflict date back to 1947, when the British partitioned the Indian subcontinent along religious lines, creating Hindu India and Moslem Pakistan. The northern Kashmir province, which bordered both China and the USSR, was primarily Moslem, but its Hindu ruler chose to join India.

For more than a year India and Pakistan fought with both guerrilla and conventional troops over the way the subcontinent was divided, until the United Nations halted the conflict. Under terms of the cease-fire, Pakistan was given one-third of the Kashmir province and India two-thirds. The province was scheduled to vote in a referendum to decide which country Kashmir would join.

The vote was never held and in December 1964 India decreed that its portion of Kashmir was to become part of India. In August 1965, Pakistani guerrillas invaded Indian Kashmir to disrupt the government and foment a revolution. Regular forces on both the Indian and the Pakistani sides intervened and a large-scale, undeclared war escalated. The conflict lasted for three weeks and ended without clear resolution of the political divisions that caused the fighting.

Order of Battle

Pakistan Air Force

Until 1956 the Pakistan Air Force used mostly British equipment and was organized along the lines of the Royal Air Force. In 1956, the United States initiated its own military aid to Pakistan, and during the late 1950s and early 1960s delivered many F-86F Sabre jets, B-57 light bombers, and F-104A Starfighter supersonic fighters. America also provided a variety of weapons, including bombs and AIM-9B Sidewinder infrared-guided air-to-air missiles.

Commanded by Air Marshal Malik Nur Khan in the mid-1960s, the Pakistan Air Force had some 15,000 personnel. On the eve of the 1965 conflict, the Pakistan Air Force included the following aircraft:

100 F-86F Sabre fighter-bombers; 25 B-57B light bombers; 12 F-104A and F-104B Starfighter fighter/interceptors; 12 T-33A jet trainer/ground-attack aircraft.[1]

The most numerous Pakistan Air Force fighter, the F-86F, was the same aircraft as that used by the U.S. Air Force in the Korean War. Although subsonic, the F-86F was a highly maneuverable dogfighter, particularly the -40 version equipped with fixed leading edges and extended wingtips that considerably increased its maneuverability.

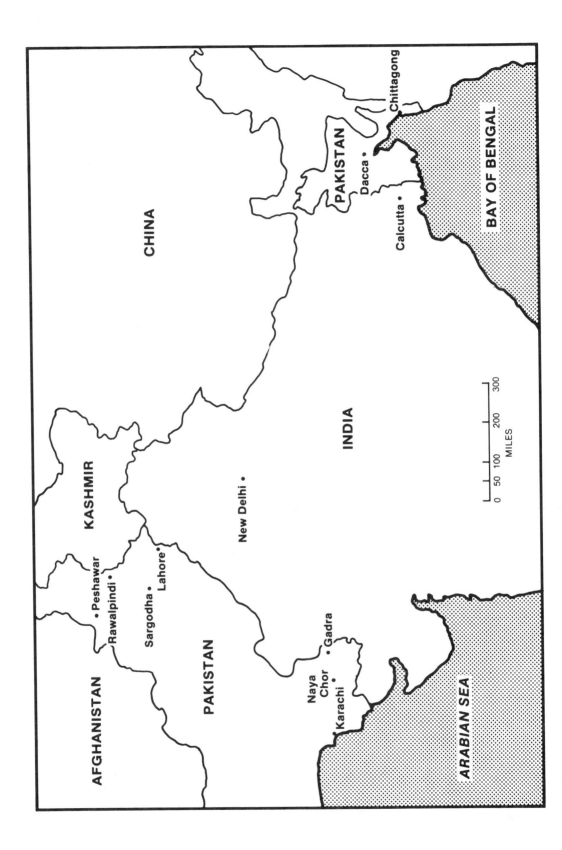

The F-86F was the most numerous fighter of the Pakistan Air Force during the 1965 Indo-Pakistan conflict. More than 100 Sabre jets had been supplied in the late 1950s by the United States as part of its mutual aid program. (W. Green)

One-quarter of the Pakistan Air Force's F-86F Sabre jets were capable of carrying the AIM-9B Sidewinder. The infrared-guided air-to-air missile significantly enhanced the aircraft's combat potential. In the ground-attack role, the Sabre could carry up to 2,000 pounds of bombs, rockets, or napalm.

The F-104A Starfighter was the Pakistan Air Force's only supersonic fighter/interceptor. Pakistan powered its F-104As with the J79-11A turbojet engines that, with their 15,800 pounds of thrust, were more powerful and more reliable than the J79-3E-3 that originally had been fitted to production A-model Starfighters.

The Pakistan Air Force's attack element was composed of 25 B-57B light bombers, a U.S.-built version of the English Canberra bomber.

The T-33A jet trainer/light attack aircraft was a two-seat version of the U.S.'s first jet fighter, the P-80. The "T-bird" was armed with two 0.5-in. machine guns and could carry up to 2,000 pounds of ordnance.

The Pakistan Air Force trained its personnel to very high standards, with pilots intensively schooled in aerobatics, tactics, gunnery, and air combat. Many Pakistan Air Force pilots gained experience on exchange duty with the RAF and other air forces. The two-year pilot training program began at the air academy at Risalpur where students attended a classroom course and then began basic flying training in T-6 Texas/Harvard trainers. Trainees flew 185 hours in the T-6 and then were assigned to Mauripur Air Base to fly T-33s in advanced training.

Those who successfully completed basic and advanced training proceeded to the fighter leader school at Peshawar to complete their training in the F-86F Sabre jet.

Indian Air Force

Following the 1962 conflict with China, the Indian government began a major program to expand its air force. Training programs were enlarged and intensified, and late in 1962 the government decided that in the future it would need 45 squadrons to defend the country adequately. Commanded by Air Marshal Arjan Singh, in 1965 the Indian Air Force included 27 fighter squadrons of 16 aircraft each, and three bomber squadrons.

In 1965, the Indian Air Force strength totaled:

8 MiG-21 fighter/interceptors; 118 Hawker Hunter fighter-bombers; 80 Mystère IV-A fighter-bombers; 50 Gnat fighters; 56 Ouragan (Toofani) fighter-bombers; 132 Vampire jet trainers/fighter-bombers; 53 Canberra bombers; and 7 Canberra reconnaissance aircraft.[2]

The Indian Air Force consisted of aircraft from several countries. In 1962, India decided to purchase the Soviet MiG-21 Fishbed as its first supersonic fighter but only a handful of the aircraft were in service by September 1965. Although the Fishbed interceptors flew patrols over Indian territory, they did not see combat.

The Hawker Hunter Mk.56 was the backbone of the Indian fighter force. The subsonic British aircraft was used as both a fighter and a fighter-bomber.

Hawker Hunter F Mk.56s lined up at the Hawker plant at Dunsford, England, prior to delivery to India in 1957. The highly-capable Hawker Hunter formed the backbone of the Indian Air Force during the 1965 Indo-Pakistan conflict. More than 110 Hunters were in service on the eve of the war. (W. Green)

The lightweight Gnat fighters were developed by Britain's Folland Air, Ltd. While Great Britain itself did not embrace the lightweight fighter concept embodied in the Gnat, its high performance and low unit cost was just what the Indian Air Force needed. In 1956, Hindustan Aircraft, Ltd., began producing the Gnat under license in India. By late 1965, three squadrons were in service in India and a fourth was being formed.

Although subsonic, the little fighter had an excellent rate of climb because of its high thrust-to-weight ratio for aircraft of its time; it also could accelerate quickly and was highly maneuverable.

The Dassault Mystère IV-A, first ordered in 1956 in response to Pakistan's procurement of the F-86F, was given the ground-attack role.

The straightwing, French-built Ouragan, known in Indian service as the Toofani, equipped a number of India's fighter-bomber squadrons.

The de Havilland Vampire was the oldest jet fighter aircraft in service with the Indian Air Force, devoted to training and to ground-attack and reconnaissance missions. Of World War II vintage technology, the Vampire was constructed of wood and metal and was powered to a top speed of 548 miles per hour by a Goblin turbojet.

The Indian Air Force's primary long-range strike aircraft was English Electric Canberra. Canberras also served in the strategic reconnaissance role.

The Indian Air Force—in 1965 an air arm of the Indian Army—was divided into three regional groups: Western, Central, and Eastern; each region had its own air command. The training and maintenance commands of the Indian Air Force were separate organizations that maintained functional control of their areas of responsibility throughout the country.

The Indian Air Force's training program was considerably expanded in order to train enough personnel to fly the planned 45-squadron air force. Student pilots were initially trained in the Hindustan Aircraft-built HT-2 light trainer at the Indian Air Flying College. Pilot trainees then went on to fly 85 hours in the T-6 Texan/Harvard trainer. Advanced training included 75 hours of flying de Havilland Vampire two-seat and single-seat jet aircraft.

The Indian Air Force had a number of SA-2 radar-guided surface-to-air missile sites protecting military and industrial targets.[3]

The Conflict

Day One: September 1

Following several border clashes, Pakistani troops marched into Indian Kashmir to claim that portion of the province. Supported by two regiments of tanks, artillery, and aircraft, the Pakistani forces overwhelmed several Indian outposts.

The Indian Air Force responded by flying 28 sorties against the invaders. Vampires and Mystère IVs bombed Pakistani columns and supply depots, allegedly destroying 14 tanks and some 30 or 40 other vehicles. Two Pakistan Air Force F-86F intercepted one flight of four Indian Vampires attacking Pakistani troops, and in the brief dogfight shot down all four.[4]

Day Two: September 2

Pakistani forces continued their drive into Indian Kashmir, capturing Chhamb and penetrating six to eight miles deeper into the territory. The advancing ground forces were supported by F-86Fs. While Indian spokesmen claimed that their fighters forced several Pakistan F-86F to turn tail following a dogfight over the battlefield, the Pakistan Air Force denied that any air battles were fought.

An Indian Air Force Vampire. A flight of four Vampires was shot down by two Pakistan Air Force F-86F Sabre jets on the first day of the war. As a result of its poor showing in air combat against the F-86F, the Vampire was withdrawn from front-line service and relegated to training and second-line duties. (Indian Air Force)

Day Three: September 3

India reported that it had checked the Pakistani offensive and inflicted severe losses. Spokesmen also reported that six Indian Gnat fighters led by Squadron Leader Prevor Keelor intercepted a flight of Pakistani F-86Fs over Chhamb and downed one; and another F-86F was picked off by antiaircraft fire.[5]

Pakistan admitted that one F-86F had been damaged but said that the aircraft, piloted by Flight Lieutenant Yousaf, successfully returned to base; Pakistan further counter-claimed that in the dogfight one Indian Gnat was shot down and two more damaged.[6] Following the dogfight, a Pakistani F-104 forced down an Indian Gnat. The aircraft landed at Pasrur airfield and was captured intact together with its pilot by Pakistani ground troops.[7]

Day Four: September 4

Pakistani forces continued to press into Indian Kashmir and advanced several miles against heavy Indian resistance. Both sides flew ground-attack sorties, and Indian Gnats flying air combat patrol again tangled with Pakistani Sabres. Four Pakistani F-86Fs bombing the Akhnoor bridge in the Chhamb area were surprised by four Indian Gnats flying seemingly out of nowhere. According to Indian sources, the Gnats shot down two of the Sabres;[8] Pakistan admitted losing one F-86F, but claimed that it had been downed by antiaircraft fire.

Day Five: September 5

With tanks, heavy artillery, and air strikes, Pakistani forces relentlessly rolled forward and captured three more Indian outposts in the Kashmir, including the town of Jaurian. India stated that two F-86Fs fired rockets and strafed the Indian air base at Amritsar—the first air raid against a target outside the Kashmir battle area.

Day Six: September 6

On September 6, several Indian Army divisions pushed into Pakistan and moved toward Lahore, the country's second largest city. The attack, which penetrated to within several miles of the city, was designed to split Pakistan to take pressure off the Kashmir sector. Indian Air Force fighter-bombers and Canberra bombers attacked trains, military vehicles, and fortifications near Lahore, and were even seen as far afield as the Pakistani capital of Rawalpindi nearly 200 miles north. Meanwhile, fighting still raged in the Kashmir as Pakistani forces continued to drive into Indian territory.

Pakistan Air Force planes bombed ground targets near the battle zone and attacked several Indian airfields and radar sites. Patrolling Indian Air Force fighters intercepted a number of the raids and were caught up in swirling air combat. In one incident, three Pakistani F-86F Sabre jets on a mission to attack the Indian Air Force airbase at Adampur were headed off by four Hawker Hunters just before reaching the airfield. According to the Pakistani flight's Squadron Leader Alam as recounted in John Fricker's *Battle for Pakistan:*

''I remember thinking what very pretty aircraft these brand new Hunters were as I ordered my section to punch tanks. The Hunters also jettisoned their drop tanks, and we turned into each other for combat. The fight didn't last long. I got my sights on the No. 4 Hunter, and after a brief burst, he flicked and went into the ground in a great ball of flame, although I'm not certain whether I hit him or not. For once, we were evenly matched numerically, although I never fought at such low altitudes again, nor often at such low speeds. The three Sabres and the three Hunters maneuvered at low altitude and slow speed, attempting to get on each other's tails.

"Before the war in our appreciation of the Hunter, we had some apprehension in our minds that, with its maneuvering flaps, this aircraft might be able to out-turn the Sabre. In this encounter, we were very close to each other—not more than about 1,000 feet—when I saw my opponent's split flaps go down. So I also lowered my flaps, although our limiting speed is rather higher—around 185 knots—and I was flying at about 200 knots at the time. But I found that the only thing it did was to slow me down—I had no problem keeping behind the chap—so I put them up again.

"We continued tail-chasing and I soon shot down my second quarry. We had started off by pulling about five g during the turns, but as the speed fell off, we got down to perhaps less than two g.

"During the scrap, I had all the other five aircraft in sight, and I watched one of my wingmen, Squadron Leader "Butch" Ahmed, score strikes on one of the Hunters in front of him. I think it was hit in the wings as white vapor was streaming from the fuel tanks. We had been in combat for five or six minutes within about 40 miles of Adampur, and I was getting worried that more Indian fighters might be sent to the scene, so I gave a call to all my flight members to return to base."[9]

Meanwhile another Pakistan Air Force Sabre strike force simultaneously heading for the Indian Air Force airfield at Halwara encountered no fewer than 10 Hawker Hunters. In spite of being so outnumbered, the three F-86F pilots maneuvered with the numerous Hunters and shot down several of them. However, the odds eventually caught up with the Sabre pilots. According to an official Indian Air Force report on the dogfight: "In the first skirmish . . . one Sabre had fallen to (Hunter pilot) Flight Officer Ghandhi's guns." Flight Officer Rathore closed in on the right, opening fire at 650 yards, and instructing his wingman Flight Officer Neb to attack the F-86F on the left. "Closing still further," continued the report, "Rathore fired again from 500 yards . . . This time the Sabre was mortally hit . . . and turned into the ground in a huge sheet of flame, five or six miles from the airfield."

Neb, still a novice pilot, closed in on the second Sabre and opened fire at 400 yards.

"The Pakistani pilot . . . pulled up sharply. Neb . . . rapidly closed in to less than 100 yards and fired again on the sharply climbing Sabre, which now presented a much better target. He saw pieces fly off the Sabre as his cannon shells found their mark on the Sabre's left wing. There was a puff of smoke which rapidly turned into a sheet of flame as the last of the . . . Pakistani Sabres disintegrated in mid-air and fell to the ground."[10]

Pakistan claimed to have destroyed a total of 22 Indian Air Force aircraft during the day's combat in the air and strikes against planes on the ground. That night, Pakistan Air Force B-57 light bombers raked a number of Indian airfields, and Indian Air Force Canberra bombers responded in kind against Pakistani airfields. The Pakistanis lost one B-57 to antiaircraft fire.

Day Seven: September 7

The seventh day was marked by heavy aerial combat. Both sides staged air raids against cities and airfields throughout India and Pakistan. India said that its planes bombed the Pakistani airbases of Sargodha and Chaklala.[11]

In an early morning strike against Sargodha, six Indian Air Force Mystère IVs caught the defenders by complete surprise. According to Pakistani reports, the raid did little damage and two of the Mystères were downed, one by antiaircraft artillery and one by a fast-acting F-104 that scrambled after the Mystères as they were exiting from the strike. In a dogfight with the four remaining Mystères, the F-104 was hit by cannon fire and the pilot bailed out.[12]

After the attack, a flight of four F-86Fs and one F-104 took up positions to cover the airfield. Squadron Leader Mohammed Alam, commander of the No. 11 Sabre squadron at

Pakistan Air Force F-104A Starfighters in formation. The most advanced fighter involved in the 1965 conflict, the F-104A was successful in combat against the slower but more maneuverable Indian Air Force fighters. (Pakistan Air Force)

Sargodha, was one of the top cover pilots. Within minutes of the previous Mystère IV attack, Pakistani ground control alerted Squadron Leader Alam of six approaching Hawker Hunters. In a spectacular dogfight lasting less than a minute, Alam singlehandedly shot down *four* of the Hunters. Recounted Alam in *Air Enthusiast* magazine:

"I picked up four Hunters diving to attack our airfield. So I jettisoned my drop tanks to dive after them through our own ack-ack. Almost simultaneously I saw two more Hunters about 1,000 feet (305 meters) to my rear, so I forgot the four ahead and pulled up to go after the pair behind. The Hunters broke off their attempted attack on Sargodha, and the rear pair turned into me. I was flying much faster than they were at this stage—I must have been doing about 500 knots (925 kilometers per hour)—so I pulled up to avoid overshooting them and then reversed to close in as they flew back toward India . . . I took the last man and dived behind him, getting very low in the process. The Hunter can outrun the Sabre—it's only about 50 knots (92 kilometers per hour) faster, but it has much better acceleration so can pull away rapidly. Since I was diving, I was going still faster, and as he was out of gun range, I fired the first of my two GAR-8 (AIM-9B) Sidewinder missiles at him. . . . In this case, we were too low and I saw the missile hit the ground short of its target.

"This area east of Sargodha has lots of high-tension wires, some of them as high as 100–150 feet (30–45 meters), and when I saw the two Hunters pull up to avoid one of these cables I fired my second Sidewinder. The missile streaked ahead of me but I didn't see it strike. The next thing I remember was overshooting one of the Hunters, and when I looked back its cockpit canopy was missing and there was no pilot in the aircraft. He had obviously pulled up and ejected, and just then I spotted him coming down by parachute . . . I had lost sight of the other five Hunters, but I pressed on thinking that maybe they would slow down . . . I had lots of fuel so I was prepared to fly 50–60 miles (80–95 kilometers) to catch up with them.

"We had just crossed the Chenab river when my wing man called out contact. I picked them up at the same time—five Hunters in absolutely immaculate battle formation. They were flying at about 100–200 feet (30–60 meters), at around 480 knots (890 kilometers per hour), and just as I reached gunfire range they saw me. They all broke in one direction, climbing and turning steeply to the left, which put them in close line astern. This, of course, was their big mistake. If you are bounced, which means a close-range approach by an enemy fighter within less than about 3,000 feet (915 meters), the drill is to call a break.

"This is a panic maneuver to the limits of the aircraft's performance, splitting the formation, getting you out of the way of an attack, and freeing you to position yourself behind your opponent. However, in the absence of one of the IAF sections initiating a break in the other direction to sandwich our attack, they all simply stayed in front of us.

"It all happened very fast. We were all turning very tightly—pulling in excess of 5 g, or just about on the limits of the Sabre's very accurate A-4 radar ranging gunsight. I think that before we had completed more than about 270 degrees of the turn, at around 12 degrees per second, all four Hunters had been shot down! In each case, I got the pipper of my sight around the canopy of the Hunter for virtually a full deflection shot.

"My fifth victim of this sortie started spewing smoke and then rolled onto its back at about 1,000 feet (305 meters). I thought he was going to do a barrel roll, which, at low altitude, is a very dangerous maneuver for the pursuer if the man in front knows what he is doing. I went almost on my back and then realized that I might not be able to keep with him, so I took off bank and pushed the nose down. The next time I fired was at very close range—about 600 feet (180 meters) or so—and his aircraft literally blew up in front of me. None of these four pilots ejected, and all were killed."[13]

This spectacular performance was witnessed by Pakistan Air Force pilots flying with Alam. A highly-experienced pilot with more than 1,400 hours in the Sabre, Alam had flown Hawker Hunters on exchange duty with the RAF and thus knew his opponents' strengths and weaknesses.

Pakistan reported that Indian aircraft widened the conflict by bombing the east Pakistani cities of Dacca, Rangpur, Chittagong, and Jessore and the western Pakistani city of Karachi. Indian spokesmen charged that Pakistani Sabre attacked the Kalaikunda airfield near Calcutta, losing three aircraft to ground fire.[14] Pakistan did not detail its losses, but reported destroying 24 Indian aircraft both in the air and on the ground.[15] Indian ground forces made a battalion-sized attack toward Sialkot to relieve pressure from the Chhamb front.

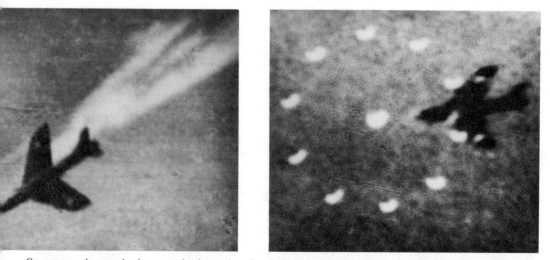

Gun camera photographs document the destruction of an Indian Air Force Hawker Hunter. On September 7, 1965, Squadron Leader Mohammed Alam shot down four Indian Air Force Hawker Hunters in less than 30 seconds near Sargodha Air Base, Pakistan. (Pakistan Air Force)

Day Eight: September 8

Fighting continued in the Kashmir, around Lahore, and broke out near Gadra (a border town about 200 miles east of Karachi). Both countries continued to support ground forces from the air and to strike at each other's airfields. Most missions designed to weaken each other's air power were not dogfights but bombing runs against airfields flown at night by Pakistani B-57s and Indian Canberras. India claimed to have destroyed 21 Pakistani aircraft during the sixth and seventh days of fighting, but said its losses were low. Pakistan Air Force Commander Air Vice Marshal Malik Nur Khan contradicted the Indian claims by saying that his force had shot down 28 Indian aircraft and destroyed 26 on the ground since the start of fighting on September 1.[16]

Day Nine: September 9

The undeclared war raged at several points along the border between India and Pakistan. The Pakistan Air Force attacked Indian Air Force airfields at night, while the Indian Air Force reportedly hit targets in and around Karachi. Pakistani spokesmen dismissed the Indian claim of destroying 21 Pakistani aircraft, saying that only five planes had been downed.[17]

Day Ten: September 10

The fighting spread to the border between East Pakistan and India where Indian police and troops battled against Pakistani soldiers, while Indian Air Force fighter-bombers reportedly struck Chittagong, Jessore, and other targets. Meanwhile, ground combat continued in the west with neither side reporting significant gains. Patrolling Pakistani Sabres and Indian Gnats tangled in air combat near Kasur, India, with both sides claiming kills.

Western military intelligence sources estimated that by the end of Day Ten Indian air losses totaled about 45 aircraft since the start of fighting, and that Pakistani losses were probably slightly higher.[18]

Day Eleven: September 11

Fighting continued and neither side was able to break the stalemate even though both countries had introduced fresh units. The Indian Air Force claimed to have shot down two F-86F Sabre jets near Amritsar during an attack on a radar site.

Day Twelve: September 12

Heavy combat continued between Amritsar and Lahore and near Sialkot as Indian forces aggressively fought to gain ground. Both sides flew ground support, air combat patrol, and night airfield attack sorties.

Day Thirteen: September 13

After a major battle with tanks and armor, Indian forces advanced around the city of Sialkot. Despite intense Pakistan counterattacks and heavy bombing from the air, Indian aircraft defended and supported the advance. Canberras went into action at night, bombing Pakistani airbases. The Pakistanis claimed to have downed two Indian Air Force aircraft by antiaircraft fire. Pakistani fighters and bombers also held their own, reportedly downing one Gnat in air combat and flying close support for ground troops and, in their turn, bombing Indian airfields.[19]

Day Fourteen: September 14

By now there was a lull in ground fighting, but air combat continued unabated. The Indian Air Force Canberras continued their night attack sorties against airfields. Pakistan Air Force F-86Fs and B-57s attacked Indian troops and targets throughout the day.

The Pakistanis admitted that one F-86F was lost in a dogfight with Indian Hawker Hunters. Pakistani spokesmen stated, however, that Pakistan had shot down 11 Indian aircraft over the previous two days; according to them, two Mystère IVs and one Hawker Hunter were allegedly downed by antiaircraft fire in the Lahore sector, five Indian aircraft were destroyed on the ground, and three (including two Hunters) were killed in air combat.[20]

Day Fifteen: September 15

While Indian forces slowly advanced toward Sialkot, there was a lull in the fighting in the Lahore sector. During the preceding week U Thant, United Nations Secretary General, had traveled to Pakistan and India to bring about a cease-fire. Both sides agreed in principle, but differed greatly on the terms. Pakistani spokesmen reported that an F-86F's AIM-9B Sidewinder downed an Indian Air Force Canberra during a night attack.

Day Sixteen: September 16

Troops locked in combat around Sialkot and Chawinda, but no significant gains were reported. Indian spokesmen claimed that since the beginning of the conflict its forces had destroyed 250 Pakistani tanks and 55 aircraft.[21] Pakistan said that it had repulsed the latest Indian effort to take Sialkot, destroying 36 tanks in the process. Pakistan Air Force Sabres again met Indian Air Force fighters in air combat with both sides claiming victories.

Day Seventeen: September 17

Conflict raged around Sialkot, in the Lahore sector, and near Chhamb. Indian Mystères and Canberra bombers flew night interdiction attacks against Pakistani airfields, holing the runways. Hawker Hunters attacked troop positions near the battle zone. Pakistan Sabres reportedly knocked out a large number of vehicles of a truck convoy on a road leading to the Sialkot battle area.[22] Pakistani B-57 bombers raided the Indian airbase at Sirsa, 90 miles west of New Delhi.

Day Eighteen: September 18

The intensity of fighting diminished considerably as a U.N. cease-fire appeared at hand. Both sides, however, fired artillery and harassed each other by air attacks. Patrolling flights of Sabre jets and Gnats met over Pakistani territory and, in the resultant dogfight, one Sabre was shot down.

Day Nineteen: September 19

Ground conflict consisted only of intermittent fire exchanged between artillery and tanks, but air combat continued. Indian Mystères flew a number of sorties over the Lahore area in close support of ground troops. Indian Gnat fighters on patrol engaged four Pakistani F-86Fs and reportedly shot down two without loss. Pakistani sources admitted that one F-86F was lost but claimed to have downed one Gnat, the pilot being captured by Pakistani troops.[23]

Days Twenty to Twenty-third: September 20–23

India and Pakistan continued to skirmish, patrol, and attack the other's territory. On September 20, Pakistani spokesmen reported that Sabre jets in the Lahore area downed two Indian Air Force fighters and lost one F-86F. The next day, a Canberra bomber returning from a raid against a Pakistan Air Force airfield was destroyed by a Sidewinder launched from an F-104.

On September 22, India accepted the cease-fire proposed by the United Nations Security Council, followed a day later by Pakistan's acceptance.

Analysis

The losses of men and equipment during 1965's three-week Indo-Pakistan conflict were considerable. Following the undeclared war, Pakistan claimed to have killed or captured 8,200 Indian soldiers, destroyed 113 aircraft, and captured or destroyed 500 Indian tanks.[24] India reported that it had killed or captured 5,259 Pakistanis and destroyed 73 aircraft and 471 tanks.[25]

India claimed to have gained possession of 670 square miles of Pakistani territory, while it admitted losing 200 square miles of its own. Pakistan said its forces gained control of 1,600 square miles of Indian territory and lost 450 square miles of its own.[26]

The actual gains and losses incurred by India and Pakistan were undoubtedly considerably less than the released figures. India listed total losses as 33 aircraft, while Pakistan admitted only 19—each figure about one-quarter the number claimed by the opposition.

Most of the air activity supported the ground forces. Pakistani B-57s and F-86F Sabres, Indian Hawker Hunters, Mystère IV-As, Canberras, and Vampires strafed, bombed, or fired rockets at defensive positions, opposing troops, and vehicles. The ground-attack aircraft carried standard ordnance, including general-purpose bombs, rockets, napalm, and ammunition for machine guns and cannon.

Neither India nor Pakistan had set up a regular cooperative close air-support system between their Army and their Air Force. Therefore, most air sorties that supported ground troops were specified armed reconnaissance missions or pre-planned attacks against positions.

Both air forces flew many battlefield interdiction sorties to bomb and strafe second-echelon armor, infantry columns, supply convoys, trains, supply positions, bridges, or other rear-area targets to weaken the enemy before they reached the main battlefield.

The Pakistan Air Force flew C-130 Hercules transports on nocturnal missions to bomb Indian troop concentrations, artillery positions, and supply dumps just behind the battle area. The rear landing ramps of several of the Hercules cargo transports were modified so that they could be opened while the aircraft were in flight. Up to 22 1,000-pound bombs were mounted on pallets that were pulled through the rear door by a parachute when the bombs were released. The Pakistan Air Force even pressed trainers into service to beef up the ground-attack force. In the daytime, T-33 jet trainers closely supported ground troops, and at night T-6 Texan/Harvard primary trainers interdicted convoys and attacked supply dumps.[27]

India initially sent elderly Vampire fighters to attack Pakistani ground positions, but after a flight of four Vampires was mauled by Sabre jets, the Indians withdrew the Vampires from combat.

Both air forces frequently attacked each other's airfields. By day jet fighters struck at airbases; by night Indian Canberra and Pakistani B-57 jet bombers flew long-range attack missions deeper into each other's territory. Although both sides claimed to have destroyed a sizable number of the other's aircraft on the ground, actual losses and damage to the airbases were impossible to ascertain.

Tactically, most attack aircraft on both sides penetrated at low level to avoid being detected by radar. The Pakistan Air Force relied on low-level flying to evade Indian light antiaircraft gunfire, radar-directed 40-mm antiaircraft gunfire, and SA-2 missiles. While the Indians fired a number of SA-2 missiles during the war, only one kill was recorded; on September 8, one SA-2 reportedly destroyed a Pakistan Air Force C-130 transport flying a night mission.[28]

Air defense and counter-air missions were flown primarily by Pakistani F-86s and F-104s and by Indian Hawker Hunters and Gnats. The Pakistan Air Force claimed to have downed 35 Indian aircraft in air combat while losing but seven Sabre jets and one F-104.[29] While the Mach-2-plus F-104s were responsible for downing two Mystère IVs and two Canberras, F-86Fs allegedly accounted for most of the kills, including 19 Hunters, six Gnats, four Vampires, one Mystère, and one Canberra.[30] (Later, Pakistan claimed to have inflicted on India losses totaling about 50 aircraft. The 22 lost in air combat reportedly were 12 Hunters, four Vampires, three Mystère IVs, two Gnats, and one Canberra.[31]

About one-quarter of the Pakistan Air Force's 100 F-86Fs were equipped to carry the AIM-9B Sidewinder. The infrared-guided, air-to-air missile had to be fired within a limited angle of the target's tail to successfully home on the heat of its jet exhaust. Designed to be most effective against such non-maneuvering targets as bombers, the Sidewinder was difficult to fire successfully in fast-turning dogfights. The Pakistan Air Force reported firing 33 Sidewinders, destroying nine Indian Air Force aircraft.[32]

Most dogfights were low-level maneuvering battles involving between two and 10 aircraft on each side. While the Pakistan Air Force had the advantage of AIM-9B Sidewinders, those missiles did not change the pilots' tactics. A missile attack was similar to gun attack, requiring only less careful aim and longer range. Since the Sidewinder's probability of kill was low, the pilot frequently had to follow up with a gun attack.

Indian Air Force Hawker Hunters scored a number of kills during the conflict but it was the Gnat that rose to fame. Nicknamed the "Sabre Slayer," the Gnat demonstrated excellent acceleration, rate of climb, and maneuverability, and it had the added benefit in that its diminutive size make it harder to spot—and once spotted it was often deceptively close. At least six F-86s allegedly fell to the Gnat's 30-mm Aden guns.[33]

The long-awaited clash between the Mach-2 MiG-21 and the F-104 did not occur as India's force of only eight Soviet Fishbeds was used solely for training.

Few significant lessons can be drawn from the 1965 Indo-Pakistan conflict.

Dueling mostly with subsonic jet fighters and bombers, Korean-War-and-earlier vintage antiaircraft guns, tanks, and artillery, both sides fought with no clear-cut strategy or purpose. From the evidence available, neither side can be called the victor. Because the conflict was unplanned, and both the United States and Great Britain embargoed arms shipments to India and Pakistan at the outset, severe shortages of spare parts and ammunition contributed to the cease-fire.

The lightweight, Indian-built Gnat was nicknamed the "Sabre Slayer" by the Indian press because of its success in air combat against PAF F-86F Sabre jets. At least six Sabres were downed by 30-mm cannon fire from Gnats. (W. Green)

CHAPTER IV

Battle for Bangladesh:
Indo-Pakistan War, 1971

Introductory Overview

Following the inconclusive 1965 Indo-Pakistan War, both countries agreed to withdraw troops from each other's territory and establish a cease-fire line patrolled by U.N. troops. In September 1966, Pakistani and Indian military leaders met and agreed to limit the concentrations of their troops near the border and to notify each other of exercises or military maneuvers.

While at peace, Pakistan and India continued to expand and modernize their military forces.

The 1971 Indo-Pakistan War had its roots in 1970, when an election was held in both East and West Pakistan to end military rule and institute a representative government. Negotiations for a united central government broke down, and the East Pakistani government declared itself in March 1971 the independent State of Bangladesh. Then began a bloody civil war between West and East Pakistan.

The Indian government saw the opportunity to capitalize on the strife and seriously weaken its long-time foe by contributing arms, supplies, and training to aid the creation of Bangladesh. By the fall of 1971, Indian troops were attacking positions in West Pakistan.

Full-scale war broke out in December 1971 in fierce combat lasting two weeks. In the end, Bangladesh was formed and India captured a substantial area of Pakistani territory. Thousands of soldiers on both sides were injured or killed, and scores of aircraft destroyed. One intriguing aspect of the conflict was the wide variety of Soviet, American, French, British, and Chinese tactical aircraft and weapons pitted against one another, and their resultant performance.

The Order of Battle

Pakistan Air Force

Following the 1965 war, Pakistan began negotiating with other countries to purchase combat aircraft to replace those lost and to increase its Air Force's overall strength. Early in 1966, Pakistan began to receive MiG-19s (known as F-6s) built in the People's Republic of China, and by mid-1967 had three squadrons.[1] An assembly line to produce MiG-19s had been set up in China prior to the break in Sino-Soviet relations in 1961.

In 1966, Pakistan began to receive the first of 90 ex-Luftwaffe Sabre Mk. 6, the Canadian-built version of the F-86. These aircraft were bought by a Swiss company from West Germany, refurbished, and supplied to Pakistan.[2] In addition to the Canadian-built Sabre Mk. 6s, Pakistan also had the F-86Fs purchased from the United States in service with one operational training unit and one fighter squadron.

The Pakistan Air Force received the Chinese-built version of the Soviet MiG-19 known as the F-6 beginning in 1966. The twin-engine fighter was armed with three powerful Nudelmann-Richter 30-mm cannon and could carry AIM-9B Sidewinder air-to-air missiles or rocket pods for ground attack missions. (W. Green)

In 1968, Pakistan purchased from France Mirage IIIE fighter/bombers. The Mirages operated with No. 5 squadron at Sargodha.[3]

The Pakistan Air Force also had a single squadron of B-57 bombers and RB-57 reconnaissance aircraft.

Seven F-104A fighters remaining from the 12 delivered in 1962 equipped one squadron for strike and interdiction missions.

In order to increase the survivability of its aircraft, Pakistan built a number of new airfields and constructed camouflaged revetments to shelter most aircraft. In addition, airfields were protected by large numbers of antiaircraft guns including U.S.-supplied quad-mounted, half-inch machine guns, and Chinese-built 14.5-mm heavy machine guns and 37-mm cannon.

Pakistan further improved its organization of ground observers, which had been so successful in warning of the approach of Indian aircraft during the 1965 conflict. Its radar coverage was expanded and the command-and-control system was upgraded by adding Soviet P-35 ground-controlled intercept radars, Plessey AR-1 low level radars, and Marconi Condor ground-controlled intercept stations.[4]

The Pakistan Air Force's primary task in the event of war was to defend Pakistani territory and ground forces from air attack. Secondary missions included interdiction of enemy airfields, transportation centers, and military targets, and close air support of Pakistani troops.

At the beginning of the conflict in December 1971, the Pakistan Air Force comprised 13 combat squadrons manned by some 17,000 personnel. One squadron of Sabre Mk. 6s was based at Dacca, East Pakistan. The 12 remaining squadrons were stationed in West Pakistan.

On the eve of the conflict, the Pakistan Air Force included the following aircraft: 40 F-86F Sabre fighter-bombers; 90 Sabre Mk. 6 fighter-bombers; 70 F-6 (MiG-19) fighters; 20 Mirage IIIE fighter-bombers; 7 F-104A/B Starfighter fighters; 16 B-57 light bombers; 4 T-33 jet trainer/ground-attack aircraft; 2 RB-57 reconnaissance planes.[5]

Indian Air Force

The Indo-Pakistan Conflict of 1965 somewhat slowed the Indian Air Force's ambitious program to expand, but by late 1971 India's own manufacturing supplemented by British and Soviet imports gave the Indian Air Force a front-line strength of 33 combat squadrons. In April 1966, the Indian Air Force, which had begun as the air arm of the Army, became an independent service, organized into Central, Western, and Eastern air commands; training and maintenance commands served all the air commands.

Operational only with a trial unit during the 1965 conflict, the MiG-21 force had expanded to seven squadrons by the end of 1971. Furthermore, Hindustan Aeronautics had established a production line for building the late-model MiG-21PF Fishbed D customized in India, known as the MiG-21FL. Fully 60 percent of the MiG-21FL was built in India itself, the remaining items being bought from the USSR because they could not be economically produced in India.[6]

Unlike the Soviet Fishbed D, which had no cannon, the Indian MiG-21FL had a lead-computing gunsight and the capability to carry the GP-9 twin-barrel 23-mm cannon. The GP-9 gunpack was carried in conjunction with the MiG-21FL's standard armament of two K-13A Atoll infrared-guided air-to-air missiles.

The most numerous fighter serving with the Indian Air Force on the eve of the 1971 conflict was the Gnat. Also produced by Hindustan Aeronautics, the Gnat's main task was to defend important airfields, military areas, and to fly combat air patrol.

Two fighter-bomber squadrons and a training unit were equipped with the HF-24 Marut, the first combat aircraft designed and built in India. The Marut was designed and produced with the assistance of Dr. Kurt Tank, the genius behind the FW-190 World War II German fighter. Built by Hindustan Aeronautics, the HF-24 Marut entered service in 1968 and served as a fighter-bomber.[7]

Also in service by late 1971 were six squadrons of Soviet-supplied Su-7B figher-bombers. Designed to make short-range, high-speed tactical nuclear attacks, the Su-7B was procured by the Indian Air Force for the conventional strike mission because it was the only aircraft then available.[8]

An Indian Air Force Su-7B takes off on a training mission. Program delays and performance shortcomings of the HF-24 Marut resulted in the Indian Air Force procuring the Soviet Su-7B supersonic fighter-bomber beginning in 1968. The Su-7B was designed to supersonically deliver tactical nuclear weapons, and thus it had only a modest range when carrying a heavier load of conventional ordnance. (W. Green)

Six squadrons of the venerable Hawker Hunter remained in service after the 1965 conflict. Released from air superiority duties when the MiG-21 and the Gnat were phased into service, Hawker Hunters were tasked with providing close air support for ground troops and interdiction missions.

The Mystère IV-A fighter-bomber, first supplied to the Indian Air Force in 1957, was still in active service 14 years later. Two squadrons flew primarily close support missions.

Long-range strike missions were the responsibility of the Canberra squadrons. Because of the bomber's slow speed, it usually flew its interdiction missions at night.

Learning from the 1965 War, the Indian Air Force considerably expanded its radar network, adding numerous Russian and Western units. Following the Pakistanis' lead, India established an extensive ground observer network linked to a command-and-control network by UHF radio.

About 20 batteries of SA-2 surface-to-air missiles protected key military and industrial areas. The missiles' low-altitude coverage was improved when the Fan Song E radar was introduced; it was capable of accurately guiding missiles at aircraft as low as about 1,000 feet.[9]

India, like Pakistan, took steps to reduce the vulnerability of her forward airfields. Aircraft were well dispersed: many were stationed at rear fields out of range of Pakistan's Sabres and Mirages. Antiaircraft defenses were strengthened around the forward airfields and protective revetments were built to shelter most aircraft. Additional engineering personnel and equipment were stationed at forward airfields to ensure that damaged runways and buildings could be quickly repaired.

The Indian Air Force operated about 625 combat aircraft crewed by some 80,000 personnel. A majority of the aircraft were earmarked against West Pakistan. About 200 aircraft were stationed at airfields surrounding East Pakistan:[10]

Seven squadrons MiG-21 Fishbed fighter/interceptors; seven squadrons Gnat fighters; six squadrons Hawker Hunter fighter-bombers; two squadrons Mystère IV-A fighter-bombers; three squadrons HF-24 Marut fighter-bombers; six squadrons Su-7B fighter-bombers; three squadrons Canberra bombers.

In addition to its air force, India had a small naval air arm that operated from its sole aircraft carrier, the I.N.S. *Vikrant*. This totaled 35 Sea Hawk fighters, 12 Alizé anti-maritime, anti-submarine warfare aircraft, two Sea King helicopters, and 10 Alouette III helicopters. The *Vikrant* carried the standard complement of the 18 Sea Hawk fighters, four Alizé aircraft, and two Alouette helicopters.[11]

Background and Goals of War

India's goals in the 1971 war were to divide and conquer its longtime foe, to help liberate East Pakistan, and to forestall offensive moves by West Pakistan. The hope was that when India attained air superiority, then the Indian Air Force would interdict Pakistani supply lines and airfields and, most importantly, provide close support for Indian ground units. To provide for more effective support, the Indian Air Force assigned tactical air centers at division and corps levels, and forward air controllers down to the brigade level. Air crews were trained in low-level navigation, close air support tactics, and communications.

The roots of this conflict dated back to 1947 when Great Britain created India and Pakistan by a division along religious lines. West Pakistan was separated from East Pakistan by more than 1,000 miles of Indian territory. Neither West nor East Pakistan had a common language, culture, or heritage; the only communal tie was religion and fear of India. Semi-industrialized West Pakistan was the home of the aristocratic Punjabis, who held most of the powerful government and industry positions. The Bengalis of agricultural East Pakistan, who produced most of the crops used for food and foreign exchange, wanted a more equal distribution of government positions and resources.

In December 1970, an election was held in Pakistan to end military rule and to institute a representative government. In West Pakistan, Zulfikar Ali Bhutto and his Pakistan People's Party emerged victorious; in East Pakistan the winner was the nationalist Awami League led by Sheikh Mujibur Rahman.

In March 1971, Awami leader Rahman declared the establishment of the independent state of Bangladesh. His followers began a series of guerrilla raids against the military government of Pakistan. For the most part, East Pakistani police and military forces supported the separatist movement. Military President General Agha Mohammad Yahya Khan reacted swiftly to this challenge by sending three divisions of troops and armor to East Pakistan to suppress the revolt. West Pakistan military forces massacred hundreds of thousands of Bengali civilians.

The attacks failed to crush the rebellion and brought about a running guerrilla war between the Pakistani military forces (most of whom came from West Pakistan) and the Mukti Bahini (People's Liberation Army, East Pakistan nationals). About 10,000,000 refugees, mostly Hindis, crossed into India. India provided arms and training to the People's Liberation Army, now heavily involved in fighting against the 80,000 Pakistani troops in East Pakistan. In addition to supplying arms and military training, by the fall of 1971 Indian troops were attacking local Pakistani positions.

On November 22, 1971, an Indian infantry brigade supported by armored vehicles penetrated several miles into East Pakistan on a mission of "active defense." Early in the afternoon, four Pakistani Sabre Mk. 6s attacked this Indian force with rockets and machine guns. Four Indian Gnat fighters challenged the Sabres. Pakistani sources claimed that two Gnats and two Sabres were downed in the dogfight with all four falling in Pakistani territory. India said that three Sabres were downed without loss, and added that two of the three pilots who bailed out were captured.[12]

Conflict along the border continued, and on November 23, 1971, Pakistan declared a state of emergency. Local attacks escalated over the following week along the border of East Pakistan, and the fighting became all-out war on December 3.

The War

Day One: December 3

On the evening of December 3, Pakistani Sabres and B-57s bombed a number of Indian airfields, railway stations, and military concentrations, continuing without remission throughout most of the night. Airfields attacked included Pathankot, Amritsar, Avantipur, Srinagar, Uttarlai, Agra, and Ambala.[13] Several hundred yards of runway at Amritsar were heavily cratered and a radar station was destroyed, but most of the other airfields suffered only minor damage. The Pakistan Air Force hoped to deal India a severe blow with its Israeli-style preemptive strike, but by attacking many targets with only a few aircraft each, the offensive had little effect. Indian aircraft were dispersed and protected in shelters and revetments, leaving runways and buildings as the only easy targets. Four Pakistani aircraft were allegedly shot down during the series of raids.

The Indian Air Force reacted swiftly to the initial attacks, striking back against Pakistani airfields and other targets in both East and West Pakistan. Canberra bombers, Su-7Bs, Hawker Hunters, and other fighter-bombers bombed Pakistan Air Force bases at Peshawar, Sargodha, Shorkot, Mauripur, and Tezgaon.[14]

Day Two: December 4

Indian ground forces advanced into East Pakistan while MiG-21s, Hawker Hunters, and Su-7Bs concentrated their attacks against the sole East Pakistan airfield at Tezgaon to try to eliminate Pakistani air cover. The 14 remaining Pakistani Sabre Mk. 6s and antiaircraft guns put up a concerted defense, claiming eight Indian aircraft. In the air, Pakistani Sabres reportedly downed five Indian aircraft with the loss of three.[15]

According to Flying Officer Hag, a Pakistani pilot in his early twenties, on the morning of December 4:

"I was told to take off and engage a formation of enemy aircraft approaching Dacca. The moment I got airborne I got a call from the controller, 'Two bogies (enemy aircraft) two miles,

3 o'clock.' My No. 2 was delayed a bit and could not join up although he managed to get airborne in time. As soon as he gained height I told him to jettison tanks and break into the bogies. I had barely finished talking to him when I saw the Su-7s split and come one behind each of us.

"I broke, dropped my fuel tanks, and hit the deck as soon as I broke. I pulled up in order to get behind the Su-7. At that moment, I saw the other Su-7 fire two missiles at my No. 2, Shamshad, but the missiles missed the target and went past his F-86. Simultaneously, the bogie which was still somewhere behind me fired a missile at me. I sensed the danger immediately and broke in time . . . Spurred as I was by the lucky escape, I maneuvered myself behind the Su-7 which was zooming past me, selected my guns, and started closing in on him. I opened fire at 1,800 feet but to no effect. So I continued the chase and kept firing till I was as close as 400 feet from the target. . . . The Su-7 pilot lit the afterburner and tried to out-distance me by sheer speed. His attempt proved futile as by then my burst had landed around his canopy. I saw his left wing and exhaust trailing smoke and the aircraft going into a spiral. A few seconds later, it hit the ground.

"The other Su-7 was still behind my No. 2; so I rolled in for it. The pilot of that aircraft lit his burner and disengaged from No. 2 before I could open fire.

"Control reported four Hunters behind us. I left the Su-7 and went for the Hunters. They were in pairs; so each of us took a pair and engaged in aerial combat. The pair I got behind split and one of them pulled away. I got behind the other Hunter, opened my guns at it from a range of 600 feet. The fire was accurate and hit the aircraft squarely. The Hunter started trailing smoke and after a couple of seconds its pilot bailed out. My No. 2 was still behind the other Hunter. He was firing at him. Meanwhile, I got a call from the controller that another Hunter was in sight. . . . My bullets had been expended and I had only one missile left. I still had a powerful weapon under the belly, so I decided to go after the Hunter which was exiting towards West Bengal. I continued the chase and went about nine to 11 miles inside the enemy territory. I was flying at about 400 feet and so was the Hunter. I went further low over tree-tops and got right behind the aircraft. As soon as I heard the missile tone confirming contact I fired the missile. I saw the missile miss initially but then in a flash of a second it went straight into the exhaust of the Hunter. The aircraft immediately turned into a ball of fire. I saw the pilot being thrown out at an angle of 45 degrees to the right. Then the parachute opened."[16]

By day's end the Indian Air Force had so severely cratered the single runway at Tezgaon that the 11 remaining sheltered Sabres were unable to take off. India acknowledged losing five aircraft but claimed destroying seven Sabres, four on the ground and three in air combat.[17]

At the conflict's outset, the Indian Navy's carrier *Vikrant* and several escort vessels were patrolling in the Bay of Bengal 100 miles off the coast of East Pakistan. The *Vikrant's* Sea Hawk fighter-bombers attacked and heavily damaged the airfield and port facilities at Chittagong.

Meanwhile, in the west, Pakistani forces pushed into Indian Kashmir. Mindful of the vulnerability of East Pakistan—defended by only four infantry divisions, one squadron of aircraft, and a single regiment of U.S.-built Chaffe light tanks—the Pakistanis hoped to take a major portion of Indian Kashmir. The hope was that the captured territory then could be used as a bargaining chip during peace negotiations.

The HF-24 Marut saw its first action on counter-air missions to bomb airfields in central West Pakistan. Maruts, Sabres, and other fighter-bombers closely supported respective ground forces. On the western front, India claimed to have destroyed 19 Pakistani aircraft (nine Sabres, five B-57s, three Mirages, and two F-104A Starfighters) for the loss of six Indian aircraft. Pakistani spokesmen said that 26 Indian aircraft had been downed while losing only two Sabre jets.[18]

Pakistan Air Force Sabres in formation. Sabre Mk. 6 pilots of the #14 squadron at Tezgaon airfield near Dacca. East Pakistan, destroyed 11 Indian Air Force aircraft attacking the base. Waves of Indian Air Force fighter-bombers severely damaged Tezgaon's runway, however, grounding the 11 surviving Sabre Mk. 6s and eliminating all air cover for the Pakistani forces in East Pakistan. (Pakistan Air Force)

Day Three: December 5

In East Pakistan, the Indian Air Force's unremitting heavy attacks against Tezgaon airfield near Dacca further damaged the runway and hangars, keeping the surviving Sabres on the ground. One Indian aircraft was downed by Pakistani antiaircraft fire. With no opposition from the air, however, Indian Air Force fighter-bombers concentrated most sorties to support advancing ground columns. Sea Hawk figher-bombers from *Vikrant* continued to attack Pakistani targets.

In the west, Pakistan Air Force fighter-bombers struck Indian airfields and provided air support for their troops' drive into the Kashmir. Aircraft also flew sorties against Indian targets in the Kashmir and in the Sind Desert along the border near central West Pakistan. Since the beginning of fighting, Pakistan claimed that its forces had downed 61 aircraft.[19]

The major missions of Indian Air Force units in the west were to attack and destroy airfields, radar sites, and ground-control sites. However, Mystère IVs, Hawker Hunters, HF-24 Maruts, and Su-7Bs, also supported Indian troops on the ground, slowing the Pakistani offensive into the Kashmir and aiding the attacks in the Sind Desert. Canberras and Hunters attacked the Karachi fuel depot, igniting numerous fires. Indian spokesmen claimed to have destroyed 47 Pakistani aircraft since the beginning of the conflict, while losing 14 fighter-bombers and one helicopter.[20]

Day Four: December 6

Sabre Mk. 6s based at Tezgaon airfield in East Pakistan were able to take to the air despite extensive damage to the runway. Four attacked Indian Army units near Comilla. Four Indian Hawker Hunters interfered with the strike, and in a series of dogfights one Hunter was reportedly shot down.[21] India claimed to have shot down one of the remaining Sabres. The Indian Air Force also flew several hundred ground-support sorties to cover advancing columns.

A Canadian C-130 cargo transport flying over Dacca was attacked and damaged by fighters. The transport, part of the U.N. force, was able to evade the fighters and landed safely in Bangkok, Thailand.

In the west, both air forces continued to bomb each other's airfields, the Pakistan Air Force attacking 10 Indian airbases while the Indian Air Force struck at five Pakistani bases. Indian aircraft again attacked oil and port facilities near Karachi, damaging them extensively. Su-7Bs, Hunters, and Canberras also supported troop advances and attacked Pakistani rail lines and convoys.

Pakistan Air Force fighter-bombers supported units pressing deeper into Indian Kashmir and bombed an Indian Navy patrol boat in the Gulf of Kutch.

Day Five: December 7

In the east, Indian units captured Jessore and thus controlled half of East Pakistan. There being no opposition from the air, Indian Air Force fighter-bombers supported advancing columns. *Vikrant* Sea Hawk fighters and Alizé anti-maritime aircraft bombed and strafed shipping, harbor facilities, and the airfields at Chittagong and Cox's Bazar.

Pakistani forces launched a major drive on the Kashmir front, advancing at least five miles deeper into Indian territory. Sabre and F-6 fighter-bombers supported the offensive, destroying tanks, guns, and defensive positions. The Pakistan Air Force continued to harass Indian airfields, but admitted that the initial raids flown on December 3 and 4 had destroyed "very few Indian aircraft, possibly none at all" because the aircraft had been dispersed and housed in revetments.

Sea Hawks prepare to take off from the Indian Navy carrier I.N.S. *Vikrant*. Sea Hawk fighter-bombers repeatedly bombed and strafed PAF airfields at Chittagong and Cox's Bazar, plus harbor and shipping facilities. Since all Pakistan Air Force Sabres had been grounded when their runways were destroyed, the Sea Hawks met only light antiaircraft opposition. (W. Green)

Indian aircraft supported units retreating before the Kashmir offensive, and struck along the Pakistani border near Rajasthan. As fighters met near the front lines, they frequently battled. Pakistani fighters reportedly shot down two Su-7Bs and one Hawker Hunter.[22] Two HF-24 Maruts tangled with four Sabres near Chor in central West Pakistan. In a head-on pass against a Sabre, one Marut shot down the F-86, scoring the type's first air combat victory.[23] Pakistan reported that Indian air attacks killed 112 civilians and injured hundreds more. Indian spokesmen reported that since the outbreak of fighting, 52 Pakistani aircraft had been destroyed for the loss of only 22.[24]

Day Six: December 8

Indian units continued to gain in the East. The Indian Air Force flew hundreds of close support sorties and joined Indian Navy aircraft from *Vikrant* in yet again attacking Pakistani airfields and shipping off the coast.

Meanwhile, the Pakistan Air Force concentrated most of its sorties to support ground forces in Kashmir and in the Sind Desert. Counter-air missions continued, mostly at night: Sabres, B-57s, and other aircraft bombed several Indian airfields and a number of military installations. Two defending Su-7Bs were allegedly shot down over Risalawala airbase.

The Indian Air Force flew dozens of strike missions in Kashmir's Chhamb area to help solidify defensive positions, attacking fuel dumps, supply convoys, and four airfields.[25]

Day Seven: December 9

Indian aircraft flew more than 100 sorties to support army columns closing a ring around Dacca. With Su-7Bs, Hunters, MiG-21s, and even Gnat fighters, it bombed and sank many river craft the Pakistanis used to transport supplies and retreating troops.

Pakistani forces fought a number of battles in an attempt to drive deeper into Indian Kashmir. In mid-day, Mirages struck Pathankot airfield and at night B-57s bombed a number of bases.

Indian air and naval units coordinated an attack on the port of Karachi, sinking a number of ships. Moreover, HF-24 Maruts and Hawker Hunters knocked out many tanks of the Pakistani 27th Cavalry Regiment in the Longewala area. Other fighter-bombers attacked the battle areas in the Kashmir and in the Sind Desert. As of the end of the first week of fighting, India listed Pakistani aircraft destroyed at a total of 73 against losses of 31, while Pakistani spokesmen claimed to have destroyed 102.[26]

Day Eight: December 10

Pakistani military command admitted that its troops in the East were outnumbered by six to one and "overstressed on the ground." It also disclosed that the Indian Air Force was providing "overwhelming air support."[27] The Indian Air Force continued to support ground forces, and helicopters transported Indian troops across the Meshna River north of Dacca to outflank retreating Pakistanis.

In the west, Pakistan began a drive toward Chhamb, supporting it by bombing convoys and trains in the Sind Desert area and in Indian Kashmir and by bombing Indian airfields day and night. The Pakistan Air Force claimed to have destroyed six Indian fighter-bombers in air battles, one a Navy Alizé shot down by an F-104 off the coast near Karachi.[28]

Indian aircraft continued to raid Pakistani airfields, although none in the west was put out of action. According to several reports, Indian bombing runs over airfields and the successive raids against Karachi were largely unchallenged. Pakistani aircraft seemed to be concentrating on bombing Indian targets in the Kashmir and Sind Desert areas. The Indian Air Force was active on all fronts supporting ground fighting, and flying air cover missions.

Day Nine: December 11

Pakistani army representatives in Rawalpindi said that the outlook in the east was "grim," but added that an Indian helicopter-borne attack in the Khulna area south of Dacca had been repulsed. A battalion of Indian paratroopers was dropped behind Pakistani lines to capture an important bridgehead, supported by heavy sorties of fighter-bombers.

Indian units counterattacked Pakistani forces in the Chhamb sector of Kashmir, but made little progress. In air combat, a Gnat allegedly downed a Pakistan Air Force Mirage.[29] B-57s continued their nocturnal bombing of several airfields while Sabres, Mirages, and F-104s attacked Indian Air Force bases three times during the day.

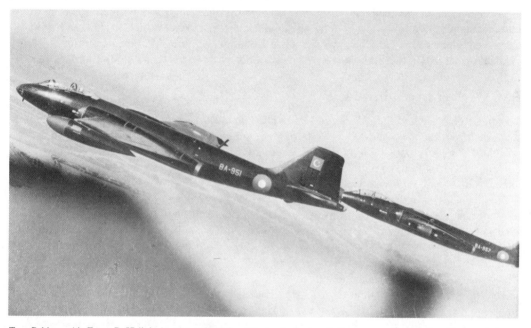

Two Pakistan Air Force B-57 light bombers climb for altitude. Such aircraft flew numerous night interdiction missions against Indian airfields. (Pakistan Air Force)

Day Ten: December 12

The ring was further tightened around Dacca, with only a few towns remaining in Pakistani hands. Hawker Hunters, MiG-21s, and Sea Hawks from the *Vikrant* repeatedly attacked Pakistani troop positions. Hawker Hunters of the Indian Air Force's Squadron #14 began flying from the airfield at Jessore, which had been captured on December 7.[30]

The long-awaited first air combat between the MiG-21 and the F-104 was fought December 12. Two MiG-21FLs were scrambled from Jamnagar airfield when forward observation posts detected several intruders approaching at low altitude. One of the F-104 Starfighters strafed the airfield, but broke off at high speed when he saw the top cover of MiG-21s. The F-104 pilot attempted to outmaneuver the pursuing Fishbeds by making a tight 360-degree turn and breaking away at low altitude. Flight Lieutenant Soni, in a MiG-21, maneuvered to close range and raked the F-104 with his GP-9 gun. The F-104 plunged into the ocean, the pilot ejecting just before the plane hit.[31]

The Indian Air Force concentrated nearly 100 sorties to support ground fighting against Pakistani positions near Chhamb, and flew numerous air combat patrol and attack missions in the Sind Desert near Naya Chor. The Pakistan Air Force retaliated by bombing several Indian airfields and flying close support near Chhamb and Rajasthan.

Day Eleven: December 13

Indian Air Force fighter-bombers and Navy Sea Hawks pounded retreating Pakistani forces and defense positions around Dacca and the remnant of East Pakistan still uncaptured.

Meanwhile, in the west the Pakistan Air Force harassed six Indian airfields from the air. During a strike against Pathankot airfield, two Su-7Bs were reportedly downed in a dogfight.[32] Sorties were flown to support ground units engaged in the Kashmir and the Sind Desert.

The Indian Force bombed and strafed Pakistani trains and convoys in northern Pakistan to interdict supply lines, and flew counter-air missions against several airfields. Hawker Hunters extensively damaged a petrochemical factory at Khairpur with rockets and cannon fire. Pakistani positions in the Sind Desert near Naya Chor were bombed and strafed.

Day Twelve: December 14

Indian troops entered the suburbs of Dacca and continued to push forward, their advance supported from the air with MiG-21FLs striking a number of key targets in Dacca; the most notable was a rocket attack on the East Pakistan governor's house. During the raid, the governor was said to have written his resignation on a scrap of paper while taking cover in a ditch.[33]

Simultaneously, in the west India began a drive against Shakargarh, a salient of Pakistani territory near Lahore that juts into India, and launched a similar effort against Naya Chor in the Sind Desert. The Indian Air Force bombed rail lines, trains, and marshalling yards in northern and central Pakistan to lessen the flow of supplies to forward units; the Indian Air Force also bombed Pakistani airfields and radar sites. One MiG-21 was downed by Pakistani antiaircraft while attacking the Badin radar station.

The Pakistan Air Force bombed airfields at Pathankot, Amritsar, and Srinagar. Sabres engaged Gnat fighters in a dogfight over Srinagar, with both sides losing planes.

Meanwhile, the Pakistanis flew large numbers of close support sorties in the Shakargarh, Sialkot, and Zafarwal areas, destroying eighteen tanks, many guns, and armored personnel carriers. A number of dogfights took their toll during the strikes. A Pakistani F-6 pilot shot down an Indian MiG-21, Sabres destroyed an Indian observation aircraft, and other Pakistani planes damaged a number of Indian fighter-bombers.

Day Thirteen: December 15

Lt. Gen. Amir Abdullah Khan Niazi, commander of East Pakistan forces, contacted Lt. Gen. Jagjit Singh Aurora, Indian commander, regarding a cease-fire, and the two agreed on terms. The Indian Air Force continued close support from the air, however, right up until the cease-fire.

India maintained pressure against the Shakargarh salient and the Sind Desert, fighting to capture as much territory as possible before the cease-fire; a Sabre and an F-6 were claimed in air combat. Indian Air Force fighter-bombers repeatedly bombed Pakistan rail lines, trains, and convoys.

Pakistani Air Force fighter-bombers supported ground units in the Shakargarh salient and in the Sind Desert near Naya Chor. In an air battle near Naya Chor, a Pakistani Sabre reportedly shot down an Indian Hunter. Pakistani interdiction missions against rail lines near Kukenen destroyed an ammunition train, and B-57 bombers blasted three Indian air bases in the north.

Day Fourteen: December 16

The largest armored battle of the war continued in the Shakargarh salient, both sides feeding in aircraft to defend their ground units from air attack. Indian Su-7Bs bombed Pakistani positions while MiG-21s flew protective cover. Pakistani Mirages and Sabres also attacked ground targets, and Sabres engaged MiG-21s in air combat; no losses were claimed.

Indian units succeeded in penetrating Pakistani territory near Naya Chor, the advance aided by air sorties. They continued to bomb the Pakistani railway but patrolling Pakistan Air Force fighters contested many of the strikes. Indian Canberra bombers again raided Karachi harbor at night. Pakistan claimed to have downed one by antiaircraft fire.

Pakistani Mirages damaged the Bhatinda railway station, while F-86 Sabres attacked Srinagar and Avantipur airfields during the day.

Cease-Fire: December 17

Having captured East Pakistan, India announced a unilateral cease-fire for 8 p.m. on December 17. In the Shakargarh and Naya Chor areas, heavy fighting continued right up to the cease-fire. Pakistani and Indian fighter-bombers flew many support sorties in both battle areas.

Sabres and MiG-21s battled over Shakargarh, and Pakistan claimed one MiG-21. Pakistani F-104s flying cover for Sabres near Naya Chor engaged more MiG-21s, and two of the Starfighters were allegedly shot down.

Pakistan Air Force Sabres, Mirages, and Starfighters raided several Indian airfields. One of two F-104s attacking Uttarlai airfield was downed by a CAP MiG-21.[34]

At 8:00 p.m. the fighting ceased.

Analysis

India emerged from the 14-day conflict as the clear victor. East Pakistan had been excised; 85,000 Pakistani soldiers were captured; and Bangladesh won independence. In West Pakistan where ground and air forces were more evenly matched, combat was intense. India captured more territory than Pakistan, but both sustained heavy losses.

India admitted to have suffered 12,000 casualties including more than 3,000 dead,[35] but other sources put the total closer to 20,000 [36] India admitted one naval vessel sunk by a Pakistani submarine and 83 tanks lost. More than 83 tanks were undoubtedly knocked out in action, with those admitted lost probably being irreparable. Pakistani casualties included 8,000 killed and 25,000 wounded.[37] India claimed to have destroyed 220 Pakistani tanks and 22 naval vessels, including two submarines, four escorts, and 16 patrol boats.[38]

Aircraft kill-to-loss claims of both air forces differ widely. India stated that it destroyed 94 Pakistani aircraft (54 Sabres, nine F-104A Starfighters, six Mirage IIIs, and 25 other aircraft) while losing only 54.[39] Pakistan, on the other hand, claimed to have destroyed 106 Indian aircraft (32 Hawker Hunters, 32 Su-7Bs, 10 Canberras, nine MIG-21s, five Mystère IVs, five HF-24 Maruts, three Gnats, one Alizé, one Mi-8, one light aircraft, and seven unidentified planes.[40] Pakistan admitted losing only 25 planes, but other sources claimed 40 aircraft from all causes.[41]

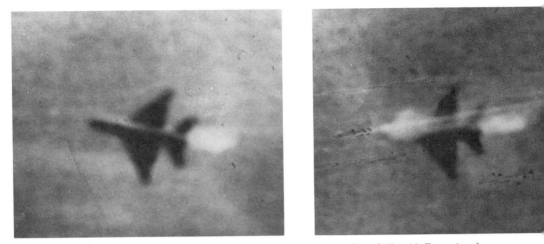

Gun camera footage released by the Pakistan Air Force shows the destruction of two Indian Air Force aircraft.

Both air forces employed aircraft primarily in the ground-attack role. The war started with a series of Pakistani counter-air missions bombing Indian airfields in the west. Throughout the two-week conflict, Pakistan continued to fly missions against Indian airfields. During the day, Pakistani Mirage IIIEs, F-104s, Sabre Mk. 6s, F-86Fs, and F-6s attacked airfields while at night B-57 light bombers were primarily used. The strikes undoubtedly did a fair amount of damage, but only five Indian aircraft were claimed destroyed on the ground.

Pakistan admitted that its initial strikes on December 3 and 4 did little damage, as most Indian aircraft were well dispersed and protected by shelters or revetments. Indian air bases were also well-defended by SA-2 missile sites and antiaircraft guns. Indian sources claimed to have shot down one Pakistani aircraft over Halwara airfield with an SA-2 missile.[42] Pakistan stated that only five of its aircraft were shot down by ground defenses near Indian bases. This low figure is suspect as Pakistan admitted losing three B-57 bombers in one night alone.[43]

The Indian Air Force and Navy flew large numbers of counter-air sorties against Pakistani airfields, and succeeded in grounding the Pakistan Air Force's #14 Sabre squadron at Tezgaon, East Pakistan, because of runway damage. Runways and facilities at Kurmitola, Chittagong, and Cox's Bazar airfields were heavily damaged. Pakistani sources disclosed that Indian fighter-bombers dropped several types of runway-blasting bombs. MiG-21FLs from India's #28 squadron flew the first offensive sorties against Tezgaon airfield and dropped rocket-boosted M-62 1,100-pound (500 kg) bombs, which left deep wide craters requiring significant repair.[44]

Another type of bomb the Indians reportedly used in West Pakistan left separate impact craters and explosion craters connected by pavement-weakening tunnels. No information has been disclosed on the characteristics of this weapon, but runways required time-consuming repair.[45] Moreover, Indian Canberras dropped ''anti-tire'' steel tripods on the runways at the Pakistani airfield of Mianwali; the tripods did not damage runways but caused a Mirage to blow a tire.[46]

While runways and facilities at Pakistani fields in the West were damaged, no airfield was put out of action more than temporarily. Antiaircraft defenses and revetments reduced the number of aircraft lost. Pakistan admitted that nine aircraft were destroyed on the ground, while India claimed 36.[47]

At the beginning of the war, Indian Canberras, Su-7Bs, Hawker Hunters, and HF-24 Maruts flew many counter-air missions attacking airfields, but later flew fewer missions as the emphasis turned to providing ground support and interdicting supply lines.

The Indian Air Force and Army had worked long and hard to develop the communications network and doctrine required for effective close air support, resulting in success. The number of Indian sorties reveal heavy emphasis on ground support. Of the 1,978 sorties flown by the Eastern Air Command between December 4 and 15, 1,178 directly supported ground units.[48] Of the 4,000 sorties flown in the west, perhaps half were ground strikes near the battle area, with the remainder divided between interdiction and combat air patrol.[49]

Indian aircraft flew numerous interdiction missions against supply convoys, freight trains, ammunition and fuel dumps, railway stations, marshalling yards, oil refineries, and harbor installations. Indian aircraft destroyed some 100 freight trains, 170 tanks, hundreds of vehicles, field guns, supply dumps, and numerous ships and small boats.[50]

Indian Navy Sea Hawks and Alizés from the *Vikrant* flew some 400 sorties during the conflict. Flying unchallenged except by Pakistani antiaircraft fire, the aircraft sank seven ships, one submarine, and dozens of small craft, and heavily damaged East Pakistani harbor installations and airfields.[51]

The Indian Air Force employed a variety of aircraft on strike missions ranging from supersonic interceptors to turboprop transports. The HF-24 Marut designed and built by the Indians proved its mettle as a fighter-bomber. With the heavy armament of four 30-mm Aden cannon, a retractable rocket launcher, and 4,000 pounds of externally carried bombs or rockets, Maruts proved deadly to convoys, trains, ammunition dumps, and other ground targets.

The Soviet-supplied Su-7B fighter-bombers flew a large percentage of the Indian Air Force ground-attack sorties, but suffered very high attrition; reportedly 32 of the 145 in service were destroyed.[52] The big aircraft had relatively poor performance when carrying external stores unless powered by afterburner, and they proved vulnerable to antiaircraft fire and to other fighters.

Hawker Hunters and Canberras flew most long-range interdiction and counter-air missions, the Hunters mostly by day and the Canberras by night. Hunters toting rockets, bombs, or—on long-range missions—only internal cannon, performed admirably; even so, 32 were claimed destroyed during the war.[53]

Although in the process of being phased out of operation, several squadrons of Mystère IV-As also flew several hundred ground-attack sorties; despite a shortage of spare parts, they were responsible for destroying large numbers of Pakistani armored vehicles, tanks, and railroad cars.

Eager to maximize damage to Pakistan, the Indian Air Force flew transports to attack targets at night. A number of Soviet-supplied An-12B turboprop transports were modified to permit them to drop bombs from the rear cargo door while in flight. In West Pakistan, An-12s using all-weather radar for guidance bombed fuel and ammunition dumps as well as troop concentrations. Transports were hit by antiaircraft fire and one was attacked by a Mirage, but all returned safely.[54]

The Pakistan Air Force used all of its aircraft in the attack role.

Most capable of the Pakistani fighter-bombers was the Mirage IIIE. India claimed that it downed six Pakistani Mirages during the conflict, most to ground fire,[55] while Pakistani sources stated that none was lost.[56] Considering that most of the 2,840 sorties flown by the Pakistan Air Force in the west were attack missions, it is reasonable to assume that a small number of Mirages was indeed lost.

The seven F-104s of #9 Squadron at Sargodha flew in the long-range strike role. As with the Mirage, Indian and Pakistani loss figures differ; Pakistan admitted losing three Starfighters while India claimed downing nine. India claimed that 10 Royal Jordanian Air Force F-104As

During the 1971 Indo-Pakistan War, Pakistani Mirage IIIEs flew both fighter and attack missions. During numerous strike sorties, the Mirages allegedly downed nine Indian Air Force aircraft with Sidewinders and 30-mm cannon. (B. Hanes)

had been flown to Pakistan on December 5. Several of them, painted in desert camouflage, were downed in the Sind/Rajasthan sector. King Hussein later admitted that Jordanian F-104As indeed had been used in the conflict.[57]

The sole Pakistani B-57 squadron repeatedly attacked Indian airfields at night. Five B-57s were lost to fighters and antiaircraft fire.

Chinese-built F-6 fighters flew very few ground attack missions because the aircraft can carry only two small rocket pods when it is fitted with fuel drop tanks.

The majority of the Pakistani close support and interdiction sorties were flown by the venerable F-86F Sabre and the Sabre Mk.6. Capable of carrying a bomb load of only 2,000 pounds when equipped with external fuel tanks, the Sabre was nevertheless able to considerably damage airfields, trains, vehicles, or other tactical targets. India claimed to have downed 54 Sabres while Pakistan admitted losing only 29.[58] Eleven were Sabre Mk. 6s that the Pakistanis themselves destroyed on the ground at Tezgaon airfield near Dacca, to prevent them from being captured.

Planes engaged in frequent air combat during the war, with most dogfights either near the forward edge of the battle area or near airfields. Despite being heavily outnumbered, Pakistan claimed to have gained air superiority over the battle areas in the west and to have prevented India's continued deep attacks. Because of Pakistan Air Force fighter cover, the Indian Air Force allegedly was forced to resort to sneak raids against border cities and railway stations. The Pakistanis said that 50 Indian aircraft were downed in air combat with the loss of only 10 Pakistani fighters.[59]

In East Pakistan, pilots of #14 Squadron flying Sabre Mk. 6s claimed shooting down 11 Indian Air Force fighters: (nine Hawker Hunters, one Su-7B, and one Gnat), losing only five Sabres before the remaining aircraft were grounded because of runway damage.[60]

In the west, the Pakistanis reported that Sabres, F-104s, F-6s, and Mirages shot down 39 Indian Aircraft with the loss of only five (one F-6, two F-104s, and two Sabres).[61]

In a long-awaited battle, the Indian MiG-21FL met the Pakistani F-104 in combat, and the Fishbed emerged the victor. India claimed that at least three F-104 Starfighters fell to the guns or missiles of its MiG-21FLs. On the other hand, Starfighters allegedly shot down a number of other Indian aircraft, including one Indian Navy Alizé on patrol near Karachi. The Pakistan Air Force's other Mach-2 fighter, the Mirage IIIE, demonstrated that it, too, was a capable air-to-air combatant, claiming nine kills with AIM-9B Sidewinder missiles and 30-mm cannon. One Mirage also fired a Matra 530 missile at an Su-7B; the Mirage pilot was forced to break away before impact, causing the radar-guided missile to go ballistic and miss its target.[62]

In the war, the Chinese-built F-6 was used in full-scale combat for the first time, and reportedly downed nine Indian Air Force aircraft. An extremely maneuverable dogfight aircraft at both low and medium altitudes, it could turn tighter than any fighter except the Sabre. Having a thrust-to-weight ratio of .85 at combat weight when in maximum afterburner, the F-6 could climb with the F-104A and could outclimb the MiG-21 to medium altitude.

Many F-6s were equipped with AIM-9B Sidewinders in addition to their normal complement of three NR-30 30-mm cannon. Wing Commander Syed Sa'ad Hatmi, who led one of the F-6 fighter squadrons, became the Pakistan Air Force's second ace. Flying Sabres in the 1965 conflict, Hatmi had claimed a Gnat and a Hawker Hunter. Flying the F-6 six years later, he downed two Su-7Bs and another Hawker Hunter.[63]

The F-86F Sabre, because of its excellent maneuverability, was able to deal with more modern fighters. The Sabre Mk. 6, fitted with an Orenda 14 turbojet engine producing 1,200 pounds more thrust than the F-86F Sabre, proved to be more than a match for Indian Air Force Hawker Hunters and Gnats. While all Sabres carried six 0.50-in Colt Browning machine guns, many were fitted additionally with AIM-9B Sidewinder missiles. In West Pakistan, some 15 Indian aircraft—including one MiG-21—reportedly fell to Sabre guns or missiles.

Pakistan Air Force F-6 firing its cannon at practice targets. The aircraft saw combat during the 1971 Indo-Pakistan conflict. Capable of brisk acceleration and a high degree of maneuverability, the F-6 also had a powerful armament of three 30-mm cannon. Many F-6s were also equipped with AIM-9B Sidewinder missiles with the result that the F-6 was a Chinese-built version of a Soviet fighter carrying American weapons. (Pakistan Air Force)

The MiG-21FL was the Indian Air Force's primary air superiority fighter in the 1971 conflict. Maneuverable and quick, the MiG-21 outfought F-104s, F-6s, and Sabres. When air superiority was attained over East Pakistan, MiG-21s flew numerous close support and airfield attack missions with rockets and bombs. (Indian Air Force)

A flight of Indian Air Force Gnats. The diminutive aircraft again proved itself a potent fighter, downing a number of Sabres in dogfights. (W. Green)

Little information is available on Pakistani tactics in air combat. While a number of Pakistan Air Force fighters were capable of carrying AIM-9B infrared-guided missiles, most kills were scored with guns. Thus, it can be assumed that most air combat involved high-g tight-turning battles.

The major effort of the Indian Air Force was to support ground forces, but many CAP and air defense sorties were flown. While the Indian Air Force claimed 94 Pakistani aircraft, no figures have been released on kills in air combat alone. Thirty-six Pakistani aircraft were claimed destroyed on the ground; the remaining 58 must have fallen to antiaircraft and fighters.

In East Pakistan, Gnats of the Indian Air Force's #24 Squadron scored the first victories on November 22, downing three Sabres. On December 4, Indian MiG-21s and Hawker Hunters engaged Sabres while fighter-bombers cratered the runways at Tezgaon and other East Pakistan air bases. Hawker Hunters of #14 Squadron claimed four Sabres in dogfights.[64]

In West Pakistan, Indian pilots reported that Pakistanis were often reluctant to engage in air combat. Indian sources said that the Pakistan Air Force concentrated on battle zones in the Kashmir province and the Sind/Rajasthan area plus the air defense of Islamabad, allowing the Indian Air Force freedom to attack strategic military and transport targets near Karachi and other important Pakistani towns. Indian antiaircraft and fighters in the west were allegedly responsible for destroying 72 Pakistan Air Force aircraft.

The MiG-21 was the most important air superiority fighter in service with the Indian Air Force. Equipped with a radar and all-weather instruments, Indian MiG-21FLs proved capable of defending air space both day and night. Maneuverable and quick to accelerate, MiG-21FLs outfought Pakistani Starfighters, F-6s, and Sabres. Most Indian MiGs were armed with only two K-13 Atoll infrared-guided missiles, but about a quarter were also equipped with the GP-9 cannon pack. Although the limited number of rounds in the GSh-23 23-mm pod allowed only a few seconds of firing time, the cannon pack was a welcome backup for the Atoll missiles, which were usually effective against only relatively docile targets.

Seven Indian Air Force fighter squadrons were equipped with the Gnat. The nimble Gnat again demonstrated its outstanding dogfight characteristics on November 22, when four Gnats of #22 Squadron intercepted Sabres and reportedly downed three in a brisk dogfight. On December 11, a Gnat was said to have downed a Mirage near Chhamb in Kashmir.

Although assigned to ground attack, Hawker Hunters and the HF-24 Maruts were able to defend themselves in the air when necessary. Hawker Hunters downed four Sabre Mk. 6s in East Pakistan and undoubtedly shot down other Pakistani aircraft in the west. On December 7, a pair of Maruts engaged four Pakistani Sabres, reportedly destroying one.

Pakistani sources reported that India was using some type of AWACS (Airborne Warning And Control System) to warn pilots of Pakistani raids and to direct Indian strike aircraft to attack. Designated Spider, the warning aircraft usually flew a racetrack patrol pattern well inside Indian territory. It was speculated that the aircraft in question was the USSR's Tu-126 Moss AWACS aircraft, manned by Russian and Indian controllers.

Because both contestants have refrained from confirming losses and discussing tactical lessons and other significant factors, it is very difficult to generalize about the air warfare phase of the Indo-Pakistan conflict. A few important events or trends, however, can be gleaned. A wide variety of Soviet, American, French, British, and Chinese tactical aircraft were pitted against one another and demonstrated positive and negative operational characteristics. The Indian-built MiG-21FL and the Chinese-built F-6 (MiG-19) demonstrated high performance in air combat, while the Su-7B fighter-bomber proved a poor tactical attack aircraft. The Mach-2 MiG-21 and Mirage IIIE performed well both in the attack and air superiority role. The subsonic F-86, Hawker Hunter, and Gnat again proved capable dogfighters.

In the west, neither India nor Pakistan attained more than local air superiority. In the east, the Indian Air Force was able to dominate the skies because of its extensive and successful attacks on Pakistani aircraft and airfields. Even though a number of Pakistani Sabre Mk. 6s survived the repeated bombings, they were unable to assist in the air battle because of cratered runways. The tactics and weapons employed by the Indian Air Force reflect the capabilities of Soviet tactical air forces Frontal Aviation units (MiG-21 and Su-7B fighters plus special anti-runway munitions), and should serve as a warning to Western planners who rely heavily on airfield-based tactical air units to make up for an imbalance in ground forces.

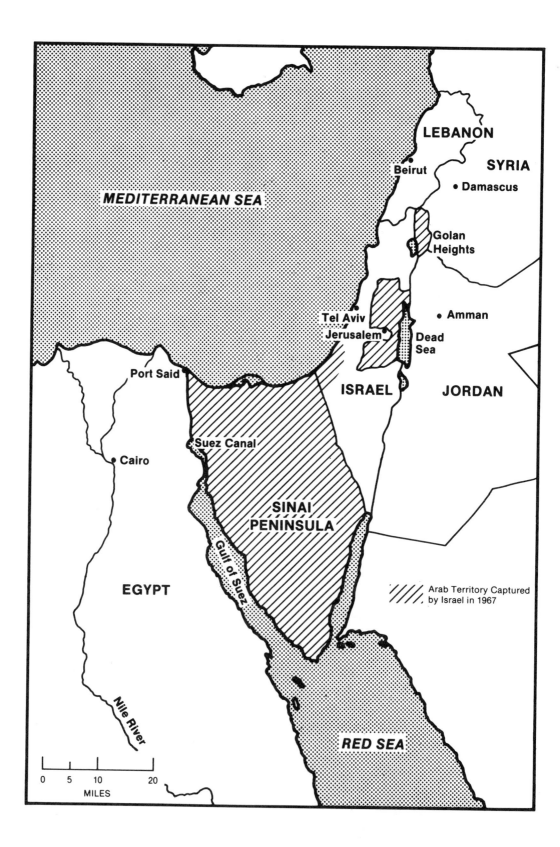

CHAPTER V

Six-Day War: Arab-Israeli Conflict, 1967

The Steps Leading to War

The precarious peace in the Middle East was shaken in 1964 at an Arab League summit conference in Cairo, where Syria, Jordan, and Lebanon agreed on a plan to divert the Jordan River to deprive Israel of precious irrigation water. As engineering efforts got under way, artillery fire and border clashes increased along the Israeli-Syrian border. In November 1964, in response to Syrian artillery fire, Israeli artillery, tanks, and aircraft attacked engineering equipment engaged in the river diversion project. More clashes occurred over the next few months, and early in 1965 Arab efforts to divert the river ended.

In 1966, the newly organized Palestinian Liberation Organization undertook repeated guerrilla raids into Israel with the tacit approval of the Syrian government. On April 7, 1967, a Syrian artillery barrage escalated into a full-scale tank and aircraft battle. In the dogfights, six Syrian MiG-21s—fully one-third of the country's total operational force of the Mach-2 fighters—were downed while the Israel Defense Force/Air Force reported no losses.[1]

As border conflicts continued, President Nasser of Egypt, criticized by his fellow Arab leaders for not lending support, expanded his forces in the Sinai and embarked on a propaganda campaign against Israel. Tensions mounted rapidly, and on May 18, 1967, Egypt demanded that the United Nations forces leave the Egyptian-Israeli border. Although neither the Arab nations nor Israel wanted all-out war, Israel countered the move on May 20 by mobilizing forces. Two days later, Nasser blockaded the Straits of Tiran, closing them to all ships bound for the southern Israeli port of Elat. The final step toward war had been taken.

Opposing Air Forces

Israel Defense Force/Air Force

In 1967, the Israel Defense Force/Air Force had a peacetime strength of about 8,000; of those, between 800 and 1,000—or about 10 percent—were pilots or pilot trainees.[2] Upon mobilization for war, the strength of the Israel Defense Force/Air Force was augmented by thousands of reserve pilots, ground crews, maintenance, and support personnel. Israel possessed more than 400 aircraft including training planes, transport aircraft, and helicopters. Half were combat aircraft that formed nine squadrons, four of interceptors and five of fighter-bombers. Moreover, 76 jet-trainer/ground-attack aircraft made up two additional squadrons to support ground forces.

Israeli Mirage IIICs. The
Mirage IIIC was Israel's primary air superiority fighter,
but it could also carry bombs
or rocket pods if called on to
attack ground targets.
(IDF/AF)

A pair of Israeli Super
Mystère B-2s fly in formation
with a 707. One squadron of
the supersonic fighter-bombers
was operational on the eve
of the Six-Day War.
(J. Margulies)

   In 1967 the strength of the Israel Defense Force/Air Force totaled:[3]
   72 Mirage IIIC fighter-bombers (three squadrons); 18 Super Mystère B-2 fighter-bombers
(one squadron); 50 Mystère IV-A fighter-bombers (two squadrons); 40 Ouragan fighter-
bombers (two squadrons); 25 Sud Vautour IIA fighter-bombers (one squadron); 76 Fouga
Magister trainers (two squadrons).
   The delta-wing Mirage IIIC, first delivered in 1963, was Israel's most potent interceptor,
ranking with the MiG-21 in performance. The Super Mystère B-2 fighter-bomber was a capable
air-to-air machine, roughly comparable to the MiG-19. The Israel Defense Force/Air Force's
primary ground-attack fighter was the Mystère IV-A. It was armed with two 30-mm DEFA
cannon and a wide variety of air-to-ground bombs and rockets.

The straight-wing Ouragan fighter-bomber was the oldest Israel Defense Force/Air Force combat aircraft in service during the Six-Day War. The Ouragan carried four 20-mm cannon and more than a ton of bombs, rockets, and other weapons.

The Sud Vautour IIA was the Israel Defense Force/Air Force's only specialized attack aircraft. Heavily armed with four 30-mm DEFA cannon, the Vautour also could carry more than two tons of ordnance both internally and externally on four wing stations.

The Israel Defense Force/Air Force's fleet of Fouga Magister trainers, pressed into service in the ground support role, carried two 7.62-mm machine guns and either 100-pound bombs or 80-mm rockets on two stores stations.

The Israeli Air Force is an arm of the Israeli Defense Force. The basic organizational structure of the Air Force is the wing—each wing composed of two or more squadrons.

The Air Force Commander serves as a professional adviser to the Israeli Chief of Staff. During the Six-Day War, the primary functions of the Israel Defense Force/Air Force were defending Israel air space from attack, gaining and maintaining air superiority over the battle area, and supporting ground and naval forces.

During 1960s, Israel was surrounded by four hostile Arab nations whose combined air forces possessed four times as many aircraft as it did. In response to this threat, Brigadier Weizman, commander of the Israel Defense Force/Air Force from 1960 to 1966, upgraded the Air Force's offensive capability by centralizing control of operations and increasing pilot training. Moreover, Weizman devised an aerial attack plan designed to destroy the Arab air forces on the ground, using surprise as a weapon against numerical superiority.[4]

By 1967, pilot training was highly intense. The enlistee joined as a student pilot at age 18 and agreed to serve five years. Student pilots trained for more than two years before qualifying for operational duty.

Pilot training was so demanding that in one 1960 class only a single pilot graduated.[5] Pilots continually engaged in realistic air-to-air and air-to-ground exercises. While the pilots learned air-to-air missile tactics, emphasis was placed on accurate cannon fire at close range. Constant practice in bombing/cannon fire, navigation, and tactics honed the skills of Israeli pilots. As they exercised ground-attack skills against model targets in the Negev Desert, frequent simulated large-scale attacks gave ground crews experience in rapidly servicing, refueling, and re-arming the aircraft—skills necessary to make the most of their limited assets.[6]

Air-to-air training stressed classic dogfighting and mutual support. The basic flight unit is two aircraft. Generally four fighters, known as a flight, comprise a minimum element for any mission. Once engaged in combat, Israeli tactics call for individual initiative; wingmen are free to engage targets and are not tied to the leader to provide protection as they were in tactical arrangements common in both World Wars and the Korean War. Pilots are urged to coordinate their individual attacks, however, in the hope of splitting up enemy formations. Defensive mutual support is stressed; pilots cover one another by warning of bogeys and engaging threatening fighters.

Air-to-air skills were tested by constant mock dogfights among Israeli pilots. The defection of two Arab pilots in 1965 and 1966 with their respective aircraft afforded an opportunity to evaluate and fly mock dogfights against adversaries' best fighters, the MiG-17 and MiG-21. This tactical insight plus rigorous training tempered the Israelis into a force of unmatched proficiency in air-to-ground and air-to-air combat.[7]

Air Force of the United Arab Republic (Egyptian Air Force)

On the eve of the Six-Day War, the Egyptian Air Force had personnel strength of approximately 20,000 and possessed nearly 600 aircraft.[8] Of those, 450 were combat aircraft grouped into more than 20 squadrons:[9]

120 MiG-21 fighter/interceptors (six squadrons); 80 MiG-19 fighters (four squadrons); 150 MiG-15 and MiG-17 fighters (five squadrons); 30 Su-7B fighter-bombers (one squadron); 30 Tu-16 bombers (two squadrons); 40 Il-28 bombers (three squadrons).

The six squadrons of MiG-21 fighter/interceptors included both the standard MiG-21F Fishbed C and the newer MiG-21PF Fishbed D models. The MiG-21PF featured an aerodynamically refined fuselage, an uprated Tumansky turbojet producing 800 pounds more thrust than the MiG-21F Fishbed C engine, and a larger air-intake shock cone housing a longer-range radar. Primary armament for the new Fishbed D was a pair of Atoll infrared-guided air-to-air missiles, replacing the Fishbed C's NR-30 cannon.

Supplementing the six MiG-21 squadrons, the Egyptian Air Force had four squadrons of MiG-19 fighters and five squadrons of MiG-15 and MiG-17 fighters. Some of the MiG-19 Farmer aircraft were operational in the Farmer C day-fighter version; others were fitted with radar in the Farmer D all-weather version. The MiG-15s and MiG-17s were used primarily in day-fighter and ground attack roles.

As of June 1967, the Egyptian Air Force had one operational Squadron of the USSR's new Sukhoi Su-7B ground attack fighter, and was planning to introduce more. The large Mach-1.6 fighter-bomber was armed with two NR-30 cannon and carried more than a ton of external stores.

Three squadrons of Il-28 twin-jet light bombers, capable of carrying a bomb load of 3,000 pounds over a radius of 1,200 miles, spearheaded the Egyptian Air Force strategic bomber force. These were augmented by two squadrons of Tu-16 medium bombers; the Tu-16 could carry a bomb load of 20,000 pounds over a radius of 1,500 miles.

Egyptian Air Force combat aircraft were stationed at some 25 airfields, mainly in the Cairo and Nile Delta regions.[10] To alert these airfields of an attack more than 20 radar stations, concentrated mostly in the Sinai Desert and in eastern Egypt, formed an advanced warning

This Egyptian TU-16 Badger medium bomber (top) was intercepted over the Mediterranean Sea by U.S. Navy fighters. A major threat to Israeli factories and cities, the TU-16 could carry a bomb load of 20,000 pounds to a radius of 1,500 miles at a speed of up to 580 mph. The Badger was operational with the Egyptian and Iraqi Air Forces. (U.S. Navy)

system.[11] Egyptian antiaircraft defense consisted of more than 1,000 Soviet-built antiaircraft guns (37-mm, 57-mm, and 85-mm) plus some 150 SA-2 surface-to-air missiles at approximately 20 sites.[12]

Although originally equipped with British aircraft and modeled after the RAF, the Egyptian Air Force switched to Soviet equipment and Soviet-style training in the mid-1950s.[13] In the initial stages, hundreds of Egyptian pilots were sent to the Soviet Union for training, while in Egypt Soviet general staff officers advised the Egyptian general staff and participated in the country's war games. Soviet advisers were present at all levels in the Egyptian armed services, and the Egyptian Air Force was modeled after the Soviet Air Force. The basic Egyptian Air Force unit was the regiment; a regiment was made up of three squadrons each equipped with between 16 and 20 aircraft.[14]

Because the expansion of the Egyptian Air Force exceeded the rate at which pilots could be trained, by 1967 Egypt was acutely short of air crews. Egyptian training techniques, aerial strategy, and tactics closely followed those of the Soviet Air Force. Egyptian pilots learned hit-and-run tactics but were not taught to be proficient in dynamic air combat.

Soviet-style intercept tactics relied on ground-based radar controllers to vector pilots into position for a quick attack. These set-piece tactics, combined with the limited number of flight hours most pilots received each month, lessened their effectiveness in traditional maneuvering air combat. About a third of all Egyptian pilots had combat experience prior to the Six-Day War, having flown missions in the Yemen Civil War of 1965–66.

Syrian Arab Air Force

In 1967, the Syrian Arab Air Force had approximately 9,000 personnel and was equipped with about 150 aircraft.[15] Combat strength included three regiments of fighters, with each of three squadrons equipped with between 12 and 16 aircraft. In one squadron, the MiG-21F day-fighter fulfilled the air-defense role; in the other two the MiG-17F served primarily as a ground attack fighter. One squadron also operated the radar-eqipped MiG-17PF in a limited all-weather air-defense role. In addition, a single squadron of Il-28 light bombers was working up to operational capability.

On the eve of the Six-Day War, the Syrian air strength totaled:[16]

36 MiG-21 fighter/interceptors (two squadrons); 90 MiG-17 fighter-bombers (four squadrons); six Il-28 bombers (one squadron).

Like Egyptian pilots, Syrian pilots also were taught Soviet techniques and tactics. Although basic pilot training was held in Syria in L-29 Delfin and MiG-15UTI trainers, most pilots learned to fly such front-line combat aircraft as the MiG-17, MiG-21, and the Il-28 in the Soviet Union and other Warsaw Pact countries. The Syrian Arab Air Force had a shortage of experienced pilots and was in the process of expanding its pilot-training program.

Royal Jordanian Air Force

The Royal Jordanian Air Force was a very small but relatively efficient organization. About 2,000 strong, it possessed fewer than 30 aircraft, all of which were based at Mafraq and Amman. A British-supplied Marconi radar system provided warning. By June 1967, the force totaled:[17]

22 Hawker Hunter Mk. 6 fighter-bombers; six Lockheed F-104A Starfighter fighters.

The backbone of the Royal Jordanian Air Force was the highly maneuverable subsonic British Hawker Hunter. The fighter was armed with four 30-mm Aden cannon; in a fighter-bomber role it could also carry up to a ton of bombs and rockets.

The Royal Jordanian Air Force had stationed six Mach-2 F-104A Starfighters in Amman for training, with 30 more on order from the United States. The Starfighters and their American instructors were flown out of Jordan just prior to the Six-Day War. When the war broke out, only 16 Jordanian pilots were available for operational missions, since many were in the United States learning to fly the Starfighters.

The organization, training, and tactics of the Royal Jordanian Air Force closely followed those of the RAF, which had established the Jordanian service. Because of its limited forces, Jordan planned to cooperate with the air forces of Syria and Iraq in attacking Israel in the event of war.

A Jordanian Hawker Hunter equipped with ferry tanks. The entire Jordanian Air Force consisted of 22 such fighter aircraft.

Iraqi Air Force

In 1967 the Iraqi Air Force had about 10,000 men[18] and an inventory of some 220 aircraft:[19]

20 MiG-21 fighter/interceptors (two squadrons); 15 MiG-19 fighters (one squadron); 20 MiG-17 fighter-bombers (two squadrons); 33 Hawker Hunter fighter-bombers (three squadrons); 10 Il-28 bombers (one squadron); 12 Tu-16 bombers (one squadron).

Guidance and support were provided by the RAF until 1958, when Soviet influence began. Following a coup d'etat that toppled the Iraqi government in 1963, British training and doctrine were reinstated. Subsequently, the Indian government took over training responsibility, and many Iraqi Air Force pilots and ground crews studied in India. Despite these shifts in political alignment, the Iraqi Air Force still closely followed the RAF structure and was one of the best-trained Arab air arms. Many Iraqi Air Force pilots had gained ground support experience in the Kurdish War of Independence. In the event of war, Iraq's strategy was to send its bomber force against Israel in cooperation with the other Arab air forces.

Conflict

Day One: June 5

Israel, anticipating Arab military moves against it, took the initiative early in the morning of Monday, June 5, and struck the first blow by staging a surprise attack against 10 Egyptian airfields. The first wave of about 40 Mirages and Mystères took off at 7:00 a.m. Israeli time (8:00 a.m. Egyptian time). Subsequent waves of 40 aircraft each followed at 10-minute intervals over the next hour and 20 minutes.

Planes heading for northwestern Egyptian airfields flew over the Mediterranean at low altitude to avoid being detected by the Arab radar network. Fighter-bombers making their way to inland targets flew low over uninhabited desert terrain, eluding detection by both radar and ground spotters.

The 10 flights, each of four aircraft operating in pairs, struck the 10 most important Egyptian airfields: El Arish, Bir Gifgafa, Cairo West, Bir el Themada, Abu Suweir, Jebel Libni, Jebel el Kabrit, Beni Suef, Inchas, and Fayid.[20] Israeli planes bombed and strafed all airfields simultaneously except for Fayid, shrouded in morning mist and which was struck several minutes later. Each flight spent 10 minutes over its target, time enough for a bomb attack and several strafing runs.

As soon as the first wave of flights broke off, the second wave attacked the airfields for a further 10 minutes. Following a 10-minute pause, the Israelis launched a second 80-minute-long series of strikes on the same air bases.

The Israelis maximized their limited assets through intense efforts. Turnaround time for the fighter-bombers on the ground was held to 10 or 15 minutes. In that short time, the ground crews rapidly patched up the majority of aircraft hit by antiaircraft fire and sent them back into service, enabling pilots to re-attack the medium-range target airfields less than an hour after their previous attack.

Israeli pilots flying the initial waves concentrated on destroying the potent Tu-16 and Il-28 bombers on the ground in order to eliminate Egypt's capability to retaliate against Israeli cities and airfields. The MiG-21 interceptors were also first-priority targets because they were capable of contesting Israel's air superiority. Secondary targets included MiG-17s, MiG-19s, Su-7B fighter-bombers, transports, and helicopters.

A TU-16 Badger burns following an Israeli air strike against an Egyptian airfield. The Badger in the revetment has had its tail surfaces shot away by cannon fire. (IDF/AF)

Attacking pilots found most of the Egyptian Air Force planes well dispersed, and many bases had dummy aircraft. Several flights of taxiing MiG-21 fighters were caught on the ground by the first-wave attacks. The attacking pilots destroyed most Egyptian aircraft with 30-mm cannon while strafing. They also cratered runways with conventional 500-pound and 1,000-pound bombs to prevent aircraft from escaping to other fields.

One of the most effective weapons, which severely damaged a number of runways, was a specially developed weapon known as the concrete "dibber" bomb. When first released, a parachute opened to steady the weapon vertically; then booster rockets drove the hard-nosed bomb deep under the runway, where its explosion erupted a much larger crater than that left by conventional bombs.[21]

Despite the suddenness of the attack, eight Egyptian MiG-21s managed to take to the air; these intercepted and shot down two Israeli fighter-bombers.[22] Twenty additional Egyptian fighters (12 MiG-21s and eight MiG-19s) based at Hurghada were also able to get airborne because their base was not attacked. Speeding north toward the primary Egyptian bases near the Suez Canal, the MiGs found the bases under attack and succumbed to Israeli fighters or crash-landed after running out of fuel before being able to render any aid.[23]

In one of a series of dogfights over Abu Suweir, an Egyptian airfield near the Suez Canal, pilot 1st Lt. Giora (his first name, Israeli security will not allow the full name of pilots to be published) was patrolling in his Mirage IIIC at 25,000 feet when he and his flight leader spotted a MiG-21 taking off. After the flight leader shot down the first plane, Giora saw another MiG-21 in the air above the base. As he later told *Aviation Week & Space Technology* magazine:

"He saw me and we began fighting. After a minute or so I was sitting on his tail and, from a range of 350 meters, I fired a one-second burst. Then his tail began to burn and he began to spin and then crashed."

Following the kill, Giora returned to Abu Suweir, where he observed two Israeli Mirages strafing Il-28 bombers on the ground. Noticing two MiG-21s closing on the Mirages from behind, Giora switched on his afterburner and attacked. "I took the right one and No. 1 (the flight leader) took the left one. At a range of 300 meters, he saw me and began to break from side to side. After a half a minute I had closed the range to 180 meters and fired a short burst. The plane exploded and crashed."

Short on fuel, Giora and his flight leader headed for their airfield in Israel.[24]

In response to the attack on Egypt, Jordan retaliated against Israel. Just after 11:00 a.m., Jordanian Hawker Hunters attacked the Israeli base at Netanya. Jordan claimed the Hunters destroyed four aircraft, but Israeli officials admitted losing only a single Noratlas transport.[25]

Half an hour later, 12 Syrian MiG-21s and MiG-17s attacked the Haifa oil refinery and strafed dummy aircraft at the airfield at Megiddo. Two MiG-17s were shot down over the airfield and a third over Tawafik.[26] Meanwhile, four flights of Mystères were raiding airfields in Syria: Damascus, Marj Riyal, T-4, and Seikal. Bombs chewed up the runways and cannon fire destroyed numerous aircraft.

At 12:15 p.m., Israel turned against Jordan, attacking the airfields at Mafraq and Amman and destroying the Mount Ajlun radar station. In 20 minutes, King Hussein lost most of his aircraft.[27] One Israeli aircraft was shot down by ground fire, the pilot parachuting into the Sea of Galilee and reportedly picked up by an Israeli patrol boat.

Throughout the afternoon and evening, Israel continued to strike Egyptian airfields. Delayed-action bombs hindered efforts to repair damaged runways. Israeli fighters also concentrated on radar installations; by the day's end, they had destroyed the 16 radar sites in the Sinai Desert as well as most of those in the Nile Delta area and in the Suez Canal zone.

While Israeli armored columns advanced, Fouga Magister aircraft flew a number of sorties against Arab troops concentrated in Egypt and Jordan. Israeli Mystères inflicted numerous casualties on an Iraqi brigade and a Palestinian battalion caught in the open while marching toward the Jordanian front.

By end of the war's first day, Jordan's air force was totally destroyed, Egypt's had suffered heavy losses, and Syria's was severely stunned. All together, 25 Arab air bases had been attacked, and Israeli pilots claimed more than 300 aircraft destroyed. Israeli losses totaled 19 aircraft: four Super Mystères, four Mystère IV-As, four Ouragans, four Fouga Magisters, two Mirages, and one Vautour. Of the 19 pilots lost, eight were killed and 11 listed as missing.[28] After the initial surprise, Egyptian antiaircraft put up intense fire, and these accounted for most of the Israeli planes lost.

According to Israeli communiques released after the war, on Day One, Israelis engaged Egyptian fighters 18 times, downing 26 Egyptian aircraft, while 16 dogfights with other Arab fighters resulted in the Israelis destroying 12 more aircraft. At least two Israeli fighters fell to Egyptian aircraft.[29]

Israeli sources disclosed that their aircraft flew about 1,000 sorties that first day.[30] Perhaps 750 were attacks against Egyptian airfields, radar sites, and combat air patrols. The remaining were flown against other Arab targets and in defending Israeli airspace.

Day Two: June 6

At dawn on June 6, an Iraqi Tu-16 bombed the Israeli town of Netanya, causing numerous casualties. As it flew over ground forces in the Jezreel Valley, the lone intruder was shot down by antiaircraft.[31]

About 9:00 a.m., Lebanon—Israel's northern neighbor—backed up its declaration of war by sending two of its Hawker Hunters into Israeli airspace north of the Sea of Galilee. The Hunters were immediately intercepted by Israeli fighters, which shot down one.[32]

The Egyptian Air Force, while badly battered, still had more than 200 operational aircraft and a substantial number of pilots. Most of the intact aircraft were in Yemen or had been shifted to bases out of the range of Israeli fighters. Egyptian MiGs conducted numerous ground attack missions on Day Two, the most effective being at dawn when Egyptian MiGs strafed an Israeli supply point in the central Sinai.

The Israelis continued to strike major Arab airfields plus smaller dispersal points where many aircraft had flown to escape attack. In retaliation for the Iraqi air strike against Netanya that morning, four flights of Israeli Mystères bombed and strafed H-3, the Iraqi air base near the Jordanian border. In addition, two flights of Mirages were sent against a more distant airfield. Here the Israelis were caught by surprise. The Mirages, flying in at low level to avoid radar detection, were bounced from above by Iraqi Hawker Hunters. In the ensuing dogfight, three Mirages were shot down with the loss of a Hawker Hunter.[33]

While continuing their attacks against airfields, as well as interdiction and reconnaissance missions, the main effort of the Israel Defense Force/Air Force shifted toward providing air support for the ground forces—primarily in the Sinai Desert. Israeli Mirages, Super Mystères, Vautours, and Ouragans joined the Fouga Magister trainers in assaulting Arab tanks, troops, and fortifications in the Sinai with bombs, napalm, rockets, and cannon fire. The Israelis also flew a number of ground support missions against Jordanian positions around Jerusalem.

Day Three: June 7

Having attained a high degree of air superiority, Israel concentrated its sorties against retreating Arab ground forces.

Egyptian MiGs flew numerous close support sorties. Six MiGs strafed the Israeli Tal Ugda (division) in mid-afternoon as it was moving into position to seal off Ismailia Pass. Israeli fighters appeared and, in the ensuing series of dogfights, one Israeli fighter and one Egyptian MiG were downed.[34]

Late that day, Lieutenant Giora participated in a mission directed against an Egyptian brigade retreating from Sharm El Sheikh toward the Suez Canal. When he arrived in the target area, the ground controller told his flight of three Mirages to salvo their bombs and engage MiGs in the western Sinai near Mitla Pass. The flight reached the area just as two MiG-17s and two Super Mystères were engaged in a dogfight at low altitude. As he recounted to *Aviation Week & Space Technology*: "We punched off our drop tanks and dove toward them, passing inside the fight. The two MiGs saw me and broke off from the Super Mystères and began to fight with me. I was all alone, since No. 1 and No. 3 in my flight had taken off after our Super Mystères, thinking that they were MiGs.

"The two MiGs and I maneuvered for about a minute and then they broke it off and dove to an altitude of 10 meters and began to run toward the Canal. We were above Bir Gifgafa then, and there's a road from there leading to Ismailia.

"So I chased after them. When I came up to 200 meters behind the rear one and was ready to fire, another funny thing happened. I heard someone shout over the radio, 'Don't shoot, they're ours!'"

In the confusion of the fight, to be certain that the planes he was pursuing were indeed MiG-17s, Giora closed in for a better look at the fleeing fighters. Sure of his identification, he dropped back to 1,000 feet.

"I fired a short burst and saw two or three pieces fly off the MiG and pass over my head. Since he was only 10 meters above the ground, I shouted that he was going to crash. But instead, he began to nose up and climb to a higher altitude. I was surprised at this, since he didn't try to maneuver.

"My speed carried me to within 40 or 50 meters beside him. I saw something very strange. The canopy of the MiG was gone and there was no one sitting in the cockpit. The pilot had ejected without my seeing him.

"The pilotless MiG continued to climb for about five seconds more, and then, having lost flying speed, it apparently stalled. It rolled over on its back and dived to the ground. When I saw him crash, I lowered the nose of my aircraft, went to low altitude and started in the direction the other MiG had taken. I didn't see him at first, and I flew as low as I could so I could spot him above the horizon. The MiGs weren't camouflaged; they were silver colored. Then I saw a glint above the horizon. At this point I noticed my airspeed indicator said I was flying at 710 knots with full afterburner.

"This was the fastest I have ever flown at low altitude. I caught the MiG-17 above the Canal near Ismailia, and then he saw me. I still don't know how he saw me. I was exactly on his tail. He broke and then we began to dogfight. It is difficult to fight a MiG-17 because it is more maneuverable and can turn tighter. I fired some bursts but they missed. At this point, my fuel was low, and the ack-ack had opened up on me. So I broke off and returned to base."[35]

Final Phase of the War

During the last three days of the conflict, Israeli fighter-bombers supported advancing ground troops by bombing and strafing Arab positions and engaging the infrequent Arab fighter sorties.

On Day Four, Egyptian MiGs concentrated their efforts against an Israeli reconnaissance column approaching the Suez Canal. By mid-afternoon, the Egyptians had flown 32 ground-attack sorties against the formation. Responding to calls for air cover, Israeli fighters intercepted the MiGs, destroying a large number of them with no Israeli losses reported.[36]

Israeli ground support and interdiction missions continued against retreating Egyptian forces.

Friday and Saturday, the fifth and sixth days of the war, a series of intense bombing and strafing sorties was directed against Syrian fortifications on the Golan Heights. The Arab countries, sponsored by the United Nations, sued for peace and the war came to an end on Saturday, June 10. Israel had defeated the much larger combined armies of its Arab neighbors, and now possessed the entire Sinai peninsula (thus barring Egypt's use of the Suez Canal); a significant portion of the Golan Heights; all of Jerusalem; and the section of Jordan that we know as the West Bank.

An Egyptian T-55 tank and two trucks destroyed by Israeli air attacks. (IDF/AF)

Analysis

Following the Six-Day War, Israel claimed to have destroyed 451 aircraft during the first 60 hours, 58 of them in air combat.[37]

Table I

Israeli Aircraft Claims

Type	Egypt	Syria	Jordan	Iraq	Total
Tu-16	30			1	31
Il-28	29	2			31
Il-14	24		5	5	34
An-12	8				8
Mi-6	10				10
Mi-4	1	3	3		7
MiG-21	100	32		13	145
MiG-19	29				29
MiG-15, 17	87	23			110
Su-7	14				14
Hunter			21	6	28
Unidentified	4				4
Total	336	60	29	25	451*

*Total also includes one Lebanese Hunter. Chart duplication by permission of *Aviation Week & Space Technology* magazine of issue dated June 19, 1967.

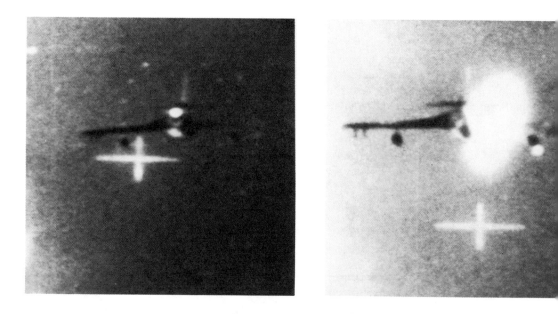

An Arab aircraft is caught in the gunsight of an Israeli fighter and subsequently destroyed. (IDF/AF)

An official list of Israeli losses was never released, but evidence indicates that Israel lost about 45 aircraft, at least three-quarters of them to antiaircraft fire. Official releases stated initially that only four Israeli fighter-bombers were downed in air-to-air combat. Several years later, Gen. Benjamin Peled, commander of the Israel Defense Force/Air Force, disclosed that 10 aircraft had, in fact, been shot down in dogfights.[38]

Israeli pilots proved to be highly capable air-to-air fighters. Their intense training has emphasized maneuvering and hit-and-run combat, with the 30-mm cannon as primary weapon. Many Israeli Mirage IIIC were equippped with the Matra 530 as well, but there were no reports of the missile being fired during the war.[39]

The Mirage IIIC was Israel's primary air combat fighter and thus was responsible for the majority of Arab aircraft shot down. The other Israeli fighters and fighter-bombers also proved their worth in air combat. Super Mystères downed Mach-2 MiG-21s and subsonic Vautours; Mystère IVs and even Ouragans were able to shoot down MiG-17s and Hawker Hunters.[40]

Table II

Arab Aircraft Shot Down During the Six-Day War

By Mirage IIIC	By Super Mystère	By Mystère IV
9 MiG-17	2 MiG-21	2 MiG-17
12 MiG-19	2 Il-14	1 Hunter
15 MiG-21	1 MiG-17	
1 Il-14		1 MiG by Ouragan
1 Il-28		
5 Hunter		1 Hunter by Vautour
5 Su-7		

Reproduction of chart permission of *Born In Battle* magazine. Total: 58 a/c shot down in aerial combat.

The Israelis highly rated the MiG-21 as a medium-altitude dogfight aircraft. With its slightly higher thrust-to-weight ratio and lower wing-loading, it was able to out-accelerate and out-turn the Mirage IIIC.[41] Israeli Mirage IIIC pilots were able to shoot down MiG-21s, however, because Arab pilots generally did not fly the aircraft to its limits of performance. The Israelis rated Iraqi pilots highly, but found others to be less skilled, with the Syrian pilots rated as the poorest performers.[42]

Many Arab MiG-21s were armed with the Soviet Atoll infrared-guided air-to-air missile. The missile was fired at Israeli fighters on at least two occasions. In one case, an Israeli Mirage IIIC patrolling over an Iraqi airbase was hit. Despite extensive damage to his tailpipe, the pilot was able to return to base.[43]

The MiG-21 was found to be highly susceptible to battle damage, having a tendency to burn or explode after being struck only a few times with 30-mm cannon fire.[44] The older MiG-17 was rated highly by Israeli pilots. With its good turning capability, it was a hard target to hit; moreover, the MiG-17 was a tough aircraft, absorbing many cannon hits before going down.[45]

By destroying Egyptian, Syrian, Jordanian, and Iraqi aircraft on the ground, Israel quickly traded surprise and skill for numerical superiority and dealt a crushing blow to Arab morale. The success of these initial strikes enabled Israel to gain air superiority and begin flying attack sorties quickly to support Israeli ground forces as well. These sorties destroyed many Arab vehicles and defensive positions, speeding up the Israeli rate of advance. Had a furious battle for air superiority been fought in the air, losses on both sides undoubtedly would have been higher and the war could have quite possibly lasted longer.

Although the war was fought with modern weapons—Mach-2 fighters, runway-blasting bombs, surface-to-air missiles, air-to-air missiles, and the like—neither electronic warfare nor advanced missiles were of overwhelming importance. At bottom, the Six-Day War was a classic conflict where careful planning, rigorous training, swift employment of forces, and tactical initiative carried the day.

Egyptian MiG-15s fly in formation. Israeli pilots rated the MiG-15 and MiG-17 as two of their toughest opponents. Highly maneuverable and capable of withstanding considerable battle damage, the early MiGs were worthy adversaries.

CHAPTER VI

The War of Attrition: Arab-Israeli Conflict, 1967-1970

Introductory Overview

The air war from 1967 to 1970 among Israeli, Egyptian, and Syrian aircraft and antiaircraft defenses is one of the lesser-known aerial campaigns. Beginning as a series of random skirmishes following the Six-Day War of 1967, by 1969 it had developed into a systematic Arab campaign of attrition against Israel.

One reason that the War of Attrition is less well-known than the other wars recounted in this book is that the conflict was fought mostly with guerrillas, commando raids, artillery barrages, and air strikes—with comparatively little activity by ground troops. Moreover, it occupied less attention in the United States at the time than did the conflict in Vietnam, because America's involvement in the Middle East conflict was comparatively limited.

Viewed in proper perspective, however, the War of Attrition is remarkable: In the three years of conflict, Israel reportedly shot down 137 Arab aircraft; Syria, Egypt, and guerrilla groups claimed to have downed more than 250 Israeli aircraft. Although the exact claims cannot be substantiated, it is likely that the number of aircraft lost in air combat exceeded the number of North Vietnamese aircraft lost in dogfights over Vietnam during the 1965–1968 Rolling Thunder campaign.

The Stage 1967

Immediately following the Six-Day War in 1967, the Soviet Union began an intensive transfusion of tactical aircraft and war materiel to the Arab nations to shore up their defeat. Late in June, Soviet President Podgorny and Chief of Staff Marshal Zakharov visited Egypt to pledge support and plan further resupply. By the end of the month the USSR reportedly had delivered more than 130 jet fighters.[1]

In an attempt to exact revenge, Egypt began some limited attacks against Israel. On July 14, 1967, Egypt and Israel exchanged artillery fire along the Suez Canal. On August 26, Israel allegedly downed an Egyptian fighter with antiaircraft.[2] Six weeks later, Israel reported shooting down a MiG-21 in a dogfight near the Great Bitter Lake.[3]

On October 21, in the sharpest escalation to date, Soviet-built surface-to-surface Styx missiles launched from Egyptian Komar patrol boats sank Israel's largest warship, the destroyer *Eilat*, while it was patrolling 12 miles off Port Said. In retaliation, Israeli artillery severely damaged two Egyptian oil refineries and a fertilizer plant near the town of Suez, while Israeli aircraft struck at naval facilities at Alexandria and Port Said.

Searching for a peaceful solution to the smoldering Middle East conflict, the United Nations on November 22 passed Resolution 242. The resolution called for Israel to withdraw from captured Arab territory; for the Arab nations to acknowledge the existence of the State of Israel; for the two sets of nations to settle the problem of the Palistinian refugees; and for them to establish demilitarized zones.

The Pressure Builds

For the first year and a half following the end of the Six-Day War of 1967, the Arabs continued to harass Israel with guerrilla raids and artillery attacks across the Suez Canal. Israel vigorously retaliated by bombing and raiding Arab military targets, industrial facilities, and guerrilla training camps. Air activity during the period was limited to occasional sorties by Egypt across the canal, and Israeli retaliation raids against Egyptian, Jordanian, and guerrilla forces. Both sides lost aircraft, but totals are difficult to ascertain from the conflicting claims.

By mid-1968, the Egyptian Army had been reorganized and expanded to the point where it included approximately 550 T-54 and T-55 tanks, 300 heavy guns, 450 field guns, 200 mortars, and more than 800 light armored vehicles.[4] The Egyptian Army stationed three of its six divisions along the Suez Canal with most of its artillery.

In 1968, the Egyptian Army established an Air Defense Command, dedicated to protect Egyptian air space. Although the air defense troops were nominally members of the army, in effect they were an autonomous branch modeled on the Soviet version. These forces manned more than 30 batteries of SA-2 surface-to-air missile sites and more than 1,000 antiaircraft guns to protect military bases, transportation centers, and other important positions. Moreover, several squadrons of Egyptian MiG-21 interceptors were incorporated into the Army's defense system to deal with intruders.

An Egyptian SA-2 surface-to-air missile site in the Sinai desert. The SA-2 Guideline missile was effective against aircraft flying at medium-to-high altitudes and could reach targets at a slant range of 23 miles and higher than 60,000 feet. (U.S. Army)

An Israeli A-4H Skyhawk on a training mission. Israel's first U.S.-built combat aircraft, the A-4 entered service in 1968. (IDF/AF)

The massive Russian resupply had brought the Egyptian Air Force to about 60 percent of its prewar strength. The Egyptians built new bases to replace the five airfields in the Sinai Desert taken by the Israelis. Several new airstrips were built by widening sections of the Cairo–Alexandria highway and by adding adjacent hangars and support facilities.[5] Moreover, the Egyptians had learned their lesson well from the Six-Day War: They constructed concrete shelters at air bases throughout Egypt.[6]

By late 1968, the Egyptian Air Force had 110 MiG-21 fighter/interceptors; 80 MiG-19 fighters; 120 MiG-15 and MiG-17 fighters; 40 Su-7B fighter-bombers; 40 Il-28 bombers; and 10 Tu-16 bombers.[7]

The Egyptian Air Force began a substantial pilot-training program both to improve skills and to increase the pool of available pilots. Training was provided by Egyptian flying personnel supported by about 100 Russian instructors, and was conducted on Yak-18, L-29 Delfin, MiG-15UTI, and MiG-21UTI trainers. Soviet advisers were present at all levels of the force, with at least one adviser stationed at each squadron. During this period, Egypt flew few offensive sorties against Israel.

Syrian forces remained relatively quiet during the buildup. By late 1968, Soviet transfusion of materiel replaced the Syrian Arab Air Force's losses from the Six-Day War. Syrian pilot trainees were also sent to the USSR. MiG-21F Fishbed C and MiG-21PF Fishbed D fighters had replaced the MiG-17 in one regiment and the Su-7B fighter-bomber was introduced into service.[8] As the Syrian force trained, it generally refrained from direct confrontation with Israel.

By late 1968, strength was as follows:[9]

60 MiG-21 fighter/interceptors; 70 MiG-15 and MiG-17 fighter-bombers; 20 Su-7B fighter-bombers.

Israel, which had lost approximately 45 aircraft, also needed new fighters and materiel. Following the war, President Charles de Gaulle of France enacted an arms embargo against Israel. As a result, Israel was unable to take possession of 50 Mirage fighters previously ordered.

Faced with a shortage of aircraft, Israel for the first time turned to the United States. Initially, America denied Israel's request for the multi-role F-4 Phantom but agreed to supply considerable numbers of the more specialized A-4 Skyhawk fighter-bomber based on the A-4F then in service with the U.S. Navy; the Israelis requested that the A-4 be modified to their specifications. The result was the A-4H, which substituted two 30-mm DEFA cannon for the U.S.-built Mk. 12 (20-mm) cannon, installed a drag chute to aid braking, and added a large square-tipped tailfin. U.S. weapons that were supplied with the Skyhawk further supplemented Israeli-manufactured weapons and the dwindling supplies of French arms.[10]

By 1968, the first Israeli Skyhawk squadron became fully operational and was immediately pressed into service to attack Arab guerrilla bases in Jordan.[11] By late 1968, the U.S. had fully delivered the Israelis' initial order for 48 A-4H fighter-bombers and two TA-4H trainers.

Near the end of President Lyndon Johnson's administration, the United States agreed to supply Israel with additional Skyhawks, 50 F-4E Phantom fighter-bombers, and six RF-4 reconnaissance aircraft. Delivery of the Phantoms was to begin late in 1969 and continue into 1970.

Israel was operating from several of the captured Egyptian air bases in the Sinai. In addition, the Israelis built several forward landing strips (closer to the battle zone) to recover damaged aircraft. The Israelis also emplaced U.S.-built Hawk surface-to-air missiles in the Sinai to protect the captured airfields and other important installations.

In 1968, strength in aircraft was as follows:[12]

65 Mirage IIIC fighters; 15 Super Mystère B-2 fighter-bombers; 48 A-4H Skyhawk fighter-bombers; 35 Mystère IV-A fighter-bombers; 15 Vautour IIA fighter-bombers; 45 Ouragan fighter-bombers.

Confrontation: Fall 1968

On September 8, 1968, the Egyptians shattered the summer calm by unleashing a series of massive artillery barrages against Israeli troops positioned along the Suez Canal. The bombardment attempted to restrict the Israeli freedom of movement.

The Egyptians had amassed more than three divisions of infantry and hundreds of pieces of artillery along the waterway.[13] Israel, on the other hand, had only a few hundred troops stationed in perhaps two dozen lightly fortified shelters serving merely as forward warning and observation posts.

The Israelis' primary defense units were highly mobile brigade-sized armored groups situated to the rear, out of artillery range. In the event of an attack, these units were to roll forward and drive Egyptian forces back across the canal. The artillery of these brigades was short-range, self-propelled howitzers incapable of providing the counter-battery fire to suppress the numerous, longer-ranged Egyptian artillery.[14]

To relieve the relentless Egyptian pressure on the front line, on October 31, Israel staged a helicopter-borne commando raid against strategic targets deep in Egypt. The commandos destroyed two Nile bridges and an electric transformer station and damaged the Naj Hammadi dam. The raid startled the Egyptians and shifted their emphasis from offense to defense; for the next four months Egypt launched no significant artillery attacks.

Israeli Chief of Staff Chaim Bar Lev directed that the strong points along the canal be expanded and strengthened with reinforced concrete. In addition, the Israelis constructed a sand barrier 20 to 30 feet high to prevent amphibious vehicles from scaling the canal's banks on the Israeli side. This line of fortifications became known as the Bar Lev line.

Arab guerrillas continued their raids along Israel's northern and eastern borders, joined occasionally by Syrian and Jordanian forces equipped with tanks, artillery, and aircraft. On February 13, two Syrian MiG-21s crossed the Six-Day War cease-fire line near El Quneitra in the Golan Heights. Israeli fighters intercepted the MiGs and reportedly shot one down.[15] Eleven days later, 18 Israeli aircraft attacked guerrilla bases outside Damascus. Syrian fighters attacked the intruders and claimed to have shot down four Israeli Mirages with the loss of two MiGs.

On March 8, Egyptian President Gamal Nasser announced a War of Attrition in which the Egyptians again took the offensive, shelling Israeli forces in the Sinai and launching commando raids against them.

Israeli commandos rush from a Super Frelon transport helicopter. On October 31, 1968, Israeli commandos transported by helicopter destroyed two bridges and a transformer station deep in Egyptian territory. (IDF/AF)

The air battles between Egyptian and Israeli fighters also escalated as both dispatched reinforcements to support ground units under fire.

Early in July, Israeli aircraft began attacking targets in the Nile valley and along the coast. Egyptian fighters contesting these attacks suffered badly; on July 2, four MiGs were reportedly shot down.[16]

In support of Egypt's attrition strategy, Syrian artillery along the Golan Heights cease-fire line went into action against Israeli bunkers and patrols. Israeli tanks and artillery replied and aircraft bombed and rocketed Syrian positions. On July 8, Syrian MiGs challenged the air strikes and were intercepted by top-cover Mirages.

In the ensuing dogfight, seven Syrian MiGs reportedly were shot down.[17] According to the Israelis, those MiGs brought total Syrian and Egyptian losses since the Six-Day War to 41, 16 destroyed in the year since June 24, 1968.[18] Brig. Gen. Aharon Yaariv noted during a news conference following the attacks: "We want the Arabs to think hard before they launch any operations."[19]

Despite intense Israeli retaliation, the Egyptians continued their artillery attacks and raids. On July 10, a company-size commando unit ambushed an Israeli armored patrol, inflicting heavy casualties. Nine days later, on the night of July 19–20, retaliating Israeli commandos destroyed installations on Green Island, a fortified outpost in the Gulf of Suez. The loss created an opening in the Egyptian radar network through which Israeli fighters swarmed to attack Egyptian antiaircraft sites, surface-to-air missile batteries, and artillery emplacements. This was the first time that Israeli fighter-bombers were heavily committed against Egyptian emplacements since the opening attack of the Six-Day War and heralded the beginning of a major campaign.

Egyptian and Israeli dogfights continued, with losses on both sides. The Egyptians claimed 19 Israeli aircraft while losing two. Israel counted five downed Egyptian fighters (two Su-7Bs, two MiG-17s, and one MiG-21) while admitting the loss of two aircraft.[20]

The Israelis continued their heavy raids against positions along the Suez Canal. On the afternoon of July 24, a large force of Egyptian fighter-bombers counterattacked Israeli artillery, command posts, and Hawk missile sites. Major Nabi, an Egyptian pilot captured after his Su-7B had fallen to antiaircraft fire, noted, ''My mission was to strike the headquarters at the northern end of the Suez Canal about 25 or 30 kilometers from the canal,'' but his plane had been struck before he had had a chance to bomb his target. Speaking to reporters in Tel Aviv, the major noted that he had received training in the Soviet Union and had tallied a total of 1,400 hours of tactical flight time in his 13-year flying career.[21]

Throughout the remaining six days in July, several bitter air battles were fought after which Egyptian opposition abruptly ceased. Having lost a significant number of aircraft in dogfights and to antiaircraft fire, the Egyptians suddenly stopped challenging Israeli air strikes or conducting their own.

Although air attacks were halted, Egyptian artillery bombardments remained intense. Throughout August, Israeli fighter-bombers continued to strike Egyptian encampments along the canal. Egyptian guns were well dug in and could take considerable punishment before being nulified. Following a heavy Israeli strike against artillery near Port Tewfik on August 19, the Egyptians claimed three aircraft while the Israelis admitted losing one Skyhawk.[22]

General Bar Lev, in a news conference on September 7, noted that since July 20 Israel had flown 1,000 sorties over enemy territory and had lost only three aircraft while the Egyptians had lost 21 aircraft in 110 sorties. This, he added, re-emphasized Egypt's inability to match Israel in air-to-air contests.[23]

On September 9 and 10, Israeli warplanes concentrated heavily on Egyptian air-defense radars and SA-2 surface-to-air missile sites, while a strong ground force undertook a commando raid across the Gulf of Suez. On September 11, the Egyptian Air Force made aggressive air strikes against positions in the Sinai. This was the strongest Egyptian attack to date.

Between 60 and 70 Egyptian fighter-bombers caused extensive damage to Israeli encampments, but at great loss to themselves; seven MiG-21s, three Su-7Bs, and one MiG-17 were shot down by fighters, Hawk missiles, and antiaircraft fire, for the loss of one Mirage over Egyptian territory.[24]

Meanwhile, on September 7, Israel received its first shipment of U.S. F-4E Phantom fighter-bombers. The large, twin-engine Phantom gave Israel a powerful new weapon for carrying the war to the Egyptian home front. In addition to being an excellent long-range attack aircraft, the Phantom was a highly capable fighter. Maj. Gen. Chaim Hertzog, former Chief of Israeli Military Intelligence, noted that acquiring the Phantom was ''probably the most important single step taken during the year to postpone the possible date of a war.''[25]

Egyptian leaders capitalized on their superior numbers, the steady supply of aircraft and equipment from Soviet stocks, and their willingness to accept moderate casualties, and consciously undertook a war of attrition to weaken Israeli resolve. Israel was very sensitive to

An Israeli F-4E Phantom II armed with six 750-pound bombs (under wings) and six 500-pound bombs (under fuselage). Due to its high speed, long range, and hefty payload, the Phantom was the primary aircraft on deep strike missions against Egyptian targets.

the loss of men and equipment, and could not, the Egyptians believed, win an extended conflict.

During a news conference on September 13, General Hertzog spoke of an answering shift in Israeli strategy: "The front line with Egypt is not necessarily the Suez Canal but the whole of Egypt."[26]

In early October, Moshe Dayan announced the beginning of a "limited air offensive" against the Egyptian air defense system. On October 6, Egyptian fighter-bombers, protected by MiG-21s, struck at four targets in the Sinai in retaliation for recent raids. Cairo claimed eight fighters destroyed for but one aircraft lost;[27] Israeli officials, however, reported downing three Egyptian MiGs.[28]

The sniping, erosive battling by the Israelis, Egyptians, and Syrians wore on through the fall. On December 25, Israel staged its longest air strike to date, pounding for more than eight hours missile and radar sites along the Suez Canal. That night, Israeli helicopter-borne commandos seized a highly-secret Soviet-built P-12 acquisition radar and transported it back to Israel in two CH-53 helicopters. (Later, it was disclosed that four ranking Egyptian Air Force officers were executed as a result of this loss.[29])

At a news conference at year-end, Moshe Dayan noted that since August, Egypt, aided by the Soviet Union, had been attempting to set up an integrated air defense network. He reported that a significant percentage of Israeli air strikes between September and December had attacked the developing network.

Summing up the year's activities, Moshe Dayan declared that the Bar Lev Line along the Suez Canal had been battered but was still fully operational. Between the end of the Six-Day War and early January 1970, Israel lost 15 aircraft on all fronts—two in dogfights and the rest to antiaircraft. Dayan added that during the same period Egypt had lost 60 aircraft to Israeli fighters, antiaircraft, and Hawk missiles.[30]

Refitting for Battle

At the end of 1969, Israel had one operational squadron of F-4E Phantoms and was in the process of establishing a second. Along with the Phantoms, the United States had shipped a limited amount of advanced electronic countermeasures equipment, including radar homing-and-warning (RHAW) receivers, jamming pods, and chaff. This, coupled with low-level tactics, enabled Israeli aircraft to fly with relative impunity in the face of Egypt's air defense system.

The several squadrons of A-4H Skyhawks in service in 1969 were augmented by a number of refurbished ex-U.S. Navy A-4E Skyhawks. Supplementing the Phantoms and Skyhawks were the remaining squadron-sized units of French-built aircraft including Vautour IIA, Super Mystère B-2, Mystère IV-A, Ouragan fighter-bombers, and several squadrons of Mirage IIICs.

The Mirage IIIC, armed with two 30-mm DEFA cannon, plus air-to-air missiles, flew top-cover and intercept missions. Besides the Phantoms and Skyhawks, also supplied were several different versions of the AIM-9 Sidewinder.[31] Israel was slow to be convinced of the value of air-to-air missiles. Its first air-intercept missile, the French-built Matra 530, was heavy, created considerable drag, and, moreover, was very expensive and not particularly effective.[32]

In the early 1960s, the Rafael Armament Development Organization, an Israeli government weapons development laboratory, designed and began developing a low-cost, simplified infrared-guided missile named Shafrir (Hebrew for "Dragonfly"). In the late 1960s, production and testing were undertaken, and the missile entered service in 1969.[33] The Shafrir and Sidewinder, like all infrared-guided (heatseeking) missiles of the time, necessitated that the pilot attack by closing on the tail of an enemy aircraft. Any violent maneuvers by the target aircraft could break the missile's homing lock by exceeding the view limits of the seeker.

While infrared-guided missiles had their drawbacks, they allowed longer-range attacks than possible with aircraft cannon alone, increasing the potential for a kill. They also permitted "fire-and-forget" tactics, which increased the attacker's survivability.

Following the French embargo, Israel initiated the Salvo Program, a project to extend the service life of the Mirage IIIC.[34] In addition, Israel Aircraft Industries (IAI) began manufacturing a version of the Mirage. The new aircraft, called the Nesher ("Eagle"), was based on the design of the embargoed Mirage 5. Powered by French SNECMA Atar 9C

An Israeli-built Shafrir missile under the wing of a Mirage IIIC fighter. The Israeli Rafael Armament Development Authority designed and produced the infrared homing air-to-air missile. (IDF/AF)

An Israeli F-4E photographed by another Phantom following bomb release against an Arab target.

turbojets (acquired covertly from France despite the embargo) and fitted with Israeli-manufactured avionics, the prototype Nesher reportedly flew in September 1969.[35]

IAI engineers, with U.S. engineering aid, began fitting an American engine into the Super Mystère fleet. The Israelis chose the Pratt & Whitney J52-P-8A (powerplant for A-4E and A-4H Skyhawks); this necessitated considerable changes to the Super Mystère airframe because the engine was shorter and lighter than the original. In addition, the airframe was strengthened and the aircraft fitted with more modern avionics.[36] The Israelis also began examining the possibility of mating the F-4 Phantom's J79 engine with the Nesher airframe.[37]

Israeli Strategy: Strike Home

Conflict along the canal continued into 1970 with nearly every day punctuated by Egyptian artillery bombardments and Israeli air strikes.

On January 7, 1970, Israel changed its tactics and staged its first major attack against a strategic target deep in Egypt. F-4 Phantoms bombed an SA-2 missile site at Dahshur, 21 miles south of Cairo, with no losses. The attack marked the first time that the American-built F-4 Phantom was committed to operations, and signaled the beginning of a new phase of the war.[38] No longer would strikes be limited to the area near the canal area, and military targets throughout Egypt were now fair game.

The Egyptian Air Force, reacting to the escalation, bombed targets in the Sinai on January 10 and reportedly destroyed a Hawk missile site. Israel denied the loss and claimed to have destroyed two Su-7Bs. Deep strikes into Egypt continued and on January 13 the El Khanka supply depot and several surface-to-air missile sites near Cairo were struck. Three days later, an Israeli fighter-bomber was shot down. Israeli spokesmen admitted it as their sixteenth loss since the Six-Day War.[39]

The intensified attacks were causing considerable damage to Egyptian targets. On January 22, President Nasser requested an urgent meeting with Soviet leaders and flew to Moscow for discussions. He acknowledged that his country's defenses were unable to withstand the Israeli attacks and requested long-range strike aircraft to counterattack Israeli cities and defense centers.

Nasser theorized that counterattacks deep into Israel would relieve pressure on the Egyptian air defense system and enable him to reconstruct it. The Soviets would not provide offensive strike aircraft or offensive missile systems, but would supply additional defensive military aid in the form of MiG-21s and surface-to-air missiles to defend civilian and economic targets.

In an attempt to reverse the trend toward a dangerous Middle East arms race, on January 31, Soviet Premier Kosygin sent a personal note to President Richard M. Nixon. The note stated that if the West could not restrain Israel from attacking virtually defenseless Egyptian economic and civilian targets, the Soviet Union would have no choice but to supply new arms to counter the raids. On February 4, Nixon called for a Middle East arms embargo, but added that the United States would supply arms to Israel to offset any edge in war capability the Arabs might gain as a result of Soviet supplies.

Israeli raids continued deep into Egypt as did Egyptian attacks against the Sinai. By late February, the Soviet air aid program to Egypt was becoming visible. Airlift traffic increased substantially, and Russian cargo ships constantly docked at Alexandria Harbor to unload at night.

An Egyptian SA-3 Goa surface-to-air missile on its transporter. Soviet-manned SA-3 batteries were emplaced around important Egyptian cities and industrial sites to counter Israeli deep-penetration raids. The SA-3 was capable of intercepting targets at low and medium altitude to a slant range of 14 miles. Egypt was first outside the Soviet Union and Warsaw Pact nations equipped with the highly-capable Goa missile system. (U.S. Army)

In early March, Israeli reconnaissance aircraft detected that new SA-2 and SA-3 missile sites had been emplaced near important targets deep in Egypt. On March 19, *The New York Times* reported that at least 1,500 Soviet soldiers and technicians had arrived in Egypt to man the new SA-3 sites. While Israeli raids had damaged many of the SA-2 sites in eastern Egypt, new ones appeared in a network parallel to the Suez Canal. The new SA-2 sites were protected by large numbers of antiaircraft guns. Soviet-manned SA-3 batteries also appeared near Cairo, Alexandria, and around the Aswan Dam.

The SA-3 surface-to-air missile (NATO code-named Goa) was a two-stage radar command-guided missile with a slant range of approximately 13 miles and a ceiling higher than 40,000 feet. The SA-3 radar system (NATO designation Low Blow) could track six aircraft simultaneously and could fire and guide several missiles against a target. Batteries were normally configured with eight missiles ready to be fired from four two-round launchers.

The SA-3 had a role similar to the U.S.-built Hawk missile system. The SA-3 was more advanced than the SA-2 in that it was capable of intercepting aircraft at low as well as high altitudes. Its Low Blow radar and its improved fire-control equipment were also less vulnerable than the SA-2's Fan Song radar.

On March 23, the United States rejected an Israeli request for 25 additional Phantoms and 100 Skyhawks. A U.S. State Department initiative to begin negotiations toward a cease fire and settlement was rejected by both sides.

Gradually, the Egyptians set up a new defensive missile screen. Centered out of range of Israeli artillery some 15 to 30 miles west of the Suez Canal between the Cairo/Ismailia Road and the Cairo/Port Suez Road, the defense network consisted of dug-in SA-2 and antiaircraft batteries linked to early-warning radar sites. In order to mutually defend one another, surface-to-air missile sites were positioned so that their ranges overlapped.[40]

Israel, recognizing the significance of the construction effort, vigorously attacked the new network. But as quickly as the Israelis destroyed the sites, the Egyptians put them back into commission. Concurrent with the missile-site suppression raids, the Israelis continued their deep penetration attacks.

During such an attack on March 25, four Egyptian MiG-21s reportedly were downed. The MiGs had intercepted a force of Mystère IV-As bombing surface-to-air missile sites and embroiled in a dogfight with Mirage IIIC escorts.[41] Cairo reported, however, that no Egyptian planes had been lost and claimed one Israeli fighter. Two days later, aircraft again tangled. An Israeli pilot describes the encounter:

"We were heading toward the canal, circling around as the attack was taking place below, when we received an order to change direction toward Egyptian planes coming from the west.

"We saw a pair of Egyptian MiGs first and then went after them to get into firing position. We looked around to see if there were other planes and saw another pair, apparently part of a foursome, all MiG-21s. They were flying at the same altitude as the first two, but in a different direction.

"Then another foursome came in to join the other MiGs. They came in, making a turn from west to south, but not a sharp turn. In other words, I closed in front of him, closing his angle and range.

"I shot and missed. The other pilot seemed to have been startled by the shot and changed his direction, from a left to a right turn. At this point I was able to get into firing position and let off a long burst. There was a gigantic explosion and I saw flames in his wings and then his forward section."[42]

Five of the Arab fighters were destroyed, bringing Egyptian losses to 85 since the end of the Six-Day War. Israeli and Syrian forces clashed heavily at dawn on April 2 when an early-morning Israeli air raid across the border escalated into a full-scale air and ground battle along

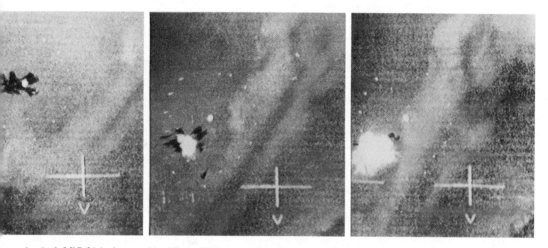

An Arab MiG-21 is destroyed by Mirage IIIC cannon fire. Israel claimed that its fighters downed more than 100 Egyptian and Syrian aircraft during the War of Attrition. (IDF/AF)

the whole length of the cease-fire line on the Golan Heights. Israel claimed three Syrian MiGs but lost its first F-4 Phantom in combat to antiaircraft fire.[43]

The Israelis continued to strike surface-to-air missile construction sites and other military targets deep in Egypt's interior. (Some nonmilitary targets also suffered; in the village of Bahr El-Bakr a primary school was accidentally hit, killing or injuring at least 50 children.)

During the first four months of 1970, the Israelis flew 3,300 sorties and dropped 8,000 tons of bombs on Egyptian targets. Moshe Dayan noted that during those attacks 80 percent of the Egyptian air defense system was knocked out.[44]

Great Soviet Commitment

By early April, the Soviets' commitment to protect Egypt against air attack was becoming increasingly evident. More than 20 batteries of improved SA-2 missiles and new Soviet-manned SA-3 missiles added depth to the existing air defense system.

The Soviet Air Force now controlled several air bases in Egypt. Israel intelligence routinely monitored radio transmissions between Arab aircraft and ground stations. Beginning in early April, the Israelis detected air-to-ground conversations in Russian, confirming their suspicion that Soviet pilots were flying air defense missions over the Nile Valley and Nile Delta regions. The Russian pilots flew the MiG-21MF (NATO code-named Fishbed J) interceptor which was capable of higher speeds than the Egyptian Air Force's MiG-21F and MiG-21PF (Fishbed C and Fishbed D); it was also equipped with an advanced all-weather Jay Bird radar, a superior fire control system, and an internal GSh-23 twin-barrel 23-mm cannon. When on April 17 Israeli pilots encountered several MiG-21s that radio monitors confirmed were being flown by Soviet pilots, the Israelis were ordered by their ground controllers to refrain from combat.[45]

In order to prevent a confrontation with either Soviet-manned MiG-21MF Fishbed J interceptors or SA-3 sites, Israel ended its deep penetration raids. Israel did not want to attack Russian-manned aircraft or surface-to-air missile sites for fear of provoking greater Soviet involvement and widening the conflict.

Soviet intervention brought the focus of the war back to the Suez Canal. On April 18, Egyptian forces, now relieved of the responsibility of home defense, opened a new offensive along the canal with massive artillery barrages and air attacks. Israeli spokesmen admitted that the April 18 air strike was the heaviest and most successful since some of the Egyptian raids against Israeli columns in the Six-Day War.[46]

Israel retaliated, destroying two MiGs in air battles between April 19 and April 21. Egyptian raids continued, however, and about 2:00 a.m. the night of April 25, two formations of Il-28 bombers penetrated deeper than 125 miles into the Sinai and bombed Israeli military targets near the town of El Arish. Israeli interceptors closed on the intruders, shooting down two.[47]

Egyptian actions reflected a new sense of confidence. On May 1, President Nasser stated, "Brothers, in the past 15 days [since April 13th] a change has taken place. Our armed forces have regained the initiative with bold military operations in the air and on land. Our determination to liberate our territory is the primary legitimate right of any nation which values its dignity."[48]

On May 12, Israeli armored forces drove five miles into Lebanon to attack guerrilla bases. Syrian aircraft intercepted the attackers, and three MiG-17s were reportedly shot down by Skyhawks.[49]

Syria acknowledged losing the aircraft but claimed three Israeli fighters. Two days later, on May 14, Israeli aircraft began pummeling positions near the canal, and claimed two Egyptian MiG-21s. The following day, another MiG-21 was downed in a dogfight and two MiG-17s by antiaircraft fire as the MiGs were attacking Israeli positions.[50]

In late May, Egypt began to reconstruct the battered air defense system near the canal in order to protect forward positions. The Israelis, perceiving the purpose, directed attacks to suppress the reconstruction effort and damaged many of the sites.

The Egyptians, in turn, staged a highly successful commando raid along the Bar Lev line, killing 13 Israelis. In retaliation, Israeli aircraft launched a week-long series of raids against Egyptian targets. Phantoms sank a destroyer and a missile patrol boat in the Red Sea, and struck repeatedly at Port Said. On June 3, Israeli aircraft allegedly downed three MiG-21s in three minutes; Egypt, however, admitted losing only one fighter and claimed two Mirages.[51]

"Stop Shooting and Start Talking"

Since mid-April, when the Israelis discovered the Russian presence in Egypt and ended strikes against the Egyptian interior, no Russian-manned defenses were known to exist in the air defense network parallel to the canal. The Soviet-piloted MiG-21MF Fishbed Js patrolled well clear of the area, and Israeli and Soviet forces were both careful to avoid direct confrontation.

In early June, Israel learned that Russian advisers were helping in the reconstruction of the surface-to-air missile defenses along the canal, and some of the new SA-2 sites were manned by mixed crews. Despite hesitation to inflict casualties on Russians, the Israelis attacked the new missile sites heavily, but the number continued to grow.

When the Soviets did not contest the raids along the canal with MiG-21s, the Israelis grew more daring. Several times Israeli aircraft feinted penetrations beyond the canal area, but each time Soviet fighters roared into the air to intercept. On June 23, Israeli helicopter-borne commandos tested the waters by raiding a camp at Bir Arida, 50 miles south of Cairo and near the Russian air base at Beni Seuf. Soviet fighters did not intercept the helicopters. Instead, the Russians began to move their fighter patrols closer to the canal.[52]

U.S. Secretary of State William Rogers announced on June 25 the beginning of a diplomatic effort for a 90-day cease-fire to encourage Israel and the Arab countries to "stop shooting and start talking." On the same day, however, Israeli jets struck military camps near Damascus and shot down a Syrian MiG-21.

The next day, Israeli and Syrian aircraft, tanks, and artillery locked in major combat at two points along Rogers' proposed cease-fire line. That morning two Syrian MiG-21s were reportedly downed when they challenged Israeli fighter-bombers; one Israeli fighter was lost, and its pilot was seen parachuting into Syria. In the afternoon, Israel claimed two Syrian MiG-17s as they attempted to strafe and bomb Israeli ground forces. Meanwhile, on the Egyptian front one MiG-17 attacking Israeli positions succumbed to antiaircraft fire.[53]

Egyptian President Nasser flew to Moscow on June 29 to confer on strategy concerning the Rogers proposal. He was willing to negotiate but wanted Russian backing.

That same night, Soviet and Egyptian technicians moved SA-2 and SA-3 batteries and supporting antiaircraft artillery into forward positions west of the Suez Canal. The following sunrise, two Israeli F-4E Phantoms fell to SA-2 missiles and Egyptian antiaircraft also claimed two Skyhawks later in the day.[54] In reaction, throughout the next week Israeli fighter-bombers heavily bombarded the new Egyptian air defense positions. The Egyptians, however, resupplied the surface-to-air missile sites in the belt west of the canal from reserves and frequently shifted them to avoid their destruction.

On July 6, Major General Bar Lev admitted that in the preceding six days Israel lost three aircraft while attacking the Egyptians' integrated air defense system.[55] The network consisted of a dozen batteries of new-model SA-2 missiles and at least two SA-3 sites, arranged in a line starting 15 miles west of the canal and extending to a point 32 miles west.

He said: "To the best of our knowledge, the SA-3 is manned by the Russians. The SA-2 is, we think, manned by Egyptians, but there are numbers of Russian officers attached to each battery who serve as more than advisers. In the whole system we feel the Russian hand in planning, directing, and operating the whole concentration."[56]

Launch of SA-2 Guideline surface-to-air missiles. On June 29-30, 1970, Egyptian and Soviet engineers moved 12 to 15 SA-2 and SA-3 sites and protective antiaircraft guns into forward positions near the Suez Canal. During the next several weeks, this cost Israel a number of aircraft, including several Phantoms and Skyhawks, trying to destroy the missiles and antiaircraft guns.

The Israelis damaged seven of the SA-2 sites but did not attack the Soviet-manned batteries. According to Bar Lev, the new weaponry shifted the balance of power along the canal seriously but not irrevocably.

In early July, the United States, rescinding its earlier position, agreed to supply Israel with more Phantoms and Skyhawks to make up the losses. In addition, rushed to Israel were additional more-advanced jamming pods capable of countering the Fan Song E radar of the improved SA-2s and the Low Blow radar of the SA-3s. In addition to these U.S.-built electronic countermeasures pods for strike aircraft, Israel sent U.S.-built Boeing C-97 Stratocruiser transports and French-built Vautour fighter-bombers, both filled with electronic equipment, to cruise the edge of the battle area to provide additional missile warning and jamming.

On July 19, Israel admitted losing another Phantom to missiles. Frustrated with the lack of success in destroying the Egyptian integrated air defense network, Israel shifted the weight of its attacks back to the Egyptian front line, heavily attacking Egyptian artillery positions, fortifications, and bunkers for the remainder of the month. Despite withstanding the pounding, Egypt too was suffering from the daily attacks. In a semi-official news report, Egyptian spokesmen admitted that in the month between 1,500 and 2,000 troops had been killed or wounded along the canal front.[57]

Until the end of July the Russians remained behind the scenes. On July 25, that all changed. The first confrontation between Israeli and Soviet pilots was triggered when MiG-21MF Fishbed Js attacked two Skyhawks. The wing of one was damaged by an Atoll air-to-air missile, but the aircraft returned to base. Five days later, a small force of Skyhawks successfully flew a simulated strike into the Nile Valley to lure Soviet interceptors into a trap. A squadron-size force of Fishbed Js chased the Skyhawks only to be ambushed south of the city of Suez by Mirage IIICs from above and Phantoms from below.

Recounted one of the Israeli pilots: "They came at us in pairs and we let them pass in order not to be sandwiched between the pairs, as they had anticipated we would. They passed one after another as couples in a procession. We waited and got in behind, now sandwiching them, and had before us 16 MiGs!

"The sky was filled with planes as the formations broke up, and the danger of collision was very acute. Also flying about were a lot of jettisoned fuel tanks, so you could hit anything if on our side. Then I saw my Number One fire a Shafrir missile and then another. Soon his target was on fire, spinning down from 30,000 feet, and the pilot bailed out fast.

"The melee continued, planes turning and twisting around, and firing guns and rockets at each other. More Israeli planes joined the battle. Breaking hard, I succeeded in getting my

Russian MiG-21MF Fishbed J photographed in flight. On July 30, 1970, a squadron-size force of MiG-21s flown by Soviet pilots was ambushed by Israeli Mirages and Phantoms. Four MiGs were destroyed with no loss of Israeli aircraft.

sights on a MiG. He had guts and turned into the fight, but I quickly realized he was inexperienced. He made elementary mistakes. Diving down to 2,000 meters, I cut him off and soon locked on my radar—then we had time. It was clear that he could not get away. At a range of 1,000 meters we fired a missile. The MiG exploded into a flaming ball but, surprisingly, flew on. We fired another missile but this was no longer necessary. The Russian plane suddenly disintegrated in the air. The pilot ejected and I observed him swing down in his parachute. Breaking off combat I returned to base."[58]

In the vicious dogfight, the Israelis shot down four of the Fishbed Js, two by Sidewinder missiles fired by Phantoms, one by a Sidewinder launched from a Mirage, and one by cannon from a Mirage.[59]

Soviet instructors and advisers had often chided Egyptian pilots for their lack of skill and aggressiveness and their failure to properly employ Soviet-style tactics. The Soviets' overbearing attitude created a rift between the advisers and their Egyptian students. When in this first major encounter, Russian pilots were soundly defeated in combat, the Egyptians reportedly were overjoyed because it vindicated their own poor showing.

Cease-Fire: August 1970

Meanwhile, behind the scenes Russian, Egyptian, American, and Israeli diplomats were negotiating. The Rogers proposal called for a three-month cease-fire followed by negotiations that would lead to Israeli withdrawal from occupied territories and Arab recognition of Israel. President Nasser announced acceptance of the proposal in a speech on July 23, 1970. The Israeli coalition government debated the plan and, on July 31, Prime Minister Golda Meir accepted the proposal as well.

One condition was that additional military units not be introduced in the cease-fire zone along the canal after August 8's truce. By August 2, to beat the deadline, the Egyptians had advanced at least five new missile batteries to within 20 miles of the canal. Israel again focused attacks on this forward air-defense system to prevent it from expanding even further.

While attacking surface-to-air missile sites over the final week of conflict, the Israelis lost another Phantom over Egypt as well as several other aircraft, most to missiles. Heavy action continued throughout the next four days as the Egyptian forces moved between 10 and 15 surface-to-air missile batteries into the canal area. Strikes continued right up to the cease-fire on about 1:00 a.m. on August 8.

Analysis

Israeli fighters patrolled along the canal and over the Golan Heights throughout the entire war of attrition. The Mirage IIICs protected strike missions and served as primary interceptor. The 30-mm DEFA cannon was the Mirage's primary weapon; as the war progressed, however, missiles—particularly the AIM-9 Sidewinder and the Israeli-built Shafrir—were used more frequently for tactical surprise and for attacks from longer range than allowed by the cannon. The American-built F-4 Phantoms served primarily as attack aircraft, but were used occasionally as fighters and interceptors. Israeli Phantoms intercepted many an intruder at night and also destroyed two Soviet-piloted MiG-21MF Fishbed Js. The Mirage and the Phantom were not the only shot down Arab aircraft; a Skyhawk pilot reportedly downed two Syrian MiG-17s.

Egyptian and Syrian pilots in Fishbed fighters retaliated by escorting raiding MiG-17 and Su-7B fighter-bombers. The skill of Arab pilots slowly improved as they learned the lessons of training and battle.

A camouflaged Mirage IIIC takes off on a training flight. The Mirages scored the majority of the Arab aircraft destroyed during the War of Attrition. (IDF/AF)

Soviet MiG-21MF Fishbed pilots damaged an Israeli Skyhawk but were badly defeated in their next major encounter. The Israelis purposely baited Russian fighters into a trap on July 30, 1970, downing four of the late-model Fishbed J interceptors and damaging a fifth with no losses.

Very little information has been released on the precise tactics of the Israeli or Arab air forces in air combat during the war. Since the battle area long the canal was relatively limited, the opponents' radar-surveillance networks generally were able to detect penetrating enemy aircraft at medium or high altitude. As a result, low-altitude tactics were used extensively by both sides.

Soviet advisers taught Arab forces to rely on their ground radar and their command-and-control network to vector fighters into surprise attacks. The Arab forces were discouraged from maneuvering combat because of the Israelis' acknowledged superiority in dogfighting.

Israeli pilots were trained to stress surprise attack, maneuvering, and aggressive tactics. Frequently, they sent decoys to gain a tactical edge. The commander of an Egyptian MiG-21 regiment admitted:

"During the War of Attrition, the Israeli Air Force had a favorite ambush tactic. They would penetrate with two aircraft at medium altitude where they would quickly be picked up on radar. We would scramble four or eight [MiGs] to attack them. But they had another dozen fighters trailing at extremely low altitude below radar coverage. As we climbed to the attack they would zoom up behind and surprise us. My regiment lost MiGs to this ambush tactic three times."[60]

Early-model Sidewinder and Shafrir missiles used by Israel plus the Atolls of the Egyptian and Syrian forces were designed to attack such nonmaneuvering aircraft as bombers. Thus, the missiles were most effective when launched at unsuspecting targets. In maneuvering high-g dogfights, the Israelis' primary weapons were cannon, frequently after a surprise first pass or if the prey detected the approaching attacker and had time to respond.

It is difficult to assess accurately the number of aircraft lost in aerial battle by either side; there are major discrepancies between the numbers each side claims and the losses each admits to. During the three-year war, Israel conceded to losing four fighters but claimed just over 100 Arab aircraft.[61] If true, in dogfights alone that meant a kill-to-loss ratio of 25 to one. Since the performance of neither the Mirage IIIC nor the F-4E Phantom was markedly superior to that of the MiG-21, the one-sided ratio must be attributed to the combination of pilot skill, superior tactics, and excellent use of weapons.

Israel further claimed at least 35 aircraft with antiaircraft fire and ground-launched U.S.-built Hawk missiles, but admits to losing 22 aircraft to surface-to-air missiles and antiaircraft fire.[62]

In contrast, Egypt claimed air defenses downed 21 Israeli aircraft during July 1970 alone; during the entire conflict from the end of the Six-Day War in June 1967 to the cease-fire on August 8, 1970, Egypt, Syria, Jordan, and Arab guerrilla groups claim a tally of more than 300 Israeli aircraft.[63]

During the conflict, both sides introduced new attack aircraft. Egypt and Syria were equipped with the Su-7B Fitter, and Israel phased into service the Skyhawk and the Phantom. Compared to most Western designs, the Fitter was limited in range and in weapons payload for its size, but in the attack role it was a substantial improvement over the MiG-17. Egypt took advantage of the Su-7B's speed and maneuverability at low altitudes, repeatedly using high-speed, low-level tactics in strikes against Israeli positions along the canal. The Israelis were able to assess the performance of the Fitter with unusual intimacy after they recovered intact an Egyptian Su-7B that crash-landed in soft sand when downed by antiaircraft fire.[64]

The subsonic A-4, which entered service soon after the Six-Day War, was the Israelis' primary ground-attack aircraft. The Skyhawk was maneuverable, simple to fly, could carry a heavy weapons load, and had a tough structure. Even so, during the War of Attrition eight Skyhawks were reportedly downed by antiaircraft fire and surface-to-air missiles, plus at least one damaged in air combat when it was struck by an Atoll missile fired from a Fishbed J.[65]

An F-4E Phanton II lands at an Israeli airfield. The F-4E served primarily as a strike aircraft but was also employed as a fighter and interceptor. (IDF/AF)

The F-4E Phantoms, serving as the long-range attack aircraft, carried the conflict to the Egyptian homeland until large numbers of surface-to-air missile batteries were erected. During the War of Attrition, nine F-4E Phantoms were reportedly lost, most falling to SA-2 missiles.[66]

Initially, Arab antiaircraft guns and the limited number of Egyptian SA-2 batteries inflicted only light losses. Israeli pilots practicing lessons learned in the Six-Day War and from Vietnam, invaded Egypt by flying in below the effective altitude of the SA-2 missile. When the Egyptians, aided by the Soviets, created an extensive air defense barrier along the canal, however, the Israelis were unable to keep it in check.

The War of Attrition was not full scale in the traditional sense, because large numbers of ground forces did not directly oppose one another. Nonetheless, the conflict was significant because the fighting was undertaken by projection forces: artillery, aircraft, antiaircraft defenses, and commando forces. As such, the war was unique because projection forces were employed alone on such a large scale over such a long period.

The see-saw battle between aircraft and antiaircraft defenses dominated the latter part of the conflict. Early on, Israeli fighters and fighter-bombers achieved air superiority and minimized the imbalance between the forces along the canal. Subsequently, with massive Soviet support, Egypt constructed parallel to the canal what was at the time one of the world's densest antiaircraft defense systems. Israeli attacks damaged this network, but were unable to eliminate it.

The August 8, 1970, cease-fire was a fortunate development for the Israelis. Continued conflict might have called for the intervention of Israeli troops across the canal to destroy the Egyptians' air defense network from the ground. Due to the growing sophisticated Egyptian/Russian air defense system, Israel was losing its capability to use air power alone to significantly direct the outcome of battle.

CHAPTER VII

The Yom Kippur War:
Arab-Israeli Conflict, 1973

Introductory Overview

The two-and-a-half-week conflict of October 1973 was the bloodiest engagement between the Arabs and Israelis since the Israeli War of Independence in 1948. One of its most remarkable aspects was that it was so carefully planned; Egypt and Syria decided to attack Israel on its highest of holy days, Yom Kippur, and trained their forces for nearly a year in virtual secrecy. When they simultaneously struck along both the Egyptian and Syrian borders the afternoon of October 6, the planning paid off; under assault from both ground and air, Israeli troops suffered heavy casualties and were forced to fall back.

The Yom Kippur War was a large-scale conventional war involving air power, hundreds of tanks, and thousands of troops. The Arabs revealed some new Soviet technological surprises: new tanks, new anti-tank missiles, and new surface-to-air missiles. The war involved some of the largest-scale air battles since the Korean conflict with extensive bombing and ferocious dogfights among dozens of planes.

The vicious war exacted heavy tolls on both sides; within 18 days, 500 planes were shot down, 1,500 tanks destroyed, and more than 10,000 men killed.

It was clear that since the cessation of the War of Attrition, the Arabs had become more expert in military tactics, including the use of surprise; their integrated air defense system on the ground was considerably strengthened. The Israelis, painfully learning new combat lessons, modified their tactics and employed new weapons. They managed to puncture the Egyptian air defense system from the ground, circumvent that of the Syrians, and gain air superiority.

Quiet Buildup, 1970–72

On September 5, 1970, less than a month after the War of Attrition cease-fire, London's International Institute for Strategic Studies reported that 45 Egyptian surface-to-air missile sites were operational in the Canal Zone—and that fully 30 of them had been emplaced since the cease-fire. In addition, Egypt received from the USSR the ZSU-23-4, a new radar-controlled antiaircraft weapon mounted on an armored, tracked vehicle.[1]

Israel bitterly complained about the continued expansion of the Egyptian air defense system. When the United States confirmed the extension, President Richard M. Nixon's administration supplied Israel with additional F-4 Phantoms, A-4 Skyhawks, new electronic countermeasures

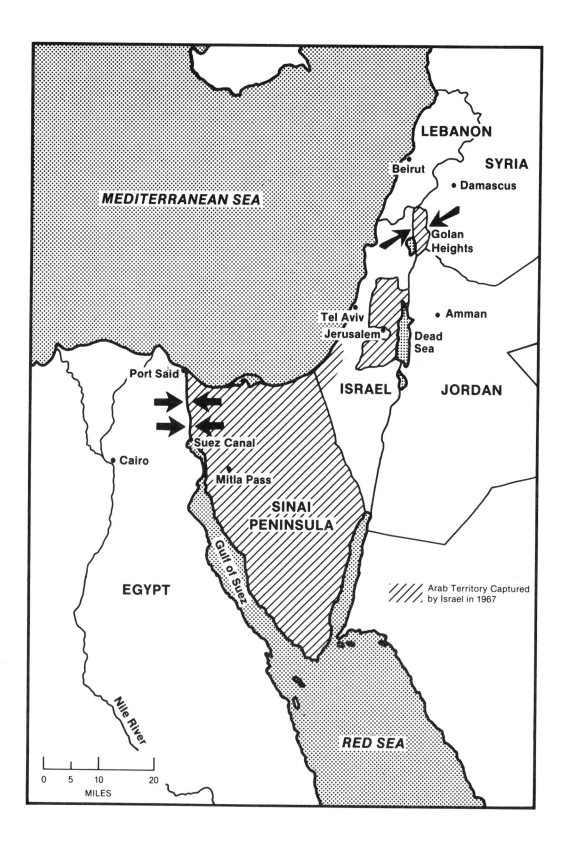

LEBANON

SYRIA

•Beirut

•Damascus

Golan
Heights

MEDITERRANEAN SEA

Tel Aviv

Jerusalem

•Amman

Dead
Sea

ISRAEL

JORDAN

Port Said

Suez Canal

•Cairo

Mitla Pass

SINAI
PENINSULA

Arab Territory Captured
by Israel in 1967

EGYPT

Gulf of Suez

Nile River

RED SEA

0   5   10   20

MILES

equipment, Shrike anti-radiation missiles, Walleye glide bombs, and unmanned BQM-34 Firebee reconnaissance drone aircraft.[2]

Talks called for by terms of the cease-fire leading toward a peaceful settlement stalled, and, in mid-September 1970, both sides clashed. On September 11, an Egyptian Su-7B flying a reconnaissance mission over the Sinai Desert was shot down by Israeli ground fire. A week later, the Egyptians countered on September 17 when an Israeli Boeing Stratocruiser on an electronic monitoring mission parallel to the canal was downed by an Egyptian SA-2 missile.[3] The next day, the Israeli attacked surface-to-air missile batteries along the canal with artillery and aircraft; the Egyptians replied with artillery.

Thereafter overt conflict ceased. For more than a year and a half until June 1972, an uneasy truce existed. Both sides continued to buy arms, and Arab guerrillas occasionally attacked Israel with the tacit approval of Syria and Egypt.

The Soviets initiated reconnaissance flights with their new MiG-25 Foxbat over the Sinai and along the Israeli coast. The flights were a constant goad since Israeli Phantoms and Mirages could not intercept the Foxbats, which flew higher than 70,000 feet at plus Mach 2.5. To return the irritation, Israel sent unmanned Firebee drones on low and fast reconnaissance missions over the Egyptian heartland.[4]

Egypt's President Nasser died on September 28, 1970. President Anwar Sadat, who succeeded him, observed that Israel was satisfied with the status quo. Sadat was under domestic and international Arab pressure to end the no-peace–no-war situation. The Suez Canal, a significant source of revenue to Egypt before the 1967 war, was still closed as a result of the fighting; and to meet its economic needs, Egypt relied heavily on subsidies from Libya, Saudi Arabia, and Kuwait.

On June 13, 1972, for the first time since the August 1970 cease-fire, Israeli and Egyptian fighters clashed. Israel reported that its fighters were flying a routine patrol over the Mediterranean when they were intercepted by Egyptian MiG-21s. Israel claimed two of the MiGs. Egypt admitted that two of its aircraft were ''hit,'' but also tallied two Israeli Mirages.[5]

One of President Sadat's first steps toward open war was expelling Soviet advisers and technicians. In July 1972, several thousand advisers left Egypt, and the Soviet Union became concerned about future relations with its client state. In an attempt to rebuild the alliance, the Soviets agreed to ship Egypt a massive supply of weapons.[6]

Arab guerrillas continued their attacks despite the cease-fire. On November 21, 1972, after a series of heavy guerrilla raids on the Golan Heights, Israeli aircraft bombed Syrian army encampments and suspected guerrilla training areas. Syria retaliated by shelling frontier civilian settlements. To counter these attacks, Israeli fighter-bombers struck at the Syrian artillery batteries and destroyed an important radar position. Syrian fighters challenged, and Israel claimed to have destroyed six Syrian MiG-21s without loss. Syrian military spokesmen admitted losing one MiG-21, but claimed to have downed two Israeli fighters.[7]

In November 1972, President Sadat made the decision to attack Israel.[8] In previous wars (1948, 1956, 1967), the aim had been to destroy the State of Israel; the goal of the new war was to be more limited: to defeat Israel on the field of battle and capture important land areas. Neither of the superpowers—the United States nor USSR—would allow a complete military victory that would lead to the annihilation of Israel or one of the Arab countries. Syria was willing to participate in an offensive against Israel in order to break the political and military stalemate, and so Egypt and Syria agreed to a two-front war.

A surprise joint attack would force Israel to fight with her limited resources on two fronts and thus increase the chances of an Arab victory. The main Egyptian objective was to cross the canal in force and establish a defensible foothold in the Sinai. Syria was to attack Israeli defenses on the Golan Heights and penetrate to the Jordan River and the shore of Lake Tiberias

(Sea of Galilee). These military objectives were designed to break the political deadlock and force Israel to begin negotiations leading to the return of Arab territory captured in the Six-Day War.

In order to succeed, Egypt and Syria planned to fight on Arab terms. A relatively static conflict fought on as wide a front as possible would thin out Israeli forces and put to full advantage the Arabs' numerical superiority. To overcome the important factor of superior Israeli skill in the air, however, the Arabs would first establish an extensive and sophisticated air defense system on both fronts. Most importantly, in order to maximize the military and political impact, the two-pronged offensive was to come as a total surprise.

The date of the attack was Yom Kippur, the Day of Atonement—the holiest Jewish holiday observed by virtually all of Israel—and therefore a time when the Israel forces would be least prepared.

Throughout the first ten months of 1973, large shipments of new Soviet arms were added to the inventories. Both Egypt and Syria had stepped up maneuvers along the borders to mislead Israeli intelligence regarding the state of Arab readiness and intentions.

Because of the acknowledged superiority of the Israeli Air Force in aerial combat, the Arabs were to rely on their powerful integrated air defense network to protect their territory and ground forces against Israeli air attacks. The Egyptian and Syrian Air Forces were to be held back from the fighting in the beginning while the Egyptian Army's air defense command and the Syrian air defense units weakened the Israeli Air Force through surface-to-air missiles and intense antiaircraft fire. The Egyptian and Syrian air forces were to strike and make hit-and-run attacks only when conditions were favorable.

During the ten months that the Arabs were secretly building up their defenses, sniping and occasional fighting still flared up along the Israeli-Arab borders. Tension on the Golan Heights mounted as Arab guerrillas continued their attacks. Each serious attack sparked a strong Israeli reprisal. On January 2, 1973, Israeli and Syrian planes battled over northern Lebanon. Israel claimed to have downed one Syrian MiG-21 and that all Israeli fighters returned home safely. Syria acknowledged the loss, but indicated the destruction of one Israeli plane.[9]

The Syrian Arab Air Force intercepted a second series of air attacks early in the afternoon of January 8, provoking a large dogfight involving more than two dozen aircraft. Again statements of losses conflicted: Israel claimed six MiG-21s while Syria, acknowledging the loss of three, claimed four Israeli fighters.

The occasional border conflicts were not confined to the Syrian-Israeli front. On February 15, Israeli and Egyptian fighters fought a brief battle over the Gulf of Suez. Egypt claimed its fighters downed one Israeli aircraft and admitted the loss of one MiG-21.[10]

On September 13, Israeli and Syrian aircraft met over the Mediterranean near Latakia. In a brief, intense, one-sided encounter, the Israelis shot down 13 Syrian MiG-21s for the loss of one Mirage.[11]

Israel anticipated a strong Syrian reaction to this defeat. On September 26th, Defense Minister Moshe Dayan inspected Israeli fortifications on the Golan Heights and as a precaution decided to position there an additional brigade of tanks, armored personnel carriers, and artillery, and put the rest of the regular Army on alert.

Immediately prior to the war, air reconnaissance and other intelligence sources warned Israel that Arab forces were massing on the borders. Because unnecessarily mobilizing the reserves would heavily drain the economy, Prime Minister Meir and her cabinet did not order full mobilization until the morning of October 6. The Israeli Air Force was prepared to undertake a preemptive attack against airfield and concentrations of Arab forces. Politically, however, a preemptive strike was undesirable because the United States had informed Israel that if she initiated any conflict aid would not be forthcoming.

Opposing Air and Air Defense Forces

Israel Defense Force/Air Force

Commanded by Maj. Gen. Benjamin Peled, the Israel Defense Force/Air Force had grown significantly in number and quality since the end of the War of Attrition. Its aircraft: 127 F-4E, RF-4E Phantom fighter-bombers; 162 A-4E, A-4H, A-4N Skyhawk fighter-bombers; 35 Mirage IIIC fighters; 40 Nesher fighter-bombers; 15 Super Mystère fighter-bombers.[12]

The Israelis had extensively modified their aircraft to meet their requirements. The A-4E and A-4H Skyhawks were being retrofitted with a new weapons delivery system consisting of a Lear Siegler inertial navigation system, Singer General Precision stabilized platform, and Elliot Automation head-up display (HUD). These new systems improved the accuracy of delivering bombs on target by several orders of magnitude, allowing the Israelis to send fewer aircraft to strike with greater confidence any given target.[13]

The A-4N, a new Skyhawk version incorporating many Israeli modifications, was also coming into service. This latest Skyhawk featured new attack avionics and a higher-thrust engine.[14]

The Mirage IIIC and the Israeli-produced Nesher were the primary air combat aircraft. Combat and attrition during training had reduced the Mirage IIIC fleet to fewer than 40 aircraft, but surviving aircraft had been overhauled and reconditioned through the Salvo service life extension program.

To overcome the effect of the French arms embargo continued from the War of Attrition, the Israel Aircraft Industries had, at considerable expense, manufactured the Nesher—a modified version of the Mirage 5. Powered by the French-built SNECMA Atar 9C engine, the Nesher was first delivered to Israel in 1972; about 40 were reportedly in service by October 1973.[15]

As soon as Nesher entered production, IAI began working on mating the Mirage airframe with the higher-thrust General Electric J79 turbojet—a project begun several years earlier. Several versions of the J79 powered Mirage, code-named Barak ("Lightning"), were completed and reportedly saw service during the Yom Kippur War.[16]

The Israel Defense Force/Air Force possessed a reasonably large stock of electronic countermeasures equipment, most supplied by the United States. The equipment reportedly included the Litton ALT-27 standoff electronic jammer, the Hughes Aircraft ALQ-71 barrage noise jamming pod, and the Westinghouse ALQ-87 noise jamming pod. In addition to such noise-emitting electronic countermeasures equipment, threat-warning sensors and chaff/flare dispensers were installed on many aircraft.[17]

All the jammers and deception devices were designed to degrade the effectiveness of search and acquisition radars, antiaircraft fire control radars, and the guidance radars for the SA-2 and SA-3 missiles.

While Israel was much better stocked with electronic countermeasures equipment than most air forces in the world in 1973, not all aircraft were fitted with radar-warning units, chaff/flare dispensers, or jamming pods. Nor was the equipment effective against the frequency range of all threat systems.

While electronic countermeasures were fairly successful in disrupting Egyptian and Syrian radar-directed missile and gun systems during the War of Attrition, the increasing density and variety of air defense weapons on both fronts made electronic countermeasures increasingly difficult to employ effectively.[18]

The Israel Defense Force/Air Force controlled all antiaircraft assets of the Israeli forces. Mirage IIIC and F-4 Phantom interceptors were the first line of air defense, but Israel also had about 400 20-mm and 40-mm antiaircraft guns and 10 batteries of Hawk surface-to-air missiles.[19]

An Egyptian MiG-21 on the taxiway of a desert airfield. In the left background is a shelter designed to protect aircraft against air attack.

Egyptian Air Force

The Egyptian Air Force commanded by Maj. Gen. Hosnay Mubarak possessed about 620 combat aircraft. Many were in storage, however. The aircraft: 210 MiG-21F, MiG-21PF, MiG-21MF fighter/interceptors; 100 MiG-17 fighter-bombers; 80 Su-7B ground-attack/fighter bombers; five Il-28 light bombers; 25 Tu-16 medium bombers.[20]

Egypt had been supplied with the late-model MiG-21MF Fishbed J capable of carrying an increased payload of air-to-ground ordnance[21]; it could fly at supersonic speeds at low altitude. Egypt also possessed a large fleet of helicopters, including 90 Mi-8s, between 20 and 30 Mi-6s, and between 70 and 80 Mi-4s.

Following the War of Attrition, the Egyptian Air Force instituted a new tactical training program designed to prepare more pilots for combat.

Students attended the Air Force Academy at Bilbeis in the Nile Delta where they underwent a two-and-a-half year academic course that included basic flight instruction on the Egyptian-built Gomhuriah piston-powered training aircraft. The students then flew 80 hours in Soviet-built Yak-18s for intermediate-level training before 170 hours of conversion and advanced training on Czech L-29 Delfin jet trainers. Graduates from the Bilbeis Academy spent one year at operational training units flying the fighters, bombers, or transports to which they were assigned. Despite the expanded training programs, however, Egypt was still short of pilots.[22]

Egyptian Air Defense Command

Commanded by Gen. Ali Fahmy, the air defense command was assigned to defend the Egyptian homeland and to protect forward troops in the field. Established in 1968 as an independent branch of the Egyptian Army, the air defense command comprised some 75,000 men, three times the Egyptian Air Force.[23]

Following the War of Attrition, Egypt greatly expanded the number of SA-2 and SA-3 surface-to-air missile sites along the Suez Canal. The weapons sites were hardened with concrete and sand.

Egyptian air defense weapons were positioned to provide overlapping coverage. The SA-2 missiles covered high-altitude approaches, while the SA-3s were set to engage aircraft at medium and low altitudes. Both of these semi-mobile systems were protected by large numbers of radar-directed and visually-sighted antiaircraft artillery guns.

In addition, new air-defense weapons introduced into service by the Soviet Union during and after the War of Attrition closed the Egyptian air-defense system's gap of vulnerability at very low altitude. One of the important weapons was the SA-6 surface-to-air missile system.

NATO code-named Gainful, the SA-6 system was designed to provide low-altitude and medium-altitude air defense for mobile forces. The SA-6 system consists of a radar/fire-control unit and four transporter/launcher vehicles each carrying three missiles. Both the radar unit and the launchers are mounted on a modified light tank chassis and has a limited degree of armored protection. The SA-6 missile has a slant range of about 17 miles against low-altitude targets and up to 35 miles against medium-altitude targets.[24]

Another new system was the ZSU-23-4 antiaircraft vehicle carrying four 23-mm guns. Mounted on a modified light tank chassis, the vehicle is equipped with the Gun Dish fire control radar. The 12-mile-range radar operates both as an acquisition and a tracking radar, incorporating a moving-target indicator to detect aircraft at low altitude. The four-barrel system has a cyclic rate of fire of 4,000 rounds per minute and an effective range of 9,800 feet. Against aircraft, the ZSU-23-4 usually fires in bursts of 50 rounds.[25]

The third new weapon against low-altitude aircraft introduced was the SA-7 Grail infrared-guided missile. The Soviet SA-7 had initially proved its effectiveness in 1972 in South Vietnam, where it was responsible for downing a significant number of helicopters and slower attack aircraft. The missile travels at Mach 1.5 and is effective up to two miles.[26]

To increase the effectiveness of these low-altitude weapons, Egypt established an extensive ground-observation network to ensure that the air defense system would function smoothly. Observers near the forward line of battle would scan the skies with binoculars for low-flying Israeli aircraft penetrating defended air space, and report them to the communications network via telephone and radio.

At the beginning of the Yom Kippur War, Egypt possessed more than 150 batteries of SA-2, SA-3, and mobile SA-6 surface-to-air missiles backed up by several thousand antiaircraft artillery guns and SA-7 launchers. More than 60 of those batteries were stationed along the

SA-6 missile launch vehicles parade through Red Square. The SA-6 surface-to-air missile has a slant range of about 17 miles and can hit targets at altitudes higher than 40,000 feet. The SA-6 was formidable during the Mideast conflict because Israel's electronic countermeasures equipment initially was unable to counter the weapon's Straight Flush continuous wave radar guidance system. (U.S. Army)

Suez Canal. Nine squadrons of MiG-21 interceptors remained on air defense command alert status.[27]

The strengthened Syrian air defense system included 12 fixed SA-2 and SA-3 batteries and 35 mobile batteries of SA-6 surface-to-air missiles. These were supported by more than 1,000 SA-7 missiles and antiaircraft guns, most concentrated on the plain immediately behind the Golan Heights.

Syrian Arab Air Force

Like the Egyptian Air Force, the Syrian Arab Air Force also had expanded its training program to produce increased numbers of pilots. And like the Egyptian air bases, most Syrian bases were equipped with protective shelters for aircraft, fuel, and munitions. The Syrian Arab Air Force strength by October 1973[28]: 200 MiG-21 fighter/interceptors; 80 MiG-17 fighter-bombers; 30 Su-7B fighter-bombers.

Over the summer and early autumn, the Syrian Arab Air Force reportedly phased into service late model MiG-21MF Fishbed J fighters and Su-7B fighter-bombers.[29]

In addition to the above, aircraft from several other Arab air forces participated in the conflict. Iraq deployed fighter-bombers to both fronts: one squadron of Hawker Hunters was stationed in Egypt, and two squadrons of Su-7Bs and one of MiG-21s flew missions from Syrian airfields. Algeria also sent one squadron of Su-7B fighter-bombers to Egypt, and Libya sent two of Mirage fighters to help Egypt.[30]

The Yom Kippur War

Day One: October 6, Yom Kippur

At 2:00 p.m., Egypt and Syria launched a simultaneous surprise attack along both the Suez Canal and the Golan Heights.

On the canal front, several thousand artillery guns, mortars, rocket launchers, and tank guns opened up a withering barrage against Bar Lev outposts and second-echelon units. Meanwhile, some 200 strike aircraft including MiG-21s, Su-7Bs, MiG-17s, and Iraqi Hawker Hunters bombed and strafed Israeli positions.

Targets included the forward airfields, headquarters for various units, communications and electronic countermeasures centers, artillery positions, Hawk missile batteries, and depots of armor and equipment.[31] Delayed-action bombs, timed to explode several hours after impact, were dropped on many targets, and according to Egyptian sources most Sinai airfields were out of action for 48 hours.

Israeli fighters scrambled from Ras Nusrani near Sharm el Sheikh and reportedly downed a number of the attacking aircraft.[32] In general, however, because of surprise, Egyptian losses were light; only a few aircraft were shot down by Israeli fighters, Hawk missiles, and antiaircraft fire.

At the canal, Egyptian engineers directed torrents of water from high-pressure hoses against the high sand wall built by the Israelis on the eastern bank, washing away gaps. Men and equipment were ferried across, and by nightfall several pontoon bridges spanned the canal.

A number of Israeli positions were hit by unguided FROG (Free Rocket Over Ground) missiles. Tu-16 bombers in the initial strikes launched Kelt standoff guided missiles against radar sites and communications centers in the Sinai. Some Kelt missiles were shot down by antiaircraft fire and by Israeli fighters, including one reportedly headed for Tel Aviv. While the missile was known to have its own crude radar guidance system, there was speculation that at least some had been fitted with an anti-radiation seeker, as two homed unerringly on Sinai radar sites and destroyed them.[33]

By late afternoon, the Israel Air Force began to press attacks on the ferries, personnel, and vehicles on both sides of the canal as well as vessels in the Gulf of Suez.

Israeli aircraft striking at Arab forces experienced dense antiaircraft fire and a number were shot down.

At dusk, a force of about 50 Egyptian Mi-8 helicopters carrying commando teams penetrated into the Sinai to attack the Israeli positions and to ambush reinforcements heading toward the front lines. The slow-moving transport helicopters suffered heavily from Israeli antiaircraft fire and fighters; 20 reportedly where shot down. Commando teams that succeeded in reaching their objectives, however, wreaked considerable damage and confusion.[34]

Meanwhile, along the Golan Heights, after an hour-long artillery barrage, three separate Syrian divisions comprising nearly 900 tanks attacked the Israeli lines held by two armored brigades of no more than 125 tanks. Syrian MiG-17s and Su-7Bs roared in, bombing and strafing Israeli headquarters, concentrations of armor, and other tactical targets, while MiG-21s protected them from Israeli fighters from above.

The Syrians concentrated on striking positions near the battle area; some Syrian fighter-bombers, however, attempted to attack deeper targets only to be met by Hawk missiles, antiaircraft fire, and interceptors.[35]

Simultaneous with the main assault, Syrian commandos, airlifted by Mi-8 helicopters, attacked the Israeli outpost on Mount Hermon. The Syrians surprised the small unit, composed mainly of observers and technicians, and captured the outpost on the first assault.

Beginning in early afternoon, large numbers of Israeli fighter-bombers struck Syrian columns with bombs, rockets, and napalm. The Phantoms and Skyhawks concentrated their attacks to slow tanks, armored personnel carriers, and other vehicles rather than suppressing the extensive Syrian air-defense system and, as a result, received heavy missile and antiaircraft fire.

Through sheer weight of numbers, the three-pronged Syrian head-on assault succeeded in pushing back the heavily outnumbered Israeli ground forces. By nightfall, the columns had penetrated 12 miles beyond the 1967 Six-Day War cease-fire line. Well equipped with night-vision equipment, the Syrians continued attacking late into the night.

Israeli interceptors succeeded in downing a number of Syrian aircraft and ground-attack aircraft had some success in bombing Syrian supply and reinforcement columns. Only three Israeli aircraft were shot down by the Syrian air defenses, which seemed to be lagging well behind their advancing armor.[36]

Day Two: October 7

At dawn of the second day of the war, Egyptian and Israeli naval units clashed. In the Red Sea near Sharm el Sheikh, Israeli patrol boats intercepted and sank several Egyptian landing craft carrying commando troops. A few hours later, Egyptian missile boats launched surface-to-surface missiles to strike Israeli shore installations in the Sinai. Israeli missile boats, helicopters, and bombers retaliated, reportedly sinking one Egyptian boat without loss.[37]

Around 6:30 a.m., the Israeli Air Force raided Egyptian airfields, bombing and strafing Beni-Suef, Bir Arido, Tanta, Mansurah, Shubrah-hit, Genaclis, and Kutamieh. As all the Egyptian aircraft were now protected by concrete shelters, the raids succeeded in little more than cratering the runways.[38] At least five of the attacking fighter-bombers, however, spun to earth when they were struck by Egyptian missiles and antiaircraft fire.

In the Sinai, most of the air effort on day two concentrated on destroying the Egyptian pontoon bridges and the infantry and armor crossing them. The attacking aircraft met a withering barrage of missile and antiaircraft fire. The heavy defenses, particularly the SA-6 with its undetectable continuous-wave radar, annihilated many aircraft. To evade the defenses, Israeli pilots used low-level, high-speed tactics. Even with low-level tactics, however, the bristling numbers of ZU-23, ZSU-23-4, and 12.7-mm antiaircraft guns plus the SA-7 shoulder-fired missiles all coordinating their fire under the guidance of forward observers exacted a heavy toll.

Egyptian Air Force MiG-17s and Su-7Bs attacked Israeli bases and columns, flying low to hit and run. Patrolling Mirage and Nesher interceptors, Hawk missiles, and antiaircraft batteries reportedly shot down 12 Egyptian attack aircraft and helicopters that day.

Egypt admitted losing 21 aircraft in the two days, but claimed 57 Israeli planes in return.[39]

Meanwhile on the Syrian front, ground, naval, and air forces of both sides were locked in fierce combat. An Israeli naval flotilla of five missile boats supported by observation helicopters engaged Syrian missile boats twice.

The Israeli flotilla reportedly sank four boats; Syria admitted losing one, but claimed sunk several of the Israeli fleet.

On the ground, the Syrian columns advanced, pressing back the Israelis, and by midday the leading units had fought their way to the edge of the Golan Heights overlooking the Jordan Valley.

To stem the tide of Syrian armor and to give reserve-force armored units time to meet the attack, large numbers of Israeli fighter-bombers flew against the Syrian columns. Mirages and Neshers shot down many attacking Syrian fighter-bombers, but Skyhawks, Phantoms, and Super Mystères suffered heavily. Caught up now and keeping pace with the advancing Syrian ground forces was the tight, integrated, air defense network of ZSU-23s, SA-6s, and other antiaircraft weapons.

Early that morning, the Israeli Air Force began a series of defense suppression attacks, using Shrike missiles and other weapons similar to those the Americans had employed in Vietnam. Several batteries of Syrian missiles and antiaircraft artillery near the front were reportedly damaged. A large number of strike aircraft were damaged or destroyed in the effort, and the attacks seemed to have little impact. The Israelis paused to appraise their ground attack tactics and decided not to directly take on the Syrian air defense network.[40]

Syria claimed 43 Israeli aircraft in the day's fighting and Israel claimed 19 Syrian aircraft. Both figures appear to be exaggerated, but both air forces indeed suffered heavy losses.[41]

Day Three: October 8

By the third day of the war, more than 80,000 Egyptian troops and several hundred tanks had amassed on the bank of the Suez Canal, and at least a dozen bridges had been constructed across it. Deep in the Sinai, Egyptian troops had dug defensive positions prickling with tanks, anti-tank guns, Sagger anti-tank missiles, and RPG-7 anti-tank rocket launchers, which had easily fought off the uncoordinated Israeli counterattacks.

Early in the morning, Egyptian fighter-bombers attacked Israeli forward air bases, Hawk missile sites, and headquarters of communications and command. Israeli and Egyptian fighters engaged in huge dogfights while fighter-bombers repeatedly strafed and bombed the pontoon bridges, Egyptian military concentrations, and the air-defense sites near Port Suez.

Israel claimed 15 Egyptian planes both in air battles and by antiaircraft.[42] Egypt, admitting the loss of 10 aircraft, claimed to have shot down 24 Israeli aircraft and helicopters.[43]

Meanwhile, on the Syrian front Israel's reserves had arrived. Air strikes helped stem the Syrian advance. Syrian MiG-17 and Su-7B fighter-bombers made a number of hit-and-run attacks, and MIG-21s and Iraqi Hawker Hunters continued to tangle with Mirages.

During the third day, Syria reported downing 34 Israeli fighters and Jordan claimed two Israeli aircraft that were trying to end run the formidable Syrian air defense system by flying through Jordanian airspace.[44] Israel reported downing three Syrian Su-20 swing-wing fighter-bombers, but photographs later showed the aircraft to be standard Su-7Bs.[45]

Day Four: October 9

Unsuccessful in counterattacks against dug-in Egyptian forces, the Israel forces consolidated their defensive line, continuing to bomb airfields, emplacements, pontoon bridges, and antiaircraft batteries near Port Said. During this day Egypt claimed 16 Skyhawks and Phantoms.[46] In the evening, Egyptian armor attempting to break out and widen the bridgehead toward Rus el Sudr exceeded their protective umbrella of surface-to-air missiles and were hammered by air attacks and counterattacking armor, losing many tanks and men.

Despite the heavy fighting with the Egyptians, it was the Syrian front that received most of the Israeli ground and air effort. Although the Syrians were being pushed back across the Golan Heights by strong armored columns, these forces retreated in good order and, when possible, counterattacked with fierce determination. Israeli air operations on the northern front were under the command of Maj. Gen. Mordechi Hod, former commander of the Israel Defense Force/Air Force. Commenting on the air war, Hod noted: "We've had complete air superiority over Golan since Sunday (the day before)." He added: "We operated 12 hours today with only occasional Syrian planes trying to intercept us. Most Israeli losses have come from ground fire and missiles, particularly the SA-6 which the Syrians had positioned just behind the battle line. These are the latest and best missiles the Russians have, better than anything the Americans encountered in North Vietnam."

While the missiles had caused many casualties earlier, General Hod said fewer were being fired. "Maybe they're running out of them," he remarked with a touch of humor. "I hope so."[47]

On the other hand, Iraqi MiG-21s and Hawker Hunters were particularly active over the Golan Heights, flying 80 sorties that day.[48] After the Syrians fired some 20 FROG long-range artillery rockets against Israeli civilian settlements, Israeli war planes began a full-fledged strategic air attack campaign, repeatedly striking at the headquarters of the Syrian Arab Air Force and at the Homs Oil Refinery north of Damascus.

Syria reportedly destroyed 23 Israeli aircraft, including three Phantoms lost in a dogfight following the air strikes.[49] While this boast was probably inflated, U.S. and Israeli sources disclosed that more than 50 Phantoms and Skyhawks had been lost since the start of the war only 100 hours earlier—more than half falling to Syrian defenses.[50]

An Israeli A-4N Skyhawk on takeoff. Israeli fighter-bombers, mostly Skyhawks and Phantoms, struck at Arab armored columns to slow their advance and enable Israel Defense Force reservists to mobilize during the Yom Kippur War. The extensive Syrian and Egyptian defenses shot down more than 50 Israeli aircraft by the end of the third day.

Day Five: October 10

The Egyptians moved additional armor and mobile batteries of SA-6 missiles and other air defense weapons into the Sinai to set up an even more powerful air defense screen. The Egyptians sent a few flights to stage limited attacks against Israeli bases in the northern Sinai, but in general most aircraft remained in their protective shelters.

Israeli ground, naval, and air units struck at the Egyptian bridgehead, meeting intense defensive fire. Israeli Air Force fighter-bombers attacked bridges, radar stations, missile batteries, and the airfields at Quwaysina and Abu-Hamed, but more often than not were repulsed.

The Egyptians claimed to have downed six Israeli planes, while Israel tallied five Egyptian aircraft.[51]

Again the major Israeli effort was concentrated against the retreating Syrian forces on the Golan Heights. Strong armored formations rolled forward, protected and supported by dozens of fighters and fighter-bombers. In addition to tactical targets near the front line, the Syrian refinery at Homs, and airfields as far inside Syria as Damascus, Haleb, Halhul, and Blei were struck. Dozens of swarming, confusing dogfights were fought over the Golan Heights as Israeli Mirages, Phantoms, and Skyhawks clashed with Syrian MiGs, Sukhois, and Iraqi Hawker Hunters.

Israel claimed that its fighters and antiaircraft fire shot down 18 Syrian aircraft during the day.[52] Syria listed 43 Israeli aircraft—clearly an inflated figure considering the evidence available.[53]

In response to the worsening situation on the Golan Heights, aircraft and ships from the Soviet Union began to resupply Syria with arms and equipment. On October 10 alone the Soviets landed 21 An-12 flights and one shipload of equipment.[54]

During the night, Israeli missile boats attacked the Syrian navy base at Minat al-Bayada. Syrian missile boats from Latakia challenged the Israeli missile boats and allegedly the Israelis sank two Syrian craft by missiles and gunfire.[55] Two foreign cargo ships were also hit and sunk as a result of the Syrian tactic of darting in and out among merchant ships anchored near the harbor.

An Israeli F-4 Phantom (far right) closes in on an Egyptian MiG-17 (left) over the Sinai, October 11, 1973. The MiG-17 was shot down seconds after this photograph was taken. (IDF/AF)

Day Six: October 11

On the Suez front, this day was one of consolidation; both sides strengthened their positions and conducted small-scale probing attacks with artillery and aircraft.

That evening, Egyptian forces attacked the Israeli naval bases at Abu Rudeis on the Gulf of Suez and Robuzu in the Mediterranean Sea, extensively damaging both installations. Later that night, naval units of both clashed off Port Said, and Gabriel missiles fired by the Israeli boats reportedly set aflame two Egyptian missile boats.

Meanwhile, Israeli armored spearheads on the Golan Heights continued to push toward Syria, at one point penetrating beyond the cease-fire line of the Six-Day War. Strategy seemed intent on knocking Syria out of the war before tackling the larger Egyptian incursion into the Sinai. Retreating Syrian forces continued to retire in good order, causing many Israeli casualties on the ground and in the air with accurate gun and missile fire. Israeli attacks occurred throughout the morning; fighter-bombers struck Syrian airfields at Blei, Seikal, Dmeir, Maza, Nasiriyak, Halhul, Damascus, and T-4 and several other strategic targets.

The Soviets continued to resupply Arab forces by air and sea, with the bulk of the materiel going to Syria. The Israelis, too, were receiving limited amounts of ammunition and missiles from U.S. stocks, flying the materiel across the Atlantic in their own El Al transports.

Six 750-pound bombs dropped from an Israeli Phantom on Syria's Nassarieh airfield on October 11, 1973. (IDF/AF)

Israeli troops examine the wreckage of an Egyptian MiG-17 downed in the Sinai on October 12, 1973. (IDF/AF)

Day Seven: October 12

Egyptian forces continued to expand on the canal's east bank, and began preparations for a major offensive to break out of the bridgehead. Aircraft saw action over the Sinai, bombing Israeli tanks and armored vehicles, headquarters, and radar stations. Israeli warplanes struck back, heavily bombing surface-to-air missile sites near Port Said and concentrations of armor near Ismailia.

Israeli pilots devised several tactics that apparently lessened the effectiveness of the SA-6 missile. Fighter-bombers carried chaff in internal dispensers, in pods, and even stuffed into airbreak cavities, and dispersed it with violent jinking maneuvers to evade tracking missiles. Helicopter-borne observers warned of missile launches to strike aircraft above, and pinpointed the site that launched the missile as a target for immediate attack. Aircraft took advantage of the low angle at which the missiles left the launcher by attacking the sites in a steep dive from high altitude, releasing bombs as they pulled up from the lowest point in the dive. The split "S" escape maneuver successfully used to shake the SA-2 and SA-3 missiles off the aircraft's tail did not seem to be nearly so effective against the SA-6 because of the newer missile's high speed and maneuverability.[56]

The Israelis heavily attacked Syrian forces, placing most emphasis upon the Syrian drive up the El Quneitra/Damascus road. Israeli warplanes pounded Syrian units and their supporting Moroccan and Iraqi contingents, and flew missions against Syrian airfields, bridges, and missile sites. Mirages, Neshers, and Phantoms met the defending MiGs, Sukhois, and Hunters in aerial combat over the front lines.

By day's end, Israeli fighters and antiaircraft reportedly shot down 16 Syrian and Iraqi aircraft.[57]

Western sources reported that in the one week since the war began, Syria had lost 80 warplanes, plus about seven helicopters. Egyptian losses totaled 82 aircraft: 49 MiG-21s, unspecified numbers of MiG-17s and Su-7Bs, and 17 transport helicopters. Israel reportedly lost 78 warplanes: 14 Phantoms, 29 Skyhawks, four Super Mystères and 28 other aircraft. Iraq admitted losing six Hawker Hunters.[58]

Day Eight: October 13

The Sinai front was again relatively quiet except for local battles and air actions.

The Soviet continued to resupply the Egyptians and Syrians; Israel pressured the United States for a similar effort to replace aircraft, tanks, and ammunition.

The heaviest fighting was still concentrated on the Syrian front as Israel continued to drive into Syrian territory. Near dawn, the Israelis battled with an Iraqi armored force comprised of some 8,000 men and 250 tanks; 70 Iraqi tanks were destroyed. In addition, Israeli helicopter-borne commandos set explosives on a bridge 60 miles northeast of Damascus, destroying it to disrupt the transport of Iraqi supplies and reinforcements to the Syrian front. The Israel Air Force continued heavy bombing, damaging Syrian airfields at Maza, Blei, Halhul, Damascus, Dmeir, and Seikal as well as missile sites and concentrations of Syrian and Iraqi armor.

After a week of Arab pressure for support, Jordan entered the war, moving its 40th Armored Brigade to the Syrian front.

Day Nine: October 14

This day dawned with full-scale bloody warfare in the Sinai. Following an intense artillery barrage and a series of early morning air attacks, Egyptian armored columns rolled forward to seize the Khatmia, Giddi, and Mitla Passes.

Libyan Mirage dropping practice bombs. During the Yom Kippur War, such aircraft staged a number of attacks on Israeli targets.

The widespread battle, involving more than 1,000 Egyptian and 800 Israeli tanks, was the largest armor engagement since World War II. While Israeli tanks and artillery exacted the heaviest Egyptian casualties, heavy Israeli air strikes broke up formations and damaged many vehicles. In the one-day battle, Egypt lost more than 250 tanks to Israel's 40. Israeli fighter-bombers also flew missions against surface-to-air missile sites west of the canal and against the airfields at Salahieh, Mansurah, and Tanta. On the Arab side, Egyptian aircraft and Libyan Mirages supported the day's tank battles.[59]

Meanwhile, the U.S. Air Force officially began its resupply flights to augment those of El Al. Air Force C-5 and C-141 aircraft carried missiles, bombs, and other war materiel across the Atlantic to restock Israel's depleted stores.

While the massive tank combat was grinding in the Sinai, fighting still raged in the Golan Heights. In an early morning battle north of Latakia, Syrian missile boats ambushed several Israeli craft, reportedly sinking two. Israel denied the loss, but did not claim to have inflicted any casualties. Arab forces, holding easily-defended terrain, prevented the Israelis from significantly advancing despite their heavy attacks. Syrian fighter-bombers continued their hit-and-run sorties against Israeli ground forces, causing considerable damage and numerous casualties.

The Israeli Air Force flew dozens of sorties to strike the Maza airfield and support the fighting on the front line.

Day Ten: October 15

Despite heavy losses in the previous days' battle, the Egyptians continued attacks to widen the bridgehead. Israeli units pounded the Egyptian tanks with artillery and tank fire, and made repeated air strikes. The Israelis also flew against the airfields at Kutamieh, Shubra-hit, and Tanta and against surface-to-air missile sites on both sides of the Suez Canal. Retaliating Egyptian fighter-bombers struck heavily at an Israeli convoy on the Sinai coastal road, destroying a number of vehicles.

Until the second half of the day, ground action in the Golan Heights was limited. In the afternoon, however, a fierce Israeli attack forced the Iraqi 3rd Armored Division to retreat several miles. In the air, numerous ground-attack and patrol missions were flown; losses from skirmishes amounted to a few aircraft on each side. The Soviet resupply effort, in effect since October 10, reached its highest point on the 15, when the Soviets reportedly delivered 550 tons of materiel.[60]

Day Eleven: October 16

The eleventh day of the Yom Kippur War began with full-scale fighting in the Sinai. Following a series of large-scale battles, Maj. Gen. Ariel Sharon's paratroopers drove in half tracks through a gap between the Egyptian 2nd Army and Great Bitter Lake. Israeli forces crossed the Suez in ferries and quickly established a bridgehead on the west bank; troops worked under fire to construct a pontoon bridge. Meanwhile, raiding columns, in Soviet tanks captured in the Six-Day War and disguised as Egyptian tanks, fanned out and destroyed Egyptian supply dumps, communications positions, and three SA-2 batteries.

Recognizing the significance of the Israelis' crossing, Egyptian forces shelled the bridgehead with artillery and bombed it. A late afternoon air strike developed into a full-scale dogfight as Israeli fighters zeroed in to engage the fighter-bombers.

In this air battle alone, 10 MiG-17s fell to the fighters and gunfire with no Israeli losses. And 10 more Egyptian fighters reportedly fell that same day to fighters, antiaircraft artillery, and Hawk missiles.[61] Egypt claimed to have destroyed 11 aircraft throughout the day with ground defenses and fighters.[62]

Along the Golan Heights to the north, an early morning counterattack by Jordanian, Iraqi, and Syrian forces became uncoordinated and was beaten back. Syrian MiGs and Su-7Bs actively bombed and strafed while Israeli warplanes in turn bombed strategic targets to the Syrians' rear.

Meanwhile, the new daily shuttle of U.S. Air Force C-5 and C-141 transports brought in missiles, ammunition, and new electronic countermeasures equipment. In addition, the U.S. rushed 25 F-4 Phantoms and a number of A-4 Skyhawks to make up the heavy losses.

Day Twelve: October 17

Heavy fighting continued both on the ground and in the air as Israel hastily constructed a pontoon bridge across the canal. Egypt counterattacked to destroy the incursion. Israeli planes bombed Kutamieh airfield, tanks, and armored vehicles, and surface-to-air missile sites—including targets near Port Said. As both sides sent in air forces over the bridgehead, numerous air battles occurred.

Both were also receiving huge quantities of weapons from their respective sponsors. During the previous eight days the Soviets had resupplied the Arabs with more than 5,500 tons of aircraft, weapons, and ammunition airlifted in some 350 cargo flights. The U.S., in addition to 25 F-4 Phantoms, conducted some 20 supply flights each day that unloaded a total of between 700 and 800 tons of bombs, missiles, and other weapons.[63]

As the fighting heated up on the canal, it remained essentially static on the Syrian front. However, artillery duels, tank ambushes, and patrol sorties continued.

Day Thirteen: October 18

Israeli aircraft bombed and rocketed Egyptian missile batteries, radar sites, the airfield at Zalahieh, and positions at Port Said; they also closely supported the division-size force in the Israeli west bank bridgehead. The Egyptian Air Force threw its full strength against the Israelis' makeshift pontoon bridges and a full-scale girder bridge built in the past several days. Israeli fighters now dominated the Sinai airspace unhindered near the bridgehead because Israeli ground forces had destroyed many surface-to-air missile sites and antiaircraft artillery batteries. MiG-17s, Su-7Bs, and armed transport helicopters bombed and strafed Israeli targets on the ground while MiG-21 fighters provided cover.

Nonetheless, Israeli fighters and antiaircraft fire exacted a heavy toll of the raiders, reportedly shooting down 27 aircraft—11 allegedly in one afternoon's battle.[64] Egypt related a different outcome, claiming 15 Israeli fighters and three helicopters.[65]

Meanwhile, on the Golan Heights Syrian MiG-17s and Su-7Bs attacked Israeli encampments and armored vehicles at several sites. Although the Israelis resisted with antiaircraft, the Air Force was fully occupied on the Sinai front on this day and thus could not counter with interceptions or air strikes.

Day Fourteen: October 19

Again the main combat was on the Suez front. Israeli forces surged forward to cut supply lines to the Egyptian 3rd Army in the Sinai. Israeli aircraft bombed Egyptian tanks, troops, and missile batteries along the canal, bridges near El Qantara, and targets in the Egyptian interior including the Tanta airfield in the Nile Delta. As Israeli ground units destroyed more missile and antiaircraft artillery sites, they created a significant breach in the Egyptian air defense system.

Egyptian fighters tried to plug the gap by intercepting Israeli aircraft and fighter-bombers and continued to fly sorties to maintain pressure on the Israelis' bridgehead. Air strikes and artillery damaged the Israeli bridges several times, but were quickly repaired.

Syrian, Iraqi, and Jordanian units attacked the eastern and southern side of the Israeli salient, the spearhead of Israeli forces jutting into Syrian territory near Sassa. Despite the fact that a number of Israeli brigades had been pulled out and sent to fight on the Sinai front, the defenses held firm. Air action was light, and Israeli spokesmen claimed but two Syrian aircraft in air battles.[66]

Day Fifteen: October 20

A Pentagon estimate of the losses on both sides to date was as follows:

Syria—149 fighters (mostly MiG-21s and Su-7Bs) and six helicopters. Egypt—113 aircraft, including 64 MiG-21s, 20 helicopters, one Tu-16, and 28 unidentified types. Iraq—21 fighters (MiG-21s and Hawker Hunters). Israel—105 aircraft, including 52 A-4 Skyhawks, 27 F-4 Phantoms, eight Mirage IIICs, five Super Mystères, and a number of helicopters and other aircraft. Most Israeli aircraft were downed by surface-to-air weapons. Only about 10 percent of the Israeli aircraft fell in air combat; non-combat accidents accounted for another 10 to 15 percent.[67]

Israel continued to send men, tanks, and vehicles across the Suez Canal. The Air Force supported the ground invasion with comparative impunity, now that Egyptian missile sites and antiaircraft batteries were minimized. Air battles were frequent as raiding Israeli fighters met defending Egyptian fighters over the canal and in the Egyptian interior. In the day's dogfighting Israel reported 11 Egyptian aircraft destroyed,[68] while Egyptian weapons claimed 15 Israeli fighters.[69]

Along the Syrian front, both sides shelled and skirmished to attain local gains. Both Israel and Syrian fighter-bombers blasted the battlefield; one Syrian aircraft was claimed by Israeli fighters during the day.[70]

Day Sixteen: October 21

Bitter, heavy air battles raged over the canal as both the Egyptians and Israelis sent large numbers of aricraft on offensive and defensive missions. Over the previous few days, Egypt launched more than 1,050 air-defense sorties to protect the interior, to fill the gap punched in the air defense network.[71]

Israeli ground forces had captured several airfields on the west bank, and transports began to land at the field at Fayid bearing supplies for the front.

Egyptian and Israeli claims for downed planes mirrored each other: 25.[72] With a large segment of the Egyptian air defenses out of action and the infusion of new U.S.-supplied aircraft, weapons, and electronic countermeasures equipment, however, it would seem likely that the Egyptians suffered a proportionately greater share of losses.[73]

On the Golan Heights, fighting flared during the morning as Syrian infantry with Jordanian and Iraqi tank support rolled forward and counterattacked Israeli forces near Sassa. At 4:00 p.m., the Israeli Golani Brigade assaulted the outpost on Mount Hermon in Syrian hands since the outbreak of the war. Helicopters transported troops to the outpost while aircraft and artillery bombarded the position. Syrian ground, air, and artillery units responded, resulting in a savage air and ground battle. Syrian fighters and fighter-bombers engaged Israeli aircraft and ground forces in fierce combat. Syrian Mi-8 helicopters hastened to bring reinforcements to the battered outpost, but the Israelis intercepted them and shot down several. On the ground, artillery shelling and fighting raged into the night.

Day Seventeen: October 22

On October 19, President Sadat had asked Soviet Premier Kosygin to convene the United Nations Security Council to initiate a cease-fire agreement. On October 21, U.S. Secretary of State Henry Kissinger flew to Moscow. On October 22, the U.N. Security Council met and passed Resolution 338 calling for a cease-fire for sundown that evening. Israel, Egypt, and Syria agreed to the plan.

Israel armored columns on the Egyptian front advanced in all areas to occupy as much terrain as possible before sundown. The Air Force repeatedly bombed ground targets along the canal and provided hundreds of sorties for tanks and other armored vehicles trying to surround the Egyptian 3rd Army.

Egyptian MiG-17 and Su-7B fighter-bombers forcefully attacked the advancing Israeli armor. Even L-29 Delfin jet trainers were armed and pressed into service. Israeli fighters and air defense weapons reportedly downed 11 Egyptian aircraft[74]; Egypt claimed 12 Israeli aircraft were downed by fighters and antiaircraft fire.[75]

The Arabs were feeling the impact of the U.S.-supplied weapons. Some 48 new F-4E Phantoms had already arrived from the U.S. Air Force's active inventory as well as a large number of A-4 Skyhawks. Several thousand advanced weapons, including Sidewinder air-to-air missiles, Shrike anti-radiation air-to-ground missiles, Walleye glide bombs, Maverick television-sensor guided air-to-ground antitank rockets, and Rockeye cluster bombs were rushed into combat. Egyptian commanders also hypothesized that U.S. pilots supplemented the Israeli pilots in combat late in the war.

Observed one Egyptian air defense officer: "These Phantom pilots we met after October 17 had a much different style to their combat tactics that we never encountered with the Israelis. Whether they were volunteer reservists or regular U.S. military pilots we don't know, but they were certainly not Israelis."[76]

Meanwhile, on the slopes of Mount Hermon Israeli troops fought to consolidate their hold. Troops of the 31st Paratrooper Brigade assaulted the outpost from the air to reinforce the Golani Brigade. Syrian helicopters also attempted to land reinforcements at their outposts, but after several were shot down including other aircraft, the Syrians terminated the attempt. Early in the evening, past the cease-fire time, the outpost on Mount Hermon was finally recaptured by a determined Israeli assault.

Day Eighteen: October 23

After a lull in action, the cease-fire was broken as the Arabs and the Israelis battled. Israeli tanks and armored vehicles again surged north and south of the canal to try to completely sever the supply lines to the Egyptian 3rd Army and capture the town of Suez. The Air Force pounded heavily the town and the positions of Egyptian 3rd army with bombs, missiles, and gunfire to pave the way for the armored columns.

Egyptian fighters intercepted a number of the Israeli attacks while fighter-bombers attacked Israeli armored spearheads that were spreading out north and south along the Egyptian west bank.

Meanwhile, in Syria the Israeli Air Force repeatedly bombed an oil depot northeast of Damascus and struck at Syrian armored columns advancing toward Mount Hermon. Syrian fighters contested the Israelis' raids in several dogfights.

Day Nineteen: October 24

With fast armor thrusts, the Israeli forces completely encircled the Egyptian 3rd Army, with warplanes supporting the columns' advance. By day's end, Israeli forces held all territory from just south of Ismailia to Adabiya, except for the town of Suez where they had been repulsed with heavy casualties.

A second lasting cease-fire took effect at 5:00 p.m.

Analysis

Israeli and Arab Strategy

The Yom Kippur War was fought primarily on the ground; however, the Israeli Air Force and Arab air forces and air defense units were heavily committed and played an important part in the overall conflict; nonetheless, because of the extensive Arab integrated air-defense network, the Israeli Air Force was less influential in the course of the battle on the ground than it had been six years earlier in the Six-Day War.

Its first priority was to defend Israel and her ground forces, and to engage and destroy Arab aircraft. While the claim that only five Egyptian, Syrian, or Iraqi air strikes penetrated Israeli defenses seems implausible, Israeli fighters, antiaircraft artillery, or missiles contested most Arab air attacks, destroying scores of planes. Israeli fighter-bombers were unable to provide effective support for ground units, however, until the Arab air-defense network was suppressed.

Israeli aircraft attacking near the forward edge of the battle area on both fronts initially suffered heavy casualties; the intensity and variety of the Arab air defense missiles and cannon were a lethal surprise.

Despite heavy losses, the Israelis continued to support their ground troops from the air, dropping bombs using low-risk delivery profiles, electronic countermeasures, and—when available—stand-off weapons. Through relentless, concentrated attacks, the Israelis temporarily suppressed the air-defense network near Port Said. Near war's end, a segment of the air defense network was destroyed by fierce ground fighting west of the canal.

A second major Israeli priority was interdiction of Arab transport, concentrations of military forces, and attacks on airfields and other strategic targets. Israel conducted a highly effective strategic air campaign against military and industrial targets in Syria. Such targets in Egypt, however, were much more heavily protected by surface-to-air missiles, antiaircraft artillery, and fighters. Israeli losses were high in proportion to the damage inflicted. During the war, the Israeli Air Force flew more than 500 sorties each day for a total of more than 10,000 sorties over the entire 18-day war.[77]

The major Arab offensive was based on ground troops and armor. The primary role of both the Syrian and Egyptian air forces was to defend their homelands from air attack. The Arab air forces' secondary mission was to attack Israeli forces and postions. Early in the war, the Syrian Air Force flew large numbers of sorties to support the advancing troops on the ground, but as the Syrians lost aircraft in air combat, their fighter-bombers were seen less frequently.

In the first few days of the war, Egyptian fighter-bombers heavily bombed Israeli airfields and command centers, but did not sustain the attacks at a high level. Except for defending home territory, ground controllers held the mass of the Egyptian aircraft in protective shelters until committing them against the Israeli bridgehead on the west bank.

The Arabs generally left defense of their forward battle area to their numerous antiaircraft missile and artillery systems rather than applying fighter cover. Very little information is available on the total sorties flown during the war. Semi-official figures in Arab publications, however, state that 6,815 sorties were flown during the war. The smaller Syrian Air Force and other Arab units probably logged fewer than half the number flown by the Egyptian Air Force. Therefore, it is reasonable to estimate that during the 18-day conflict Arab sorties totaled between 9,000 and 10,000.[78]

Losses and Resupply

The exact number of aircraft lost by each side can not be accurately determined. Israel claimed that Arab forces lost 451 aircraft.[79] According to Israeli sources, more than 370 Egyptian, Syrian, and Iraqi fighters, one Tu-16 bomber, and some 40 Arab helicopters fell to the guns and missiles of Israeli fighters in dogfights, for the loss of only four Israeli fighters.[80]

Maj. Gen. Benjamin Peled, commander of the Israel Defense Force/Air Force during the war, stated that altogether Israel lost 115 aircraft: four fighters in air combat, another one shot down accidentally by an Israeli fighter, 10 by accidents or unknown causes, 48 by surface-to-air missiles, and 52 by antiaircraft fire. Peled added that overall, Israel lost one aircraft per 100 sorties—a figure that compared quite favorably with the loss rate in the Six-Day War of four per 100 sortie.

Egyptian military officials have challenged General Peled's claim that only four Israeli aircraft were downed in dogfights. The commander of one three-squadron MiG-21 regiment indicated that his unit alone scored 22 kills in air combat, and as evidence has released gun-camera footage displaying several of the kills.[81]

Altogether, Arab forces claimed to have shot down several hundred Israeli aircraft, most falling to ground-based air defenses. At a news conference on October 21, Egyptian Maj. Gen. Issad Din Mulhtar reported that, on the Sinai front, Israel lost 303 fighters and 25 helicopters. When asked why this figure combined with Syrian claims exceeded the total number of aircraft believed to be in service, Mouhtar replied that the Israelis had started the war with 550 aircraft, not with the 450 generally quoted.[82]

U.S. intelligence sources estimated that Arab missiles and antiaircraft artillery claimed 80 percent of the Israeli aircraft shot down, air combat 10 percent. According to the same sources, 242 Egyptian aircraft, 179 Syrian aircraft, and 21 Iraqi aircraft were destroyed by all causes.[83]

While both sides suffered heavy losses, the Soviet Union and later the United States ferried in massive amounts of equipment. Soviet An-12 and An-22 transports flew 934 round trips to Egypt and Syria carrying missiles, ammunition, crated aircraft, and other materiel. In addition, an extensive sealift operation supplied an unknown quantity.

U.S. Air Force C-5 and C-i41 cargo transports flew 566 round trips to Israel, totaling 22,395 tons. Israeli El Al cargo aircraft carried a further 5,500 tons, and an American sealift operation delivered an additional unknown amount. Israel received more than 80 A-4 Skyhawks, 48 F-4E Phantoms, a dozen C-130 transports, and a number of CH-53 transport helicopters.

In addition, the United States supplied such sophisticated weapons as Sidewinder infrared-guided air-to-air missiles, Shrike anti-radiation missiles, Walleye glide bombs, Maverick television-sensor-guided air-to-ground antitank rockets, and TOW (Tube-launched Optically-guided Weapon) short-range anti-tank missiles.[84]

Arab Air Defense Network

One most frequently discussed aspect of the Yom Kippur War was the effectiveness of the Arab air defenses. Batteries of SA-2 and SA-3 surface-to-air missiles supported by mobile SA-6 and SA-7 missiles, plus ZSU-23-4 and other artillery systems covered Arab airspace with interlocking defenses from ground level to higher than 60,000 feet.

Israel was aware that the Arabs had an extensive air defense network, but was surprised by new weapons and their sheer numbers. The SA-2 and SA-3 missile systems were known quantities, but the SA-6 missiles and the ZSU-23-4 antiaircraft guns were nasty surprises. The SA-6 missile's radar was not susceptible to the Israeli electronic countermeasures equipment designed to disrupt the radars of the SA-2 and SA-3.

In addition, the missile's great speed and maneuverability made it more difficult for Israeli fighters to evade through violent twists and turns. The ZSU-23-4 with its high firepower destroyed a significant number of Israeli aircraft. Because the good weather and the generally barren terrain over both the Sinai and the Golan Heights allowed Arab operators to sight approaching aircraft very early, optically aimed antiaircraft cannon also downed many Israeli aircraft.

Such antiaircraft artillery as the ZSU-23-4 above were credited with downing a significant number of Israeli aircraft. (U.S. Army)

The density of the air defense networks on both fronts, however, posed a problem for Arab as well as Israeli aircraft. Even though Egyptian and Syrian aircraft were equipped with Identification Friend or Foe (IFF) equipment, a number of friendly aircraft were shot down in the heat of battle. Iraqi, Libyan, and other Arab air force units not supplied with adequate IFF lost even more planes to Arab air defenses.[85]

While Soviet-supplied surface-to-air missiles downed more than 40 Israeli aircraft, some 2,100 missiles were fired to score those kills.[86] According to Peter Bougart writing in 1977 in *International Defense Review,* an average of 55 SA-6 missiles were fired for each kill.[87] If correct, the SA-6 performed about the same as the older SA-2 against U.S. aircraft seven years earlier over North Vietnam (one kill for every 60 launches).

The SA-6 surface-to-air missile proved its potency as an antiaircraft weapon by destroying several dozen Israeli aircraft.

The SA-7 shoulder-fired missile, although a nuisance to the Israelis, scored few vital blows. The Arabs fired large numbers of the infrared-guided missile but, while the missiles damaged more than 30 Israeli aircraft, they downed only two. Aircraft at high speed were relatively immune to the SA-7 because they could outpace the short-range tail-homing missile.

To counter the new Arab air defenses, the Israel Defense Force/Air Force modified tactics, employed chaff, installed new U.S. supplied electronic countermeasures equipment, and repeatedly staged extensive defense-suppression attacks. While all these efforts reduced Israeli losses, the Arab air defenses continued to claim victims all through the war. Aggressive sabotage from the ground, particularly the Israeli offensive west of the Suez near war's end, proved to be the most effective way to blunt the air defense threat.

On the Golan Heights, Israeli ground offensive took a different tack: It forced Syrian and other Arab units to fall back so that their air-defense assets were thinned out along the expanded defensive line. This ground action, when combined with judicious air attacks at low-risk profiles, electronic countermeasures, defense-suppression strikes, and the strategic interdiction campaign, finally weakened the Syrian air-defense system.

Israeli Air Defenses

Although most media attention both during and after the war centered on Arab air defenses, Israel also possessed an effective air defense network. The Israel Defense Force/Air Force operated 10 Hawk missile batteries and several hundred 20-mm and 40-mm antiaircraft guns.

Israeli fighters downed many Arab attackers, but batteries of Hawk missiles, dug into reinforced sites around headquarters, air bases, and other likely targets, also claimed more than a dozen Arab planes. The radar-guided system of Hawk missiles, supplied by the United States, was several times more effective than the Soviet-supplied surface-to-air missiles. The Israelis' mobile and fixed 20-mm and 40-mm antiaircraft cannon also shot down a number of Arab aircraft and succeeded in destroying several Kelt missiles.

Firing of a U.S.-built Hawk surface-to-air missile. Israeli Hawk missiles and antiaircraft guns scored against a large number of Arab aircraft during the Yom Kippur War. (U.S. Army)

According to the Israeli magazine *Born In Battle*, the following Arab aircraft were downed by antiaircraft fire and surface-to-air missiles[88]:

Type Aircraft	by AAA	by SAM
MiG-17	19	5
MiG-21	10	1
Su-7	6	3
Hawker Hunter	3	1
Mirage	0	1
Helicopters	2	2
Total	30	13

Reproduction of data with permission of *Born In Battle* magazine.

When the U.S. was resupplying Israel's stores, it provided the U.S. Army's mobile forward air defense weapon, the Chaparral. The Chaparral system consists of four Sidewinder infrared-guided missiles mounted on a tracked vehicle.

The missile is aimed and fired by a gunner tracking the target through an optical sight. An Israeli Chaparral battery downed a Syrian MiG-17 over the Golan Heights near the end of the war.[89]

Striking Ground Targets

The war began when Egyptian and Syrian Su-7Bs and MiG-17s bombed and strafed Israeli airfields, headquarters, and supply centers. As the war raged on, Iraqi Hawker Hunters and Libyan Mirages also struck Israeli military positions in the Sinai.

During the final week of the war, the Egyptians heavily attacked the bridgehead on the west (Egyptian) bank of the Suez Canal. Cairo sources reported to *Aviation Week & Space Technology* that the Egyptian Air Force fought 18 battles over the bridgehead. In the last week of the war alone, the Egyptians flew more than 2,500 sorties trying to destroy the Israeli bridges and concentrations of armor and troops. The Egyptians sent anything into the air that could bomb: MiG-17s, Su-7Bs, and even L-29 Delfin jet trainers and Mi-8 transport helicopters.

Although the various Arab air forces used a variety of tactics to attack Israeli positions, they usually preferred fast low-altitude, low-angle strafing or rocket runs. In general, MiG-17s and Su-7Bs peppered the ground with cannon fire and unguided rockets; bombing attacks were in the minority.[90]

With the exception of the Libyan Mirages, Arab attack aircraft did not have the performance, payload capacity, or weapons delivery systems equal to Israeli fighter-bombers. Limited experience of most Arab pilots also reduced the Arabs' ability to provide effective close support to their ground troops or strike at Israeli rear-area targets.

Despite heavy losses to Israeli air defenses, the Arabs continued to fly strike sorties. Low-level attacks frequently caught Israeli defenses unprepared, and these strikes were successful in causing many casualties and considerable damage.

Smoke rises from bomb craters on an Arab runway. Israeli attacks against airfields damaged runways but destroyed few aircraft because most were harbored in concrete shelters.

The Israelis flew the Phantom primarily for strategic interdiction—bombing airfields, Arab resupply convoys, surface-to-air missile sites, and other strategic targets in rear areas.

Depending upon the tactical situation, the F-4 Phantom also flew close-support and air-superiority missions. One of the Phantom's more difficult missions was offensive counter air against Arab airfields.

After the devastation of the Six-Day War in 1967, the Egyptians and Syrians had built concrete shelters for all aircraft, weapons, fuel and command posts, and staunchly defended them with fighters, missiles, and artillery. The Israelis managed to destroy about 20 fighters and transports in attacks on Syrian airfields but succeeded in only cratering the runways of Egyptian airfields.

Although the Phantom proved to be highly capable in both attack and air combat during the 2½-week war,[91] the extensive Arab air defense system and Arab fighters downed some 35 F-4s.

The Israelis flew the A-4 Skyhawk mainly to provide close air support for ground troops. The Skyhawk (and to a lesser extent the Phantom) initially slowed the Arab offensive both in the Sinai and along the Golan Heights, to give Israeli reserves precious hours to mobilize. Most Skyhawk bombing runs were near the forward edge of battle area where Arab air defenses were bristling; consequently, the Skyhawk suffered the heaviest losses. During the 18-day war, no fewer than 52 were shot down.[92]

The light-attack bomber proved to be quite tough. Many Skyhawks returned to base with damage that would have downed other fighter-bombers. The older, lower-powered A-4E, A-4F, and A-4H models were lost noticeably more often than the higher powered A-4N,[93] which could maneuver tightly and sustain high speed at low altitude even when it was heavily loaded with armament.

The Israelis' single squadron of Super Mystère B-2s was pressed into service to supplement the Skyhawks for close support. The Super Mystère suffered high losses relative to the small numbers in service, six being downed.

During the Yom Kippur War, the Israel Defense Force/Air Force fought with its full range of air-to-ground weapons. Most frequently, general-purpose bombs were carried by strike aircraft. Cluster bomb units were dropped on surface-to-air missile sites, antiaircraft gun emplacements, convoys, and large-area targets. Shrike anti-radiation missiles were frequently fired at surface-to-air missile radars. Even napalm and unguided rockets were used against ground forces.[94]

Late in the conflict, the United States supplied Israel with a variety of "smart" weapons including Maverick television-camera guided missiles and laser-guided bombs. These weapons proved quite effective. Although introduced only in the final days of the war, the Maverick missile allegedly destroyed between 30 and 50 Arab tanks, other vehicles, and bunkers.[95]

The Israel Defense Force/Air Force has not officially released any reports on the strike tactics it continuously evolved while attempting to circumvent and destroy the intense Arab air defenses. It is known, however, that Israeli planes attacked SA-6 batteries from high-angle dives; they struck other tragets inside the Arab defenses at low level and then "popped up" to release bombs while evading surface-to-air missiles.[96]

Air Combat

Air-to-air combat during the Yom Kippur War was highly intense. Large-scale dogfights between as many as 40 to 60 aircraft occurred over the Sinai Desert, the Suez Canal, and the Golan Heights. Many were fought at low level as fighters tangled with opposing ground-attack aircraft and their escorts.

The primary air combat fighter of the Syrian, Egyptian, and Iraqi forces was the MiG-21. Armament and performance of the many MiG-21 models in service varied, but all could carry the Soviet K-13 Atoll infrared-guided air-to-air missile.

Arab pilots found it difficult to make the limited-performance missile lock on to a highly maneuvering fighter-size target, even from an optimum firing position.[97] Early-model MiG-21F Fishbed C and late-model MiG-21MF Fishbed J were equipped with the NR-30 30-mm cannon and GSh-23 23-mm cannon respectively. The cannons were fired with some success from gentle turns, but during a banking maneuver of more than 2.75 gs, the lead-computing gyroscopic gunsight had a tendency to tumble out of balance, leaving the pilot to aim only by eye.[98]

Egyptian MiG-21PF Fishbed D fighters also reportedly employed the Soviet K-5 Alkali radar-guided missile. As with the K-13 Atoll, however, this early-generation missile was difficult to fire in a fast-moving dogfight. As a result, Arab pilots flying MiG-21s were often able to get into firing positions, but were unable to shoot down Israeli aircraft because of technical limitations of their missile or gun-aiming systems.

Egyptian MiG-21s with a full complement of air-to-air and air-to-ground weapons on display at an Egyptian airfield. A late-model MiG-21MF Fishbed J is flanked by two earlier-model MiG-21PF Fishbed D interceptors.

Iraqi Hawker Hunters were sent on air combat missions. The maneuverable fighter was heavily armed with four 30-mm Aden cannon, but it did not have the acceleration or the thrust of the Phantom or Mirage or Nesher and it did not carry air-to-air missiles.

Arab pilots were primarily taught Soviet-style tactics of ground-control intercept, with limited emphasis on tactical initiative. Egyptian pilots were taught low-altitude/low-speed dogfight tactics by Pakistan Air Force instructors.[99] As day-to-day flying was restricted by alerts, maintenance, and the desire to conserve aircraft, however, the pilots did not get the training and the hours of practice needed to become highly proficient, especially against such skilled adversaries as the Israelis.

While on patrol, Egyptian fighters flew in the classic formation known as "Finger Four."[100] Finger Four, devised by the Luftwaffe in World War II, consists of two pairs of fighters flying in a slight V-formation in positions similar to the position of one's fingertips in the outstretched hand. The aircraft fly several hundred yards apart, giving each room enough to maneuver and to keep watch on one another's tail. When engaged in combat, the Finger Four formation breaks up into the two original pairs, each being composed of an attacker and his protective wingman.

The Syrians frequently sent mixed formations of MiG-17s and MiG-21s on its air combat patrols. Two MiG-21s were trailed by two MiG-17s in a loose formation.[101]

Israel was not able to stop Arab incursions into her airspace, but established clear superiority over those areas of the Golan Heights, the Sinai Desert, and the west bank where Arab air defenses were not concentrated. In dogfights alone, Israel Defense Force/Air Force officials claimed to have shot down more than 370 Egyptian, Syrian, Libyan, and Iraqi fighters while losing only four Israeli aircraft—a kill ratio greater than 90 to one.[102]

Other reports listed the Israel Defense Force/Air Force as having downed about 335 Arab aircraft.[103] The U.S. Air Force estimated that 10 percent of Israeli aircraft were lost in air combat (115, thus about 12 fighters were believed to have been downed by Arab fighters). Given this more conservative estimate, the Israeli/Arab kill-to-loss ratio would still be about 30 to one. Skilled pilots, efficient command and control, high-performance aircraft, and superior air-to-air weapons all contributed to the Israelis' extremely one-sided kill ratio.

The extensive Israeli surveillance system and centralized command-and-control network was a significant factor in the air superiority battle. Israeli Air Force operations were directed by a single commander who had the necessary data and communications facilities to deploy and instantly redirect his forces to meet changing threats.

While efficient command, control and communications contributed to the effectiveness of the Israeli air defense effort, the Arabs applied measures that reduced the advantage. The Soviet-trained and supplied Arab forces were equipped with electronic systems that could monitor and jam Israeli radio communications.

The Israelis' force of Mirage IIIC and Nesher fighters was tasked with air superiority and strike escort responsibilities. Armed with two Israeli-made DEFA cannon and two Shafrir or Sidewinder air-to-air missiles, these fast, maneuverable delta-wing dogfighters scored most of the Israelis' air combat kills.

The Mirage IIIC (above) and Israeli-built Nesher (not shown) served as the primary air superiority aircraft. Armed with two 30-mm cannon and two infrared-guided air-to-air missiles, the fighters were credited with a majority of Israel's 1973 air combat victories. Note the eight circular kill markings under the cockpit windows. (J. Margulies)

Israeli F-4E Phantoms flew both air superiority missions and strike missions during the Yom Kippur War. This Phantom is credited with one air combat kill. (IDF/AF)

The F-4 Phantom also frequently found itself in air-to-air combat. The Phantoms were usually armed with AIM-7E Sparrow missiles, AIM-9 Sidewinder missiles, plus an internal 20-mm cannon.

Israeli pilots noted that they owed much to the excellent performance of both the Shafrir and the late-model Sidewinder missiles.[104] The infrared-guided Shafrir, developed by the Israeli Rafael armament development laboratory, proved highly effective even in the demanding environment of a high-g dogfight. Armed with a 24 lb. warhead triggered by both impact and proximity fuses, the missile had a remarkable success rate of 56 percent.[105]

Late-model AIM-9 infrared-guided Sidewinder missiles from the United States also used extensively in the conflict, performed comparably well. Nearly 200 of the Arab aircraft destroyed were downed by the Shafrir or Sidewinder infrared-guided missile.[106]

In general, Israeli fighters sought to use their infrared missiles first and then close to short range to fire their cannon. In the large, confusing air battles, Israeli pilots used missiles more frequently than the cannon becaue they quickly broke away after each attack to preserve their own skin. Even so, according to Israeli General Peled, more than 50 Arab aircraft fell to Israeli cannon fire.[107]

Compared to the infrared heat-seeking missiles, the radar-guided AIM-7 Sparrow missile scored more modestly, accounting for only about seven air-to-air kills. Israeli officials reported that the Sparrow had a success rate of 42 percent, indicating that perhaps 17 had been fired.[108] The Sparrow, carried by the F-4 Phantom, required more preparation to fire than the infrared-guided missiles, and also required that the pilot keep his radar locked onto the enemy target until the Sparrow scored home.

The Israel Defense Force/Air Force has never released information on its tactics, particularly those of air-to-air combat. However, an interview with an Israeli wing commander who flew as a pilot in the Yom Kippur War revealed that Israeli tactics were quite similar to those of the U.S. Navy.[109]

The basic U.S. Navy air combat tactic practiced today is called Loose Deuce. In the Loose Deuce tactic, aircraft fly in a line abreast, laterally separated by between three-quarters to one-and-a-half miles. In contrast to older tactical formations such as Finger Four or Fluid Four, where each attacking aircraft was closely defended by a wingman, both members of a Loose Deuce pair act alternately as attacker and defender. Teamwork is essential. One fighter engages the target while the other positions itself to protect the attacker and to be ready to take over the offensive. Each engages the target alternately until scoring a kill. Should enemy reinforcements interfere with the attack, the free fighter of the Loose Deuce pair can engage them to protect his partner.

The Egyptians and the Syrians had the advantage of prior planning, greater numbers, and surprise. They used these elements to drive back Israeli ground forces, destroy large numbers of vehicles and aircraft, and inflict sizable casualties. The Israelis used their superior aircraft to overcome the formidable odds, and eventually came to hold the upper hand in the air and on the ground.

CHAPTER VIII

Continuing Middle East Conflicts: 1973-1983

Introductory Overview

While the cease-fire agreement among Israel, Egypt, and Syria ended the large-scale Yom Kippur War on October 24, 1973, local skirmishing continued along both borders well into 1974. In 1974, after much negotiation between all the countries aided by U.S. Secretary of State Henry Kissinger, the United Nations established a buffer zone along the Suez Canal and along the Golan Heights. In 1979, Israel and Egypt signed a permanent peace treaty, in which Israel would return the Sinai to Egypt in return for Egypt's recognition of the State of Israel. The return of the Sinai was completed in April 1982.

While the fighting between Israeli, Egyptian, and Syrian forces thus ceased in 1974, in the following years Arab guerrillas, based primarily in camps inside the borders of Lebanon, continued to attack Israeli outposts—dramatically increasing their assaults after the Israeli-Egypt peace treaty of 1979. Israel retaliated by periodically bombing and then in 1982 destroying guerrilla base camps in southern Lebanon through direct attacks by ground forces.

In 1981 Israel, in order to prevent an Arab country from gaining the potential for a fission bomb, attacked a French-built nuclear power plant near Baghdad, extending hostilities to Iraq.

Meanwhile, the Middle East wars have not been limited to Arab-Israeli conflicts. In 1977, Egyptian and Libyan forces clashed, and, in September 1980, a long grinding war began between Iran and Iraq.

Skirmishing 1973-1979

While the cease-fire of October 24, 1973, ended large-scale conflict, over the following weeks Egyptian and Israeli forces continued to clash in local skirmishes. On November 11, both sides signed an agreement establishing a solid cease-fire and opening the way to exchange of prisoners. In late November, 241 Israelis and 8,031 Egyptians were repatriated.

Nonetheless, violations of the second cease-fire along the Sinai front escalated as both nations sought to reaffirm their resolve. On December 6, patrolling Israeli and Egyptian fighters met in the air over the Gulf of Suez. In the resulting dogfight, Egypt claimed one F-4 Phantom while Israel allegedly scored a MiG-21 fighter.[1]

In early January 1974, Secretary of State Kissinger shuttled between Cairo and Tel Aviv, attempting to end the fighting and negotiate a more permanent peace. On January 17, Egypt and Israel both agreed to withdraw troops to an established cease-fire line and ended all fighting.

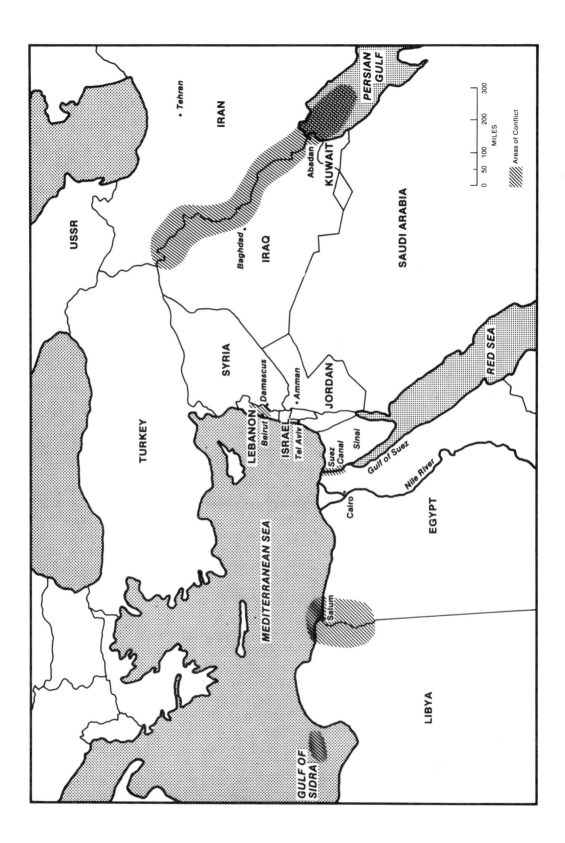

Meanwhile, along the Sinai front the October 24 cease-fire ending the Yom Kippur War remained in effect on the Golan Heights for the first two weeks. On November 6, however, Syria claimed that Israeli aircraft attacked Syrian radar sites with Shrike missiles.[2] The two countries sporadically fired artillery and dueled with tanks over the next several months but, by mid-January 1974, all was quiet.

Suddenly, on January 26, Syrian artillery once more pounded Israeli troops and vehicles. Israeli forces responded and small-scale battling wore on daily for the next two months. Dr. Kissinger met with Syrian President Hafez al-Assad and Israeli Prime Minister Golda Meir and tried to bring about a cease-fire and a plan to negotiate a more permanent peace, but to little avail.

On April 6, the Israeli Air force flew into action against Syrian forces for the first time since the Yom Kippur War. Fighting continued for the next two days and on April 8, Syria claimed to have shot down an Israeli F-4 Phantom. Israel acknowledged losing a Phantom, but noted that a malfunction had caused the jet to catch fire and the two crewmen had bailed out over Lebanon.[3]

On April 13, Syrian infantry supported by heavy artillery tried to storm the Israeli outpost on Mount Hermon. Israeli planes bombed the attackers while artillery backed the dug-in Israeli infantry; by late afternoon, the Syrians were driven back down the slopes.

On April 19, Mount Hermon became the focal point of a major air battle. In a vicious dogfight, Syria announced that its fighters scored seven Israeli jets and its air defenses 10 more, for the loss of only one MiG. Israel admitted that two planes fell to antiaircraft fire, but that its fighters picked off two Syrian aircraft.[4]

News reporters, visiting the Syrian slopes of Mount Hermon on April 24, witnessed several Israeli bombing runs against Syrian troops and vehicles, observing one striking aircraft falling in flames after being hit by a Syrian missile.[5]

After five days of relative calm, Syrian MiG-17s roared in formation over the mountain and bombed the Israeli outpost and artillery shells rained down heavily. Retaliating Israeli fighters tangled with the MiG-21s that flew a protective patrol for the MiG-17 bombers, shooting down four with air-to-air missiles and cannon fire.[6]

Dr. Kissinger returned to Damascus and Tel Aviv to try to end the fighting. Prime Minister Meir and President Assad still substantially disagreed on the terms of a disengagement treaty, but negotiations began to progress.

After a month of intense talks, on May 30 both Syria and Israel finally agreed to a cease-fire and troop disengagement.

While the fighting between the armed forces of Israel, Egypt, and Syria thus ceased in 1974, guerrillas continued to terrorize and kill Israelis—sniping that has continued into the 1980s. Israel established a policy of preemptive and retaliative attacks against guerrilla base camps, primarily along the Lebanese border: hundreds of bombing runs were flown and dozens of ground raids staged into Lebanon to destroy Palestinian bases and operations.

Middle East Air Forces

Since 1974, the air forces of Syria, Egypt, and Israel have been considerably upgraded.

Syria

The Syrian MiG-21, Su-7B, and MiG-17 fighters downed during the Yom Kippur War were replaced and supplemented by the Soviet Union with more advanced MiG-21, MiG-23, and MiG-25 fighters and swing-wing Su-20 Fitter C fighter-bombers. Moreover, Syria developed an expanded pilot-training program to build a larger reserve. Soviet, North Korean, and

Egyptian and U.S. Air Force F-4E Phantoms over the pyramids. Egypt was supplied with Phantoms as part of a U.S. aid package following the Egyptian-Israeli peace treaty of 1979. (U.S. Air Force)

Vietnamese advisers reportedly instruct and pay particular attention to weapons training, tactics, and flying skills.[7]

Egypt

The Egyptian Air Force, once an almost totally Soviet-style force, has been rapidly reequipping with Western tactical systems.

Egypt has numerous squadrons of Soviet-built MiG-21 Fishbed and Su-7 Fitter B still in service. The Egyptian Air Force also is equipped with several squadrons of Mirage IIIE/ Mirage 5 purchased from France, F-4E Phantoms provided by the United States, plus a large number of F-6s (MiG-19s) and F-7 (MiG-21s) supplied by the People's Republic of China. The United States has supplied F-16 fighters and Egypt is building Alpha Jet trainers and plans to purchase French Mirage 2000 fighters.

Egypt and Israel have not fought in the air since clashing over the Gulf of Suez on December 6, 1973. It is worth noting, however, that Israel has not been the only Egyptian adversary. In 1977, the Libyans opened hostilities with their Arab neighbor Egypt.

Following the Yom Kippur War in 1973, relations between Egyptian President Sadat and Libyan leader Col. Muammar el Qadaffi deteriorated. On July 21, 1977, after several border conflicts, Libyan and Egyptian tanks and armored vehicles clashed near the Egyptian village of Salum on the Mediterranean coast. Libyan aircraft bombed Egyptian outposts, with two planes reportedly falling to air defenses. The next day, Egyptian fighter-bombers including swing-wing Su-20s bombed and strafed the Libyan airfield El Aden near Tobruk. Air raids, dogfighting, and ground attacks raged for several days until Kuwait and other Arab governments called for a cease-fire.

Egyptian air attacks destroyed several Libyan military positions, including three radar stations and a half dozen aircraft at El Aden. Libya claimed to have downed a large number of Egyptian aircraft with interceptors and air defenses; Egyptian spokesmen admitted that two of the new Su-20 fighter-bombers had been lost.[8]

Israel

By the 1980s, the Israel Defense Force/Air Force was substantially more powerful than at the beginning of the Yom Kippur War. The air superiority element was upgraded by the addition of U.S.-built F-15 Eagle and F-16 Fighting Falcon fighters and Israeli-built Kfir tactical aircraft. The Kfir is the Israeli version of the Mirage 5 powered by the Phantom's General Electric J79 engine. the Israelis also bought several American-built E-2C Airborne Warning and Control System (AWACS) aircraft, which can survey and control strike missions while standing off miles from the battlefield. All Israeli combat aircraft now have electronic countermeasures including systems for detecting enemy radars, dispensers for chaff and flares, and jamming pods.

The Israelis have also added many new weapons and changed tactics to cope with the Arab air defense threat. The Israeli Army now provides much of its own firepower support with new self-propelled artillery, surface-to-surface unguided rockets, and the American-built Lance missile. The Lance missile by Vought Corporation is normally built to carry a nuclear warhead.

Kfirs on the production line at Israel Aircraft Industries. The aircraft scored its first air combat victory on June 27, 1979, when it downed a Syrian MiG-21 with a Shafrir infrared-guided, air-to-air missile. (IDF/AF)

Israeli Lance missiles carry a non-nuclear cluster-bomb-type warhead containing 836 BLU-63 bomblets whose fragments can pepper an area half a mile across, ripping holes in vehicles and buildings, and effectively knocking out missile sites. Israel also has a force of Hughes 500D and AH-1S helicopters carrying TOW anti-tank missiles for supporting ground forces.

Israel has also developed a television-guided air-to-ground missile called LUZ-1, which can be fired miles away from battle. Also on hand for standoff attacks are the U.S.-built Shrike missile, Maverick missile, laser-guided and electro-optically guided bombs.[9]

Egypt/Israeli Peace Treaty, 1979—And Reactions

Israel and Egypt negotiated for five years. Finally, in the spring of 1979, the two signed a treaty. Under its terms, Israel would return the Sinai to Egypt in exchange for recognition of Israel as a sovereign state—terms fulfilled by April 1982.

After the treaty's signing, such Arab guerrilla groups as the Palestinian Liberation Organization (PLO) dramatically increased their assaults against Israel. In retaliation, Israel increased its aerial reconnaissance and bombing runs over terrorist camps, primarily in Lebanon. Since the 1975-76 Lebanese Civil War, Syria maintained a 30,000-man peacekeeping force in Lebanon. Syrian planes began flying protective patrols over garrisons in central Lebanon to demonstrate Syria's unacceptance of the Israelis' renewed air strikes.

On June 27, 1979, a force of F-4 Phantoms and A-4 Skyhawks flew north from Israeli bases to attack suspected guerrilla facilities near Sidon and Tyre in southern Lebanon. The attack aircraft were protected by a force of F-15 Eagle and Kfir fighters. An Israeli E-2C AWACS aircraft orbiting off the Lebanese coast monitored the mission. When between eight and 12 Syrian MiG-21 fighters tried to attack the strike aircraft, they were immediately engaged by the covering Eagles and Kfirs. One F-15 pilot recounted the engagement in *Born In Battle* magazine: "Definite identification: Tallyho! enemy aircraft! We headed for them at once—we all knew that whoever got in close fastest would down the first MiG. Within seconds, I was on the tail of one, in fire position. Locking the IR missile, I fired immediately. The MiG never even had a chance to break away—my missile got it at close range and it exploded in mid-air. I had apparently hit the fuel system. I broke away at once, toward the second MiG—but it wasn't there any more. While I'd been blasting 'my' MiG out of the sky, my buddies had taken care of four more!"

Another F-15 pilot related his version: "We took off, fully armed for air-to-air combat, to cover the attacking aircraft. We linked up with the Kfirs on the way and climbed to 20,000 feet. Up there, the air is clear and there's no condensation. We patrolled the length and breadth of the "Battle Triangle," knowing all the time that we could run into MiGs at any moment. Over Sidon, we received orders to head north—enemy aircraft were heading for us at 15,000 feet.

"The radar showed two MiG formations advancing on us—one attacking, one covering. The MiGs were no more than 10 miles from our strike aircraft. Hitting the afterburners, we swooped down on them. They tried to break away when they saw what we were up to—but they never had much chance to do so: we had already locked onto most of them, splitting them up between us like wolves dividing their prey. 'My' MiG was one of the second formation. The F-15 pilots hit the MiGs the moment they came within range. I wanted to make sure of my MiG and closed in, not waiting for him to approach me. By the time I got within firing range, three of the MiGs were already spiralling down. I slowed down, aimed, and fired a missile, and climbed above it—so my aircraft wouldn't be inadvertently damaged. My # 2 confirmed my kill.[10]

A fifth MiG-21 was jumped by Kfir and shot down with a Shafrir infrared-guided air-to-air missile.

According to an Israeli communiqué, five MiG-21s had been destroyed and two others damaged in two fast dogfights, each lasting only two or three minutes.[11]

Syria admitted losing four aircraft, but also claimed two Israeli fighters.

Over the summer of 1979, Syria strengthened its air defenses and continued MiG patrols over Lebanon. Israel continued reconnaissance missions over Lebanon despite the increased Syrian defenses. On September 19, 1979, the Syrians fired first: MiG-23 Floggers launched air-to-air missiles at an Israeli RF-4 Phantom reconnaissance aircraft. The Phantom was able to evade the missiles and return to base.[12]

Five days later on September 24, MiG-21s attempted to interfere with another Israeli reconnaissance mission. The MiG-21s were detected by an E-2C AWACS aircraft that alerted several F-15 Eagles flying cover. The F-15s were vectored by the E-2C to intercept the MiG-21s.

According to an Israeli F-15 pilot in *Born In Battle*: ''The [radar] screen showed a large formation of MiGs at 11 o'clock, altitude 30,000 feet. In fact, there were three MiG-21 [Fishbed J] foursomes, armed with AA-8 missiles, headed straight for our aircraft in scattered assault formation—just like the last time. We jettisoned our fuel tanks, ignited our afterburners and accelerated into real face-to-face combat. . . .

''From the minute I locked my radar onto ('my' MiG), the whole thing was a piece of cake. I was sitting on his tail, my Shafrir missile locked onto the heat of his powerplant. I closed in on him and fired the Shafrir. It hit him in the tail, but the aircraft didn't explode—it just stopped dead in mid-air! As I overtook the MiG, I saw the dome open and the pilot bail out.''[13]

An Israeli F-15 sports two kill markings. Israeli Eagles have downed numerous Syrian fighters including MiG-21s, MiG-23s, and MiG-25s. (IDF/AF)

Altogether in the brief battle four of the MiG-21 Fishbeds were shot down. Syria admitted losing four fighters, but added that two Israeli aircraft were also downed."[14],[15]

As Arab guerrillas continued raids along the Israel border into 1980, Israel stepped up the number of its ground and air patrols and the intensity of its air strikes into Lebanon.

Israeli and Syrian aircraft continued to clash. On December 31, 1980, a force of between four and six MiG-21s attempted to attack aircraft returning from a strike against terrorist bases in southern Lebanon. Israeli fighters intercepted the Syrian aircraft over southern Lebanon and reportedly downed two with missiles.[16]

The latest U.S.- and Soviet-built aircraft clashed for the first time on March 13, 1981, when a Syrian MiG-25 Foxbat attacked an Israeli RF-4 reconnaissance aircraft. The Syrian Foxbat was shot down by a radar-guided Sparrow air-to-air missile fired from an Israeli F-15 fighter—the first time that the Mach-3 MiG-25 had been intercepted and shot down.[17]

Further confrontations between forces of the two nations were inevitable as Israel supported Christian factions in Lebanon, and as Syrian and Palestinian groups endeavored to expand their spheres of influence. On April 28, 1981, Israeli fighters intercepted and shot down two Syrian helicopters ferrying Palestinian forces into position to attack a Christian mountaintop strong point.[18]

In retaliation the following day, Syria moved SA-6 surface-to-air missile batteries into the Bekaa Valley on the border between Lebanon and Syria. Israel threatened to bomb the missile sites if they were not removed, but Syria responded by increasing the number of missiles in Lebanon and in Syria just over the Lebanese border.

Israel continued to fly reconnaissance and strike missions over southern Lebanon and launched remotely-piloted reconnaissance drones over the Bekaa Valley. On May 14, Syria claimed to have shot down one of the unmanned drones. On May 25, Israel admitted three drones had been downed, but denied losing any manned aircraft.[19]

Three days later, Israeli warplanes attacked Libyan-manned surface-to-air missile units south of Beirut. the units were probably SA-9 batteries. The SA-9 is a short-range infrared-guided air defense missile mounted on an amphibious armored vehicle. Similar in concept to the U.S. Army's Chaparral missile, the SA-9 can destroy targets up to an altitude of 15,000 feet at a range of four miles.

Attacking the Reactor

On June 7, 1981, six Israeli F-15s and eight F-16s took off from Etzion Air Base in the Sinai Desert to undertake a mission that would shock the world. Israel, anxious to prevent an Arab country the capability of building a fission bomb, sent fighter escort F-15s carrying missiles and external fuel tanks, along with F-16s carrying Sidewinder infrared-guided missiles, fuel tanks, and two one-ton bombs. The planes flew low and fast, following a carefully planned route around Jordan through Saudi Arabia and into Iraq—to bomb the Iraqi nuclear reactor power plant 12 miles southwest of Baghdad.

Despite their low-altitude flight profile, the aircraft were detected by Jordanian radar and challenged by radio. The Israeli pilots answered in perfect Arabic and convinced the controllers that they were a Jordanian or Saudi training flight.

About 50 minutes after takeoff, the aircraft sighted the reactor dome. The F-16s popped up for their bomb runs while the F-15s covered them from below. The F-16s, opposed only by ineffectual light antiaircraft fire, dove to release their ordnance, directing all 16 of their bombs into the reactor dome and surrounding buildings. The multitude of one-ton high-explosive bombs collapsed the covering dome, destroying the reactor and severely damaging several surrounding buildings.

Israeli F-16A Fighting Falcons such as this bombed the Iraqi nuclear reactor near Baghdad in June 1981. The aircraft has also engaged in air combat against Syrian aircraft and achieved more than 40 air combat victories.

The attack moved with such speed that surface-to-air missile sites positioned around Baghdad to protect the capital neither challenged the attackers nor did interceptors scramble to give chase. The F-15s and F-16 returned home, flying at high altitudes over Iraq and Jordan to maximize their range. Despite the now-open violation of Jordanian airspace, no antiaircraft missile fire or fighters rose to contest them. Following the raid, it was disclosed that for more than 18 months the pilots had practiced for the mission in secret drills that included flying dozens of sorties against a simulated reactor building in the Israeli desert.[20]

Reacting to the raid, the U.S. government embargoed the delivery of military aircraft to Israel because of its policy of supplying arms only for Israel's self-defense.

Israel continued to fly regular reconnaissance and strike sorties over Lebanon throughout the summer of 1981.

On July 17, Israeli strike aircraft bombed the headquarters of the PLO in downtown Beirut. The attack killed more than 300 people and wounded more than 800, most of them civilians.[21] The PLO and other guerrilla groups responded by stepping up their activities by firing numerous rockets and artillery shells at Israeli border settlements.

The United States, reconsidering its embargo, reacted to the Beirut raid by continuing its embargo of F-16s to Israel. Further, Philip C. Habib, President Ronald Reagan's special envoy to the Middle East, initiated efforts to secure a cease-fire between the PLO and Israel. These attempts were successful and the two groups declared a cease-fire on July 24, 1981.

Despite the cease-fire, Israel continued to fly reconnaissance flights over Lebanon to monitor the activities of terrorist groups and the disposition of Syrian forces, especially those manning the SA-6 missile batteries in the Bekaa Valley. Syrian MiG-25s attempted to intercept an RF-4 reconnaissance aircraft on July 29, 1981, and escorting Israeli fighters shot down one of the Mach-3 Foxbats—the second in six months.[22]

Invasion of Lebanon

During the spring of 1982, following a period of relative calm, shelling and guerrilla raids occurred with increasing frequency along the Israeli-Lebanon border. Tension rose and Ariel

Sharon, Israel Defense Minister, announced that unless terrorist activities ceased, Israeli ground forces would cross into Lebanon and wipe out the PLO.

On June 4, 1982, Shlomo Argov, Israeli ambassador in London, was shot and critically wounded by an Arab terrorist. In retaliation, the following day Israeli warplanes staged more than 60 airstrikes against PLO targets throughout southern Lebanon. The PLO responded by barraging Israeli settlements with artillery and rocket fire.

Israeli armored task forces crossed the border at 11 a.m. on June 6, beginning a large-scale invasion of southern Lebanon. The operation, known in Israel as "Peace for Galilee" was designed to eliminate the PLO and other terrorist groups, dislodge Syrian units which occupied much of central Lebanon, and demilitarize that area of southern Lebanon within rocket or artillery range of Israeli towns and settlements. Some 60,000 troops and more than 500 tanks advanced north along three major routes. Each multi-division task force was heavily supported by artillery, attack helicopters, and air strikes.[23]

The 15,000 PLO fighters in southern Lebanon were equipped with more than 100 tanks and hundreds of heavy cannon and rocket launchers, but this force was no match for the powerful Israeli units. Fighting was intense but the PLO was inexorably pushed back or overrun.

On the second day, Israeli forces clashed with tanks of the Syrian 85th Armored Brigade. Israel announced that it would not attack Syrian units unless they fired first.[24] Following this declaration, PLO forces retreated behind Syrian units and intermingled with their supply columns to lessen the probability of being attacked by artillery or air strikes. Syria reacted by moving additional forces into the country, strengthening surface-to-air missile defenses in the Bekaa Valley, and providing air cover for units in central Lebanon.

Fighting continued on June 8 between Israeli forces and the PLO along the coast road near Sidon. An armored battle developed as Israeli forces pushed north against Syrian armored and commando units in central and eastern Lebanon. Syrian aircraft met Israeli fighters over the battlefield and six MiG fighters were reportedly downed in three separate engagements; no Israeli fighters were admitted lost.[25]

On June 9, Israeli forces continued to push north against PLO and Syrian resistance. At 2:00 p.m., Israeli aircraft, working in concert with artillery, attacked the Syrian defense system in the Bekaa Valley. The Syrian defenses were formidable: fifteen SA-6, two SA-3, and two SA-2 missile batteries with some 200 ready-to-launch missiles and supporting antiaircraft guns were concentrated in the valley and along the Syrian border.[26] However, the Israelis had worked almost a decade on techniques to counter the Arab air defense network that had stung them so badly in the 1973 war.

Long-range artillery and surface-to-surface rockets pounded the missile and gun systems and simultaneously a variety of jamming and deception techniques were employed to blind Syrian radars and confuse the seekers of infrared homing missiles. Israeli fighter-bombers then blasted the surviving Syrian air defense sites with missiles and bombs. Ten of the nineteen Syrian batteries were knocked out within the first ten minutes and the Israelis claim to have destroyed seventeen batteries and damaged two during the attack without losing a single aircraft.[27]

The Syrians reacted with a force of more than sixty MiG-21 and MiG-23 fighters to drive away the Israeli fighter-bombers. Israeli F-15s and F-16s flying cover for the strike aircraft engaged the Syrian MiGs, resulting in one of the most far-ranging and intense dogfights since World War II. The Israelis claim to have destroyed 29 Syrian aircraft without a loss. Syria admitted losing 16 aircraft but declared victories over 26 Israeli warplanes.[28]

The Soviet Union was so surprised at the effectiveness of the Israeli attacks that it immediately dispatched Col. Gen. Yevseny S. Yuvasov, Deputy Commander of the Soviet Air Defense Force, and a team of experts to Syria to investigate.[29]

During the next twenty-four hours, Syria rushed additional missile batteries, tanks, and troops into Lebanon to halt the advancing Israeli forces and reconstitute an effective air defense umbrella. Israeli warplanes pounded the reinforcements and new air defense sites and reportedly shot down 26 Syrian MiGs and three attack helicopters.

Air and ground action between Syrian and Israeli forces continued on June 11; however, the fighting ended at 12 noon when a cease-fire went into effect. Eighteen Syrian aircraft were said to have been destroyed during a series of morning air battles.

By June 12, Syria reportedly had lost in air combat more than 80 MiG-21, MiG-23, SU-22 aircraft and five helicopters. No Israeli aircraft were admitted to have been lost to Syrian aircraft but one A-4 Skyhawk and two helicopters were said to have been downed by ground fire.[30]

The PLO hadn't been included in the cease-fire so battles raged on. Armored columns linked up on the outskirts of Beirut and slowly edged into the city, pushing out the PLO. There was a lull in air combat but Israeli aircraft continued to fly hundreds of ground support sorties. Heavy fighting again broke out between Syrian and Israeli units and on June 24 Israeli warplanes destroyed a SA-6 site in the Bekaa Valley. The same day, Israeli fighters intercepted and downed two Syrian MiG-23 Floggers.

The battle for Beirut continued for more than a month and on July 24 an Israeli F-4 was shot down by a Syrian SA-6 missile. Several Syrian missile batteries including at least one sophisticated SA-8 Gecko system were said to have been knocked out by Israeli retaliation raids. The SA-8 is one of the latest Soviet air defense weapons and the first which mounted a fire-control radar and missile launcher on the same vehicle. The radar-guided missile can hit targets at a range of more than six miles and an altitude of 21,000 feet.[31]

In late August 1982, the PLO and Syrians agreed to evacuate Beirut and a multi-national force including the Lebanese army entered the city to restore peace. Israeli forces pulled back to a line south of Beirut.

Despite these positive events, Israeli warplanes continued to attack Syrian missile batteries. On August 3, a Syrian MiG-25 Foxbat flying over Beirut was shot down by a Hawk surface-to-air missile. The on-again, off-again cease-fire has been observed by Israel and Syria since October 1983 but fighting has continued between rival Lebanese factions and outside occupation forces.

To counter the Israeli warplanes, the Soviet Union reportedly has placed several SA-5 surface-to-air batteries in Syria. The weapon poses a threat to aircraft flying over Israel itself due to its 180-mile range and 100,000-foot maximum altitude. The deadly chess game in the Middle East continues.[32]

Analysis

Knocking Out the SAMs

The aspect of air warfare that undoubtedly attracted the most attention involving the 1982 Lebanese conflict was the destruction of the Syrian air defense system. The Israelis crippled the Syrian air defense system in the Bekaa Valley; for obvious reasons the amount of damage inflicted and the precise techniques and equipment employed have yet to be fully revealed. However, a number of details concerning the engagements have surfaced. According to U.S. sources, Israel destroyed 23 Bekaa Valley SAM installations including numerous advanced SA-6 and SA-8 systems.[33]

This was accomplished because the Israelis did their homework. For more than a year since SA-6s were installed in the valley remotely piloted vehicles (RPVs) equipped with electronic and optical sensors monitored the SAM batteries and provided up-to-date reconnaissance.

The tactics employed to destroy the Syrian air defense system were similar to those used in Vietnam by U.S. forces but with innovations. Jamming and deception were extensive and radar and infrared decoys were deployed by rocket, drone, and manned aircraft.

According to Israeli Lt. Gen. Rafael Eiton: "(SAM) battery sites were not only under ground force artillery range but within the range of our new family of computer-guided surface-to-surface missiles; in advance of direct attacks we used long-range artillery. So when we more or less neutralized the effectiveness of each battery, we came in with heavy aerial bombardment, destroying every site."[34] Aircraft fired Shrike anti-radiation missiles and a number of reports spoke of a new Zeev (Wolf) surface-to-surface missile equipped with an anti-radiation seeker.[35]

Some sources suggest that Israeli losses were understated. U.S. officials said that at least two A-4s and an F-4 appear to have been lost by Israel and that seven other aircraft including an F-16 had been crippled by ground fire or SAMs.[36] Much of the blame for the destruction of the Bekaa Valley air defense system lies with the Syrians. It appears from available information that the Syrians did not capitalize on their tactical advantages. Once positioned in the Bekaa Valley many missile batteries did not reposition or extensively dig in to improve their survivability.

Radar emission control was another shortcoming. Many radars were activated to track drones, giving away their operating frequency and position. The lack of dummy emitters and decoy SAM batteries reduced radar longevity. The Syrians reportedly did utilize heavy smoke to screen positions once the attack began but, given the open nature of the terrain and extensive information available from previous RPV missions, this was of little help.[37]

While defense suppression missions attracted much attention, Israeli F-4E Phantoms, Kfirs, A-4 Skyhawks, and F-16s flew hundreds of attack sorties against PLO and Syrian positions and other tactical targets.

Air Superiority

In the period from the invasion of Lebanon to the end of large-scale fighting in August, Israeli fighters reportedly shot down 85 Syrian jets plus a number of helicopters. The bulk of these were destroyed between June 8 and 11 in a series of massive dogfights over the Bekaa Valley.

Waves of Syrian MiG-21, MiG-23 fighters, and Su-22 strike aircraft flew into Lebanon to challenge Israeli warplanes and ground forces. When the aircraft entered Lebanon, Israeli fighters, mostly F-15s and F-16s, attacked, resulting in huge multi-plane dogfights.

The F-16 Fighting Falcon, in Israeli service for less than two years, was responsible for the destruction of 44 Syrian aircraft. About 40 Syrian planes were accounted for by Israeli F-15s. These kills gave Israeli F-15s a 58 to 0 track record against Syrian MiGs. One Syrian jet was downed by an Israeli F-4. The majority of the Syrian losses were MiG-21s but a substantial number of MiG-23s and several SU-22 fighter-bombers and helicopters were also shot down.[38]

According to U.S. sources, fewer than seven percent of the kills were achieved with cannon fire. Most Syrian aircraft were hit by infrared homing missiles. These included the Shafrir, recently introduced Python 3 (both made in Israel), and several versions of the AIM-9 Sidewinder. The all-aspect AIM-9L was said to have performed magnificently. The radar-guided AIM-7F Sparrow, which arms the F-15, was also used with considerable success.[39]

Factors contributed to the topsided air combat exchange ratio included reliability and effectiveness of Israeli warplanes and weapons, highly-trained Israeli pilots, and innovative tactics.

Key factors contributing to the success of both the anti-SAM and air-to-air victories were Israeli reconnaissance and command-and-control networks. Information from drones, including mini-RPVs (such as the Israeli Scout and Mastiff), EC-707, E-2C Hawkeye early warning aircraft, tactical RF-4E, OV-1D, and RC-12D reconnaissance aircraft, and ground-based sources was transmitted in real time to the command system.[40] Decisions were made and quickly disseminated to pilots and field commanders. In the air combat area, Israeli commanders knew when Syrian aircraft took off, their course, and number. One can assume that tactical communications between Syrian aircraft and ground controllers were also monitored and jammed.

Iran-Iraq War, 1980

On September 22, 1980, war erupted between Iraq and Iran. The two have a long history of mutual distrust and hostility that can be traced back over many past Arab-Persian conflicts. Iran, under Shah Mohammad Reza Shah Pahlavi, built up a formidable military force as part of his drive to be policeman of the Persian Gulf and its surrounding area.

The Shah took advantage of his strength in 1975 and coerced Iraq into signing a treaty that gave Iran control of disputed territory along the Iran-Iraq border. That territory ran along the Shatt-al-Arab, the waterway through which the Tigris and Euphrates rivers flow into the Persian Gulf. The waterway is Iraq's only access to the gulf.

Iran and Iraq have major oil storage and transportation terminals on their respective sides of the Shatt-al-Arab. President Saddom Hussein of Iraq was humiliated by the treaty giving Iran so much power and land, and vowed to reverse the situation.

With the 1979 Iranian revolution, which had ousted the Shah and elevated Ayatollah Khomeini to power, and the resultant embargo of supplies and parts for Iran's U.S.-built and British-built tanks, warplanes, and ships, President Hussein saw an opportunity to turn the

An F-4E Phantom II of the Imperial Iranian Air Force trailing its drag chute on landing. Thirty-two F-4D and 177 F-4Es were acquired by Iran beginning in 1966. The F-4D and F-4E Phantom IIs flew most of the Iranian Islamic Revolutionary Air Force's (the Iranian Air Arm's post-revolution name) long-range strike missions during Iran/Iraq war.

tables. On paper, Iran still had a much more powerful military force than Iraq, but the pro-Shah military leadership had been decimated by the revolution.

The pre-revolution strength of the Imperial Iranian Air Force was said to be more than 440 combat aircraft, including: 188 F-4D/E Phantom II fighter-bombers (10 squadrons); 166 F-5E/F Tiger fighter-bombers (eight squadrons); 77 F-14A Tomcat fighter/interceptors (four squadrons); 14 RF-4E Phantom II reconnaissance aircraft (one squadron).

In addition to the powerful air force, Iran had a 150,000-man army equipped with 1,500 late-model British-built and U.S.-built tanks, large numbers of armored personnel carriers and artillery pieces, and more than 200 AH-1J missile-armed attack helicopters. Backing up the air force was a substantial air defense system composed of many radars, Hawk and Rapier surface-to-air missile sites, and antiaircraft artillery.[41]

The Iranian revolution had considerably reduced the personnel strength of the military; moreover, a significant portion of Iran's tanks, aircraft, and ships were inoperative due to the lack of spare parts and a shortage of trained personnel.

At war's beginning in September 1980, a year after the Iranian revolution, perhaps 200 combat aircraft of the newly-named Iranian Islamic Revolutionary Air Force were operational, amounting to about half the aircraft.[42]

Iraq's forces, however, were in fighting trim. The Iraqi Air Force included more than 300 combat aircraft: 12 Tu-22 bombers (one squadron); 10 Il-28 light bombers (one squadron); 80 MiG-23 Flogger B fighter-bombers (four squadrons); 40 Su-7B fighter-bombers (three squadrons); 40 Su-20 fighter-bombers (four squadrons); 15 Hawker Hunter fighter-bombers (one squadron); 115 MiG-21 fighter/interceptors (five squadrons).

Moreover, large numbers of Mirage F-1, MiG-23, and MiG-27 fighter-bombers were on order.

The Iraqi army, 200,000 strong, included 2,500 Soviet-built and French-built tanks, plus thousands of armored personnel carriers and artillery. Iraq also had a sizable air defense network, with 23-mm and 57-mm antiaircraft guns and batteries of SA-2, SA-3, and SA-6 surface-to-air missiles.[43]

On September 22, 1980, Iraqi aircraft bombed ten Iranian air bases, radar sites, and other positions while several armored columns penetrated Iranian territory. President Saddom Hussein intended to regain full control of the Shatt-al-Arab and the disputed 240 square miles of border territory. Another major goal of Hussein's invasion was to eliminate the Ayatolla Khomeini's Islamic Shite population that was at odds with his government.

Initially, Iraqi armored units made gains, but were slowed by determined Iranian resistance. Air strikes and ground combat continued through the fall of 1980, but stalled as a stalemate with the onset of the winter rains and snows and both sides intent to reduce casualties and equipment losses.

In January 1981, the Iranians launched a counter-offensive, but gained little ground. Throughout the spring while the fighting continued, a nine-member Islamic conference team shuttled between Baghdad and Tehran trying to arrange a cease-fire. Neither side, however, would agree to end the fighting.

Reacting to the raids, Iran flew repeated missions against Iraqi oil storage areas, supply dumps, and airfields. Strike aircraft penetrated to their targets at low altitude, eluding radar detection. On most sorties, the pilots passed only once over the target to drop their bombs, and then turned to escape at high speed toward home base. These tactics allowed Iranian aircraft to slip past the Iraqi radar early-warning system that controlled large numbers of MiG-21 and MiG-23 interceptors plus SA-2, SA-3, and SA-6 surface-to-air missiles.

When alerted in time, Iraqi surface-to-air missile and antiaircraft artillery batteries did shoot down a sizable number of aircraft. But the Iranian pilots, as a result of their U.S. training, were aware of the missile-evasion maneuvers employed by the U.S. Air Force and Navy during the Vietnam war, and many Iranian F-4s and F-5s were able to outmaneuver Iraqi surface-to-air missiles.

While official information on Iranian aircraft losses has not been released, it is thought that at least 100 aircraft were lost during the first year of conflict. Iraqi antiaircraft artillery and small arms reportedly accounted for the majority, with a significant number lost due to accidents and maintenance problems.[44]

Iraq relied on the same low-level strike tactics to evade Iranian radar and Hawk missiles and thus dogfights have been few. On occasion, patrolling fighters and strike aircraft have encountered one another and engaged in air combat, with losses on both sides.

The Iraqi Air Force had initiated the war on September 22. Immediately following those initial attacks, the Iraqis dispersed their aircraft to airfields in western Iraq, Kuwait, Jordan, and Saudi Arabia to minimize losses to counterattacks. Later in the war, most of these aircraft returned to their bases.

Iranian retaliatory raids against Iraqi airfields continued with some success; on April 6, 1981, Iranian fighter-bombers bombed and strafed four Iraqi air bases including Haj Sen, just 30 miles from the Jordanian border. Iran claimed to have destroyed several bombers on the ground in the attacks.

Iraqi fighter-bombers plus Tu-22 and Il-28 bombers occasionally struck Iranian rear-area targets, heavily bombing some industrial complexes near Tehran. As a result of battle damage and the lack of spare parts, the Iranian network of radar surveillance and command-and-control has lost considerable effectiveness.

Thus, most Iraq raids went unchallenged by interceptors or by Hawk or Rapier surface-to-air missiles. As the fighting raged on, most Iraq attack sorties appeared to have been directed against targets close to the battle area—a tactic that closely follows Soviet doctrine. That tactic calls for air units to provide close support for advancing ground forces.

Iraqi fighters bested Iranian aircraft in air combat on several occasions. Reportedly, Iraqi MiG-21s have been armed with French-built Matra 550 Magic infrared homing air-to-air missiles.[45] The weapons are far more effective than the MiG's normal complement of Atoll missiles.

As of early 1981, Iraqi losses were estimated in excess of 100 aircraft, most falling to Iranian antiaircraft artillery fire and a few lost in accidents. Since Iraq, unlike Iran, was still able to purchase spare parts and aircraft from French and Soviet sources, it could replace a substantial part of its attrition.[46]

During the summer and fall of 1981, Iran initiated a series of counterattacks against Iraqi forces. These drives made considerable gains including the recapture of Abadon in late September. Skirmishing continued but neither side was able to make any real headway. However, the attrition warfare exacted a considerable toll; by early 1982, the adversaries had lost an estimated 70,000 killed and 150,000 to 200,000 wounded.[47]

In March 1982, Iran launched a major attack in the Desful area 150 miles north of the Persian Gulf. In a week of heavy fighting, Iranian forces pushed the defenders back more than 20 miles, killed or captured about 20,000 Iraqis, and captured or destroyed more than 600 tanks and armored vehicles. Iran reportedly used its remaining tactical aircraft sparingly and relied primarily upon attack helicopters for close support. Iraq flew more than 150 sorties a day over the battle zone, but their effectiveness was said to have been reduced by heavy antiaircraft fire from cannon, machine guns, and SA-7 missiles.[48]

To sustain the war of attrition both sides needed new supplies of weaponry and spare parts. Iraq received weapons from the Soviet Union and France, training and logistic support from Egypt and Jordan, and money from Saudi Arabia and other gulf countries.

Iran on the other hand had lost the use of much of its U.S.- and British-built aircraft, tanks, artillery, and missile systems due to the embargo of spare parts and ammunition. Israel supplied Iran some equipment and military supplies but persecution of Iranian Jews and U.S. pressure slowed this flow to a trickle. Iran increasingly relied upon Libya, Syria, and North Korea for arms; however, these countries supplied large numbers of light weapons and only a limited amount of heavy hardware such as artillery, tanks, and aircraft.[49]

Iran, however, had several advantages: a large pool of manpower and religious fervor. Khomeini and his "religious" generals launched major infantry attacks in July, September, October, and November, which captured little territory and resulted in tens of thousands of casualties, primarily among recently recruited teenage soldiers. Iraq had learned lessons from earlier combat and made more effective use of its artillery, armor, strike aircraft, and helicopter gunships. Iraq struck back by heavily bombing Iranian oil facilities and international flag tankers at Kharg Island in the Persian Gulf and by firing Scud surface-to-surface missiles at such area targets as Iranian sorties.

Despite heavy casualties in the summer and fall offensives, Iran again staged a spring offensive, this time north of Desful. Formidable drives in early February and April 1983 made gains but Iraqi armor, supported by artillery, strike aircraft, and attack helicopters again stopped the attacks and inflicted substantial Iranian casualties.

Early in 1983 both Iran and Iraq began to receive new tactical aircraft, both from the same source. Egypt has procurred sizable numbers of Chinese built F-6s (MiG-19s) and F-7s (MiG-21s) and is supplying these aircraft types to Iraq for use against Iran. These fighters, plus deliveries of French Mirage F-1s, Super Etendards, and Soviet-built warplanes have considerably strengthened the Iraqi Air Force. Iraqi pilots have been increasingly effective because they are using such new weapons as the Exocet antiship missile and innovative tactics taught by French, Egyptian, and Indian instructors.

Iraq has also strengthened its air defense system through the addition of Roland and additional Soviet-built SAMs and hundreds of antiaircraft guns including numerous ZSU-23-4s.[50]

In late 1984, it was estimated that Iran had fewer than 75 operational American-built F-14, F-4, and F-5 fighters due to combat losses and canabilization. However, the Islamic Revolutionary Air Force has received Chinese-built F-6 (MiG-19) tactical aircraft from North Korea and reportedly continues to receive spare parts and assistance from Israel which help maintain the dwindling numbers of U.S.-built tactical aircraft. Iranian air power was often quite effective early in the conflict; however, losses and the poor supply situation have severely reduced its participation in combat.[51] The fourth anniversary of the war's beginning has come and passed and Iran and Iraq were still fighting a war of attrition with no end in sight.

Not all conflict in the Middle East has been between warring local factions. In August 1981, two Libyan Su-22 Fitter fighter-bombers tangled with two U.S. Navy F-14 Tomcat fighters on combat air patrol protecting the U.S.S. *Nimitz*.

The *Nimitz* was participating in a U.S. Sixth Fleet missile-firing exercise in international waters in the southern Mediterranean, which included operations in the Gulf of Sidra that borders Libya. On August 18, Libyan fighters flew more than 40 missions into or near the exercise area. These penetrations were met by fighters from the Sixth Fleet carriers *Nimitz* and *Forrestal*, and were turned away.

Early the next morning, August 19, two Libyan Su-22 Fitters were detected by two F-14s on combat air patrol 60 miles south of the *Nimitz*. As the four aircraft closed, one of the Su-22s fired a missile (presumed to be a Soviet-built Atoll) from its wing station.[52]

The F-14 pilots saw the launch and both broke away to evade the missile. Immediately after, F-14 pilot Comdr. Henry M. Kleeman, squadron leader of the VF-41 Black Aces, and his RIO

A Libyan Su-22 Fitter similar to this one photographed over the Mediterranean fired an air-to-air missile at two U.S. Navy F-14s on August 19, 1981.

Lt. David J. Venlet, and wingman pilot Lt. Lawrence M. Musczynski and his RIO Lt. James P. Anderson, engaged the two Su-22s and shot both down with AIM-9L Sidewinders.[53]

The crews of the F-14s reacted under normal peacetime rules of engagement, which allow the pilot of an aircraft fired upon to strike back in self-defense. Following the brief engagement, Libya claimed that eight F-14s had bounced the two Su-22s that were on a routine patrol, and that one F-14 had been shot down.[54]

Three F-14s of U.S. Navy Squadron VF-41 in echelon. Two F-14s flying on combat air patrol over the Mediterranean were fired on by two Libyan Su-22 Fitters on August 19, 1981. The F-14s engaged the two Fitters and downed both with AIM-9L Sidewinders.

After the dogfight, the Sixth Fleet maneuvers continued and Libyan fighters continued to probe the exercise area but without further incident.

With the multitude of political and religious factions, the economic importance of oil, and the unstable nature of politics in the Middle East, it would not come as a surprise if the use of offensive and defensive air power, both in air-to-air and air-to-ground combat, continued for years.

The Middle East as a battleground bears watching, not only for the political and economic importance of shifts in power, but also because it may well be the military testing ground for advanced aircraft, weapons, and tactics of the major arms-producing nations, in much the same way that previous confrontations have been both in the Middle East and in Vietnam.

The U.S. Navy F-14 victors over the Libyan Fitters. From left, Radar Intercept Officer Lt. David Venlet and his pilot, Comdr. Henry Kleeman; pilot Lt. Larry Muscyznski and Radar Intercept Officer Lt. James Anderson.

CHAPTER IX:

Battle for Malvinas:
Falkland Islands Conflict, 1982

B etween April 2 and June 14, 1982, Argentina and Great Britain fought a short and vicious war to determine who controlled a group of remote islands situated off the Argentinian coast and inhabited by fewer than 2,000 people.

The roots of the conflict date back to the independence of Argentina from Spain in the early 1800s. The islands had, at various times, been claimed and inhabited by the French, Spanish, and British. In 1829, Argentina established a colony that lasted until 1833 when Britain reasserted control and evicted Argentinian settlers. The Falklands subsequently became a part of the British Empire.

In 1945, Argentina reasserted its claim to the islands. Two decades later, the United Nations initiated negotiations between Britain and Argentina concerning the future of the islands. These discussions continued without major agreement until April 2, 1982, when Argentine forces invaded.

The primary goal of Argentina and Britain in the conflict was to capture, hold, and control the Malvinas/Falkland Islands and South Georgia Island. Though British ground forces ultimately won the terrain, naval forces were required to transport soldiers and equipment to the islands while airpower was essential to protect friendly units and hinder enemy forces.

The Argentine Air Forces Fuerza Aerea Argentina (FAA), Argentine Naval Air Arm Aviacion Naval Argentine (ANA), Royal Navy, and Royal Air Force played major roles in the 1982 South Atlantic conflict. Important air warfare aspects included: the first combat use of V/STOL tactical aircraft; the first use of air-launched, sea-skimming anti-ship missiles against warships of a major navy; the first widespread use of sea-based surface-to-air missile systems; and the first sustained air attacks since World War II against naval forces.

Chronology of Events

March 19—About 60 Argentine civilians employed by a salvage company landed on South Georgia Island and raised the Argentine flag. Although the islanders asked the workers to depart, 10 remained and continued to disassemble an obsolete whaling station.

March 26–28—Argentine naval units undertook possession of the Falkland/Malvinas and South George Islands. The three separate task forces included the Argentine aircraft carrier *Veinticinco de Mayo* (equipped with eight A-4Q Skyhawks, four S-2E trackers, and a number of helicopters), seven destroyers, three frigates, and numerous amphibious ships and transports.

March 30—Reacting to the increasing tensions between Great Britain and Argentina, the Royal Navy ordered the nuclear submarines HMS *Spartan* and HMS *Superb* to prepare to deploy to the South Atlantic.

April 2—Argentine troops landed at Port Stanley. Following a brief firefight, Gov. Rex Hunt surrendered and all 84 British Royal Marines were taken prisoner.

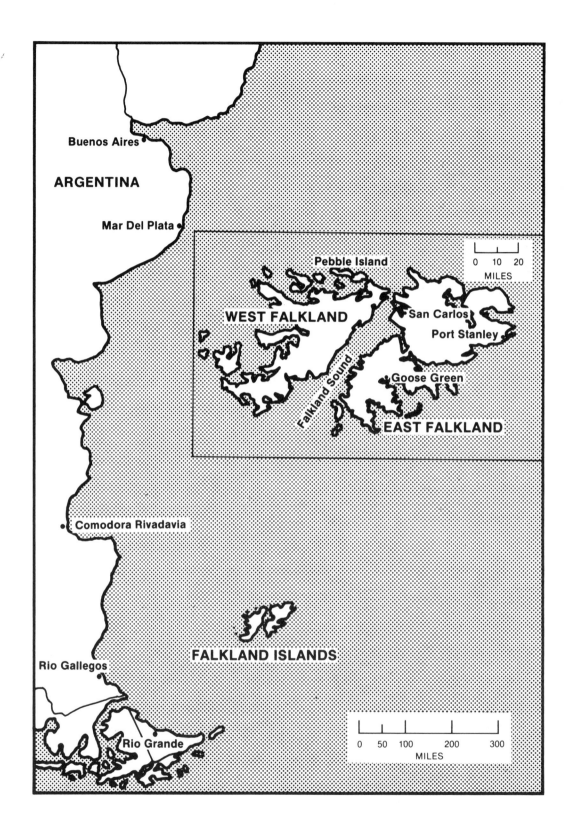

Buenos Aires

ARGENTINA

Mar Del Plata

Pebble Island

0 10 20
MILES

WEST FALKLAND

San Carlos

Port Stanley

Falkland Sound

Goose Green

EAST FALKLAND

Comodora Rivadavia

FALKLAND ISLANDS

Rio Gallegos

Rio Grande

0   50 100   200   300
MILES

April 3—Argentine forces were helicoptered to South George Island. The 23-man Royal Marine detachment surrendered after having shot down an Argentine Puma helicopter and damaged the Argentine Frigate *Guerrico*.

In 1982, the Furerza Aerea Argentina (FAA) was one of the strongest air forces in South America. In addition to a sizable number of American-, British-, and French-built tactical aircraft, the FAA operated several dozen twin-turboprop IA-58 Pucara ground attack aircraft produced in Argentina. The light attack aircraft is powered by two 1,022 shp Turbomeca Astazou turboprops and has a normal loaded weight of 14,300 lb. The Pucara can attain maximum speed of 323 mph and is armed with two 20-mm cannon and four 7.62-mm machine guns and up to 3,307 pounds of bombs and rocket pods.

The FAA inventory included Mirage IIIEA and similar Israeli-built Dagger supersonic fighters and U.S.-built A-4P Skyhawk fighter-bombers. (Known as the Nesher in Israeli service, the Dagger Mirage-like fighters were built in Israel and saw combat in the 1973 Arab-Israeli War.) The Skyhawk force also included refurbished A-4B/C previously operated by the U.S. Navy. Long-range attack missions were the responsibility of a small element of British-built Canberra light bombers. Support for the tactical aircraft was provided by C-130 Hercules transports and similar KC-130 refueling tankers.

The air element of the Argentine Navy, Aviacion Naval Argentina (ANA), operated from shore bases and the Navy's single aircraft carrier, the 16,000-ton *Veinticinco de Mayo*. The ANA operated A-4Q Skyhawks (refurbished A-4B) and was phasing into service a dozen French-built Super Etendard strike aircraft armed with the AM-39 Exocet anti-ship missile. In addition to fighter-bombers, the ANA flew Italian-built Aeromacchi MB 339 jet trainers that could undertake attack missions.

Argentine Air Force (FAA): 20 Mirage IIIEA; 30 Dagger; 60 A-4P Skyhawk; 60 IA-58 Pucara; 9 B-62 Canberra; 7 C-130; 2 KC-130.

Argentine Naval Air Arm (ANA): 10 A-4Q Skyhawk; 5 Super Etendard; 10 Aeromacchi MB-339.[1]

Following the invasion, Argentine C-130s and naval craft began transporting men and materiel from the mainland to set up extensive defenses. Most of the Argentine forces were stationed at Port Stanley (renamed Puerto Argentino after capture). The port's 4,000-ft. (1,200-

An Argentine-built IA-58A Pucara light attack aircraft displayed with a variety of the armament which the twin turboprop can deliver. More than two dozen of these STOL attack aircraft were sent to the Falkland Islands to provide air support for defending troops. A-4B jet attack aircraft of the Argentine Air Force are visible in the background. (Argentine Navy)

m) runway was too short to accommodate fully-loaded combat aircraft but was acceptable for STOL transports and light strike aircraft.

The FAA sent several dozen Pucara light attack aircraft to the islands to provide close support. The ANA sent T-34C trainers and MB-339 jet-powered light strike aircraft.

Logistics support for the Argentine Army and Marine troops was provided by Army Aviation UH-1H, CH-47 Chinook, Puma, and A 109 helicopters, and Skyvan transports and helicopters of the Argentine Coast Guard.

The sizable force of strike aircraft, helicopters, and transports was based at Port Stanley (Puerto Argentino), Goose Green (BAM Condor), Pebble (Borbon) Island, and several other grass fields in the Falklands.

Air defense was provided by one Roland fire unit, Tiger Cat, Blowpipe, and SA-7 SAMs plus numerous 40-mm, 35-mm, and 20-mm antiaircraft. These weapons were primarily concentrated around Port Stanley with many also at Goose Green and Pebble Island. The multiservice contingent of aircraft was under the command of Brig. Gen. Mario B. Menendez, island garrison commander. An air operations and air defense planning staff working with several radars coordinated air activities.

The FAA and ANA moved many tactical aircraft to southern Argentina within range of the Falklands to provide air cover and strike support should Britain attempt to retake the islands. FAA Canberras shifted to Comodoro Rivadovia; Mirage IIIEAs, A-4P Skyhawks, and Daggers operated from Rio Gallegos; Rio Grande was home base for Daggers, A-4P Skyhawks, and A-4Q Skyhawks and Super Etendards of the ANA.[2]

The flexibility of this sizable force was considerably hampered because combat operations would take place at ranges in excess of 450 miles. (For example, Rio Grande was 437 miles and Comodoro Rivadovia 596 miles from Port Stanley.) Such distances required external fuel tanks, reduced payload, and allowed for a maximum of five minutes combat time. The FAAs two KC-130 tankers could refuel A-4P/Q Skyhawks and Super Etendards but Mirage and Dagger aircraft lacked air-refueling capability.[3]

April 5—The invasion took the British Government by surprise. Since the Falklands were 7,100 miles southwest of the U.K. and the closest base, Ascension Island, was more than 3,900 miles from Port Stanley, naval forces need be the primary element of any effort to recapture the Islands.

A hurriedly-assembled task force including the aircraft carriers HMS *Hermes* and HMS *Invincible*, several destroyers, frigates, and more than a dozen support ships departed England. The air strength of the task force included 20 Sea Harriers from naval squadrons 800, 801, and 899 (12 embarked on *Hermes* and eight on the smaller *Invincible*) and dozens of Sea King, Wessex, Lynx, and Wasp helicopters.[4]

Ascension Island became the focal point for South Atlantic-bound ships and aircraft. VC-10, C-130 transports of the RAF, and leased Belfast aircraft moved high-priority cargo to the island from where it was transferred to the fleet. At one time, seventy percent of the RAF Victor tanker force was stationed at Ascension Island. These tankers provided fuel for transports, tactical aircraft, ferry flights, Nimrod reconnaissance sorties, and Vulcan bomber attack missions. During April, several dozen ships left England for the South Atlantic to strengthen the task force with additional combat troops and supplies.

April 22—British troops helicptered to South Georgia Island to scout future landings. Following the loss of two helicopters in a blizzard, the scouts and aircrew were recalled.

April 25—Helicopters from a small British task force detected and attacked the Argentine submarine *Santa Fe* near South Georgia Island. The submarine, damaged by helicopter-fired missiles, sank in the Grytriken Harbor. British troops, put ashore by helicopter, attacked under the cover of naval gunfire and forced the Argentine garrison to surrender.

The Royal Navy aircraft carrier HMS *Hermes* steams in formation with the Sea Wolf-armed guided missile frigate HMS *Broadsword*. Both ships saw extensive action during the Falkland Islands conflict. (Royal Navy)

A Royal Navy Sea Harrier from 809 Squadron armed with two AIM-9L Sidewinders prepared to launch on an air combat patrol from HMS *Hermes*. Sea Harriers scored 23 confirmed victories over Argentine aircraft during the conflict. Twenty of these were achieved with the highly-capable AIM-9L Sidewinder infrared homing air-to-air missile. (British Aerospace)

May 1—A Vulcan bomber flying from Ascension island dropped 21 1,000-lb. bombs on Port Stanley airfield at 3:45 a.m. One bomb hit the runway and the others damaged aircraft and support facilities. At dawn, Sea Harriers bombed the Port Stanley and Goose Green airfields and, later in the day, a British destroyer and two frigates bombarded Argentine positions around Stanley. Argentine Skyhawks, Daggers, Mirages, and Canberras flew 56 sorties against British vessels,[5] during which HMS *Arrow* was damaged by a bomb.

Two FAA Mirage IIIEAs flying cover for strike aircraft engaged Sea Harriers. 1st Lt. Carlos Perona described subsequent events:

"My radar showed two 'bandits' coming in head-on—Sea Harriers. Our Mirages and the British aircraft crossed each other, and I began a scissors maneuver in an attempt to six o'clock one of our adversaries. The Sea Harrier has the ability to decelerate rapidly, and when I glanced to one side, I saw one of the bandits within 150-meters of my aircraft. I followed it visually until it disappeared from sight, and it was at that moment that I felt a tremendous impact. My Mirage began to shudder violently and control was lost . . . I had no recourse but to eject from my crippled plane. As I hung from my chute I saw my Mirage hit the water."[6] The FAA admitted the loss of four aircraft to Sea Harriers and antiaircraft.

May 2—Four Argentine Navy task forces patrolled the area between the mainland and the Falklands, outside the British-established 200-mile exclusion zone. The Royal Navy nuclear attack submarine HMS *Conqueror* torpedoed and sank the Argentine cruiser *General Belgrano* patrolling outside of the exclusion zone.

May 3—British Lynx helicopters attacked an Argentine tug and patrol craft after Sea King helicopters were fired upon. Sea Skua missiles, fired in combat for the first time, sank the tug and severely damaged the patrol vessel.

May 4—A British Vulcan bomber again attacked the airfield at Port Stanley followed up later by Sea Harriers that also raided the airfield at Goose Green. During the Goose Green attack, a Sea Harrier was shot down by antiaircraft and the pilot killed.

Later in the morning, ANA Super Etendards armed with AM-39 Exocet anti-ship missiles made a successful attack on the British fleet. HMS *Sheffield* was hit and abandoned several hours later as fires threatened to set off ammunition magazines. The ship sank on May 10 while under tow.

The Royal Navy guided missile destroyer HMS *Sheffield* after being hit by an air-launched Exocet sea skimming antiship missile. The destroyer was gutted by fire and later sank while under tow in heavy seas. (Royal Navy)

May 9—Sea Harriers strafed and damaged an Argentine trawler shadowing the British fleet. The vessel later sank after the crew had been captured. An Argentine Puma operating over Port Stanley was destroyed by a Sea Dart fired from HMS *Coventry*.[7]

May 12—FAA Skyhawks escorted by Mirage fighters struck at British ships and hit HMS *Glasgow* with a 1,000-lb. bomb which passed through the ship's hull without exploding. Of 12 A-4s which attacked the *Glasgow* and HMS *Brilliant*, two were reportedly destroyed by Sea Wolf missiles and a third crashed while taking evasive action.[8]

May 14—British Commandoes raided the airfield at Pebble Island in the East Falklands, destroying 11 aircraft and a radar station.

May 18—The container ship, *Atlantic Conveyor*, arrived in the South Atlantic with six GR MK 3 Harriers, eight Sea Harriers, and ten helicopters. Within the next twenty-four hours, four Sea Harriers had been ferried to *Invincible* and the ten remaining fighters (four Sea Harriers and six GR MK 3s) to *Hermes*. Total British air strength included 31 aircraft, one Sea Harrier having been lost in action and two to accidents.[9]

May 21—British troops landed on the Falklands at San Carlos Bay. Argentine aircraft from the islands and mainland flew more than 75 sorties against British ships and shore positions. The fighter-bombers had to run the gauntlet of Sea Harriers, ship-launched Sea Dart, Sea Wolf, Sea Cat SAMs, and antiaircraft fire.

These naval defenses were soon augmented by land-based Rapier missile batteries, Blowpipe missiles, and machine guns. Argentine Navy A-4 pilot Capitande Corbeta Alberto Jorge Philippi related the events of his May 21 attack against British shipping in San Carlos Bay: "We deployed three airplanes. The targets were the ships that were supporting the San Carlos landing. We knew that the attack would be carried out without escort and without the existence of air superiority.

"One hundred miles before arriving at the coast of Gran Malvina, I ordered a descent to 100 feet over the island. We followed course 069° until the south entrance of the San Carlos Strait, where we accelerated to 450 knots, flying at no more than 50 feet.

"Arriving at Bahia Ruiz Puente, I saw at 11 o'clock among the rocks the masts of a frigate that seemed to have detected us and appeared to be leaving rapidly from the coast toward the center of the channel with a course of approximately 240°. I signaled the target to my companions, they had already seen it, and I ordered us to open attack. I veered toward the right in order to take cover in the [radar] echo of the coast and in order to attempt to blend in with the dark rocks. When the angle of fire was adequate, I turned to slope toward the frigate [HMS *Ardent*] with the point of my left wing almost scraping the waves, and when I finished the turn, I was already in position to fire, crossing from the port quarter to the starboard bow. Before I carried out the attack, I saw the bow gun, the cannons on the ship's sides, and the Sea Cat missile fire.

"At 1,000 to 1,500 meters from the target, I ascended to 300 feet and I concentrated to arrange the crosshairs of my sight on the stern, without thinking of anything else; it was aligned. When the center of the crosshairs was superimposed on the target, I pressed the button that launched the bombs, I increased speed and commenced a violent turn to escape to the right, descending in order to once again fly just above the waves, later turning to the left. Meanwhile, I listened to the voice of my fellow pilot Jose Cesar Arca shouting, "Very good, Sir." I looked over my left shoulder and saw the frigate with much smoke in the stern and a splash 20 meters from its starboard bow. We escaped by the same route.

"In a couple of minutes an attack arrived, and a shout by Marquez stopped my heart, "Harrier! Harrier!" Immediately I ordered external cargoes ejected and to escape with the hope of reaching refuge in the clouds that were in front of us. But I felt an explosion in my tail and the nose of the airplane elevated uncontrollably; I needed the support of both hands on the stick

Five A-4Q Skyhawks of the Argentine Naval Air Arm in formation. The naval Skyhawks, which flew most of their missions from land bases during the conflict, succeeded in sinking the HMS *Ardent*, but suffered heavy losses to Sea Harriers and antiaircraft fire. (Argentine Navy)

that was unresponsive. I looked to the right and saw a Sea Harrier at 150 meters coming in for the kill. I communicated and said, ''I am going to eject; I am well.'' I reduced speed, opened the speed brakes, placed my left hand on the lower ejection handle and fired it. I felt a forceful explosion when the canopy was ejected, and immediately there was a forceful pain in the nape of my neck. My final thought before passing out was, ''I am falling like a rock.'' When I recovered consciousness I was hanging from my parachute, in a cloud, with drops of rain moistening my face, and I had lost the helmet and the mask. I landed 100 meters from the coast and unfastened the parachute. I swam arm over arm to the coast. I arrived so tired that I was not able to walk. I tried to rest.''[10]

Argentine pilots braved the fire and sank HMS *Ardent* and damaged four other ships with bombs. However, the cost was high. Britain reportedly shot down 15 fighter-bombers, including eight destroyed by Sea Harriers.[11]

For their part, RAF GR Mk 3 Harriers undertook numerous air strikes, and one was lost to a Blowpipe SAM over Port Howard.[12] Two Royal Marine Gazelle helicopters were also destroyed by ground fire near San Carlos.

May 23—Argentine aircraft pressed home attacks that caused serious damage to the HMS *Antelope*, hit by four bombs. The British claimed six Argentine Mirages and an A-4.[13]

May 24—One of the bombs on *Antelope* exploded during an attempt to defuse it, and the ship caught fire and later sank. Waves of Skyhawks and Mirages attacked British ships and positions near San Carlos. The fighter-bombers damaged LSTs *Sir Galahad* and *Sir Lancelot*, but eight were downed by British defenses. Three of these were achieved by a single flight of Harriers. Lt. Comdr. Andrew Ault, commanding office of Royal Navy 800 Air Squadron, discussed the battle: ''I was operating from the HMS *Hermes* to the east of the Falkland Islands. We arrived over, and we had just established ourselves on combat air patrol when my wingman and I were vectored towards an incoming Argentine raid. The ship controlling us directed us on to the aircraft, and it was excellent weather conditions. We sighted four attacking Mirages, and we had to maneuver very hard to achieve the kill . . . we were down at two hundred, at five hundred fifty knots. I fired two missiles in very quick succession against two targets. The missiles guided, and I was trying for a gun kill on the third while all the Mirage aircraft had, of course, jettisoned their fuel tanks and bombs and were in a hard turn . . . I was trying for a gun kill on the third, when my wingman fired over my shoulder and his missile scored. He achieved a kill on the third man. The fourth man managed to escape back toward the mainland.''[14]

May 25—On Argentine National Day, FAA and ANA aircraft flew dozens of sorties and scored a number of victories against the British fleet. FAA Skyhawks attacked *Broadsword* and *Coventry*, patrolling north of West Falkland Island to detect and warn of incoming strikes. *Broadsword* was damaged by a bomb. *Coventry* was hit by at least three 1,000-lb. bombs, capsized, and sank within one hour.

Two Super Etendards, each carrying one AM-39 Exocet and one fuel tank, air-refueled from a KC-130 to extend their range enough to attack. The aircraft subsequently launched their missiles at what they thought was an aircraft carrier, the containership *Atlantic Conveyor*. Fires out of control, the ship was abandoned with the loss of 12 lives. Its cargo of six Wessex and three Chinook helicopters and tons of important supplies were destroyed in the fire. Britain claimed destruction of seven Argentine A-4.[15]

May 27—British paratroopers attacked Argentine positions at Darwin/Goose Green, and a GR Mk 3 Harrier providing close support was downed by antiaircraft. The pilot ejected successfully. Mirage and Skyhawk fighter-bombers hit the San Carlos beachhead and British ships off shore. Two Skyhawks were reportedly destroyed.

May 28—British paratroopers captured Darwin and met heavy resistance at Goose Green. Harriers and Pucaras provided close support for their respective forces. A Pucara was downed by a Blowpipe missile but another Pucara shot down a British Scout helicopter.[16]

May 30—Two ANA Super Etendards, one armed with an AM-39 Exocet, joined four FAA Skyhawks for a coordinated attack against the task force. Following launch of the Exocet, the Skyhawks swept in to bomb with two reportedly shot down by naval SAMs. The Argentines insist they hit a carrier while the British deny any damage. (British sources indicated that the Exocet was destroyed by a lucky shot from the HMS *Avenger's* 4.5 in. gun.)[17] Some reports had it that the attacks were against the hulk of the *Atlantic Conveyor* and sank her.[18]

An RAF Harrier was damaged by antiaircraft fire during a strike against Port Stanley and the pilot successfully ejected over the ocean when fuel was exhausted. That night, a Vulcan from Ascension Island attacked and damaged with Shrike missiles the antenna of an Argentine search radar.[19]

June 1—Harriers and Sea Harriers continued to strike at the Port Stanley garrison as British troops advanced to occupy key positions around the town. A Sea Harrier was shot down while flying at 13,000 ft. over Port Stanley, the victim of a Roland SAM.[20]

June 5—The British laid down an 850-ft. airstrip of aluminum matting at the San Carlos beachhead. The forward strip served as a refueling point for patrolling Sea Harriers and a ground-loiter position for Harriers on call for close air support.

A Sea Harrier takes off from the steel mat runway established as a forward operating site near the San Carlos beachhead. This strip increased the effectiveness of Harriers and Sea Harriers since they could refuel and ground loiter near the battle zone. (British Aerospace)

June 8—Argentine forces detected an attempt to land troops in Buff Cove, seven miles south of Port Stanley. Four Skyhawks and two Daggers bombed the landing ships *Sir Tristram* and *Sir Galahad*, causing fires, extensive damage, and more than 100 casualties including more than fifty dead. Air attacks also took place against British ships in Falkland sound. The frigate HMS *Plymouth* was hit by four 1,000-lb. bombs that did not explode, and a landing craft was sunk with the loss of six men.

Ten Argentine aircraft were claimed including several late in the day that fell to Sea Harriers. Lt. David Smith described the dogfight: "Later that afternoon, as I flew patrol overhead at ten thousand feet, I once against witnessed the awful sight of the *Sir Galahad* fiercely ablaze, pouring out masses of thick, oily smoke. It was a quite incredible sight, one etched with so many others on my mind forever. The whole of the after section was literally glowing red with the intense heat from the fire.

"As the sun set in the North West with angry colors, we noticed a small landing craft heading towards the disaster area from Goose Green. Just as we were carrying out a combat turn over it, Moggy (Flight Lt. Dave Morgan) shouted over the R. T.: 'Good God! Its being attacked—three—no four Mirages—follow me down, Dave.' With that he rolled upside down and pulled hard for the surface, almost disappearing in the rapidly gathering gloom. I slammed the throttle to full power and dived down after him in a desperate attempt to stay visual with his aircraft. As we leveled out at wave-top height, with the Harrier shrieking loudly as my airspeed topped 600 knots, I saw two bright flashes as Moggy fired his missiles. I followed the two white smoke trails and saw two huge fireballs as the Mirages disintegrated and impacted the sea. I was now in the quite dreadful situation of seeing several aircraft ahead but not being able positively to identify Moggy and get a clear shot. Mog then suddenly opened up on the two retreating Mirages with his cannons, and, from the water kicked up by his bullets, I was able to pick out one of the 'bogeys.' I pointed the missile at him and there was the usual growl in my ears as it acquired him. A quick press of the 'accept' button on the stick and a green circle appeared in the head-up display, accompanied by a chirp noise in my headset. The circle followed the Mirage despite his speed and incredibly low altitude and, rolling back the safety flap, I fired.

"There was a bright flash and a roar as the missile launched, fairly rocking the aircraft in its wake. Surely the Mirage was too low, too fast, too far away . . . I watched with a sort of helpless fascination. At that moment everything seemed to stay quite still, although in the real world my Sea Harrier was belting along at more than ten miles a minute, a few feet above the waves.

"Then the darkness was lit up by another fierce flash and fireball. He must have been flying so low that the missile impact and ground impact seemed almost simultaneous. Then, as the reality of the situation returned, a quick glance at my fuel gauges showed I was already on dangerous ground and I pulled the aircraft up to the vertical to attain the sanctity of high altitude. There was still the long return to the ship to fly, with a difficult night recovery at the end of it."[21]

June 12—British troops surrounded Port Stanley and made a night assault against defensive positions five miles from the town. The HMS *Glamorgan* providing gun fire support was hit as it was withdrawing by a land-based Exocet. The missile hit the ship's aft deck and destroyed a helicopter, hangar, and Sea Cat missile launcher, killing 13 and wounding 17. The ship remained sea worthy and returned to service following repairs 36 hours later.

June 13–14—British troops made strong night assaults against positions around Port Stanley. Argentine aircraft flew several sorties, losing a Mirage and Canberra while British Harriers began using laser-guided bombs against enemy positions. On the morning of June 14, Argentine forces formally surrendered and the fighting ended.

Analysis

With the cease-fire on June 14, 1984, the fighting between Argentina and Great Britain ended. Argentina had been unable to hold the islands. Britain's naval task force enforced a blockade and landed troops who, following numerous battles, recaptured South Georgia and the Falkland Islands.

Britain positioned several thousand troops, Phantom and Harrier fighter aircraft, air defense missile batteries, and several warships in the Falklands in the event of renewed hostilities. Argentina restrained from further military action and began purchasing aircraft, naval vessels, and ground equipment to make up its losses.

During the conflict, Argentina suffered almost 2,000 casualties including more than 700 killed. Losses included the cruiser *General Belgrano*, submarine *Santa Fe*, and a half dozen patrol craft/trawlers and cargo ships. Argentina admitted the loss of 79 FAA and ANA aircraft, 49 said to have been destroyed in combat.[22] Britain claims that it destroyed or captured 103 Argentine aircraft. During the conflict, 255 British civilians and military personnel were killed and more than 700 wounded. Two destroyers, two frigates, one landing ship, and one leased civilian container ship were sunk and more than a dozen warships and transports damaged. Aircraft losses included nine Harriers/Sea Harriers and 25 helicopters. Three Harriers, two Sea Harriers, and 12 helicopters were destroyed by hostile action.[23]

Air warfare in the conflict involved a mix of well-proven and new, high-technology weapon systems. The war saw the combat initiation of the Harrier/Sea Harrier V/STOL tactical aircraft and widespread use of missile systems. It was also the first conflict since World War II that included heavy, sustained air attacks against naval forces. While the successful use of the AM-39 Exocet air-to-surface anti-ship missile attracted much attention, most British and Argentine strike sorties were made with conventional "iron" bombs, rockets, and cannon.

Argentine Strike Operations

Argentina began attacking British targets on May 1 and flew about 300 strike sorties against ships, amphibious operations, and land targets until the cease-fire. Mirage/Dagger and Skyhawk fighter-bombers that performed a majority of the strike sorties were equipped with day-only, manually-operated weapons aiming systems and limited navigation equipment. To accurately deliver weapon loads of bombs or rockets, Argentine pilots had to penetrate British aircraft and missile defenses and overfly the target.

Skyhawk and Mirage/Dagger pilots could spend only a few minutes of combat time since they were operating at their extreme range. Time was further limited since targets frequently had to be sought out because of limited reconnaissance data and poor weather. Another detrimental factor was the necessity for high-speed, low-level flight profiles to survive the heavy defenses.

Despite these drawbacks, Argentine pilots repeatedly hit ships and land targets with bombs, rockets, and cannon fire. Free-fall bombs sank four ships (two frigates, one destroyer, and one assault ship) and damaged ten others. Fewer than half the bombs that hit ships exploded since the low-level delivery techniques did not allow time enough for the bombs to arm themselves. According to British sources, at least six more ships would have been destroyed if those bombs had detonated.[24]

The ANA began the war with five Super Etendard fighter-bombers and several AM-39 Exocet air-to-surface, anti-ship missiles. The Super Etendards flew five missions, fired five missiles, and hit the *Sheffield*, *Atlantic Conveyor*, and, according to Argentine sources, a British aircraft carrier.[25] *Sheffield* and *Atlantic Conveyor* were gutted by fire and later sank. A sixth Exocet fired from land damaged the *Glamorgan*.

The AM-39 Exocet air-launched missile allowed the low-flying Super Etendards to attack from beyond the range of sea-based radar and close-in defenses.[26] The missile, however, did have drawbacks as its seeker locks onto the first large radar target detected. Thus, the weapon could not be used to attack shipping in Falkland Sound during the San Carlos assault because the surrounding hills provided a larger radar return than the ships offshore.[27]

An Argentine Naval Air Arm Super Etendard takes off with an Exocet air-to-surface antiship missile. The Super Etendard/Exocet combination was responsible for the destruction of the destroyer HMS *Sheffield* and containership *Atlantic Conveyor* and proved the most effective Argentine antiship weapons system. (Argentine Navy)

FAA Pucara and ANA Aeromacchi MB-339A light strike aircraft operating from islands flew numerous attack and reconnaissance sorties during the conflict. Pucaras performed many close support missions against British troops during and after the San Carlos landing. ANA MB-339A jet aircraft flew reconnaissance and strike sorties from the Port Stanley airfield and reportedly damaged with rockets and cannon fire a British warship on May 21.

Argentine transport and reconnaissance aircraft supported the fighter-bombers by tracking the British fleet, providing navigation aid to strike aircraft, and resupplying the islands. Aircraft in these roles included 707, C-130, Fokker F-28, and L188 Electra transports, P-2 Neptune ASW aircraft, and civilian Lear Jets.

In addition to sinking or damaging several ships, Argentine strikes forced British carriers and most of the task force to patrol well east of the islands, beyond range of Argentine strike aircraft. This degraded the effectiveness of British air cover and naval gunfire.

With skill and courage, Argentine Air Force and Navy pilots penetrated the British defenses and hit numerous land and naval targets. They paid a heavy price: Argentina admitted the loss of 40 pilots and aircrew and 49 aircraft in combat. An additional 30 aircraft were said to have been lost to non-combat causes.[28] Britain claimed to have shot down 72 Argentine aircraft with an additional 31 destroyed on the ground or captured.[29]

According to Argentine sources, the FAA launched 445 combat sorties, 272 of which reached their targets. The ANA successfully flew 50 combat sorties.[30] During the 322 combat sorties that penetrated British defenses, between 49 and 72 aircraft were shot down. This translates to average attrition rate per sortie of between 15 and 22 percent.

British Air Defense Operations

The British established a multilayered screen of defenses around their task force and ground units following the San Carlos landings. Sea Harriers from the two aircraft carriers flew

Combat Air Patrol (CAP) along the likely avenues of approach for Argentine attack. These aircraft formed the outer perimeter of the air defenses.

Since the small British carriers lacked the capability to carry airborne early warning aircraft, it was necessary to position ships equipped with surveillance radars near the Falklands to give advance warning of strike aircraft and direct Sea Harriers flying CAP.

In the air intercept role, the Sea Harrier carried two AIM-9L Sidewinder air-to-air missiles and two 30-mm Aden cannon. When equipped with two external fuel tanks, the Sea Harrier had a flight time of approximately 90 minutes that allowed 30 to 45 minutes of CAP time.[31]

Air-to-air combat between British and Argentine aircraft began on May 1 when two Sea Harriers and two Mirages engaged in a dogfight. The Mirages fired missiles at the Sea Harriers (either AIM-9B Sidewinders, Matra 550s, or Matra 530s) but a Sea Harrier scored first with an AIM-9L Sidewinder. Most subsequent Sea Harrier air combat victories were against bomb-carrying Mirage/Daggers and A-4 Skyhawks at low altitude and high speed.

Sea Harriers logged more than 1,100 CAP sorties and were credited with the destruction of 20 Argentine aircraft.[32] No Sea Harriers were lost in air combat. Confirmed kills included 12 Mirage/Daggers, five A-4 Skyhawks, one Canberra, one Pucara, and one helicopter.[33]

The AIM-9L Sidewinder was credited for the destruction of 16 Argentine aircraft, with another four falling to 30-mm cannon. Most Sidewinder shots were from the rear hemisphere. The missile achieved a very respectable success rate of 61 percent (16 kills for 26 launches).[34]

The Sea Harrier performed excellently despite the fact that it is subsonic; equipped with pulse-only radar incapable of detecting low-flying targets over land; and has limited range and payload performance.[35] Due to the limited number of fighter aircraft available (never more than 25 Sea Harriers in the South Atlantic at one time) and the lack of airborne early warning platforms, the British were unable to gain air superiority and thus prevent losses.[36]

Aircraft that penetrated the outer screen of Sea Harriers entered the free-fire missile engagement zone. The Falkland Islands conflict witnessed the first widespread employment of naval surface-to-air missiles systems.

Area air defense was provided by seven ships armed with Sea Dart surface-to-air missiles. The ramjet-powered, medium-range, radar-guided missile was effective against aircraft at medium and high altitudes and at ranges of more than 25 miles. It was credited with the destruction of eight Argentine aircraft.[37]

Sea Dart received substantial negative publicity due to the fact that two Type 42 destroyers were sunk by air and missile attacks. The system experienced problems detecting and tracking low-flying aircraft and missiles, especially those operating over land. However, it must be pointed out that the weapon system was designed to provide area defense against aircraft penetrating at medium and high altitude and that such other systems as Sea Wolf—designed to counter low flying targets—were responsible for close-in defense.

Two County Class destroyers armed with area defense Sea Slug missiles were included in the task force. Little information has been released on the use of the Sea Slug in the Falklands. However, it is known that the system was judged to be obsolete and was being phased out because of its limited rate of fire and lack of effectiveness against low-flying targets.[38]

Close-in defense was provided by 17 ships armed with Sea Cat and two armed with Sea Wolf surface-to-air missiles. The small, lightweight Sea Cat was generally thought to be obsolete since it required manual optical guidance via radio and had limited range. However, the missile was credited with eight victories.[39]

Two ships of the task force were armed with the Sea Wolf missile system developed to provide self-defense against missile attack. Sea Wolf demonstrated its effectiveness against low-flying aircraft and was credited with five victories with the expenditure of only a small number of missiles.[40] The Sea Wolf system had problems with ground-clutter interference and was quickly modified in the field to improve performance.

Most British combat ships mounted 4.5-in., 20-mm, 40-mm cannon, and many were hurriedly equipped with numerous mountings for machine guns. (Hand-held Blowpipe missiles were even fired from the decks against attacking aircraft.)[41] Cannon and small arms on ships and land were credited with seven kills.[42]

Following the San Carlos invasion on May 21, 12 Rapier surface-to-air missile units were landed to provide air defense. The Rapier system protected the landing area for a week and then were moved forward to cover troops advancing toward Port Stanley. The system was credited with 14 confirmed kills.[43] The man-portable Blowpipe point-defense missile system was credited with destroying nine Argentine aircraft including a number of Pucaras attacking during the British assault at Goose Green. Special Air Service "commando" troops were equipped with U.S.-built light-weight Stinger infrared guided antiaircraft missiles and reportedly scored a Pucara during the conflict.[44]

(Jeffrey Ethell and Alfred Price in their comprehensive study of the Falkland Islands conflict *Air War South Atlantic* contend that the official British white paper seriously overstated the actual Argentine losses to surface-to-air missiles and guns. Ethell and Price state that they could confirm only 20 of the 52 SAM and gun kills claimed. The authors point to the few Argentine pilots captured, limited amount of aircraft wreckage, and historical precedents for inflated antiaircraft claims [particularly when the aircraft were to have crashed at sea] to substantiate their position.)[45]

A Sea Wolf surface-to-air missile is launched from a British *Broadsword*-class guided missile frigate. The Sea Wolf missile system was credited with the destruction of five Argentine aircraft during the Falkland Islands conflict. (British Aerospace)

British Strike Operations

The first British air attack of the conflict was made on the early morning of May 1 when a Vulcan bomber—more than 3,300 miles each way from Ascension Island—dropped 21 1,000-lb. bombs on the Port Stanley airfield. Subsequently, Vulcans flew two additional airfield bombing attacks and two strikes with Shrike anti-radar missiles in an attempt to destroy Argentine surveillance radars.

While the Port Stanley runway was damaged, following repairs, Argentine flight operations resumed. The anti-radar missions succeeded in damaging and destroying some radars; however, antiaircraft fire over Port Stanley did not diminish appreciably.

Several hours after the first Vulcan attack, Sea Harriers struck at the Port Stanley and Goose Green airfields with 1,000-lb. bombs and BL755 cluster munitions. Strikes continued but following the loss of a Sea Harrier and pilot to antiaircraft over Goose Green on May 4, tactics were modified.

To reduce vulnerability to the heavy concentration of antiaircraft weapons encountered at Port Stanley and Goose Green, Sea Harriers took to loft bombing. This type of delivery was very inaccurate but was designed to keep pressure on the Argentine troops while limiting losses. Sea Harriers on CAP used their 30-mm Aden cannon on May 9 and 16 to strafe Argentine trawlers and patrol craft.

Royal Air Force GR Mk. 3 Harriers arrived in the South Atlantic on May 18 to augment the overly-committed force of Sea Harriers. The Harriers, which operated from the *Hermes* and later from a forward operating site near San Carlos, took over most of the responsibility for ground-attack operations.

The aircraft flew attacks against airfields at Port Stanley, Goose Green, and Pebble Island, close support strikes, and preplanned strikes against enemy positions. The most common ordnance employed was the 1,000-lb. bomb although BL755 cluster bombs, 2-in. unguided rockets, and laser guided bombs were also delivered.

A Sea Harrier is launched from HMS *Hermes*. The tight packing of aircraft, support equipment, and ordnance can be seen from this photograph. The *Hermes* normally carried a complement of five Sea Harriers and nine Sea King ASW helicopters. During the Falkland Islands campaign, the *Hermes* initially operated with 12 Sea Harriers and 18 Sea King helicopters. (British Aerospace)

Argentine IA-58A Pucaras captured in various states of disrepair at Port Stanley airfield. (British Aerospace)

The Harriers and Sea Harriers operated routinely against several well-defended targets. Goose Green was defended from air attack by six twin-barrel Rheinmetall 20-mm cannon supported by an Israeli-built ELTA radar, two 35-mm Oerlikon cannon directed by a Skyguard radar, and SA-7 shoulder-fired missiles. On May 4, a Sea Harrier making an attack was shot down by 35-mm cannon. Port Stanley sported even heavier defenses, including more than twenty 20-mm and 35-mm cannon, several fire-control radars, Tiger Cat and Roland antiaircraft missile batteries, and hand-held SA-7 and Blowpipe SAMs.[46]

Five Harrier and Sea Harriers were lost to ground defenses during the conflict. One Sea Harrier was lost to AAA over Goose Green on May 4, while a second was shot down by a Roland over Port Stanley on June 2. Sea Harriers flew some 90 attack sorties during the conflict.[47] Harrier losses included an aircraft destroyed by an Argentine Blowpipe or cannon fire on May 21, and two downed by antiaircraft fire on May 27 and May 30. The RAF Harriers flew a total of 126 attack sorties over the Falklands.[48] The aggregate loss rate for Sea Harrier/Harrier strike operations was 2.3 percent (five losses in 216 sorties).

British helicopters were also involved in strike operations. Royal Navy Lynx helicopters fired the semi-active, radar-guided Sea Skua in combat for the first time, sinking two patrol craft and severely damaging another. Wasp and Wessex helicopters engaged and sank the Argentine submarine *Santa Fe* with depth charges and AS-12 missiles. A number of British helicopters were destroyed in combat including three Garelles downed by ground fire and a Scout shot down by a Pucara.[49]

The war pitted the armed forces of Britain and Argentina against one another in a war neither side wanted to fight. The conflict is worth examining because it was the first combat test of many weapons systems and as such demonstrates the evolving nature of air warfare.

CHAPTER X

Conclusion

Throughout its history, air warfare has always been a complex activity. A World War I pilot flew frail wire, wood, and canvas biplanes faster than 100 miles per hour and had to adroitly maneuver behind an enemy aircraft to shoot at it with his machine guns.

Aircraft were the leading edge of technology, but a pilot had few aids. He detected his prey visually and fired at it over a fixed sight at short range. He worried as much about getting lost over the field of battle or mechanical and structural failure as he did about enemy fighters or ground gunners. Bombing was, in most cases, simply dropping the projectile over the side.

World War II began with faster, more-reliable monoplanes, but the fighter pilot's tasks were still quite similar to those of his World War I predecessor: rove the battle zone, detect enemy aircraft, and down them at close range with machine guns and cannon. Attack aircraft had internal bomb bays, simple delivery aids, and more effective weapons. As the war progressed, radar brought about ground-controlled intercepts, operationally feasible night fighting, more accurate day and night antiaircraft fire, and blind bombing. The pilot had new gunsights, radar systems, and even electronic countermeasures equipment to operate. There were more threats to evade from enemy aircraft similarly equipped.

The Korean War involved faster swept-wing jet fighters that necessitated new tactics and operational procedures. While jet-vs.-jet air combat received much of the attention, propeller-driven fighter-bombers flew a majority of the missions to bomb and strafe ground targets.

During the 1950s and 1960s, new equipment and weapons under development in a number of countries significantly redirected the military pilot's mode of operation. Electronics, aerodynamics, and propulsion technology had matured to the point where missiles became the new weapons of offensive and defensive air warfare. First used in combat by Nationalist Chinese F-86 Sabre pilots against Communist Chinese MiGs in 1958, the air-to-air missile (in this case, the infrared-guided AIM-9B Sidewinder missile) extended the radius of combat beyond the 3,000-foot operational range of aircraft-borne machine guns and cannon.

Radar systems and radar-guided missiles such as the AIM-7 Sparrow, Matra R-530, and AA-1 Alkali extended the pilot's reach to targets several miles away and added the capability of destroying enemy aircraft under all weather conditions.

Moreover, Ajax, Bloodhound, Guideline, and Hawk missile systems were designed to be ground-launched against aircraft. Most people first became aware of the potential of radar-guided surface-to-air missile systems when Francis Gary Power's U-2 reconnaissance aircraft was shot down over the Soviet Union in 1960. The infrared or radar-guided air-to-air "wonder weapons" caused many military theorists to postulate an end to close-in dogfights. Surface-to-air missiles, furthermore, would sweep the skies clean of enemy aircraft coming within their range.

So great was this conviction that the Soviet MiG-21PF Fishbed D and the initial models of the American F-4 Phantom II were designed to carry missiles only; the cannon or machine guns that had been the principal weaponry of earlier fighters, such as the MiG-15 and F-86, were discarded.

Vietnam was the first true testing ground for tactical air-to-air and surface-to-air missiles and for air-to-ground guided bombs.

The crucible of combat demonstrated that the theorists had greatly overestimated the effectiveness of tactical air-to-air missiles. Early in the Vietnam War, U.S. Navy F-4 Phantoms equipped with only air-to-air missiles and no guns fired more than 50 missiles without shooting down a single North Vietnamese MiG. Missiles had limited firing and maneuvering envelopes and complicated systems that did not stand up well to the rigors of combat.

Furthermore, if an enemy penetrated inside the air-to-air missile's minimum range, or if a pilot exhausted his supply of missiles, he found himself without a weapon. As a result of this early experience, today's modern fighters—including the F-16, F/A-18, the latest MiGs, the Mirage 2000, and the Tornado F. Mk 2—are all equipped with cannon with high rates of fire and projectiles of great lethality. Missiles have become the primary air-to-air weapon, but the highly-reliable cannon remains in the spectrum of weapons at a pilot's disposal.

Combat showed that surface-to-air missiles were also less effective than initially expected.

Even before the U.S. became familiar with the Soviet-built SA-2 Guideline surface-to-air missile and learned to counter it with electronic countermeasures, the best performance the missile could demonstrate was downing one U.S. aircraft for every 55 missiles fired. Pilots found that if they could see a surface-to-air or air-to-air missile in time, they could outmaneuver it.

While destroying the enemy fighter or attack aircraft is the aim of defensive air warfare, the goal of offensive air power usually is ordnance on target. During the past several decades, a number of countries have investigated means to more accurately deliver weapons, and to do so outside the lethal envelope of short-range antiaircraft fire and surface-to-air missiles. Two basic paths have been taken to develop accurate and survivable weapon delivery systems: precision-guided weapons and sophisticated aircraft weapon-delivery systems.

Precision-guided weapons date back to World War II, but their full promise was not fulfilled until the 1960s when guidance technology came of age. One of the first highly-effective surface attack weapons was the Walleye glide bomb used by the U.S. Navy in Vietnam. While not without limitations, laser-guided and television-guided missiles and free-fall bombs proved to have a very high probability of destroying their targets during the Vietnam and later conflicts.

High-performance bombs and missiles capable of destroying targets from both low and high altitude and at great standoff ranges—such as the Tomahawk cruise missile, Exocet anti-ship missile, and GBU-15 long-range glide bomb—have since been developed and widely deployed.

Despite the shortcomings of air-to-air and surface-to-air missiles, the advent of such missiles significantly altered battle tactics. In diving to low level to avoid SA-2 missiles launched by the North Vietnamese, American pilots frequently flew into intense antiaircraft fire, losing hundreds of aircraft. To counter the SA-2 and artillery antiaircraft defenses, aircraft were fitted with radar receivers, chaff and flare dispensers, and electronic countermeasures to detect and confuse the missile and gun radar guidance systems. In addition, special teams of ''Wild Weasel'' aircraft were formed to destroy ground-based defenses with bombs, rockets, and Shrike radar-homing missiles.

Missile-armed North Vietnamese interceptors, following the guidance of ground radar operators, were able to surprise U.S. aircraft with high-speed attacks and escape before the escort fighters could deter or destroy them.

The missiles and their associated radar threats considerably complicated the task of combat pilots and military mission planners. Pilots, in addition to navigating, flying, searching for, and attacking ground targets or enemy aircraft, now also had to monitor radar homing and warning (RHAW) sensors, listen to transmissions from ships or aircraft radar systems for warnings of approaching MiGs, operate electronic countermeasures equipment, and visually watch out for undetected flying "telephone poles" or marauding MiGs.

North Vietnam's heavy air defenses damaged or downed many aircraft; furthermore, they lessened the effectiveness of those that were untouched by forcing pilots to divide attention among a multitude of tasks. While evading surface-to-air missiles, antiaircraft artillery, or MiGs, pilots got lost, were forced to jettison their bombs and/or fuel tanks, or bombed the real target with much less accuracy than they had the target on the practice range.

Support systems, required to ensure that the bombers reached their target, proliferated: electronic countermeasures pods and equipment, escort fighters, radar-jamming planes, shipborne and airborne early warning systems, and refueling tankers reduced the numbers of aircraft available to carry bombs, complicated the tasks of mission planners and maintenance personnel, and drove up the cost of delivering each bomb on target. In short, the advent of missiles helped to make air warfare dramatically more complex and expensive.

As one might expect, as the limitations of the early missiles became evident, efforts were undertaken to correct the deficiencies. Now in the 1980s the latest generation of tactical missiles is far more capable than the early Sidewinder, Sparrow, Falcon, Atoll, and SA-2 that were employed with moderate success in the early phase of the Vietnam conflict. The more-advanced missiles employed during the Falkland/Malvinas Islands and Mideast conflicts of 1982 demonstrated a higher probability of success than the earlier-generation weapons used in the conflicts of the 1960s.

Research-and-development efforts continue to produce missiles that are ever more precise and versatile, and that can be fired under an ever-wider variety of conditions and still have a high probability of destroying their target. The U.S. Army's Patriot surface-to-air missile system and the U.S. Air Force/Navy's AIM-120 AMRAAM air-to-air missile are current examples of sophisticated, high-probability of kill missile systems that are nearing operational status. However, it must be pointed out that tactics, countermeasures, aircrew, weapons operator training, and political factors still significantly affect how well weapons systems perform in battle. These new weapons would be expensive failures if used improperly by poorly trained crews.

The all-important measure of aircrews of any nation, regardless of the technological level of its aircraft and weapons, is the proficiency and the tactics with which the aircrew is able to maneuver and utilize its weapons systems to defeat the enemy. Through training, ideally the crew melded with the aircraft into an integral team of man and machine, whose performance is honed to a fine edge through tactics. Training and tactics therefore play an interrelated role: training to achieve proficiency in tactics, while tactics themselves often evolve from vigorous training.

The essentials any air force's training comprises instruction ranging from the basics on how to operate an aircraft and its weapons systems to the ultimate integration of the man and machine in combat tactics. Once a pilot, radar intercept officer, or weapons system operator reaches basic proficiency in his machine and knowledge of tactics, constant practice is demanded to maintain that level of performance.

Another factor is the increasing complexity of aircraft and their weapon systems, which not only lengthen the time required for a pilot or weapons operator to reach a basic level of proficiency, but also increase the need for constant practice in the variety of roles and tactics the aircraft must perform.

Modern technological marvels, without an adequately trained crew, are just so much metal sitting on the apron.

If any one conclusion can be drawn from the discussions of all the conflicts from 1965 to the 1980s, it is that success in air warfare is achieved through a complex interweaving of a number of factors, many of which are beyond the control of the individual pilot. Among the important elements are aircraft performance, avionics, weapons, pilot training, enemy defenses, morale, tactics, the type of conflict, the number of opponents, and the political restrictions affecting the rules of engagement. Frequently it has been demonstrated in air warfare that skill, aggressiveness, and tactics can overcome being superior numbers and quality.

The downing of North Vietnamese MiG-17s by propeller-driven U.S. Navy A-1 Skyraiders or, turning the tables, the loss of a number of Mach-2 F-4 Phantom jets to subsonic Korean War vintage MiG-17s, are examples of overcoming technical odds with skill and tactics.

Air warfare is a dynamic see-saw battle. Opponents are continually experimenting with new equipment, tactics, and concepts to improve their forces' performance. Egyptians and Syrians knew from experience in the Six-Day War of 1967 and the following War of Attrition that they could not compete with the Israel Defense Force/Air Force for air superiority or air-delivered firepower with pilots and fighter aircraft alone.

Massive numbers of Soviet air defense missiles and guns were rolled up to the battlefield to deny the Israeli Air Force freedom of the skies and provide offensive firepower. The Arabs capitalized on their strength in manpower and equipment during the Yom Kippur War of 1973 and exacted a heavy price in blood and aircraft.

Later in the conflict, it was the Arabs who suffered heavy losses as they were forced to throw aircraft against the Israeli ground forces that had penetrated into their rear areas. Pilot vs. pilot, pilot vs. antiaircraft artillery gunner or missile launch officer, the battle was played out in thousands of individual engagements. Equipment, training, and tactics continue to improve because planners see air warfare as an essential element of military posture.

In the event of an international conflict in the near future, what would air warfare be like? It is almost impossible to answer this question unless the time period, opponents, and scenario are specified. A high-intensity NATO-vs-Warsaw Pact conflict would be quite different from a conflict in the Middle East or a war between two third-world countries in Asia. However, as the aircraft and weapons involved influence the nature of a battle, we can look at some present trends and make some general observations.

Recently produced tactical aircraft run the gamut from large interceptors and attack aircraft armed with long-range air-to-air or air-to-surface missiles to the small jet trainer/attack aircraft armed with cannon, bomb, rockets, and short-range missiles. Many of these new tactical aircraft have a high thrust-to-weight ratio, and many also have relatively low wing loading.

Enhanced acceleration, turning performance, increased fuel fraction, and payload capability combined with more-reliable and capable fire-control systems and armament make the latest tactical aircraft highly lethal weapon systems.

Advanced fighter/attack aircraft of the 1980s carry a wide array of avionics equipment. In order to aid the pilot(s) in operating all these systems, the aircraft's cockpit—the interface between the man and the machine—has significantly evolved.

Some aircraft, such as the F-14A Tomcat and Tornado F Mk. 2 interceptors and the F-15E, Tornado, and Su-24 strike aircraft, include a pilot and a weapon systems operator to handle the wide variety of mission tasks. The designers of the F-15 Eagle, F-16 Fighting Falcon, F/A-18 Hornet, Mirage 2000, and other single-seat tactical aircraft rely on computers, sophisticated cathode ray tube displays, eye-level head-up displays, and easy-to-reach controls to reduce the pilot's workload so that a single pilot can operate the aircraft.

Given the increasingly complex nature of the air-warfare environment, the trend of computers and avionics systems taking over tasks for the pilot will undoubtedly continue.

Today, experiments are under way to equip tactical aircraft with avionics systems that react to voice commands from the pilot.

Current efforts are directed at allowing the pilot to change radar modes, sensor modes, and call up different weapon systems by voice command. One day we might even see situations similar to that suggested in the excellent air-combat novel *Firefox* by Craig Thomas, where a fighter's weapons were launched and guided by a pilot's thought impulses without his ever having to push a button.

The move/counter-move game between fighter and attack aircraft and antiaircraft defenses (which include radars, surface-to-air missiles, antiaircraft artillery, and interceptors/fighters) continues unabated. Following the Vietnam conflict, the stakes were raised during the Yom Kippur War of 1973. The conflict fitted the latest Soviet air-defense systems against the newest U.S.-built offensive and defensive equipment. The Middle East conflicts continued after the 1973 war with the result that Israeli forces equipped with U.S. and Israeli-built weapons have fought Syrian and PLO units armed by the Soviet Union.

The Falkland/Malvinas Islands conflict and Iran/Iraq War have also served as the testing ground for a variety of military systems and new tactics. Advanced systems continue to enter service with the military forces around the world; even more-capable systems are now being developed.

In the past, target detection and missile guidance relied primarily on radar and infrared systems. Current electronic countermeasures such as chaff and jammers plus such infrared countermeasures as flares and infrared deception devices are designed to defeat threats employing those guidance techniques. Future aircraft, however, will need to be equipped with detectors and jammers effective against threats that employ wholly-new modes of guidance. The recently deployed Swedish RBS 70 manportable surface-to-air missile guides the missile home by having it ride up a laser beam to the target. None of the (known) airborne detection and warning sensors presently on operational aircraft can alert the pilot to an attack by an RBS 70.

To deal with sophisticated present-day and future antiaircraft systems such as guns, missiles, and perhaps even laser or particle beam weapons, aircraft designers and systems designers will have to incorporate new concepts. Remotely piloted vehicles (RPVs) will take on greater responsibilities for such missions as reconnaissance and defense suppression; perhaps one day they might even routinely fly weapons delivery and air combat missions. RPVs have already proven themselves during the Vietnam conflict, Yom Kippur War, and 1982 Mideast conflict as capable and survivable sensor platforms for reconnaissance over extremely high-threat areas.

Further into the future, tactical aircraft may be forced by the lethal combat environment to operate at either very high or very low altitude and at sustained supersonic speed. Armed with long-range standoff weapons, missiles that can shoot down at low-altitude enemy aircraft, and masked by stealth design features and sophisticated electronic countermeasures systems, future tactical aircraft could perform the functions of our familiar stable of aircraft in the face of science-fiction-like laser and missile threats.

No matter how far one pushes the bounds of our imagination, one must not forget that, throughout history, for every revolutionary weapon invented, an adversary eventually devised a defense or counterweapon. Advantage, parity, disadvantage—like a chess game—rival factions have always maneuvered to change the military status quo.

Appendix I:

Aircraft and Weapons, 1965

This appendix discusses the aircraft, weapons, and fire-control systems in service in 1965; Appendix II discusses those of the 1980s. Both are intended to be working indexes—that is, designed to provide background information and data so that the reader can compare various aircraft and their weapons.

Fire Control

Pilots rely on their fire-control equipment to detect and attack a target. The equipment fitted to 1965-era tactical aircraft differed widely. Interceptors and all-weather attack aircraft carried a sophisticated radar for detecting other aircraft and ground targets. Fighters carried equipment that ranged from a simple non-computing reflector gunsight to a highly-effectual radar.

Because the design engineers of the F-5A Freedom Fighter wanted to keep the fighter simple, the aircraft had the most basic fire-control equipment. A non-computing fixed-reticle optical sight was provided for air-to-air and air-to-ground weapons delivery.[1] The reflector gunsight consisted of an image projector with a glass screen jutting above the edge of the plane's instrument panel. On the screen, a pilot saw a circular sighting reticle several inches in diameter and a central aiming dot, which indicated the point toward which the aircraft and its fixed guns were aimed.

When firing from a position directly behind the target, all the pilot had to do was to center the aiming dot on the target and shoot. Since most air combat takes place between turning aircraft, however, the pilot had to estimate at what point ahead of the target he would need to focus on and fire at in order to score a hit. This lead, or distance between the point where the target actually is at the time of firing and the point at which the target will be on impact, is known as the deflection angle. The circular sighting reticle around the central aiming dot gave the F-5A pilot an indication of the correct lead required for his shells to hit a target crossing his path at a relative speed of up to 100 knots. The pilot had to estimate the distance to the target and its crossing speed, and fire according to an estimated deflection angle. It was a basic system that placed a great deal of the responsibility for accurate shooting on the pilot, but when the pilot was well-trained, alert, and responsive it worked.

The lead-computing gyroscopic gunsight was the next level of fire-control assistance. This gunsight gave the pilot a continuously-updated indication of the proper point at which to fire in order to hit a turning aircraft. Developed by the British during World War II, the lead-computing gunsight was similar to the reflector sight, but included a gyroscope that measured the firing aircraft's own rate of turn. Since the deflection angle required to hit the target was proportional to the fighter's rate of turn, the gyroscopic information was used to move the sighting reticle in such a way that it displayed the required lead.

To account for the changing range between fighter and target, also necessary to compute the proper deflection angle during an attack, the pilot used a control on his stick or throttle to modify the size of the reticle so that it would remain the same size as the target's wing span no matter how its distance varied. Because the wing span of potentially threatening aircraft is generally known, the lead-computing gyroscopic gunsight can calculate the target's range, combine it with turn-rate data, and display the proper lead angle.

The lead-computing gyroscopic gunsight was installed on British and American fighters toward the end of World War II. Initially, it was not well received; but as pilots found they could fire more accurately at high deflection angles or at long range, they began to appreciate its ability to score kills even under marginal conditions.

While the lead-computing gyroscopic gunsight was a significant improvement over the non-computing reflector sight, it was not without its drawbacks. In order to compute the deflection angle, the attacking pilot had to maintain a steady turn for a period of between one second and four seconds—a long time in a confusing dogfight.

The MiG-17 was fitted with an ASP-3N gyroscopic gunsight. The sight could measure ranges between 492 feet and 2,600 feet and took between one and four seconds to compute the lead angle. Since the lead angle was calculated based on both the speed of the target and the projectile's time of flight, the ASP-3N included a barometric unit that compensated for the projectiles' different speeds depending on the air density at the altitude at which the cannon was fired.[2]

During the early 1950s, a new computing gunsight was introduced that used a ranging radar to find accurate range data. The radar was boresighted—that is, fixed so that it pointed straight ahead along the axis of the plane—to search ahead of the aircraft. When it detected a target, the radar tracked the enemy aircraft and fed the information to the fire-control computer. The computer housed gyroscopes that figured the tracking solution for accurately firing the weapons in much the same way as a lead-computing gyroscopic gunsight. Again, the information was translated into a reticle that displayed the proper lead angle. With the radar-ranging gyroscopic gunsight, the pilot had only to track the target, fly on a pursuit course after the target, and fire.[3]

The radar-ranging gunsight system was first used on three models of the F-86 (A, E, and F) fighter during the Korean War. The F-100 Super Sabre included AN/ASG-17 fire-control radar to supply range data to the A-4 gunsight.

The radar had a search range of between 1,800 and 9,000 feet. When the radar locked on to a target, an indicator on the instrument panel lit up, and range to the target was displayed on the gunsight. At low level, the radar reacted to reflections of its own signal from the ground, and the pilot then fell back on using the manual circular sighting reticle for ranging.[4]

The MiG-21F, MiG-19s, MiG-17F, Mystère IV-A, Super Mystère B-2, F-104A, F-104C, and F-86 Sabre fire-control systems included a radar-ranging gunsight plus a back-up gyroscopic gunsight for use at low level and in case of radar failure.

The F-4B Phantom incorporated a comprehensive weapon system that could detect and track a target under all weather conditions—even in an environment in which electronic countermeasures are being applied—and successfully fire its missile. To accomplish this task, the Phantom was equipped with an Aero 1A fire-control system that included the AN/APQ-72 that can detect targets within a range of about 50 miles.

To aid the pilot and the radar intercept officer in detecting targets, the F-4B was equipped with an AN/AAA-4 infrared sensor. Housed in a streamlined pod under the nose, the infrared sensor detected heat emission from jet aircraft and, under unusual ideal conditions, the sensor could even detect an aircraft at greater range than the radar. The infrared sensor operated in search mode and track mode, and could provide bearing and elevation data, but no information on the range of the enemy aircraft. The radar and infrared sensor were electronically linked to each other and could be used in tandem for improved search-and-track capability. The infrared sensor was not subject to electronic countermeasures and, because of its passive nature, it could not be detected.

During an attack, the AN/APQ-72 radar operated in conjunction with the whole AN/APA-126 radar set group that computed steering and fire-control information for the pilot. Once the missile was fired, the radar set group illuminated the target with continuous-wave radar to provide the radar-guided Sparrow missile a target on which to guide.[5]

The Aero 1A system was complex, and in the F-4 Phantom a radar intercept officer (RIO) was included back seat of the pilot to operate both the radar and the infrared sensor and to assist the pilot in navigation.

The AN/APQ-72 was a pulse-modulated type radar. The radar transmitted a burst of energy in front of the aircraft; when the signal struck an object such as an aircraft, it was reflected back. Because the speed of the transmitted pulse was known, the radar could measure the time between the transmission of the pulse and its return; it would then calculate the distance to the target.

When operating at low altitudes or when aimed down at low-flying targets, a pulse radar receives many echos from the ground. The large number of pulses returning from ground features obscure the small signal from the target. Such ground clutter limits the accuracy of the fire-control system of the Phantom (and that of such other 1950s-generation fighters as the Mirage III, the Lightning, the SAAB Draken, or those MiG-21 Fishbed fighters equipped with pulse modulation radars) to an altitude approximately identical with that of the target or to attacks from below the target.

Guns

Historically, machine guns and cannon were the primary air-to-air weapons. In the 1950s, many engineers, scientists, and military strategists theorized that missiles would replace the rapid-firing machine gun or the cannon as the primary air-to-air weapon. Several models of the British Lightning, F-4 Phantom, and MiG-21 Fishbed were not equipped with any cannon at all because the missiles they carried had longer range and were thought to be more effective.

Frequently overlooked in the debate were the many advantages of gun systems. For example, they could be used at close range, at low altitude, and against hard-to-hit maneuvering targets, domains where missiles are less effective. Most gun systems have an ammunition capacity that allows for more kill opportunities per flight than the limited number of missiles usually carried aboard a fighter. A stream of bullets cannot be decoyed or drawn off by electronic countermeasures. Compared to missiles, cannon are relatively inexpensive to produce and fire. On the other hand, while gun systems offer lower-cost-per-kill capability, they are limited to an effective tactical range of only a few thousand feet.

What then are the characteristics of an ideal aircraft gun system?

1. Its projectiles will have a short time of flight. The faster the shell or bullet travels, the easier a pilot can take aim. High-velocity projectiles will have long range, enabling pilots to engage an enemy quicker.

2. The firing mechanism will be able to operate at a high rate of speed. The more projectiles a gun fires, the greater the probability of a hit.

3. Its projectiles will have maximum lethality. Given a hit, the projectile—through force of impact, blast, fragmentation, or incendiary effect—must extensively damage the aircraft's structure, its controls, its fuel system, or its pilot.

4. Its projectiles will be ballistically efficient. Ammunition must have low drag so that its impact energy remains high and dispersion low.

5. Overall, the system will be effective yet compact. Because a fighter aircraft demands the utmost in

maneuverability and responsiveness, the gun system must be lightweight, compact, reliable, and easy to reload and repair.[6]

A balance must be found between the gun's maximum rate of fire and the projectiles' lethality. The first models of the World War II Spitfire fighter were armed with eight 0.303-in. machine guns. In a two-second burst the Spitfire's guns fired 320 bullets, giving the aircraft a very high probability of scoring a hit on the target.

Later-model Spitfires were armed with two 20-mm cannon and four 0.303-in. machine guns. In a two-second burst from the two cannon and four machine guns simultaneously, 21 cannon shells plus 160 0.303-in. bullets were fired. The 20-mm cannon eventually replaced the light machine gun because it had greater range and, given a hit, the 20-mm explosive shell did far more damage than the 0.303-in. bullets of the light machine gun. The rate of fire was sacrificed in favor of a greater weight of fire.

Machine guns usually carried a mixture of solid slugs known as ball ammunition, plus armor-piercing ammunition and incendiary ammunition; the latter types of ammunition could destroy the structure or controls of an aircraft, ignite an aircraft's fuel supply, or injure its pilot. Cannon usually carried rounds of armor-piercing, incendiary, or high-explosive ammunition. High-explosive ammunition blows up on impact; if it is equipped with a time-delay fuse, it penetrates deeply and then explodes inside the aircraft, causing extensive blast and fragmentation damage.

The weapons installed in the fighter aircraft of the 1950s and early 1960s ranged from the 0.5-in. (12.7-mm) Colt-Browning machine gun (six of which were fitted to the F-86 Sabre) to the N-37, the 37-mm cannon that armed the MiG-15 Fagot and MiG-17 Fresco. Most Soviet aircraft carried either 23-mm or 30-mm cannon while most Western aircraft were equipped with 20-mm or 30-mm weapons.

To demonstrate the different characteristics of cannon, we will briefly examine the systems on 1965-era French, Soviet, and U.S. fighters.

Mirage IIIC
> Two 30-mm DEFA 552 cannon;
> 125 rounds per gun;
> Rate of fire: 2,400 rpm;
> Firing time: 7–8 seconds;
> Weight of fire in two-second burst: 80 projectiles,
> 41.5 lb. (18.8 kg).

MiG-19 Farmer (guns can be fired individually, in pairs, or three at once)
> Three NR-30 30-mm cannon;
> 73 rounds per gun;
> Rate of fire: 2,700 rpm (900 rpm per gun);
> Firing time: 5 seconds (3 guns firing);
> Weight of fire in a two-second burst: 90 projectiles,
> 81 lbs (36.7 kg).

F-4B/C Phantom
> SUU-16A (M-61-A1) 20-mm gun pod;
> 1,200 rounds;
> Rate of fire: cyclic—6,000 rpm, practical in two-second burst—5,250 rpm;
> Firing time: 13–16 seconds;
> Weight of fire in two-second burst: 175 projectiles,
> 38.6 lb (20 kg).

Time of Flight and Range

With its high initial velocity the 20-mm projectile fired by the M-61 Vulcan cannon has a shorter time of flight and a slightly greater firing distance with lower bullet dispersion than the 30-mm DEFA and NR-30 cannon. However, the ideal cannon firing range is between 1,000 and 3,000 feet. Firing at a target at greater than 3,000 feet introduces an excessive lead angle, reduced visibility, and the possibility that the shell will not hit the target with enough energy to cause the impact fuse to detonate—all of which reduce the probability of a kill.

Rate of Fire and the Probability of Hits

In a two-second burst the M-61 Vulcan cannon fires 175 projectiles; three NR-30 cannon fire 90 projectiles; and two DEFA cannon fire 80 projectiles. Therefore, the probability of scoring a hit with a single M-61 cannon is approximately twice that of the three NR-30 cannon or the two DEFA cannon. However, the tighter dispersion of the M-61 cannon requires more accurate aiming. The shotgun effect of a more dispersed stream of bullets can be an advantage, particularly when firing at a hard-to-hit maneuvering target.

Probability of Destruction

The M-61 Vulcan cannon fires armor-piercing/incendiary and high explosive/incendiary projectiles. The 3.5-ounce high explosive/incendiary projectile has a relatively thin-walled steel casing containing 0.031 ounces of explosive. The nose fuse detonates the charge on impact.

The 30-mm DEFA air-to-air projectile is an 8.3-ounce thin-walled steel shell containing 1.76 ounces of high explosive. The blast and incendiary power of the DEFA projectile is enhanced by its delayed-action fuse that allows the projectile to penetrate the aircraft before exploding.

The NR-30 30-mm projectile weighs 14.4 ounces. This air-to-air projectile is assumed to have a high-explosive charge.

While the M-61 Vulcan 20-mm cannon has a higher probability of hitting the target than either the French or Soviet cannon, the DEFA and NR-30 projectiles have a far greater probability of scoring a kill given a hit. Because of greater size, larger explosive charge, and delayed-action fuse, the French 30-mm DEFA round is approximately three times as powerful as the U.S. 20-mm shell; moreover, the Soviet NR-30 30-mm projectile has almost twice as much impact force and high-explosive charge as the 30-mm DEFA.

The SUU-16/A Vulcan gun pod with the M-61 cannon was fitted to the F-4 Phantom on the aircraft's centerline station. The 1,600-lb. gun pod was found to adversely affect the Phantom's speed and maneuverability as well as reducing available stores stations for other ordnance. Inertial loads exerted on the pod during maneuvers caused the bullets to disperse, and the non-computing gunsight on the F-4B and the F-4C was found to be less than ideal.

Air-to-Air Missiles

Air-to-air missiles are generally divided into two basic groups: short-range missiles designed for use in aerial combat against fighters over distances up to several thousand feet, and medium- or long-range missiles for use against bombers or other targets several miles away.

Short-range air-to-air missiles generally home in on their target through infrared or heat-seeking guidance. Early infrared-guided missiles were relatively simple weapons consisting of a tubular airframe with control fins at the front end and stabilization wings at the rear. The infrared seeker and flight-control section was situated behind a transparent nose window. A contact and proximity fuse, warhead, and solid-fuel rocket motor were fitted behind the guidance section.

Infrared missiles are light, relatively cheap, require no radar or sophisticated fire-control equipment, and have a short minimum range. Moreover, infrared-guided missiles are "fire-and-forget" weapons—that is, once the missile is fired and is homing in on its target the attacking aircraft can break away and engage another target.

Early infrared seekers used uncooled lead sulfide photoelectric cells to detect heat emitted from the target's jet-engine exhaust. The limited sensitivity of the seeker required that the attacker position himself behind the target aircraft, usually within 30 degrees either side of the target's tail. Because a target's infrared energy could be absorbed or diffused by atmospheric carbon dioxide, water vapor, rain, or clouds, infrared-guided missiles were most effective when employed in fair weather. The sun, or the sun's glint off snow or water, or hot spots on the ground could create false targets that would deceive the missile's seeker. More than once an infrared missile has homed in on the sun's reflection on clouds. While an infrared-guided missile is impervious to electronic countermeasures, it can be diverted from its target by the timely deployment of a high-temperature flare.

To overcome many of these complications, pilots of fighters equipped with early heat-seeking missiles were trained to fire the missiles only at medium or high altitudes, where the missiles were less likely to be attracted to heat sources on the ground. In fact, the pilots discovered, an infrared missile launched at high altitude where the air is thin not only avoided the confusion of secondary signals, but also greatly increased the missile's range and speed.

Once infrared-guided missiles were used in combat, pilots began to discover ways to evade them. The key element was recognizing its approach early enough to execute a sharp turn. Because most infrared-guided missiles are limited in both the ability to scan wide angles of the sky for a target and the ability to turn at high speeds, they could not readily follow an aircraft turning quickly at a tight angle. With sufficient warning, a pilot under attack could break hard, turn, and escape.

A relatively simple weapon to employ, an infrared-guided missile can be attached to any aircraft that has a launch rail and an electrical firing circuit. The pilot maneuvers the craft into firing position and then energizes the missile's seeker. Once the heat or infrared homing seeker has acquired the target, the pilot hears an audio tone in his headset. If the tone remains steady for three or four seconds, indicating that the seeker has firmly locked onto the target, the pilot may then launch the missile; he may immediately turn and engage a second target—thus "firing and forgetting." Meanwhile, the missile's guidance-and-control system guides the missile to the target; upon close approach or impact with the target, the warhead explodes.

Medium-range and long-range radar-guided air-to-air missiles are generally larger, more complex, and more expensive than infrared-guided missiles. The basic difference between the two types of missiles is their relationship to the launch aircraft. Once launched, an infrared-guided missile independently homes on its target. Radar-guided missiles, on the other hand, require that the radar of the launching aircraft continuously illuminate the target to ensure that the missile homes true. A receiving antenna in the missile's nose detects the reflected radar energy and the missile adjusts its course to the target proportionately. Pilots of aircraft equipped with radar-guided missiles may not engage a second target until after the attempt on the first is completed.

Semiactive radar guidance has several advantages over infrared homing systems. An aircraft having radar guidance can attack a target in all weather conditions and from all aspects, not just from the rear.

Furthermore, if the radar system is powerful enough, these attacks can be over a very long range. The attacking aircraft can choose the target it will shoot down even in confusing dogfights with dozens of aircraft that may deceive an infrared-guided missile. And if a pilot discovers mid-attack that he has mistakenly launched a missile against a friendly aircraft, he can terminate the attack before any damage is done. Radar missiles usually carry a sizable warhead and both a contact and proximity fuse.

On the negative side, the aircraft that attacks with a semiactive radar homing missile must keep the radar locked onto the target until the missile hits home. If the radar's lock is broken, the missile will no longer be guided, but will act as any other ballistic projectile: following a course determined by its initial velocity, air resistance, and gravity, it will miss the target.

The radar guidance systems of early missile systems were quite susceptible to electronic countermeasures; moreover, because of the clutter of radar signals returned from the ground, their effectiveness was limited at low altitude or when looking down at low-flying targets. The early radar-guided missiles required a relatively long time to lock on to the target and fire. They also had a large "dead zone" at close ranges where they could not be fired, lessening their effectiveness in dogfights.

While most radar-guided missiles are relatively maneuverable, an alert pilot can defeat an attack by turning hard at the proper point in a missile's approach. It the break is too early or not hard enough, the missile will be able to correct its intercept course. If the turn is too late, the aircraft could be damaged by fragments from the missile's warhead detonated by the proximity fuse.

Because of the radar equipment that must be carried by the fighter, radar-guided missile systems take up a great deal of space and weight and require a sizable amount of electric power. The F-4B Phantom carries a radar intercept officer whose primary function is to operate the AIM-7 Sparrow missile's radar and fire-control system. When the Phantom is going to attack, the RIO detects and tracks the target with the aircraft's radar and then locks on to it. Once the RIO attains lock-on, the fire-control computer provides steering information to the pilot on his radar display. An AIM-7E Sparrow radar-guided missile's sensors are warmed up, tested, and readied for firing.

Once the enemy aircraft is within range, a warning light on the screen notifies the pilot. The pilot pulls the trigger to activate the missile's power supply. Just prior to being ejected from the aircraft, the missile receives pre-launch guidance data from the fire-control system. The motor of the rocket fires and the missile's signal-seeker antenna searches for radar energy reflected from the target and locks on to it. At a safe distance from the launching aircraft, the missile's warhead is mechanically and electrically armed. The pilot and the RIO continue to fly toward the target, keeping it illuminated by radar energy. As the missile passes near the target, its radar proximity fuse detonates its warhead; in the event of a direct hit, its contact fuse triggers the explosion.[8] Only then is the Phantom free to turn away and engage another target.

Missile Fuses

The most important sections of an air-to-air missile are the fuses and the warhead. The guidance and control section can be highly accurate, but if the warhead does not detonate at the proper time, the missile is of little use.

The primary requirement of a good missile fuse is that it detonates the warhead at the proper distance from the target to cause maximum damage. The high-closing velocity and the trajectories of the launching and target aircraft and of air-to-air missiles require that the fuse operate under severe conditions.

Since air-to-air guided-missile systems cannot always ensure a direct hit even given a successful interception, a proximity fuse (now found in most missiles) detonates the warhead as the missile passes near the target. A proximity fuse measures the range to the target and the velocity at which the missile is closing with the target; at the appropriate distance for maximum effectiveness, the fuse sets off the warhead. Radar-guided missiles generally employ radar-activated proximity fuses, which monitor the relative motions of the missile and the target. Most infrared-guided missiles use infrared-activated proximity fuses which detect heat emissions from the engine, exhaust plume, or airframe.

Because proximity fuses rely on information received from the target, they are vulnerable to countermeasures. Radar-activated proximity fuses are subject to jamming or deception. Judicious use of electronic countermeasures can prevent the warhead from firing, or can cause it to detonate a safe distance before reaching the target. Infrared-activated proximity fuses can be deceived away from the aircraft or detonated prematurely by such decoys as flares. Designers of guided-missile fuses consider the potential countermeasures and attempt to design the missile fuse to ignore or overcome these problems.[9]

Air-to-air missiles are usually equipped with an impact fuse: the force of the missile striking the target sets off an inertial fuses that detonates the warhead. Impact fuses are generally used as backup firing mechanisms for air-to-air missiles equipped with proximity fuses. Some missiles, such as the infrared-guided AIM-4D Falcon, had only an impact fuse and thus had to hit the target to destroy it.

Missile Warheads

The fragmentation warhead is the most common air-to-air missile warhead. Because of a high-explosive charge, fragments of the warhead's casing spall off at high velocity, damaging or destroying the target on impact. The number, size, and velocity of the fragments can be controlled by numerous factors—design and shape of the warhead, the construction material, and the explosive-to-casing mass ratio of the warhead.

The casing of many warheads has grooves that cause the casing to shatter in a way that forms many small fragments. Alternatively, some warheads house pre-formed fragments; in addition, there may be a specially-shaped bursting charge to ensure greater uniformity in the fragments' size and dispersion. Such warheads are sometimes known as blast/ fragmentation devices because the pressure wave created by the detonation works in conjunction with the spalling fragments to damage the target. The AIM-9B Sidewinder, the AA-2 Atoll, and the Matra 530 are among the air-to-air missiles fitted with blast/fragmentation warheads.[10]

The continuous-rod warhead is another explosive device frequently installed in air-to-air missiles. The warhead's high-explosive charge is surrounded by a series of rods that are welded together at alternate ends. The explosive charge has been shaped and sized so that when it detonates the rod bundle will expand into a ring. The ring of rods continues to expand until it reaches its maximum diameter whereupon the rods break into fragments. Because of their weight and high velocity, the rods or their fragments extensively damage an airframe's structure. The AIM-7 Sparrow and several versions of the AIM-9 Sidewinder missile employ continuous-rod warheads.[11]

Air-to-Ground Weapons

Bombs

The form of air-to-ground ordnance used most frequently in the 1960s was the free-fall bomb. The weight of bombs in service varied from 250 pounds to 3,000 pounds. Generally, the high-explosive content of a bomb amounted to about half its total weight.

A bomb is classified by its composition and its intended mission. Bombs with a thin-walled casing and a large amount of explosive are designed to destroy targets primarily by the pressure of their blast; they are known as demolition weapons. Bombs with thick, internally-scored casings are designed to fragment when detonated to destroy targets by puncturing them; they are known as fragmentation weapons. The most commonly-used weapon is the general-purpose bomb, designed to produce both high blast pressure and many fragments.

Another form of free-fall bomb is the napalm bomb or fire bomb that carries flammable napalm that spatters on detonation, clings to whatever its splashes against, and spontaneously ignites.

Conventional bombs can be fitted with a parachute or with fins that spring out when they are airborne to increase their drag and steepen their trajectory, so that they explode well behind and below the aircraft that dropped them. With such high-drag weapons, the attacker can safely release the bombs from low altitude and not be caught in their blast.

Cluster Bombs

Cluster bombs attempt to overcome delivery inaccuracies by saturating the target area with large numbers of bomblets. Cluster-bomb weapons, such as the U.S. Air Force CBU 1A and 2A, consist of a canister on the aircraft, fitted with numerous tubes filled with bomblets. During an attack, the pilot flies directly over the target at low altitude and ejects bomblets from the canister through the tubes. The bomblets fall in a dispersed rectangular area several hundred feet long and some 75 to 150 feet wide.

Other types of cluster-bomb weapons (such as the U.S. Air Force CBU-52 or U.S. Navy Rockeye) consist of a canister filled with a large number of bomblets and fitted with an opening fuse.

After the canister itself is ejected from the aircraft, the nose fuse splits it open, dispensing the bomblets on the target. The advantage of this type of cluster-bomb weapon is that the pilot does not necessarily have to expose himself to enemy fire by flying directly over the target, but can loft the weapon—albeit with reduced accuracy.

Cluster-bomb weapons can carry a wide variety of bomblets. Three of the most common types are hand-grenade-size projectiles for use against personnel; beer-bottle-size shaped-charge projectiles that detonate into high-temperature slugs for use against tanks and armor; and projectiles that can function in both anti-personnel and anti-tank roles.

Unguided Rockets

Unguided rockets are essentially small bombs equipped with a rocket motor to give them greater range, but no guidance system for homing in on their target. Rockets were widely employed in the 1960s. They ranged in diameter from the Soviet 57-mm rocket through the European 68-mm rocket and U.S. 2.75-in. (70-mm) rocket to the European 100-mm rocket and U.S. Navy 5-in. (127-mm) rocket. Rockets can be fitted with several different types of warhead including anti-personnel/anti-materiel blast warheads, incendiary warheads, shaped-charge anti-armor warheads, and anti-personnel flechette darts. Unguided rockets were usually carried on the plane's external pylons in cylindrical pods frequently fitted with a plastic covering to reduce their aerodynamic drag.

Guided Missiles

Heavy losses of aircraft to antiaircraft artillery during Korean War close-support missions highlighted the need for a guided missile that could be fired from beyond the range of light antiaircraft weapons. In response to this requirement, the U.S. developed the Bullpup air-to-ground guided missile. Developed during the 1950s and entering service in 1959, the Bullpup's streamlined airframe carried a 250-lb. warhead and was propelled by a solid-fuel rocket motor. The pilot launched the missile, and then guided it to the intended target via joystick radio control. Later models of the Bullpup were powered by a storable liquid-fuel rocket and carried a larger 1,000-pound warhead.

The French AS-30 air-to-surface guided missile was quite similar to the Bullpup in its configuration and guidance system. The joystick-control technique, however, had several drawbacks: it required the pilot to observe and carefully guide the missile all the way to impact—requirements that could not always be met over a seething battle area.

The U.S. Navy developed the Shrike air-to-surface guided missile, whose guidance system homed in on the emissions of radar sites on the ground. The Shrike was a modified version of the Sparrow air-to-air missile, incorporating the Sparrow's own airframe and passive radar seeker, a somewhat larger (145-lb.) blast/fragmentation warhead, and a smaller rocket motor. To knock out a radar site, a pilot dove toward the target radar, waited for indication that the Shrike's seeker head had locked onto the radar signals, and then fired the missile. If the pilot wanted to take advantage of the Shrike's maximum range of about 25 miles (40 km), he lofted the Shrike unguided missile toward the target, and the seeker would lock onto the target radar during the missile's descent. The Shrike's major limitation was the narrow frequency range to which its seeker could respond, requiring the pilot to carry several Shrike missiles, each tuned to a different frequency range, if he were to knock out several different types of target radars. In addition, if the operator of the target radar detected the missile in flight, he could turn off his radar and cause the Shrike to lose guidance and miss altogether.

Guns

The aircraft in service during the early 1960s could use their internal air-to-air cannon or externally mounted cannon pods to strafe targets on the ground. Guns could be quite effective against such soft targets as trucks or personnel. Guns were useful when a plane could swoop low to attack lightly-defended targets, but proved to be less than desirable if targets were protected by heavy antiaircraft defenses.

Fighter Attack Aircraft, 1965[12]

Aircraft	Crew	Wing Span (ft)	Length (ft)	Empty Weight (lb)	Normal Loaded Weight (lb)	Combat Weight (50% Fuel + Weapons) (lb)	Wing Area (ft²)	Engine(s)	Thrust Military Power (lb)	Thrust Afterburning (lb)	Maximum Speed (Mach mph)	Combat Thrust To Weight Ratio AB / Mil	Combat Wing Loading (lb/ft²)	Combat Radius (mi)	Weapons Air-to-Air Air-to-Ground
F-4B Phantom II USA	2	38.3	58.3	28,000	44,000	38,000	530	2 General Electric J79-GE-8 Turbojets	10,900	17,000	M.2.7 1,500	.89 .57	72	200– 600	4 AIM-7 AAMS 4 AIM-9 AAMS 16,000 lbs.
F-5A Freedom Fighter USA	1	25.3	47.2	8,700	13,600	11,800	170	2 General Electric J85-GE-13 Turbojets	2,720	4,080	M 1.48 979	.69 .46	69	150– 500	2 20mm Cannon 2 AIM-9 AAMS 6,000 lbs.
F-8E Crusader USA	1	35.2	54.2	19,000	29,000	25,000	385	1 Pratt & Whitney J57-P-20 Turbojet	10,700	18,000	M 1.7 1,120	.72 .42	65	400– 600	4 20mm Cannon 4 AIM-9 AAMS 4,000 lbs.
F-104C Starfighter USA	1	21.6	54.8	14,080	19,000	16,000	196	1 General Electric J79-GE-7 Turbojet	10,000	15,600	M 2.2 1,390	.97 .62	82	200– 500	1 20mm Cannon 4 AIM-9 AAMS 4,000 lbs.
F-100D Super Sabre USA	1	38.7	49	21,000	32,000	28,000	400	1 Pratt & Whitney J57-P-214 Turbojet	11,200	16,950	M 1.3 924	.62 .40	72	300– 550	4 20mm Cannon 2 AIM-9 AAMS 7,500 lbs.
F-86F Sabre USA	1	39.1	37.5	11,125	15,175	13,000	313	1 General Electric J47-GE-27 Turbojet	5,910	—	M 0.9 599	.40	48	200– 450	6 0.5 in Guns 2 AIM-9 AAMS 2,000 lbs.
A-6A Intruder USA	2	53	54.6	25,600	37,000	29,000	529	2 Pratt & Whitney J52-P-6 Turbojets	9,300	—	M 0.87	.63	55	300– 1,000	15,000 lbs.
F-111A USA	2	31.9	73.5	45,000	82,800	55,000	525	2 Pratt & Whitney TF-30-P-1 Turbofans	10,750	18,500	M 2.2 1,390	.67 .39	105	500– 1200	20,000 lbs.
B-57B USA	2	63.9	65.5	30,000	48,000	40,000	960	2 Wright J65-W-5 Turbojets	7,220	—	585	.36	42	400– 800	4 20mm Cannon 7,000 lbs.

Aircraft								Engine							Armament
A-7A Corsair II USA	1	38.6	46.1	16,000	32,500	29,000	375	1 Pratt & Whitney TF-30-P-1 Turbofan	12,200	—	698	.42	77	300–800	2 20mm Cannon / 2 AIM-9 AAMS / 15,000 lbs.
A-4E Skyhawk USA	1	27.5	41.3	9,600	20,000	13,500	260	1 Pratt & Whitney J52-P-6A	8,500	—	M 0.8 640	.42	77	250–500	2 20mm Cannon / 8,200 lbs.
F-105D Thunderchief USA	1	34.9	64.4	27,500	38,100	34,300	385	1 Pratt & Whitney J75-P-19 Turbojet	17,200	26,500	M 2.2 1,390	.77 / .50	89	200–800	1 20mm Cannon / 2 AIM-9 AAMS / 14,000 lbs.
MiG-21PF Fishbed D USSR	1	23	44	12,000	17,000	15,000	247	1 Tumansky R-11 Turbojet	10,000	13,670	M 2.1 1,300	.89 / .66	60	150–400	1 23mm External Cannon / 2 AA-2 AAMS / 1,000 lbs.
MiG-19S USSR	1	30	48.9	13,000	17,500	16,000	250	2 Tumansky RD-9B Turbojets	5,842	7,165	M 1.3 905	.89 / .73	59	150–450	3 30mm Cannon
MiG-17F Fresco USSR	1	31.5	36.2	9,100	12,000	10,000	243	1 Klimov VK-1A Turbojet	5,950	6,990	M 0.95 627	.61 / .55	44	200–400	1 37mm Cannon / 2 23mm Cannon / 2,000 lbs.
Su-7B Fitter A USSR	1	29.9	57	19,000	26,450	22,950	—	1 Lyulka AL-7F Turbojet	15,400	22,000	M 1.7 1,055	.96 / .74	—	150–300	2 30mm Cannon / 4,000 lbs.
Il-28 Beagle USSR	3	70.3	57.9	28,400	46,300	40,000	654	2 Klimov VK-1 Turbojets	5,950	—	559	.30	61	200–800	4 23mm Cannon / 5,000 lbs.
Mirage IIIC France	1	27	48.5	14,640	19,440	16,680	375	1 SNECMA Atar 9B Turbojet	9,370	13,225	M 2.1 1,380	.81 / .58	45	180–500	2 30mm Cannon / 1 Matra 530 / 2 AIM-9 AAMS / 2,000 lbs.
Super Mystère B2 France	1	34.5	46.3	15,400	20,200	18,000	377	1 SNECMA Atar 101G Turbojet	7,445	9,700	M 1.1 743	.53 / .41	48	200–450	2 30mm Cannon / 55 58mm Rockets in fuselage pack / 2,000 lbs.
Mystère IV-A France	1	36.5	42.1	12,500	16,300	14,000	344	1 Hispano Suiza Verdon 350 Turbojet	7,700	—	M .94 620	.55	40	200–400	2 30mm Cannon / 2,000 lbs.

(Continued on next page.)

Fighter Attack Aircraft, 1965[12] (continued)

Aircraft	Crew	Wing Span (ft)	Length (ft)	Empty Weight (lb)	Normal Loaded Weight (lb)	Combat Weight (50% Fuel + Weapons) (lb)	Wing Area (ft²)	Engine(s)	Thrust Military Power (lb)	Thrust After-burning (lb)	Maximum Speed (Mach mph)	Combat Thrust To Weight Ratio AB	Mil	Combat Wing Loading (lb/ft²)	Combat Radius (mi)	Weapons Air-to-Air Air-to-Ground
Ouragan France	1	40.2	32.4	9,100	15,000	11,000	250	1 Hispano Suiza Nene 104B Turbojet	5,070	—	584		.46	44	200–400	4 20mm Cannon 2,000 lbs.
Vautour IIA France	1	49.6	51.1	22,000	35,000	30,000	484	2 SNECMA Atar 101E Turbojets	7,716	—	684		.51	61	400–800	4 30mm Cannon 5,300 lbs.
Lightning F.Mk6 U.K.	1	34.8	55.2	28,000	39,000	35,000	475	2 Rolls Royce Avon 302C Turbojets	11,100	16,300	M 2.2 1,380	.93	.63	73	200–350	2 30mm Cannon 2 Red Top, Firestreak AAMS 2,000 lbs.
Hawker Hunter U.K.	1	33.6	45.7	12,760	17,750	15,500	349	1 Rolls Royce Avon 203 Turbojet	10,050	—	M .94 620		.64	44	200–400	4 30mm Cannon 2,000 lbs.
Sea Hawk U.K.	1	39	40.2	10,300	13,200	11,500	278	1 Rolls Royce Nene 103 Turbojet	5,400	—	587		.46	41	150–350	4 20mm Cannon 2,000 lbs.
Gnat India	1	22.1	29.6	4,850	8,600	7,000	137	1 Bristol Orpheus 701 Turbojet	4,520	—	695		.64	51	100–300	2 30mm Cannon 1,000 lbs.
HF-24 Marut India	1	29.5	52	13,600	24,000	21,900	301	2 Bristol Orpheus 701 Turbojets	4,850	—	M 1.1 800		.44	73	200–400	4 30mm Cannon 48 Int. Rockets 4,000 lbs.
J-35F Draken Sweden	1	30.9	46.9	16,800	25,450	22,000	529	1 Swedish-Built Rolls Royce Avon Turbojet	12,790	17,600	M 2.0 1,320	.80	.56	42	200–600	1 30mm Cannon 2 Rb27, 2 Rb28 AARMs 4,000 lbs.

Air-to-Air Missiles 1965[13]

Missile	Guidance & Control	Propulsion	Warhead	Length (ft)	Weight (lb)	Diameter (in)	Wing Span (ft)	Maximum Speed (Mach)	Range (mi)
AIM-9B Sidewinder USA	Infrared Homing	Solid Propellant Rocket	10 lb fragmentation	9.3	155	5	1.1	2.5	0.5–2
AIM-9D Sidewinder USA	Infrared Homing	Solid Propellant Rocket	22.1 lb continuous rod	9.4	195	5	1.1	2.5	0.3–2
AIM-4D Falcon USA	Infrared Homing	Solid Propellant Rocket	Contact Fuze	6.6	134	6.4	1.8	3	0.5–6
AIM-7E Sparrow USA	Semi-active Radar Homing	Solid Propellant Rocket	66 lb continuous rod	12	440	6.4	1.6	4	1–10
AA-2 Atoll USSR	Infrared Homing	Solid Propellant Rocket	fragmentation	9.1	154	4.75	1.7	2.5	4
Firestreak UK	Infrared Homing	Solid Propellant Rocket	50 lb fragmentation	10.4	295	8.75	1.4	3	0.7–5
Red Top UK	Infrared Homing	Solid Propellant Rocket	68 lb fragmentation	11.5	330	8.75	2.4	3	7.5
Matra R 530 France	Infrared or Semi-active Radar Homing	Solid Propellant Rocket	60 lb fragmentation	R 10.7 IR 10.5	R 424 IR 427	10.35	3.6	3	R 10 IR 7

Aircraft Cannon, 1965[7]

Weapon	Muzzle Velocity (ft/sec)	Rate of Fire (rpm)	Projectile Weight (oz)	Weight of Fire Per Gun Two Seconds Burst (lbs)	Ammunition	Aircraft Armed With The Cannon
0.5 in—USA Colt Browning	2,840	1,000	1.62	33 rds 3.3	b API	6—F-86
20-mm MK-12—USA	3,320	1,200	3.5	40 rds 8.8	HEI API	4—F-8
20-mm M-39—USA	3,380	1,500	3.5	50 rds 11	HEI API	4—F-100 2—F-5A
20-mm—USA M-61 Vulcan	3,380	4,000 6,000	3.5	100 rds 22 175 rds 38.6	HEI API	1—F-104 1—F-105
30-mm—France DEFA 552	2,690	1,200	8.3	40 rds 20.75	HE HE	2—Mirage IIIC 2—Super Mystère 2—Mystère IV-A
30-mm—UK ADEN	2,590	1,400	9.7	46 rds 28.2	HE	4—Hunter 2—Gnat 2—Lightning
23-mm—USSR NR-23	2,213	850	7	28 rds 24.5	b HE	2—MiG-17
37-mm—USSR N-37	2,213	400	24	13 rds 21.3	HE	1—MiG-17
30-mm—USSR NR-30	2,502	900	14.4	30 rds 27	HE	3—MiG-19 2—Su-7B

Gun Antiaircraft Weapons, 1965[14]

Weapon Type Country	Vehicle Mount	Rate of Fire: Cyclic Per Minute	Effective Range— Anti-aircraft (ft)	Guidance	Gun	Muzzle Velocity (ft/s)
KS-19M USSR	Towed	15–20	20,000	Optical/ Radar	100-mm	2,950
KS-12 USSR	Towed	15–20	20,000	Optical/ Radar	85-mm	2,600
S-60 USSR	Towed	100–110	15,000	Optical/ Radar	57-mm	3,280
M-38/39 USSR	Towed	100–180	9,000	Optical	37-mm	2,890
ZU-23 USSR	Towed	800–1,000 per barrel	8,000	Optical	Twin 23-mm	3,182
ZPU-4 USSR	Towed	600 per barrel	4,500	Optical	Quad 14.5-mm	3,200
Bofors Sweden	Towed	120	8,000	Optical/ Radar	40-mm	3,000

Missile Antiaircraft Weapons, 1965[14]

Weapon Type Country	Length (ft)	Diameter (ft)	Weight (lbs)	Range min/max (mi)	Altitude min/max (ft)	Guidance	System	Vehicle
SA-2 USSR	35.1	1.67	5,000	2/21	3,000/60,000	Radar Command	Battery = one radar, six launchers	—
SA-3 USSR	22	1.4	1,400	1/13	300/44,000	Radar Command	Battery = one radar, eight launchers	—
Hawk USA	16.5	1.1	1,383	1/20	100/38,000	Radar	Battery = two radars, 18 launchers	—

Appendix II

Aircraft and Weapons of the 1980s

Appendix II discusses the fighter aircraft, weapons fire-control systems, and other important aircraft systems in service or under development in the 1980s. The technology, equipment, and philosophical changes from 1965 to the 1980s can be discerned by comparing aircraft, weapons, and systems in this appendix with those discussed in Appendix I.

Fire Control

The fire-control systems on the aircraft in production in the 1980s have a wide range of sophistication. The system installed in the light-weight Ajeet fighter consists of the Ferranti ISIS F-195R-3 gyroscopic gunsight that can be used for air-to-air or air-to-ground attacks. Unlike most early gyroscopic gunsights, which required the pilot to continuously adjust the reticle size to the apparent size of the target's wingspan, the Ferranti ISIS gunsight has three range settings. While this modification somewhat reduces the gunsight's accuracy, it is simpler for the pilot to operate and it relieves his workload.[1]

The Kfir C2's fire-control system is more elaborate than that of the Ajeet, but restricts itself to targets within the visual range. The Kfir C2's fire-control system includes a head-up display, a weapons delivery system, a flight control computer, and a ranging radar.

The head-up display optically projects necessary flight information and weapons delivery data within the pilot's field of view on the head-up display on the windshield, permitting him to read it without interrupting his concentration on the target. The head-up display is connected to the flight control and weapons delivery computers, to the digital display computer, and to the radar. During a normal flight, the head-up display charts the same information that appears on cockpit instruments, such as air speed, heading, and altitude.

Inside the Kfir's nose is an Israeli-built Elta EL/M-2001B radar, a relatively simple range-only instrument suitable for air-to-air and air-to-ground attacks. Ranging data from the radar enters the aircraft's fire-control computer and, after processing, the data appears as an aiming reticle on the head-up display. The reticle's position relative to the position of the target aids the pilot in accurately firing the aircraft's 30-mm cannon, or its Sidewinder or Shafrir missiles. The same system can be used to provide air-to-ground weapons delivery information.[2]

The F-14 Tomcat, designed as a fleet defense interceptor and air-superiority fighter, has a digitally controlled, multi-sensor fire-control system providing the capability to intercept multiple targets at long range in any kind of weather. The AWG-9 fire-control system consists of a high-capacity digital computer, a multi-mode pulse-Doppler, and an optical television sight unit with displays for the pilot and the radar intercept officer.

The heart of the AWG-9 system is the radar, which uses both simple pulse and pulse-Doppler modes to detect targets at greater range than any other radar previously mounted in a fighter. The radar notes the presence of large aircraft up to 200 miles away and fighter-sized targets more than 100 miles away. When in the pulse-Doppler mode, the radar's processing computer measures the frequency of a returning pulse against the transmitted pulse to detect the target's velocity toward or away from the aircraft.

Targets moving at the same relative speed as the aircraft are assumed to be signals reflected from the ground and are automatically filtered out by the radar, thus eliminating ground clutter. Targets moving toward or away from the aircraft, on the other hand, generate a Doppler shift frequency of the pulses returned; by noting the variation in the transmitted and the reflected signal, the radar can pinpoint the location and velocity of the target in the line of sight. The chief drawbck of the pulse-Doppler radar mode is that targets moving across or abeam of the tracking aircraft disappear from the display since they do not exhibit the Doppler effect and are thus filtered out. When they disappear, the F-14 Tomcat's radar intercept officer can either wait for the target to reappear or choose to shift into the simple pulse mode, which is able to detect and track targets moving abeam or at a low speed.

The radar can operate in a number of pulse and pulse-Doppler modes. In the pulse-Doppler search mode the AWG-9 has a maximum detection range two-and-a-half times farther than that of the F-4J Phantom counterpart.

While using the pulse-Doppler single-target track, the Tomcat's RIO has maximum tracking range against a target; he can track a target and attack at long range with the Phoenix or the Sparrow missile at maximum range. The major drawback is that once the RIO locks on and fires, all other targets on the radar screen disappear while the radar illuminates the target to guide the missile home.

The AWG-9 was the first fighter radar to overcome this disadvantage at medium ranges by tracking one target while simultaneously searching for another. In this track-while-scan mode, either member of the crew may launch the Phoenix missile and track up to 24 other targets at the same time. The radar searches across its field of view every two seconds and then switches back to the semiactive illumination mode, providing midcourse guidance for the missile.

The AWG-9 fire-control computer stores a target's last known position, predicts its estimated present position, and assigns a threat priority number to the six most threatening targets. Up to six Phoenix missiles can be guided to separate targets. Unfortunately, the track-while-scan mode can only be used to launch the Phoenix missile.[3]

In many Tomcats an optical television sight unit is mounted under the nose. A camera with a magnification of up to ten times, the television sight unit visually detects aircraft at much longer range than the unaided eye. The sight unit may operate in conjunction with the radar or independently.

Radar information is displayed on two-cathode-ray tubes, both in the rear of the cockpit. Television images or raw radar data can be displayed on the small five-inch cathode-ray tube. The F-14 Tomcat's RIO in the back seat uses the larger cathode-ray tube to monitor the tactical situation, and to track and attack targets.

Hughes Aircraft Co. initially designed the 1965 state-of-the-art AWG-9 to be highly resistant to electronic countermeasures; but as advances are made in the Soviet systems, Hughes currently is developing enhancements to the AWG-9 system's performance and upgraded electronic countermeasures capability.

The combined performance of the AWG-9 radar and the Phoenix missile system in operational tests has demonstrated their capability. In November 1973, an F-14 Tomcat launched six Phoenix missiles in just over 30 seconds against six individual targets. Four of the missiles scored direct hits. The F-15, F-16, F/A-18, JA-37 Viggen, Mirage 2000, Tornado F MK 2, and several new Soviet fighters are equipped with pulse-Doppler radars and missile systems that can hit low-flying targets.

Electronic Countermeasures

In the late 1950s and early 1960s, few fighter aircraft employed electronic countermeasures equipment. Radar warning devices were unreliable; jamming systems were bulky and required an inordinate amount of power. Available electronic countermeasures equipment was generally installed only on strategic bombers and large tactical attack aircraft.

This situation changed in the mid-1960s when the U.S. Air Force and Navy fighters and attack aircraft in combat over North Vietnam faced Soviet-supplied radar-directed antiaircraft artillery and SA-2 surface-to-air missile systems. The U.S. military undertook crash programs to equip its tactical aircraft with radar homing-and-warning (RHAW) receivers, flare and chaff dispensers, and jamming equipment that could counter the North Vietnamese air defense systems.

To destroy surface-to-air missiles and antiaircraft artillery, the Air Force and the Navy developed Wild Weasel and Ironhand aircraft. Select numbers of Air Force F-100s, F-105s, and F-4s, and Navy A-4s and A-6s were equipped with special receivers and weapons that could readily seek out and destroy surface-to-air missiles and radar-guided antiaircraft artillery. Such electronic countermeasures equipment significantly reduced the number of U.S. aircraft lost over North Vietnam.

Following the Vietnam War, U.S. Navy sources estimated that aircraft electronic countermeasures equipment had reduced its losses from attack by surface-to-air missiles by a factor of five. Since between 1966 and November 1972, Navy losses to the SA-2 totaled 85 aircraft, the installation of electronic countermeasures equipment prevented the loss of some 340 aircraft to surface-to-air missiles. In addition, Navy researchers estimated that support and self-protection jamming prevented a further loss of approximately 200 Navy aircraft to radar-directed antiaircraft artillery.[4]

During the Yom Kippur War of 1973, the SA-6 surface-to-air missiles, the ZSU-23-4 antiaircraft artillery, and other weapons in the dense Arab air defense networks caught the Israel Defense Force/Air Force by surprise. The need for immediate air support to contain the Arab advance precluded large-scale defense suppression missions; consequently, Israeli losses were high during the first few days of the conflict. Some of the factors that reduced losses significantly included: air and ground attacks against surface-to-air missiles and antiaircraft artillery; overall modified tactics; the introduction of guided standoff weapons; and increased use of electronic countermeasures pods, chaff, flares, and standoff jamming.

A fighter's job is to dominate the skies over the battle zone and destroy ground targets. In practice, this means a fighter must prevent enemy aircraft from interfering with friendly military units, and must clear the way for friendly attack aircraft to operate unchallenged. A fighter must detect, engage, and destroy enemy aircraft while effectively evading such enemy air defenses as surface-to-air missiles and antiaircraft artillery.

If we consider how the sophistication and density of Soviet and Warsaw Pack air defense systems in Europe have increased and also consider the large number of nations that operate sophisticated Eastern and Western-produced air-defense systems, a first-rate fighter of today requires at least a minimal electronic countermeasures capability to successfully fulfill its mission.

More and more fighters and atack aircraft are being equipped with radar homing-and-warning receivers to inform the pilot that his own aircraft has been illuminated on the radar screen of an airborne or ground-based search-and-tracking system.

A basic RHAW system includes a number of receiving antennas, a signal processor and a cockpit display. This last indicates the bearing and type of radar signal being reflected off the pilot's own aircraft by an enemy radar. An audio tone in his headset also alerts him that he has been detected by radar.

Advanced RHAW systems can identify multiple threats, assign a priority to each, and display them all, simultaneously controlling the release of chaff or flares. In some fighters, the RHAW is programmed to control internal jamming equipment as well.

The AN/ALR-69 radar homing-and-warning system in the F-16 Fighting Falcon consists of a cathode-ray tube display in the cockpit that indicates the aximuth of the attack, a threat display unit, a signal processor, and four detection antennas. A computer memory of signals built into the hardware automatically identifies the type of threatening radar: whether it be a search radar, an antiaircraft artillery guidance radar, a missile radar, an airborne intercept radar, or even an unknown type.

An alphanumeric symbol on the azimuth indicator informs the pilot of the type of threat, its position, and its range. If an enemy missile launch is imminent or a missile already in flight, the asimuth indicator warns the pilot. Prior to the mission, the pilot can select a number of radar warning system modes; the aximuth display will show either the five highest priority threats or up to 16 radar indications.[5]

F-16 Fighting Falcon's electronic countermeasures equipment includes an AN/ALE-40 chaff and flare dispenser set that may be activated by the radar warning system under threat.

Prior to a mission, the dispenser is programmed to release specified quantities of chaff or flares either manually or automatically, given an indication from the radar warning system.[6]

The ALR-56 RHAW on the F-15 Eagle gives the pilot an audio warning of radar illumination by a threatening source and an identifying alphanumeric symbol appears on the display. Moreover, the ALR-56 controls the aircraft's internal ALQ-135 jamming system that is effective against a wide range of threatening radars. Because the pilot is armed with a RHAW receiver, he is aware of radiating airborne and ground threats and can begin evasive maneuvers, ultimately reducing the advantage of an enemy aircraft equipped with a long-range radar.

Chaff and flare decoys are low-cost and proven passive electronic countermeasures that, when effectively dispensed, protect an aircraft from radar-guided or infrared-homing missiles. Chaff consists of fine wires, glass fibers, or aluminum foil cut to one half of the wavelength of a threat radar. When released into the slipstream of an aircraft, chaff quickly billows into a cloud that reflects a return signal to the threat radar.

By using several different lengths, the chaff can effectively counter a wide band of radar frequencies. Depending upon the amount ejected, the radar will be unable to detect the true position of the target or may sense a number of false targets. Chaff can break the radar lock-on of an air-to-air missile or a surface-to-air missile and may possibly cause the missile's proximity fuse to detonate the warhead harmlessly well away from its intended target.[7]

Though cheap and proven, chaff does have drawbacks. Dispensers on aircraft of fighter size generally contain only a small number of chaff payloads, enough for self-protection but too little to deploy a large-scale carpet of chaff to screen the penetration of other aircraft.

More serious is the fact that, within a few seconds of release, chaff comes to rest in the air and begins to dissipate. As a result, radar systems with moving target indicators or pulse-Doppler filters can sift out stationary or slow-moving chaff clouds from the true target. However, the high initial velocity of the chaff can momentarily confuse even pulse-Doppler and continuous-wave fire-control systems.

A high-temperature flare can effectively decoy an infrared-homing surface-to-air missile or an air-to-air missile because most missile infrared sensors are unable to differentiate between a flare and the jet exhaust of an aircraft. To be effective, however, the flare must generate a larger infrared signature than the aircraft and it must be ejected at the proper time and on a trajectory that will lead the threatening missile away from the aircraft. Flare decoys can be placed in the same dispensers used for chaff and thus can provide fighters with protection against both radar-guided and infrared-homing threats.[8]

Because a flare's spectral signature does not accurately match that of the exhaust from a high-speed aircraft, researchers in many countries are working on new flares that more closely mimic the spectral signature of jet-engine exhaust, to fool infrared-guided missiles fitted with filters that reduce their susceptibility to flares.

Another technique in use includes infrared countermeasure pods that can mislead a missile's sensitive infrared seeker by generating false infrared signals to deceive the missile's lead-computing guidance system. One of the areas receiving a great deal of attention currently is the development of threat warning sensors to alert the pilot of an attack by an infrared homing weapon.

Tail warning sensors have been developed but their high false-alarm rate render the currently existing devices unusable. Advanced infrared sensors and active radar tail-warning systems are under development and could be fitted to fighters in the near future.[9]

Ground attack aircraft can fly at high speed, maintaining low-level profiles and delivering their ordnance with minimum exposure. Fighters, on the other hand, cannot restrict themselves to a single flight profile if they are to do their job well. Air battles will be fought over and around forward air defense weapons. To survive in the face of sophisticated air-defense systems, fighter aircraft will have to evade them, be accompanied by aircraft with electronic countermeasures capability such as the EF-111A, EA-6B, or be equipped internally or externally with some form of active electronic countermeasures equipment.

Active electronic countermeasures or jamming interferes with the radar data that air-defense weapons or fighter aircraft fire-control systems rely on to accurately detect, track, and attack an airborne target. Noise jamming involves transmitting a strong radar signal on the same frequency as the threat radar. If the exact frequency of the radar is known, continuous noise transmitted on the same frequency will prevent the operator from receiving an accurate radar echo.

This technique is known as point or spot jamming. While early radar relied on single-frequency operation, almost all recent Soviet and Western surveillance and fire-control radars incorporate frequency agility—that is, they regularly and randomly switch between different transmitting frequencies. The ability to change transmission frequencies considerably reduces the effectiveness of spot jamming.

To counter radars that can change their transmission frequencies, barrage jamming is employed. Barrage jamming involves transmitting noise on all frequencies of a radar's operating bandwidth. This technique requires far greater power than spot jamming, thus decreasing the power transmitted on each individual frequency. Yet another type of jamming, sweep jamming, sequentially attacks multiple bands, essentially combining the high power of spot jamming with the wide coverage of barrage jamming.

In addition to the brute force of noise jamming, active electronic countermeasures equipment can transmit false signals to mislead threatening radars. One effective device is the deception repeater. Here the instrument receives a signal from the search or fire-control radar of an enemy, stores it briefly, and retransmits it.

The enemy radar receives a weak echo from the target followed by a stronger pulse. This technique can either create false targets or feed false range and azimuth information to the enemy radar operator, and in some cases both these objectives are obtained. Deception-repeater type jammers are particularly effective against antiaircraft artillery and surface-to-air missiles' fire-control radars.[10]

Such modern jamming systems as the AN/ALQ-119 or AN/ALQ-131 combine both noise and deception techniques. Electronic countermeasures equipment can be internally mounted or enclosed in a pod carried externally on a fighter's stores stations.

Electronic countermeasures pods are generally less expensive and more adaptable than internal systems, but external pods take up stores stations that could otherwise carry ordnance, cause drag, and reduce maneuverability; furthermore, when the pods are mounted externally their scanning angles are limited due to shadowing by fuel tanks and other pylons. Internal systems generally weigh less and have no aerodynamic penalty, but are more expensive and more difficult to modify to meet changing threats.[11]

As a result of its Vietnam experience, the United States has produced the largest number and greatest diversity of active electronic countermeasures jamming equipment. Initially, the U.S. Air Force relied primarily on noise jamming pods while the Navy opted for internally-mounted deception jammers. Today, the Air Force, the Navy, and the Marine Corps all employ both pods and internal systems. The F-14 Tomcat is equipped with an internal ALQ-100 multi-band deception jammer; an additional ALQ-129 jammer is slated for installation in the near future. The F-15 Eagle's internal tactical electronic warfare system includes the ALQ-135 jamming system under the automatic control of the ALR-56 radar homing and warning receiver. The ALQ-135's power management system automatically apportions available jamming power between the most threatening radars to provide the most effective jamming technique for each threat.

The Air Force's F-16 Fighting Falcon can carry the ALQ-119 and ALQ-131 jamming pods. There is a possibility that an internal jamming system might round out the aircraft's defenses. Belgian Mirage 5s have been equipped with sophisticated RAPPORT II (Rapid Alert and Programmed Power-Management Of Radar Targets) internal electronic countermeasures system, which is functionally similar to the F-15 Eagle's ALQ-135. A more advanced version of the Mirage 5's electronic countermeasure suite, known as the RAPPORT III, will be retrofitted to Belgian-owned F-16s and could be fitted to U.S. and NATO F-16s.[12]

The French firm of Thomson-CSF has produced several electronic countermeasures pods that can be attached to French Air Force Mirages and those of export customers. New systems are still under development for the Mirage 2000.

SATT Elektronik and Svenska Radio have produced several pod and internal jamming systems suitable for use on Swedish Air Force Viggens. The SATT AQ-31 jamming pod reportedly has been exported to India for use on its MiG-21 Fishbeds and other tactical aircraft.

Companies in England and Israel are producing active electronic countermeasures equipment, but little information has been released about the systems.[13]

Almost no information is available regarding the electronic warfare equipment in service with Soviet aviation forces. Since the Soviet Navy and Army are well equipped with both offensive and defensive electronic countermeasures systems, one must assume that their tactical air forces have similar equipment.

Air-to-Ground Weapons

The most significant development in air-to-ground weapons since the 1965 time period (see Appendix I) was the development and introduction of highly-accurate guided free-fall bombs and rocket-powered missiles.

Television-Guided Bombs

During the mid-1960s the U.S. Air Force and Navy increased their efforts to develop guided bombs to destroy well-defended discrete targets such as bridges, which proved to be so difficult in Vietnam. The U.S. Navy concentrated on television-guided weapons, and in 1967 introduced the Walleye I television-guided glide bomb in combat. A-4 Skyhawks flying from carriers in the Gulf of Tonkin employed the 1,100-pound bomb against bridges, buildings, and other high-value targets.

To deliver the Walleye I (and its larger cousin the 2,400-pound Walleye II), the pilot visually detected the target on his cockpit monitor and centered the aiming cross-hairs on it. The Walleye's television camera locked onto the target image and, after release, automatically guided the weapon to the target.

The U.S. Air Force also developed an electro-optically guided bomb. Known as HOBOS (Homing Optical Bombing System), the weapon consisted of a standard Mk. 84, 2,000-pound bomb or an M 118, 3,000-pound bomb fitted with a television camera and a guidance package in a nose cap; in addition, the bomb had aerodynamic strakes mounted on its side and a tail section containing stabilization and guidance fins. HOBOS operates in basically the same manner as the Walleye glide bomb.

Hundreds of HOBOS and Walleyes were used with considerable effectiveness in Vietnam, destroying or severely damaging between 70 and 80 percent of all targets attacked. The Walleye glide bomb was also successfully employed by the Israel Defense Force/Air Force in the Yom Kippur War in 1973.

Laser-Guided Bombs

The most widely deployed free-fall guided weapon in service in the free world is the laser-guided bomb. The weapon consists of a laser seeker and a control unit with movable guidance fins up front, a conventional bomb in the middle, and fixed stabilizing fins at the rear. The original laser-guided bombs, developed as Project Paveway, come in 500-pound, 750-pound, 1,000-pound, 2,000-pound, and 3,000-pound versions.

Laser-guided bombs seek their target through a semiactive-homing technique. A target is illuminated by a laser that can be aimed by a soldier on the ground, by the aircraft dropping the bomb, or by another aircraft. The laser seeker at the nose of the bomb passively homes onto laser energy reflected from the target.

Some 25,000 laser-guided bombs were employed by U.S. forces in Vietnam and demonstrated a high degree of accuracy. France has developed laser-guided bombs and it is assumed that the air forces of the Soviet Union are armed with similar precision-guided weapons. More than 15 countries have bought laser-guided weapons from the United States.

While television-guided and laser-guided bombs performed well in Vietnam and in the Middle East, they are not without drawbacks. Being free-fall weapons, both types must be launched within a relatively narrow ballistic path toward the target. If the bomb is launched from too far or too low, there will not be sufficient energy for the guidance fins to correct its flight path and strike the target. Since most guided bombs must be dropped from medium altitude and in good weather, the launch and guidance aircraft are potentially vulnerable to surface-to-air missiles and heavy antiaircraft artillery.

Guided Missiles

The Maverick and Martel television-guided rocket-powered missiles were the logical addition to the free-fall guided bombs. The 462-pound Maverick operates similarly to the HOBOS bomb; once the television monitor in the missile's nose locks onto the target it can be launched with no further action required of the pilot. The Maverick missile was supplied to Israel near the end of the Yom Kippur War in 1973. The Israeli Air Force reportedly fired 69 at Arab tanks and bunkers with a high rate of success.

The Martel, built jointly by the British and French, detects the target with its television sensor before it is launched, but the pilot or weapons system operator must fly the missile to its target via a data link that sends continuously updated commands to correct its trajectory.

The Maverick missile has been modified to make it a more versatile weapon. The U.S. Marine Corps is procuring a version of the missile fitted with a laser seeker and a larger 300-pound blast/fragmentation warhead for close support on the ground. Both the U.S. Air Force and the Navy are buying a version of the Maverick with an imaging infrared guidance system that can be used during the day, night, and in adverse weather. Operating as a television camera sensitive to infrared wave lengths, the missile's seeker can detect and lock onto such targets as tanks, aircraft, or ships—all of which are warm compared to the surrounding landscape.

The Soviet armed forces are known to possess a number of such tactical air-to-surface missiles as the AS-7 and AS-9.

Unguided Free-Fall Weapons

While conventional high explosive bombs have changed little since the mid-1960s, several of new free-fall unguided weapons have been developed.

Cluster Bombs

The United States and Israel used U.S.-built cluster bombs in both Vietnam and Middle East respectively to suppress air defenses and destroy large-area targets (see the air-to-ground weapons section in Appendix I). Since the 1960s, the U.S. has developed a wide variety of cluster bomb systems and warheads.

To increase the Rockeye's accuracy when lofted or released from long range, the weapon can be fitted with a laser guidance seeker and a proximity fuse to initiate the release of the bomblets when the weapon nears the target.

The U.S. Air Force has developed a series of laser-guided cluster bomb weapons. In addition to instantaneous-destruct antipersonnel or anti-armor warheads, the cluster bomb's dispenser can release time-delay bomblets or special mines that can destroy trucks, armor, or personnel over a period of hours. The munitions dispenser can be fitted with either a laser guidance kit or television guidance seeker and fins for accurate long-range attacks.

Great Britain and France have developed, respectively, the BL755 and Belugy cluster bombs that dispense antiarmor/antipersonnel bomblets. These can be released from aircraft at low or medium altitude and can pepper large areas with bomblets.

West Germany has taken a different approach in developing the BD-1 bomblet dispenser for its Phantom and Tornado attack aircraft. The BD-1 is a large container holding several hundred bomblets. As the aircraft passes over the target, bomblets are blown out of the sides of the dispenser by compressed air. Because of the large number of bomblets and the dispensing method, the BD-1 can saturate an area as wide as 600 feet and as long as 4,000 feet. The weapon can carry a wide range of different types of bomblets, including shaped-charge antiarmor bomblets, fragmentation bomblets, mines, and special hard-target bomblets.

Anti-Runway Bombs

France, USSR, Israel, Great Britain, Spain, and the United States have all deployed or developed special weapons for cratering runways. Before special anti-runway weapons were developed, ordinary bombs had to be dropped from medium altitude and level flight or from a high angle to penetrate and seriously damage the runway. These delivery tactics are very dangerous because of antiaircraft defenses. Low-altitude attacks using retarded (high-drag) weapons was safer, but the low impact speed of retarded bombs limited their capability to penetrate concrete or protective structures.

The French-built Durandal anti-runway bomb is delivered from a high-speed/low-level flight. When released, a retarding parachute deploys to slow the bomb to ensure that the aircraft is safely away. After several seconds, the parachute is loosed and a booster rocket ignites to drive the bomb downward to increase its impact velocity. The bomb penetrates the runway and the warhead explodes, creating a wide, deep crater.

The British are developing the JP233 dispenser that releases anti-runway munitions and delayed-action mines. The USSR has developed runway blasting bombs, which were quite effective when the Indian Air Force attacked Pakistani airfields during the 1971 Indo-Pakistan War.

Fuel Air Explosives

Fuel air explosives, a recent concept, dispense a cloud of fuel to form an explosive vapor. When the vapor density is distributed over the target area, time-delay detonators are fired, creating a highly-destructive shock wave. Fuel air explosives are three to five times more destructive than a similar weight of TNT. Late in the Vietnam War, the U.S. Navy and the Marine Corps employed CBU-55B fuel air explosive weapons in Vietnam for preparing helicopter landing zones and clearing mines.

Fighter Attack Aircraft 1980s[14]

Aircraft / Crew	Wing Span (ft)	Length (ft)	Empty Weight (lb)	Normal Loaded Weight (lb)	Combat Weight (50% Fuel + Weapons) (lb)	Wing Area ft²	Engine(s)	Thrust Military Power (lb)	Thrust After-burning (lb)	Maximum Speed (Mach / mph)	Combat Thrust To Weight Ratio (AB / Mil)	Combat Wing Loading (lb/ft²)	Combat Radius (mi)	Weapons Air-to-Air / Air-to-Ground
F-4E Phantom II USA	2	38.3	62.8	32,200	47,300	40,000	530	2 General Electric J79-GE-17 Turbojets	11,870	17,900	2.27 / 1,500	.89 / .59	75	250–750	1 20mm Cannon / 4 AIM-9 AAMS / 4 AIM-7 AAMS / 16,000 lbs
F-5E Tiger II USA	1	26.7	48.2	11,000	15,400	12,800	187	2 General Electric J85-GE-21 Turbojets	3,500	5,000	1.6 / 1,065	.78 / .58	69	150–500	2 20mm Cannon / 2 AIM-9 AAMS / 2,000 lbs
F-14A Tomcat USA	2	38.1 / 64.1	61.9	40,000	58,500	50,000	565	2 Pratt & Whitney TF30-P-412A Turbofans	13,400	20,900	2.34 / 1,545	.84 / .54	88	250–700	1 20mm Cannon / 4 AIM-9 AAMS / 4 AIM-7 or 6 AIM-54 AAMS
F-15C Eagle USA	1	42.8	63.8	28,000	44,500	37,800	608	2 Pratt & Whitney F100-P-100 Turbofans	14,300	23,800	2.5 / 1,650	1.25 / .75	62	250–600	1 20mm Cannon / 4 AIM-7 AAMS / 4 AIM-9 AAMS / 15,000 lbs
F-16A Fighting Falcon USA	1	31	50.5	15,140	23,400	20,000	300	1 Pratt & Whitney F100-P-100 Turbofan	14,300	23,800	2.0 / 1,320	1.2 / .72	66	250–600	1 20mm Cannon / 6 AIM-9 AAMS / 15,000 lbs
F/A-18A Hornet USA	1	37.5	56	23,350	36,000	30,000	400	2 General Electric F404-GE-400 Turbofans	10,600	16,000	1.8 / 1,190	1.0 / .70	71	200–600	1 20mm Cannon / 2 AIM-9 AAMS / 2 AIM-7 AAMS / 15,000 lbs
MiG-21 bis Fishbed USSR	1	23.5	44	12,000	20,000	16,000	247.5	1 Tumansky R-25 Turbojet	11,000	16,500	2.1 / 1,386	1.0 / .66	65	175–400	1 23mm Cannon / 4 AA-2 AAMS / 2,000 lbs
MiG-23 Flogger USSR	1	26.8 / 46.7	55.1	25,000	34,000	31,000	400	1 Tumansky R-29B Turbojet	17,635	25,350	2.2 / 1,450	.82 / .56	78	200–500	1 23mm Cannon / 2 AA-7 AAMS / 2 AA-8 AAMS / 5,000 lbs

Aircraft / Country						Engine						Armament
Mirage F-1C France	1	27.6 / 49.2	16,300 / 25,000	21,000	269	1 SNECMA Atar 9K-50 Turbojet	15,800	M 2.2 / 1450	.75 / .52	78	200–500	2 30mm Cannon / 2 550 AAMS / 2 530 AAMS / 8,000 lbs
Mirage 2000 France	1	29.5 / 49.1	16,500 / 30,000	21,000	430	1 SNECMA M53-3 Turbojet	19,800	M 2.2 / 1,450	1.0 / .62	46	200–500	2 30mm Cannon / 2 550 AAMS / 2 530 AAMS / 11,000 lbs
Tornado F Mk 2 UK	2	28.1 45.4 / 59.3	31,500 / 48,000	36,000	322	2 Turbo union RB199 Mk 103 Turbofans	16,000	M 2.57 / 1,500	.83 / .44	100	200–600	1 27mm Cannon / 2 AIM-9 AAMS / 4 Skyflash
JA-37 Viggen Sweden	1	34.7 / 56.7	27,000 / 37,000	33,000	561	1 Volvo Flygmotor RM-813 Turbofan	28,100	M 2.0 / 1,320	.88 / .50	64	300–600	1 30mm Cannon / 2 AIM-9 AAMS / 2 Skyflash / 8,000 lbs
Sea Harrier FRS Mk 1 UK	1	25.2 / 47.6	12,500 / 21,700	19,200	201	1 Rolls Royce Pegasus 104 Turbofan	—	M 0.9 / 720	1.1	95	100–400	2 30mm Cannon / 4 AIM-9 AAMS / 5,000 lbs
Kfir C2 Israel	1	26.9 / 51	16,000 / 24,000	20,600	375	1 General Electric J79-GE-17 Turbojet	17,900	M 2.2 / 1,405	.87 / .57	54	200–500	2 30mm Cannon / 2 AIM-9 or Shafrir AAMS / 8,000 lbs
Ajeet India	1	22.1 / 29.6	5,100 / 2,800	6,800	136	1 Rolls Royce Orpheus Turbojet	—	0.9 / 665	.69	.50	100–250	2 30mm Cannon / 2,000 lbs
Super Etendard France	1	31.4 / 46.9	14,200 / 25,300	20,000	305	1 SNECMA 8K-50 Turbojet	—	1.0 / 745	56	65	200–400	2 30mm Cannon / 2 550 AAMS / 4,500 lbs
AV-8B Harrier II USA	1	30.4 / 46.3	13,000 / 22,000	19,000	230	1 Rolls Royce Pegasus II Turbofan	—	0.90 / 680	1.1	82	200–650	1 25mm Cannon / 4 AIM-9 AAMS / 9,200 lbs
Jaguar UK/France	1	28.5 / 50.9	15,500 / 24,000	20,000	260	2 Rolls Royce/Turbomeca Adour Turbofans	8,400	1.6 / 1,055	.84	77	250–600	2 30mm Cannon / 2 AIM-9 or 550 AAMS / 10,000 lbs

Aircraft Cannon 1980s[15]

Weapon	Muzzle Velocity (ft/sec)	Rate of Fire (rpm)	Projectile Weight (oz)	Weight of Fire Per Gun Two Seconds Burst (lb)	Ammunition	Aircraft Armed With The Cannon
M-61A1 USA Vulcan 20-mm	3,690	6,000	2.9	175 rds 31.7 lbs	HEI API	F-4E, F/A-18 F-14A, A-7, F-15ABCD, F-16AC
GSh-23 USSR 23-mm	2,263	3,000	7.0	100 rds 44.1 lbs		MiG-21MF MiG-23B
DEFA 554 France 30-mm	2,690	1,800 1,100	8.3	60 rds 31.1 lbs	HE	Mirage F1 Super Etendard Mirage 2000
Mauser Bk 27 FRG 27-mm	NA	1,700	NA	NA	NA	Tornado
Oerlikon KCA Sweden 30-mm	3,530	1,350	12.7	45 rds 35.7 lbs	HEI API	JA-37 Viggen

Air-to-Air Missiles 1980s[16]

Missile	Guidance & Control	Propulsion	Warhead	Length (ft)	Weight (lb)	Diameter (in)	Wing Span (ft)	Maximum Speed (Mach)	Range (mi)
AIM-9L/M Sidewinder USA	Infrared Homing	Solid Propellant Rocket	25 lb fragmentation	9.4	190	5	2.08	2.5	5
AIM-7F/M Sparrow USA	Semi-active Radar Homing	Solid Propellant Rocket	88 lb continuous Rod	12	503	8	3.3	3.5	30+
AIM-54 Phoenix USA	Semi-active/ Active Radar Homing	Solid Propellant Rocket	132 lb fragmentation	13.1	838	15	3.0	3	70+
AIM-120 AMRAAM USA	Inertial/ Active Radar Homing	Solid Propellant Rocket	fragmentation	11.7	325	7	2.4	3	30+
Advanced AA-2 ATOLL USSR	Infrared or Semi-active Radar Homing	Solid Propellant Rocket		IR 9.1 R 9.6	IR 155 R 190	4.75	1.7	2+	4+
AA-6 ACRID USSR	Infrared or Semi-active Radar Homing	Solid Propellant Rocket		IR 19.3 R 20.6	IR 1,430 R 1,870	15.7	7.3	3+	IR 15 R 30
AA-7 Apex USSR	Infrared or Semi-active Radar Homing	Solid Propellant Rocket		IR 13.8 R 14.7	IR 650 R 705	10.2	4.5	3+	IR 10 R 25
AA-8 Aphid USSR	Infrared Homing	Solid Propellant Rocket		6.5	120	5.1	1.8	2.5	5
Matra 550 Magic France	Infrared Homing	Solid Propellant Rocket	27.6 lb fragmentation	9	198	6.2	2.1	2+	6
Matra Super 530 France	Semi-active Radar Homing	Solid Propellant Rocket	66 lb fragmentation	11.5	529	10.2	2.1	4	20+
Skyflash UK	Semi-active Radar Homing	Solid Propellant Rocket	66 lb fragmentation	12	425	8	3.3	3.5	25+
Shafrir Mk 2 Israel	Infrared Homing	Solid Propellant Rocket	24.3 lb fragmentation	8.1	209	6.3	1.8	2+	4

Gun Antiaircraft Weapons 1980s[17]

Weapon Type Country	Vehicle Mount	Rate of Fire: Cyclic Per Minute	Effective Range— Anti- aircraft (ft)	Guidance	Gun	Muzzle Velocity (ft/s)
ZSU-23-4 USSR	PT-76 Chassis	4,000	9,000	Radar/ Optical	4—23-mm	3,182
Vulcan USA	M-113 APC	3,000	5,000	Optical/ Ranging Radar	20-mm	3,380
DIVAD USA	M-48 Tank Chassis	600	10,000	Radar/ Optical	2—40-mm	3,362
Gepard FRG	Leopard Tank Chassis	1,100	10,000	Radar/ Optical	2—25-mm	3,854
Reinmetal 202 MK 20 FRG	Towed	2,000	5,000	Optical	2—20-mm	3,444
AMX-DCA France	AMX-30 Tank Chassis	600	10,000	Radar/ Optical	2—30-mm	3,542

Antiaircraft Missile Systems 1980s[18]

Weapon Type Country	Length (ft)	Diameter (ft)	Weight (lb)	Range min/max (mi)	Altitude min/max (ft)	Guidance	System	Vehicle
SA-6 USSR	20.3	1.1	1,210	1/16	100/60,000	Radar	Battery = one radar, nine launchers	4 Tracked, armored per battery
SA-7B USSR	4.1	.23	20.2	.2/2.5	–/10,000	Optical/Infrared	Shoulder-launched	—
SA-8 USSR	10.5	.69	440	.5/6.75	–/21,000	Radar	Six launchers and radar	Missile system on six-wheel amphibious vehicle
SA-9 USSR	5.5	.36	66	.5/3.7	–/15,000	Optical/infrared	Four launchers on one vehicle	Missile system on four wheel amphibious vehicle
Improved HAWK	16.7	1.1	1,405	1/25	100/45,000	Radar	Battery = two radars, 18 launchers	Towed limited mobility
Chaparral USA	9.2	.4	190	.2/3.1	–/10,000	Infrared	Four launchers eight reloads	Four launchers on a tracked vehicle
Stinger USA	5	.22	22.3	.2/3	–/10,000	Infrared	Shoulder-launched	—
Rapier UK	7.21	.4	94	.3/4.5	–/10,000	Radio Command	Towed or tracked	Towed—two vehicles, four launchers, Tracked—one vehicle, eight launchers
Blowpipe UK	4.5	.25	24.5	.3/2	–/10,000	Radio Command	Shoulder-launched	
Sea Cat UK	4.9	.62	143	.3/3	–/10,000	Radio Command	Three- or four-round launchers	Ship-mounted
Sea Wolf UK	6.2	.60	180	.3/4	–/15,000	Radio Command	Six-round launcher	Ship-mounted
Sea Dart UK	14.5	1.2	1,210	1/25	300/50,000	Radar Command	Two-round launcher	Ship-mounted
Roland FRG/France	7.8	.5	139	.3/3.8	–/20,000	Radio Command	Two-launchers, 8-10 reloads	Tracked or wheeled vehicle

Notes

Chapter I

1. Sharp, Ulysses S. Grant, *Strategy for Defeat*, Presidio Press, San Rafael, Calif., 1978, p. 39.
2. Cagle, Malcolm, "Task Force 77 in Action Off Vietnam," *U.S. Naval Institute Proceedings*, 98, No. 831, p. 69.
3. Ibid. p. 70.
4. Sharp, op. cit., pp. 42–43.
5. O'Ballance, Edgar, *The Wars In Vietnam*, 1954–1973, Ian Allan Ltd., London, 1975, p. 70;
   Cagle, op. cit., p. 71.
6. Sharp, op. cit., p. 43.
7. Cagle, op. cit., p. 72.
8. Sharp, op. cit., p. 46.
9. Berger, Carl, et al., eds., *The United States Air Force in Southeast Asia*, Office of Air Force History, Washington, D.C., 1977, p. 34.
10. O'Ballance, op. cit., p. 74.
11. Sharp, op. cit., pp. 66–67.
12. Berger, op. cit., p. 69.
13. Ibid., pp. 69–71.
14. Futrell, Frank, R., *Aces and Aerial Victories*, Office of Air Force History, Washington, D.C. 1976, p. 16.
15. Lavelle, A. J. C., ed., *The Tale of Two Bridges and the Battle for Skies Over North Vietnam*, USAF SEA Monograph Series, Washington, D.C., 1976, pp. 127–128.
16. Ibid., p. 122.
17. O'Ballance, op. cit., p. 82.
18. Berger, op. cit., p. 75.
19. Momyer, William W., *Airpower In Three Wars*, unlisted, p. 220.
20. Sharp, op. cit., p. 77.
21. "SAMs Down F-4C, Damage Three Others," *Aviation Week & Space Technology*, 2 August 1965, p. 27.
22. Futrell, op. cit., pp. 5–7.
23. Momyer, op. cit., p. 130.
24. Knaack, Marcelle S., *Encyclopedia of U.S. Air Force Aircraft and Missile Systems*, Office of Air Force History, Washington, D.C., 1978, pp. 130–131.
25. Van Dyke, John M., *North Vietnam's Strategy for Survival*, Pacific Books, Palo Alto, Calif., 1972, p. 66.
26. O'Ballance, op. cit., p. 83.
27. "SAMs Down F-4C, Damage Three Others," *Aviation Week & Space Technology*, op. cit., p. 27.
28. Sharp, op. cit., pp. 105–111.
29. Berger, op. cit., p. 74.
30. Sharp, op. cit., p. 103.
31. Knaack, op. cit., p. 130.
32. Lavelle, op. cit., pp. 135–137.
33. Van Dyke, op. cit., p. 58.
34. Ibid., p. 80.
35. Momyer, op. cit., pp. 90–91.
36. Ibid., pp. 178–179.
37. Futrell, Frank R., et al., op. cit., p. 27.
38. Cagle, op. cit., p. 82.
39. Van Dyke, op. cit., p. 64.
40. Momyer, op. cit., p. 119.
41. Van Dyke, op. cit., p. 64.
42. Berger, op. cit., p. 82.
43. Van Dyke, op. cit., p. 66.
44. Lavelle, op. cit., p. 138.
45. Senate Armed Services Committee Hearings FY 1974, 13–20 March 1973, pp. 4251–4465.
46. Drendel, Lou, *And Kill MiGs*, Squadron/Signal, Warren, Mich., 1974, pp. 29, 56.
47. Futrell, op. cit., p. 35.
48. Ibid., p. 37.
49. Ibid., p. 37.
50. Futrell, op. cit., p. 39.
51. Van Dyke, op. cit., p. 58.
52. Sharp, op. cit., p. 160.

53. Cagle, op. cit., p. 98.
54. Futrell, op. cit., p. 12.
55. Cagle, op. cit., p. 98.
56. O'Connor, Michael, "Aces of the Yellow Star," *Air Combat*, Vol. 7, No. 1, 1979, pp. 20–22.
57. Futrell, op. cit., p. 66.
58. Sharp, op. cit., p. 204.
59. Ibid., p. 200.
60. Momyer, op. cit., p. 136.
61. Momyer, op. cit., p. 222.
62. Berger, op. cit., pp. 126–127.
63. *The Encyclopedia of the World's Combat Aircraft*, Bill Gunston, Chartwell Books, Inc., New York, 1976, p. 217.
64. *Encyclopedia of U.S. Air Force Aircraft and Missile Systems*, U.S. Government Printing Office, pp. 223–261.
65. Senate Armed Services Committee Hearings FY 1974, 13–20 March 1973, pp. 4389–4407.
66. Miller, Barry, Electronic Warfare Special Report, *Aviation Week & Space Technology*.
67. Senate Armed Services Committee Hearings FY 1974, 13–20 March 1973, pp. 4251-4265.
68. Goertz, Maj. Robert D., USAF, "An Analysis of Air-to-Air Missile Capability in Southeast Asia," *Air Command & Staff College Papers*, June 1968, p. 70.
69. Goertz, op. cit., p. 1.
70. Ibid., p. 41.
71. Ibid., p. 58.
72. Ibid., p. 28.
73. Ibid., p. 59.
74. Ibid., p. 46.
75. Ibid., p. 14.
76. *The U.S. Air Force Operations In Southeast Asia*, U.S. Government Printing Office, 1976, p. 71.
77. Senate Armed Services Committee Hearings FY 1974, 19 March 1973, pp. 4475–4497.
78. Senate Armed Services Committee Hearings FY 1974, 13–20 March 1973, pp. 4299–4307.
79. *The U.S. Air Force In Southeast Asia*, p. 71.

Chapter II

1. Lavelle, A. J. C., ed., *Air Power and The 1972 Spring Invasion*, U.S. Air Force SEA Monograph Series, Washington, D.C., 1976, p. 3.
2. Ibid., p. 1.
3. Personal Interview by David Parsons with Lt. Comdr. Randall Cunningham, July, 1979.
4. Futrell, Frank R., et al., *Aces and Aerial Victories*, Office of Air Force History, Washington, D.C., 1976, p. 13.
5. Ibid., p. 85.
6. O'Ballance, Edgar, *The Wars in Vietnam, 1954–1973*, Ian Allan Ltd., London, 1975, p. 167.
7. Lavelle, op. cit., pp. 4–9.
8. Palmer, Dave R., *Summons of the Trumpet, U.S.–Vietnam in Perspective*, Presidio Press, San Rafael, Calif., 1978, p. 248.
9. Ibid., p. 252.
10. O'Ballance, p. 167.
11. Senate Armed Services Subcommittee Hearings FY 1975, 22–29 March 1974, p. 4897.
12. Lavelle, *Airpower*, p. 51.
13. Momyer, William W., *Airpower In Three Wars*, U.S. Government Publication, p. 236.
14. O'Connor, Michael, "Aces of the Yellow Star," *Air Combat*, Vol. 6, No. 5, 1978, p. 21.
15. Lavelle, A. J. C., ed., *The Tale of Two Bridges and the Battle for the Skies Over North Vietnam*, USAF Monograph Series, Washington, D.C., 1976, pp. 160–164.
16. O'Connor, Michael, op. cit., p. 21.
17. Lavelle, *Tale of Two Bridges*, pp. 88–92.
18,19. Personal interview by David Parsons with Cunningham, op. cit.
20. Lavelle, *Tale of Two Bridges*, op. cit., pp. 85–86.
21. Lavelle, *Airpower*, p. 51.
22. Ibid., p. 34.
23. Ibid., p. 97.
24. O'Ballance, op. cit., pp. 169–170.
25. Drendel, Lou, *Phantom II*, Squadron/Signal, Warren, Mich., 1977, p. 46.
26. Futrell, op. cit., pp. 20–23, 102.

27. Ibid., p. 170.
28. Drendel, Lou, *And Kill MiGs,* Squadron/Signal, Warren, Mich., 1974, p. 56.
29. Futrell, op. cit., p. 106.
30. Futrell, op. cit., p. 108.
31. Futrell, op. cit., pp. 109–110.
32. O'Ballance, p. 177.
33. Lavelle, *Tale of Two Bridges,* op. cit., p. 175.
34. Lewy, Gunther, *America In Vietnam,* Oxford University Press, New York, 1978, p. 412.
35. McCarthy, James R., and Allison, George B., *Linebacker II: A View From the Rock.* Robert E. Rayfield, ed., USAF SEA Monograph Series, Washington, D.C., 1976, pp. 17–20, 70.
36. Ibid., pp. 56–80.
37. Ibid., p.33.
38. Ibid., p. 68.
39. Ibid., pp. 41–56.
40. Ibid., p. 42.
41. Ibid., pp. 61–65.
42. Futrell, op. cit., pp. 111–112.
43. McCarthy, op. cit., p. 77.
44. Ibid., pp. 83–89.
45. Ibid., pp. 83–84.
46. Ibid., pp. 92–93.
47. Futrell, op. cit., p. 113.
48. McCarthy, op. cit., pp. 99–100.
49. Ibid., pp. 100–101.
50. Ibid., p. 110.
51. Ibid., p. 110.
52. Ibid., pp. 110–111.
53. Ibid., pp. 113–116.
54. Ibid., pp. 121–123, 145.
55. Ibid., pp. 151–153.
56. Ibid., p. 155.
57. Futrell, op. cit., p. 115.
58. Data Compiled From: *Aces and Aerial Victories,* Office of Air Force History, 1976; *Armed Forces Journal,* May 1974; *And Kill MiGs,* Squadron/Signal Publications, 1974; and *Combat Losses to MiG Aircraft in Southeast Asia 1965–1972,* Center for Naval Analysis Paper 78–0397 via Freedom of Information Act.
59. Momyer, op. cit., p. 157.
60. Cooper, Bert H., "Navy/Marine Corps F/A-18 Aircraft: A Survey of Major Issues," Library of Congress, 11 November 1981, p. 6.

Chapter III

1. Fricker, John, "Thirty Seconds Over Sargodha," *Air Enthusiast,* June 1971, p. 16.
2. Ibid.
3. Singh, Pushpindar, *Aircraft of the Indian Air Force,* The English Book Store, New Delhi, 1974, p. 150.
4. *New York Times,* 2 September 1965.
5. *Facts on File,* Volume XXV, No. 1297, p. 313.
6. Fricker, John, *Battle for Pakistan, The Air War of 1965,* Ian Allan Ltd., London, 1979, p. 77.
7. Ibid.
8. Chopra, Pushpindar S., "Gnat," *Air International,* August 1974, p. 74.
9. Fricker, *Battle for Pakistan,* op. cit., p. 111.
10. Ibid., p. 99.
11. *New York Times,* 7 September 1965.
12. Fricker, *Battle for Pakistan,* op. cit., p. 111.
13. Fricker, "Thirty Seconds Over Sargodha," op. cit., p. 18.
14. *New York Times,* 8 September 1965.
15. *Facts on File,* op. cit., p. 314.
16. *New York Times,* 9 September 1965.
17. Fricker, *Battle for Pakistan,* op. cit., p. 150.
18. *New York Times,* 11 September 1965.

19. Fricker, *Battle for Pakistan,* op. cit., p. 150.
20. Ibid.
21. *New York Times,* 17 September 1965.
22. *New York Times,* 18 September 1965.
23. Fricker, *Battle for Pakistan,* op. cit., p. 153.
24. *Newsweek,* 4 October 1965, p. 45.
25. Ibid.
26. Charturvedi, N. S., Air Marshall, *History of the Indian Air Force,* Vikas Publishing House, New Delhi, 1978, pp. 146–147.
27. Fricker, *Battle for Pakistan,* op. cit., pp. 164–165.
28. Singh, op. cit., p. 150.
29. Fricker, "Thirty Seconds Over Sargodha," op. cit., p. 19.
30. Shores, Christopher, *Fighter Aces,* Hamlyn Publishing Group, London, 1975, p. 148.
31. Fricker, *Battle for Pakistan,* op. cit., p. 185.
32. Ibid.
33. Shores, op. cit., p. 147.

Chapter IV

1. "Pakistan Air Force Built Around MiG-19," *Aviation Week & Space Technology,* 2 December 1968, p. 43.
2. Hunt, David, "Recollections of the Canadair Sabre," *Air Enthusiast,* April 1972, p. 203.
3. "Pakistan Air Force Built Around MiG-19," op. cit., p. 45.
4. Fricker, John, "Post-Mortem on an Air War," *Air Enthusiast,* May 1972, p. 229.
5. International Institute for Strategic Studies, *Military Balance,* 1971–1972, p. 50.
6. Singh, Pushpindar, *Aircraft of the Indian Air Force,* The English Book Store, New Delhi, pp. 143–44.
7. Chopra, Pushpindar S., "Harnessing the Storm Spirit," *Air Enthusiast,* May 1973, pp. 215–222.
8. "Quantity or Quality? The Indian Dilemma," *Air International,* October 1975, pp. 174–75.
9. Singh, Pushpindar, op. cit., p. 150.
10. *Military Balance,* op. cit., 1971–72, p. 46.
11. Chopra, Pushpindar S., "Indian Ocean Air Power," *Air Enthusiast,* December 1972, p. 275.
12. Chopra, Pushpindar S., "Gnat," *Air International,* August 1974, p. 75.
13. Chopra, Pushpindar S., "Journal of an Air War," *Air Enthusiast,* April 1972, p. 197.
14. Ibid., p. 180.
15. Shaheen, "The PAF at War," *Journal of the Pakistan Air Force,* May–August 1972, p. 5.
16. Shaheen, "An Unmatched Feat in the Air," *Journal of the Pakistan Air Force,* May–August 1972, p. 16.
17. Chopra, "Journal of an Air War," op. cit., p. 180.
18. Ibid., *New York Times,* 5 December 1971.
19. *New York Times,* 6 December 1971.
20. Ibid.
21. Shaheen, "The PAF at War," op. cit., p. 6.
22. Ibid.
23. Chopra, "Harnessing the Storm Spirit," op. cit., p. 216.
24. "India-Pakistan Air War, *Flight International,* 16 December 1971, p. 991.
25. Ibid.
26. Ibid.
27. *New York Times,* 11 December 1971.
28. Shaheen, "The PAF at War," op. cit., p. 8.
29. Chopra, "Journal of an Air War," op. cit., p. 183.
30. Chaturvedi, Air Marshal N. S., *History of the Indian Air Force,* Vikas Publishing House, New Delhi, 1978, p. 162.
31. Chopra, Pushpindar S., "India and the MiG-21," *Air Enthusiast,* July 1973, p. 7.
32. Shaheen, "The PAF at War," op. cit., p. 9.
33. Singh, Pushpindar, op. cit., p. 145; Chopra, "Journal of an Air War," op. cit., p. 206.
34. Chopra, "India and the MiG-21," op. cit., p. 11.
35. International Institute for Strategic Studies, *Strategic Survey 1971,* p. 52.
36. Rikhye, Ravi, "Why India Won the 14-Day War," *Armed Forces Journal International,* April 1972, p. 41.
37. *Strategic Survey,* op. cit., p. 52.
38. Ibid.

39. Chopra, "Journal of an Air War," op. cit., p. 177.
40. Shaheen, "The PAF at War," op. cit., p. 11.
41. *Military Aviation News,* No. 124, February 1972, p. 102.
42. Singh, op. cit., p. 150.
43. Fricker, op. cit., p. 260.
44. Ibid., p. 228.
45. Ibid., p. 228.
46. Singh, op. cit., p. 114.
47. Fricker, op. cit., p. 260.
48. Chopra, "Journal of an Air War," op. cit., p. 172.
49. Ibid.
50. Ibid.
51. Chopra, "Indian Ocean Air Power," op. cit., pp. 275–79.
52. Fricker, op. cit., p. 231; Shaheen, "The PAF at War," op. cit. p. 11.
53. Ibid.
54. Singh, op. cit., p. 133.
55. Chopra, "Journal of an Air War," op. cit., p. 177.
56. Fricker, op. cit., p. 232.
57. Chopra, "India and the MiG-21," op. cit., p. 10.
58. Fricker, op. cit., p. 260.
59. Shores, Christopher, *Fighter Aces,* Hamlyn Publishing Group, London, 1975, p. 155.
60. Fricker, op. cit., p. 260.
61. Shaheen, *The Battle of Air Forces: A Comparative Study of the PAF and IAF Successes in War,* p. 19.
62. Fricker, op. cit., p. 229.
63. Shores, op. cit., p. 155
64. Ibid.

Chapter V

1. *New York Times,* 8 April 1967.
2. O'Ballance, Edgar, *The Third Arab Israeli War,* Anchor Books, Hamden, Conn., 1970, p. 50.
3. Figures are approximate; numbers differ considerably, Goldman, Richards, and Rubenstein, Murray, *Shield of David,* Prentice Hall, Inc., Englewood Cliffs, N.J., 1978, p. 96.
4. Weizman, Ezer, *On Eagles' Wings,* Macmillan & Co., N.Y., 1976, pp. 173–199.
5. "Feasibility Study to Predict Combat Effectiveness for Selected Military Roles: Fighter Pilot Effectiveness," McDonnell Douglas Reports.
6. O'Ballance, op. cit., p. 55.
7. Wetmore, Warren C., "Mock Dogfights Sharpened Israeli Pilots," *Aviation Week & Space Technology,* 3 July 1967, p. 24.
8. O'Ballance, op. cit., p. 56.
9. Goldman and Rubenstein, op. cit., p. 96.
10. O'Ballance, op. cit., p. 57.
11. Ibid., p. 57.
12. Ibid., p. 58.
13. "Arab Air Power," *Air International,* June 1977, p. 281.
14. Ibid., p. 291.
15. O'Ballance, op. cit., p. 62.
16. Goldman and Rubenstein, op. cit., p. 97.
17. O'Ballance, op. cit., pp. 60–61.
18. Ibid., p. 61.
19. Goldman and Rubenstein, op. cit., p. 97.
20. Churchill, Randolph S., and Churchill, Winston S., *The Six Day War,* Houghton Mifflin Co., 1967, p. 91.
21. Barker, A. J., *Six Day War,* Random House, 1974, p. 66.
22. Churchill, op. cit., p. 93.
23. O'Ballance, op. cit., p. 66.
24. Wetmore, Warren C., "Israeli Mirage Pilot Describes MiG Kills," *Aviation Week & Space Technology,* 17 July 1967, p. 76.
25. O'Ballance, op. cit., p. 70.
26. *New York Times,* 6 June 1967.

27. Nadau, Safron, *From War to War: The Arab-Israeli Confrontation,* Pegasus Books, New York, 1969, p. 328.
28. Wetmore, Warren C., "Israelis Air Punch Major Factor In War," *Aviation Week & Space Technology,* 3 July 1967, pp. 18–23.
29. O'Ballance, op. cit., p. 82.
30. Churchill, op. cit., p. 93.
31. Ibid., p. 76.
32. Ibid., p. 76.
33. Wetmore, "Israelis Air Punch Major Factor in War," op. cit., p. 23. According to other sources, the penetrating aircraft were in fact Vautours.
34. O'Ballance, op. cit., p. 82.
35. Wetmore, "Israeli Mirage Pilot Describes MiG Kills," op. cit., p. 81.
36. O'Ballance, op. cit., p. 82.
37. "Massive Resupply Narrows Israeli Margin," *Aviation Week & Space Technology,* 19 June 1967, p. 16.
38. Ibid., p. 16.
39. Sella, Amnon, "The Struggle for Air Superiority," October 1973–December 1975, *RUSI Journal,* May 1975, p. 31.
40. Wetmore, "Air Attacks by Israelis Leave Fiery Wake," op. cit., p. 22.
41. "The Six-Day War," *Born In Battle* magazine, p. 21.
42. Wetmore, Warren C., "Israelis Class MiG-21 as Efficient High Altitude Fighter," *Aviation Week & Space Technology,* 31 July 1967.
43. Wetmore, "Mock Dogfights Sharpen Israeli Pilots," op. cit., p. 24.
44. Wetmore, Warren C., "Israelis Display Soviet-Built Atoll Missile," *Aviation Week & Space Technology,* 24 July 1967, p. 65.
45. Wetmore, "Mock Dogfights Sharpen Israeli Pilots," op. cit., p. 22.
46. Ibid., p. 27.

Chapter VI

1. "Massive Resupply Narrows Israeli Margin," *Aviation Week & Space Technology,* 19 June 1967, p. 16.
2. O'Ballance, Edgar, *The Electronic War in the Middle East,* Anchor Books, Hamden, Conn., 1974, p. 26.
3. Ibid., p. 27.
4. International Institute for Strategic Studies, *Military Balance,* 1968–69, p. 44.
5. O'Ballance, op. cit., p. 71.
6. Kolcum, Edward, "Soviets' Shifting Middle East Balance," *Aviation Week & Space Technology,* 18 May 1970, p. 14.
7. *Military Balance,* op. cit.
8. "Arab Air Power," *Air International,* September 1977, p. 149.
9. *Military Balance,* op. cit., p. 46.
10. Goldman, Richard, and Rubenstein, Murray, *Shield of David,* Prentice Hall, Englewood Cliffs, N.J., 1978, p. 151.
11. "Israel Preparing for the Next Round," *Air Enthusiast,* December 1971, p. 344.
12. *Military Balance,* op. cit., p. 45.
13. O'Ballance, op. cit., p. 31.
14. "Artillery Comes Into Its Own," *Armed Forces Journal International,* October 1973, p. 62.
15. *New York Times,* 14 February 1969.
16. *New York Times,* 2 July 1969.
17. *New York Times,* 9 July 1969.
18. *New York Times,* 9 July 1969.
19. Ibid.
20. *New York Times,* 26 July 1969.
21. Ibid.
22. O'Ballance, op. cit., p. 85.
23. Ibid.
24. *New York Times,* 12 September 1969.
25. *New York Times,* 14 September 1969.
26. Ibid.
27. *New York Times,* 7 October 1969.
28. Ibid.

29. Kolcum, Edward, "Soviets Shifting Middle East Balance," *Aviation Week & Space Technology,* 12 May 1970, p. 21.
30. O'Ballance, op. cit., p. 87.
31. Beck, M. O., "State of the Art," *USAF Fighter Weapons Review,* Winter, 1974. In 1969 F-4 Phantom IIs could accommodate AIM-9B, D, E, G Sidewinder air-to-air missiles.
32. Goldman, Richard, and Rubenstein, Murray, op. cit., p. 150.
33. Gunston, Bill, *The Illustrated Encyclopedia of the World's Rockets & Missiles,* Crescent Books, N.Y., 1979, p. 213.
34. "Israel's Pride of Lions," *Air International,* November 1976, p. 220.
35. Ibid.
36. Goldman, Rubenstein, op. cit., p. 80.
37. "Israel's Pride of Lions," *Air International,* November 1976, p. 220.
38. "Israel Preparing for the Next Round," *Air Enthusiast,* December 1971, p. 347.
39. O'Ballance, op. cit., p. 104.
40. O'Ballance, op. cit., p. 109.
41. Kolcum, Edward, "Vietnam Lessons Helped Israel Build Mideast Air Supremacy," *Aviation Week & Space Technology,* 25 May 1970, p. 18.
42. *New York Times,* 28 March 1970.
43. *New York Times,* 3 April 1970.
44. Whetten, Lawrence, *The Canal War: Four Power Conflict in the Middle East,* MIT Press, Cambridge, Mass., 1974, p. 95.
45. Wakebridge, Charles, "Electrons Over Suez," *Ordnance Magazine,* May–June 1972, p. 475.
46. *New York Times,* 20 April 1970.
47. *New York Times,* 26 April 1970.
48. Whetten, Lawrence, "June 1967 to June 1971: Four Years of Canal War Reconsidered," *New Middle East,* June 1971.
49. *Skyhawk,* War Data, Eshel Dramit, Ltd., Israel, pp. 39–41.
50. *New York Times,* 16 May 1970.
51. *New York Times,* 4 June 1970.
52. Whetten, *The Canal War,* op. cit., p. 19.
53. *New York Times,* 27 June 1970.
54. *New York Times,* 1 July 1970.
55. *New York Times,* 7 July 1970.
56. *New York Times,* 12 July 1970.
57. Whetten, *The Canal War,* op. cit., p. 20.
58. *Israel's Air Force, The Air War in the Mid East, Born In Battle* magazine No. 2, Eshel Dramit, Ltd., Israel p. 50.
59. *Air Enthusiast,* op. cit., p. 344.
60. Hotz, Robert, "Offense, Defense Tested in 1973 War," *Aviation Week & Space Technology,* Both Sides of the Suez Special Issue, p. 42.
61. *Aerospace Historian,* "A Short History of the Israeli Air Force," written by the Israeli Air Force, pp. 10–17.
62. "The Israeli Air Force," *Air Force Magazine,* August 1976, p. 36.
63. *Aerospace Historian,* op. cit., p. 17.
64. Aviation Advisory Service, *MILAV News,* January 1971.
65. *Air Enthusiast,* op. cit., p. 344.
66. Ibid., p. 346.

Chapter VII

1. Whetten, Lawrence, "June 1967 to June 1971: Four Years of Canal War Reconsidered," *New Middle East,* June 1971, p. 26.
2. Aviation Advisory Service, *MILAV News,* NL 118/8/71, August 1971, p. 15.
3. *New York Times,* June 14, 1972.
4. Whetten, Lawrence, *The Canal War: Four Power Conflict in the Middle East,* MIT Press, 1974, pp. 216, 218.
5. *New York Times,* 14 June 1972.
6. Dupuy, Trevor N., *Elusive Victory: The Arab Israeli Wars 1947–1974,* Harper & Row, 1978, p. 390.
7. *New York Times,* 22 November 1972.
8. Dupuy, op. cit., p. 387.
9. *New York Times,* 3 January 1973.

10. *New York Times,* 16 February 1973.

11. Herzog, Chaim, *The War of Atonement,* Little Brown, 1975, p. 255.

12. Figures are approximate. Sources differ considerably. (1) *Aviation Week & Space Technology,* 22 October 1973; (2) International Institute for Strategic Studies, *Military Balance,* 1973–74; (3) *Strategy & Tactics,* March/April, 1977.

13. Nordeen, Lon, "Israeli's Look to the Ground to Survive In The Air," *Astronautics and Aeronautics,* September 1978, p. 14.

14. *Born In Battle* magazine, "The Air War in the Middle East," Eshel Dramit, Ltd., 1978, p. 59.

15. "Jane's All The World's Aircraft Supplement," *Air Force Magazine,* October 1976, p. 41.

16. "Israel's Pride of Lions," *Air International,* November 1976, p. 221.

17. Tahtinen, Dale R., "The Arab-Israeli Military Balance Since October 1973," American Enterprise Institute for Public Policy Research, Washington, D.C., 1974, p. 4.

18. "Weapons for the Black Box War," *Flight International,* 5 May 1979, p. 1476.

19. International Institute for Strategic Studies, *Military Balance,* 1973–74, p. 33.

20. Ibid.

21. Brindley, John F., "Aircraft Profile, Mikoyan MiG-21 ("Fishbed")," *Variants,* Profile Publications Ltd., 1972, p. 89.

22. "Arab Air Power," *Air International,* June 1977, p. 294.

23. "Middle East Market," *Flight International,* 3 March 1975, p. 42.

24. Zaloga, Steven J., *Modern Soviet Armor,* Prentice Hall, 1979, p. 86.

25. Zaloga, op. cit., p. 81.

26. "Airpower and the 1972 Spring Invasion," *USAF Southeast Asia Monogram Series,* p. 44.

27. Ibid., p. 36.

28. International Institute for Strategic Studies, *Military Balance* 1973–74, p. 36.

29. Ibid., p. 36.

30. Hotz, Robert, "Egypt Plans Modernized Air Arm," *Aviation Week & Space Technology.* Both Sides of the Suez Special Issue, p. 30.

31. Both Sides of the Suez Special Issue, op. cit., p. 59.

32. "The Air War in the Middle East," op. cit., p. 59.

33. Lake, Julian S., Hartman, Richard V., "Air Electronic Warfare," *U.S. Naval Institute Proceedings,* October 1976, p. 48.

34. Nicolle, David, "The Holy Day Air War," *Air Enthusiast,* May 1974, p. 242.

35. Dupuy, Trevor N., op. cit., p. 450.

36. Nicolle, op. cit., p. 242.

37. Dupuy, op. cit., p. 554.

38. The Israeli Air Force in the Yom Kippur War, *Israeli Ministry of Defense,* Publishing House, 1975, p. 16.

39. *New York Times,* 8 October 1973.

40. "Yom Kippur–10 Years Later," *Defense Update,* No. 42, Eshel Dramit, Ltd., 1983, p. 21.

41. *New York Times,* 8 October 1973.

42. Nicolle, op. cit., p. 243.

43. *New York Times,* 9 October 1973.

44. *New York Times,* 9 October 1973.

45. Ibid.

46. *New York Times,* 10 October 1973.

47. Ibid.

48. *New York Times,* 11 October 1973.

49. Nicolle, op. cit., p. 244.

50. *New York Times,* 10 October 1973.

51. *New York Times,* 11 October 1973.

52. Ibid.

53. *New York Times,* 11 October 1973.

54. International Institute for Strategic Studies, *Strategic Survey,* 1973, p. 27.

55. Dupuy, op. cit., p. 559.

56. *The Yom Kippur War,* Insight Team of the London Sunday Times, Doubleday & Co., New York, 1974, pp. 184–89.

57. Israeli Air Force, op. cit., p. 48.

58. "Soviet Air Sparks Arab Gains," *Aviation Week & Space Technology,* 15 October 1973, p. 13.

59. Israeli Air Force, op. cit., p. 57.

60. Quandy, William B., *Soviet Policy in the 1973 War,* Rand Corporation Paper, RI864-178, May 1976, p. 24.

61. *New York Times,* 17 October 1973.
62. Israeli Air Force, op. cit., p. 74.
63. *New York Times,* 18 October 1973.
64. Israeli Air Force, op. cit., p. 80.
65. Nicolle, op. cit., p. 247.
66. Israeli Air Force, op. cit., p. 85.
67. "Israeli Aircraft, Arab SAMs in Key Battle," *Aviation Week & Space Technology,* 22 October 1973, pp. 15–16.
68. Israeli Air Force, op. cit., p. 86.
69. Nicolle, op. cit., p. 247.
70. Israeli Air Force, op. cit., p. 86.
71. El Badri, Maj. Gen. Hasson, and el Magdoub, Maj. Gen. Taha, and el Din Zohdy, Maj. Gen. Mohammed Din, *The Ramadan War 1973,* TN Dupry Associates, Dunn Loring, Va., 1978, p. 158.
72. Israeli Air Force, op. cit., p. 89.
73. *New York Times,* 22 October 1973.
74. Israeli Air Force, op. cit., p. 95.
75. Nicolle, op. cit., p. 248.
76. Hotz, Robert, "Egypt Plans Modernized Air Arm," *Aviation Week & Space Technology,* Both Sides of the Suez Special Issue, p. 33.
77. Dupuy, op. cit., p. 549.
78. Ibid., p. 550.
79. Israeli Air Force, op. cit., p. 114.
80. Coleman, Herbert J., "Israeli Air Force Decisive in War," *Aviation Week & Space Technology,* 3 December 1973, p. 18.
81. Hotz, Both Sides of the Suez Special Issue, op. cit., p. 33.
82. Nicolle, op. cit., p. 252.
83. Nicolle, op. cit., p. 248.
84. International Institute for Strategic Studies, *Strategic Survey,* 1973, p. 27.
85. Hotz, Robert, "Offense, Defense Tested in 1973 War," *Aviation Week & Space Technology,* Both Sides of the Suez Special Issue, p. 39–40.
86. Israeli Air Force briefing to Aviation & Space Writers Association, Hatzor Air Force Base, Israel, 8 June 1978.
87. Bougart, Peter, "The Vulnerability of the Manned Weapon System," *International Defense Review,* June 1977, p. 11.
88. "Air Defense Equipment In Israel," *Born In Battle* magazine, Issue No. 23, 1982, p. 23.
89. Hewish, Mark, "World Missiles," *Flight International,* 29 May 1976, p. 1442.
90. *Selected Readings In Tactics: The 1973 Middle East War,* U.S. Army Command & General Staff College, RB 100-2, Vol. 1, pp. 5–13.
91. Coleman, op. cit., p. 8.
92. Ibid.
93. *Armed Forces Journal International,* May 1974, p. 20.
94. *Selected Readings In Tactics,* op. cit., pp. 5–13.
95. Ibid.
96. Ibid.
97. Hotz, Both Sides of the Suez Special Issue, op. cit., p. 36.
98. Ibid.
99. "Middle East Market," *Flight International,* 13 March 1975, p. 420.
100. Hotz, Both Sides of the Suez Special Issue, op. cit., p. 42.
101. Palit, D. K., *Return to the Sinai,* Palit & Palit Publishers, New Delhi, India, 1974, p. 157.
102. Coleman, op. cit., p. 18.
103. *Armed Forces Journal International,* April 1974, p. 32.
104. "Anything Else Is Rubbish," USAF Fighter Weapons Review, Summer, 1975, p. 11.
105. Hotz, Robert, "Israeli Air Force Faces New Arab Arms," Both Sides of the Suez Special Issue, p. 8.
106. Briefing: Aviation & Space Writers Association, Hatzor Air Force Base, Israel, 8 June 1974.
107. *Armed Forces Journal International,* op. cit., p. 32.
108. Nordeen, Lon, conversations with B. Peled; Aviation & Space Writers Association Israeli Tour, 9 June 1978.
109. Nordeen, Lon, conversations with IDF/AF Wing Commander, Hatzor AFB, Aviation & Space Writers Association Israeli Tour, 8 June 1978.

Chapter VIII

1. *New York Times*, 7 December 1973.
2. *New York Times*, 6 November 1973.
3. *New York Times*, 9 April 1974.
4. *New York Times*, 20 April 1974.
5. *New York Times*, 25 April 1974.
6. *New York Times*, 30 April 1974.
7. *Air International*, "Arab Air Power IV," September 1977, p. 150. *Air International*, "Arab Air Power I," June 1977, p. 294. *Air International*, "Airscene," August 1979, p. 54.
8. *New York Times*, 25 July 1977; *Newsweek*, 1 August 1977, p. 29; *Time*, 1 August 1977, p. 20.
9. Nordeen, Lon, "Israelis Look to the Ground to Survive in the Air," *Astronautics & Aeronautics*, September 1978, pp. 13–14.
10. *Born In Battle* magazine, Issue No. 13, 1980, pp. 4–6.
11. *Time*, 9 July 1979, p. 34; *The Jerusalem Post*, International Edition, 1–7 July 1979.
12. *Aviation Week & Space Technology*, 1 October 1979, p. 13.
13. *Born In Battle* magazine, Issue No. 13, 1981, p. 11.
14. *Aviation Week & Space Technology*, op. cit., 1 October 1979, p. 13.
15. *New York Times*, 25 September 1979.
16. *St. Louis Post Dispatch*, 31 December 1980.
17. *Jerusalem Post*, 1 March 1981.
18. *St. Louis Post Dispatch*, 10 May 1981.
19. *New York Times*, 26 May 1981.
20. *Newsweek*, 22 June 1981, pp. 22–28; *Time*, 22 June 1981, pp. 24–38.
21. *New York Times*, 18 July 1981.
22. *Manchester Guardian*, 30 July 1981.
23. Walker, Bryce, *Fighting Jets: The Epic of Flight*, Time–Life, Alexandria, Va., 1983, p. 162.
24. "A Terrible Swift Sword," *Newsweek*, 21 June 1982, p. 21.
25. Herzog, Chaim, *The Arab–Israeli Wars: War and Peace in the Middle East*, Random House, New York, 1982, p. 389.
26. Mayo, Maj. Charles E., "Lebanon: An Air Defense Analysis," *Air Defense Artillery*, Winter, 1983, p. 22.
27. Ibid.
28. "A Terrible Swift Sword," op. cit., p. 24.
29. Cordesman, Anthony H., "The Sixth Arab-Israeli Conflict: Military Lessons for American Defense Planning," *Armed Forces Journal International*, August 1982, p. 30.
30. Herzog, op. cit., p. 389.
31. Lacouture, Capt. J. E. (U.S. Navy, Ret.), "The Critical Importance of Electronics in Modern War," *Wings of Gold*, Winter, 1982, p. 44.
32. *Chicago Tribune*, Israel and the Syrian SAMs, 7 January 1983, p. 17.
33. *The Wall Street Journal*, "US Arms Used in Lebanon War Outstrip Soviets'," 5 August 1982, p. 4.
34. Cutler, Paul S., "Lt. Gen. Rafael Eiton: "We Learned Both Tactical and Technical Lesson in Lebanon," *Military Electronics/Countermeasures*, February 1983, p. 100.
35. Robinson, Clarence A., Jr., "Surveillance Integration Pivotal in Israeli Success," *Aviation Week & Space Technology*, 5 July 1982, p. 17.
36. Ibid.
37. *Flight International*, "Syrian SAMs Lacked Protection," 21 August 1982, p. 404.
38. *The Wall Street Journal*, op. cit.
39. *Flight International*, "Bekaa Valley Combat," 16 October 1982, pp. 1108–1111.
40. *Aviation Week & Space Technology*, "Israel to Boost Combat Aircraft Strength," 14 February 1983, p. 17.
41. International Institute for Strategic Studies, 1980–1981, *Military Balance, Aerospace International*, December 1981/January 1982 issue, p. 62.
42. "Iraq Tank Guns Stop Missile Helicopters," *Aviation Week & Space Technology*, 24 November 1980, p. 66.
43. *Military Balance*, op. cit., p. 62.
44. "The War in the Oil Fields," *Newsweek*, 6 October 1980, pp. 28–38.
45. "Missile Survey," *Flight International*, 30 May 1981, p. 1640.
46. Iraqi losses estimated. About 80 were estimated to have been destroyed September 1980 to January 1981. "The Iran–Iraq War: The First Round," Edgar O'Ballance, *Parameters Magazine*, March 1981, pp. 54–59.
47. Cordesman, Anthony H., "Lessons of the Iran–Iraq War: The First Round," *Armed Forces Journal International*, April 1982, p. 32.

48. Cordesman, Anthony H., "Lessons of the Iran–Iraq War: Part Two, Tactics, Technology and Training," *Armed Forces Journal International*, June 1982, p. 70.

49. Owen, David Roger, "Lessons of the Iran–Iraq War," *Armada International, No. 3 1982, p. 46.*

50. Robinson, Clarence, Jr., "Iraq, Iran Acquiring Chinese–Built Fighters," *Aviation Week & Space Technology*, 11 April 1983, p. 16.

51. Ibid., p. 16.

52. "To the Shores of Tripoli," *Newsweek*, 31 August 1981, pp. 14–16.

53. Brown, David A., "Libyan Incident Spurs Deployment Shift," *Aviation Week & Space Technology*, 31 August 1981, pp. 14–21.

54. "Sixth Fleet F-14s Down Libyan Su-22s," *Aviation Week & Space Technology*, 24 August 1981, pp. 20–21.

Chapter IX

1. Fricker, John, "The Falklands Air Claims and Losses Analyzed," *Air International*, May 1983, pp. 244–245.

2. Huertas, Salvador Mafe, "South Atlantic Air War . . . The Other Side of the Coin," *Air International*, May 1983., p. 220.

3. Ibid., p. 216.

4. Braybrook, Roy, "V/STOL in the South Atlantic: Employment and Lessons," *Military Technology*, April 1983, pp. 80–81.

5. Huertas, p. 221.

6. Ibid., p. 220.

7. Fricker, p. 249.

8. Morison, Samuel L., "Falklands (Malvinas) Campaign: A Chronology," *U.S. Naval Institute Proceedings*, June 1983, p. 122.

9. Squire, Peter, Wing Comdr., "Falklands War From the Pilot's Seat, Biggest Threat: AA and Small Arms," *Astronautics & Aeronautics*, May 1983, p. 99.

10. Scheina, Dr. Robert L., "The Malvinas Campaign," *U.S. Naval Institute Proceedings*, Naval Review Issue, 1983, pp. 111–113.

11. "Lessons of the Falklands," Summary Report, February 1983, Department of the Navy, p. 19.

12. Jackson, Paul, "Strike Force South," *Air International*, April 1983, p. 170.

13. "Lessons of the Falklands," p. 19.

14. Thorn, Jim, "Falklands Interview," *Australian Aviation*, December 1982, p. 60.

15. Morison, p. 123.

16. Ethell, Jeffrey, "Flying the Pucara," *Air Progress*, May 1983, p. 41.

17. Fricker, p. 258.

18. Morison, p. 123.

19. Protto, Angel Armando, "The Electronic 'Lazarillo,'" *Aeroespacio Revista Nacional Aeronautica y Espacial.*

20. Fricker, p. 246.

21. Smith, Lt. David, "Royal Navy Operating SEA Harriers in the South Atlantic," *Naval Forces*, No. VI, Vol. III, 1982, pp. 75–76.

22. Ethell, Jeffrey, and O'Leary, Michael, "The Other Side, Argentine Air War," *Air Progress*, May 1983, p. 55.

23. "The Falklands Campaign: The Lessons," December 1982, British Government document.

24. Menaul, Air Vice Marshal Stewart W. B. (Ret.), "The Falklands Campaign: A War of Yesterday?" *Strategic Review*, Fall 1982, pp. 87–88.

25. Scheina, p. 114.

26. Walker, Paul F., "Smart Weapons in Naval Warfare," *Scientific American*, May 1983, p. 57.

27. Nutwell, Comdr. Robert M., "Postscript: The Falklands War," *U.S. Naval Institute Proceedings*, January 1983, p. 83.

28. Ethell, O'Leary, p. 55.

29. "V/STOL in the Roaring Forties," British Aerospace Publication, January 1983, p. 33.

30. Ethell, O'Leary, p. 55.

31. "Lessons of the Falklands," p. 27.

32. The Falklands Campaign: The Lessons, p. 45.

33. V/STOL in the Roaring Forties, p. 33.

34. Ibid., p. 32.

35. Cordesman, Anthony H., "The Falklands Crisis: Emerging Lessons for Power Projection and Force Planning," *Armed Forces Journal International*, September 1982, p. 34. Cordesman goes on to state that the Sea Harriers would have been unable to provide effective air defense without the highly-effective AIM-9L Sidewinder.

36. Roberts, Brad, "The Military Implications of the Falkland/Malvinas Islands Conflict," Congressional Research Service, The Library of Congress, 17 August 1982.
37. Richards, Frank, "Guided Weapons in the Falklands," *Air Pictorial,* March 1983, p. 89.
38. Gunston, Bill, *The Illustrated Encyclopedia of the World's Rockets & Missiles,* Lalamander Books, Ltd., London, 1979, p. 188.
39. "The Falklands Conflict Part 2, Missile Operations," *International Defense Review,* September 1982, p. 1154.
40. Lessons of the Falklands, p. 31.
41. Moore, Lt. Col. Brian W., "The Falklands War: The Air Defense Role," Air Defense Artillery, U.S. Army, Winter, 1983, p. 20.
42. The Falklands Campaign: The Lessons, p. 45.
43. "Rapier's Falklands Performance Praised," *Flight International,* 25 December 1982, p. 1799.
44. The Falklands Campaign: The Lessons, p. 45.
45. Ethell, Jeffrey, Price, Alfred, *Air War, South Atlantic,* Sidgwick & Jackson. London 1983, p. 225.
46. Alano, Rolando L. "St. Barbara, What a Debut," *Aeroespacio Revista Nacional Aeronautica y Espaciol,* pp. 44–55.
47. V/STOL in the Roaring Forties, p. 33.
48. Jackson, op. cit., p. 172.
49. Jackson, Paul, "Task Force Air Force," *Air International,* May 1983, pp. 228–230.

Appendix I

1. T.O. 1F-5A-1 *Manual* Section IV, p. 25.
2. Unpublished paper, *Soviet Sights,* by Lt. Col. Ross Whistler, USAFR.
3. Instructional Test, *Fire Control System, F-100,* Chapter 2/1 p. 19.
4. T.O. 1-F-100D(1)-1 *Manual* Section IV, pp. 50–53.
5. *McDonnell Digest,* September 1960, pp 12–22.
6. General Electric publicity material on M-61 and M-61A1 Vulcan Cannon.
7. LeTecke Kanony Upovalecnew Obdodi, *Czechoslovakian Military Magazine,* LTK 1978, pp. 789–90; also Soviet Aircraft Cannon, *International Defense Review,* February 1979, pp. 161–62.
8. Sparrow III *Weapons System Familiarization,* BR 10326, May 1978, Raytheon Co., Missile Systems Division.
9. *Principles of Guided Missiles and Nuclear Weapons,* Naupers 10784A, pp. 55–64.
10. Dr. Montred Held, Air Target Warheads, *International Defense Review,* May 1975, pp. 719–24.
11. Ibid.
12. Aircraft statistical data compiled from a variety of sources including *Janes's All The World Aircraft,* various issues *Combat Aircraft of the World* by John W. R. Taylor, G. P. Putnam's Sons, New York, 1969; *The Encyclopedia of the World's Combat Aircraft* by Bill Gunston, Chartwell Books, Inc., New York, 1978; *Soviet Aircraft of Today* by Nico Sgarlato, Squadron/Signal Publications, Mich. 1978; *World Military Aircraft Since 1945* by Robert Jackson, Scribners & Sons, New York, 1979.
13. Air-to-air missile information compiled from a variety of sources including *Jane's Weapons Systems* various issues; *Rockets and Missiles* by Bill Gunston, Crescent publications, New York, 1979; *Missiles of the World* by Michael J. H. Taylor and John W. R. Taylor.
14. Gun, missile antiaircraft weapon data from a variety of sources including *Jane's Weapons Systems,* various issues, and *Brassey's Artillery of the World* by Shelford Bidwell, Bonanza Books, New York, 1977.

Appendix II

1. Ferranti, *ISIS Gunsight Information Brochure.*
2. IAI "Kfir C-2" *Aviation & Marine,* October 1978, pp 51–60.
3. Wallis, A. J., "AWG-9/Phoenix Further Improvements on the Way," *International Defense Review,* 6/78, pp. 892–96.
4. *Aviation Week & Space Technology,* 29 October 1973, p. 17.
5. *F-16-1 Manual.*
6. Ibid.
7. Sundaram, G.S., "Expendables in Electronics Warfare–Proven Decoys for Survival," *International Defense Review,* 6/76, pp. 1045–50.
8. Brune, Neil, "Air Defense Suppression Expendables," *Military Electronics, Countermeasures,* August 1978, pp. 22–28.
9. "Planners Seek Effective Visual Defense," *Aviation Week & Space Technology,* 27 January 1975, pp. 88–95.

10. "Jammers Add Effectiveness, Complexity," *Aviation Week & Space Technology,* 22 January 1975, pp. 63–77.
11. Walsh, Bill, "Pods vs. Internal," *Countermeasures,* February 1976, pp. 16–34.
12. Spaino, John, "Rapport Jammer Design Criteria," *Defense Electronics,* March 1980, pp. 29–38.
13. Richardson, Douglas, "Weapons for the Black Box War," *Flight International,* 5 May 1979, pp. 1476–95.
14. Aircraft statistical data from various sources including *Jane's All The World's Aircraft* various issues; *The Encyclopedia of the World's Combat Aircraft* by Bill Gunston, Chartwell Books, New York, 1978; *Aircraft of the Soviet Union* by Bill Gunston, Osprey Publications, 1983; *Modern Air Combat* by Bill Gunston and Mike Spick, Crescent Books, New York, 1983.
15. Aircraft cannon data from several sources including *Jane's Weapons Systems* various issues; "Soviet Aircraft Cannon," *International Defense Review,* February 1979, pp. 161–162.
16. Air-to-air missile information is from several sources including *Jane's Weapons Systems* various issues; *Rockets and Missiles* by Bill Gunston, Crescent Publications, New York, 1979; "World Missile Survey," *Flight International,* 5 February 1983.
17. Gun antiaircraft weapons information from *Jane's Weapons Systems,* various issues; *Brassey's Artillery of the World,* Shelford Bidwell, Bonanza Publications, 1977, New York.
18. Missile Antiaircraft systems data from *Jane's Weapons Systems.*

Glossary

AAA	Antiaircraft artillery.
ACM	Air combat maneuvering.
AFTERBURNER	An auxiliary burner attached to the tail pipe of a jet engine for injecting fuel into the hot exhaust gases and burning it to provide extra thrust.
AIM	Air-intercept missile.
AIM-4	Falcon family of air-to-air missiles, infrared-homing and radar-guided.
AIM-9	Sidewinder air-to-air missile, infrared-homing.
AI RADAR	Airborne intercept radar carried by a fighter for finding and tracking targets.
AIRCREW	Officers and airmen who pilot or man an aircraft in the air.
ATOLL	Soviet-built air-to-air missile, similar to U.S. AIM-9 infrared-homing missile.
BALLISTIC	Unguided trajectory governed by the physics of mass, initial velocity, and gravity; a rocket or unguided missile flys a ballistic trajectory when propellant thrust is terminated.
BARCAP	Barrier combat air patrol; fighter cover between the strike force and an area of expected threat.
BINGO	Minimum fuel quantity reserve established for a given geographical point to permit aircraft to return safely to its home base, an alternate base, or an aerial refueling point.
BOGEY	Unidentified or enemy aircraft.
BREAK	An emergency turn in which maximum performance is desired instantly to destroy an attacker's tracking solution.
CAP	Combat air patrol; an aircraft patrol over an objective area, the force being protected, the critical area of a combat zone, or an air defense area to intercept and destroy hostile aircraft before they reach their target.
CBU	Cluster bomb unit.
CINCPAC	Commander-in-Chief Pacific.
CHAFF	A type of radar reflector that consists of narrow metallic strips of various lengths to create false signals on radar scopes.
DISCO	Radio call sign for EC-121 aircraft which provided airborne navigational assistance, borner warnings, and MiG warnings.
DOGFIGHT	An aerial battle, between opposing fighters, involving considerable maneuvering and violent aerobatics on both sides.
ECM	Electronic countermeasures; the prevention or reduction of effectiveness in enemy equipment and tactics used by electromagnetic radiation; some activities exploit the enemy's emissions of these radiations.
ECM pod	Pylon or fuselage-mounted container that houses multiple transmitters and associated electronic devices; a self-protection device for aircraft penetrating an electronically-controlled ground-to-air defense system.

FAN SONG	NATO designation of fire control radar associated with the SA-2 surface-to-air missile.
FARMER	NATO designation for the MiG-19.
FISHBED	NATO designation for the MiG-21.
FRESCO	NATO designation for the MiG-17.
GCI	Ground-controlled intercept.
IFF	Identification, friend or foe; an aircraft transponding beacon receiving radar information distinguishing friend from foe.
INFRARED-GUIDED MISSILE	A heat-seeking missile that homes in on the heat of an enemy fighter's jet exhaust.
IRONHAND	Nickname for a flight with special ordnance and avionics equipment, with a mission of seeking and destroying enemy surface-to-air missile sites and radar-controlled antiaircraft artillery sites.
JCS	Joint Chiefs of Staff.
JINKING	Constant maneuvering in both the horizontal and vertical planes to present a difficult target to enemy defenses by spoiling the tracking solution.
KILL	An enemy airplane shot down by military action while in flight; the pilot of the downed aircraft often is not actually killed in the process.
LINEBACKER	A series of JCS-directed U.S. Air Force strikes against targets in North Vietnam; Linebacker I began May 9, 1972, ended October 22, 1972; Linebacker II ran from December 18 to 29, 1972.
LOW BLOW	NATO designation for the fire-control radar associated with the SA-3 surface-to-air missile.
MACH	Properly, Mach's Number, after Austrian physicist Ernst Mach (1838–1916). The speed of sound, which varies with altitude and temperature. At sea level the speed of sound is nominally 762 mph, or Mach 1. Therefore, Mach 2 is twice the speed of sound, or 1,524 mph. But the figure diminishes with altitude: Mach 1 at 10,000 feet is 735 mph and is further reduced to 662 mph at 40,000 feet.
MiG	The Mikoyan/Gurevich series of Soviet jet fighter aircraft.
MiGCAP	Combat air patrol directed specifically against MiG aircraft.
MILITARY POWER	Maximum unaugmented (no afterburner) thrust of the aircraft engine.
POP-UP	A rapid climbing maneuver from low altitude or other position of concealment used to gain advantage for weapons delivery; also a maneuver used by enemy aircraft which involved a steep climb from a low altitude area of concealment to an inbound aircraft or flight of aircraft.
RED CROWN	Call sign for U.S. Navy radar-equipped ship stationed in the northern Gulf of Tonkin, which performed ground-controlled intercept functions.
RHAW	Radar homing and warning; on-board aircraft equipment to warn pilot of active enemy defenses.
ROLLING THUNDER	Nickname for JCS-directed U.S. Air Force strikes against targets in North Vietnam in 1965; began as gradual reprisals rather than hard-

hitting military campaigns, but gradually escalated into major air strikes as the war continued; phases of Rolling Thunder; Phase I, March 2—May 11, 1965; Phase II, May 18—December 24, 1965; Phase III, January 31—March 31, 1966; Phase IV, April 1—December 14, 1966; Phase V, February 14—December 24, 1967; and Phase VI, January 3—November 1, 1968.

SAM	Surface-to-air missile.
SA-2	Soviet-built radar-guided surface-to-air missile effective against aircraft at medium to high altitude.
SA-3	Soviet-built radar-guided surface-to-air missile system effective against aircraft at medium to low altitude.
SA-6	Mobile SAM system mounted on tracked vehicles. Soviet-built radar-guided surface-to-air missile system effective against aircraft at medium to low altitude.
SA-7	Soviet-built infrared-guided man-portable surface-to-air missile system.
SHRIKE	Nickname for AGM-45 air-to-ground radar-seeking missile.
SIDEWINDER	AIM-9 infrared-guided air-to-air missile.
SIX	Six (6) o'clock position or area; refers to the rear or aft area of an aircraft.
SPARROW	AIM-7 radar-guided air-to-air missile.
THUD	Nickname for the F-105 Thunderchief fighter-bomber.
THACH WEAVE	(See Weave)
WEAVE	A formation in which the two elements of a flight or the two members of an element continuously cross each other's flight path, normally in the horizonal plane, to increase visual coverage of each other's rear area.
WILD WEASEL	F-100F/F-105F aircraft equipped with RHAW and anti-radiation missiles, enabling them to home on SA-2 and antiaircraft artillery radar guidance signals and to mark their location.

Bibliography

"Air Defense Equipment In Israel," *Born In Battle* magazine, Eshel Dramit, Ltd., Issue No. 12, 1982, p. 23.

"Airscene," *Air International*, August 1979, p. 54.

"Airpower and the 1972 Spring Invasion," *USAF Southeast Asia Monogram Series*, pp. 36–44.

Alano, Rolando L., "St. Barbara, What a Debut," *Aeroespacio Revista Nacional Aeronautica y Espaciol*, pp. 44–55.

"Anything Else Is Rubbish," *USAF Fighter Weapons Review*, Summer, 1975, p. 11.

"Arab Air Power," *Air International*, June 1977, pp. 281, 291, 294; September 1977, pp. 149–150.

Armed Forces Journal International, April 1974, May 1974, pp. 20, 32.

"Artillery Come Into Its Own," *Armed Forces Journal International*, October 1973, p. 62.

Aviation Advisory Service, *MILAV News*, 1/71, NL 118/8/71, p. 15.

Aviation Week & Space Technology, 22 October 1973, pp. 15–16; 1 October 1979, p. 13.

Barker, A. J., *Six Day War*, Random House, 1974, p. 66.

Beck, M. O., "State of the Art," *USAF Fighter Weapons Review*, Winter, 1974. In 1969 F-4 Phantom IIs could accommodate AIM-9B, D, E, G Sidewinder air-to-air missiles.

"Bekaa Valley Combat," *Flight International*, 16 October 1982, pp. 1108–1111.

Berger, Carl, et al., eds. *The United States Air Force in Southeast Asia*, Office of Air Force History, Washington, D.C., 1977, pp. 34, 69, 70, 71, 74, 75, 82, 126–127.

"The Air War in the Middle East," *Born In Battle* magazine, Eshel Dramit, Ltd., 1978, p. 59, Issue No. 13, 1980, pp. 4–6, Issue No. 13, 1981, p. 11.

Bougart, Peter, "The Vulnerability of the Manned Weapon System," *International Defense Review*, June 1977, p. 11.

Briefing: Aviation & Space Writers Association, Hazor Air Force Base, Israel, 8 June 1974.

Brindley, John F., "Aircraft Profile, Mikoyan MiG-21 ("Fishbed")," *Variants*, Profile Publication Ltd., 1972, p. 89.

Brown, David A., "Libyan Incident Spurs Deployment Shift," *Aviation Week & Space Technology*, 31 August 1981, pp. 14–21.

Braybrook, Roy, "V/STOL in the South Atlantic: Employment and Lessons," *Military Technology*, April 1983, pp. 80–81.

Cagle, Malcolm, "Task Force 77 in Action Off Vietnam," *U.S. Naval Institute Proceedings*, 98, No. 831, pp. 69, 70, 72, 82.

Chaturvedi, N. S., Air Marshal, *History of the Indian Air Force*, Vikas Publishing House, New Delhi, 1978, pp. 146–147, 162.

Chopra, Pushpindar S., "Gnat," *Air International*, August 1974, pp. 74–75.

———— "Harnessing the Storm Spirit," *Air Enthusiast*, May 1973, pp. 215–222.

———— "India and the MiG-21," *Air Enthusiast*, July 1973, pp. 7, 10, 11.

———— "Indian Ocean Air Power," *Air Enthusiast*, December 1972, pp. 275–279.

———— "Journal of an Air War," *Air Enthusiast*, April 1972, pp. 172, 177, 180, 183, 206.

Churchill, Randolph S., and Winston S., *The Six Day War*, Houghton Mifflin Co., 1967, pp. 76, 91–93.

Coleman, Herbert J., "Israeli Air Force Decisive In War," *Aviation Week & Space Technology*, 3 December 1973, pp. 8, 18.

Cooper, Bert H., "Navy/Marine Corps F/A-18 Aircraft: A Survey of Major Issues," Library of Congress, 11 November 1981, p. 6.

Cordesman, Anthony H., "The Falkland Crisis: Emerging Lessons for Power Projection and Force Planning," *Armed Forces Journal International*, September 1982, p. 34.

———— "Lessons of the Iran–Iraq War: The First Round," *Armed Forces Journal International*, April 1982, p. 32.

———— "Lessons of the Iran–Iraq War: Part Two Tactics, Technology and Training," *Armed Forces Journal International*, June 1982, p. 70.

———— "The Sixth Arab–Israeli Conflict: Military Lessons for American Defense Planning," *Armed Forces Journal International*, August 1982, p. 30.

Cutler, Paul S. Lt. Gen. Rafael Eiton: "We Learned Both Tactical and Technical Lessons in Lebanon,"

Military Electronics/Countermeasures, February 1983, p. 100.

Data Compiled From: *Aces & Aerial Victories*, Office of Air Force History 1976; *Armed Forces Journal*, May 1974; *And Kill MiGs*, Squadron/Signal Publications, 1974; and *Combat Losses to MiG Aircraft In Southeast Asia 1965–1972*, Center for Naval Analysis Paper 73-0397 via Freedom of Information Act.

Drendel, Lou, *And Kill MiGs*, Squadron/Signal, Warren, Mich., 1974, pp. 29, 56.

———— *Phantom II*, Squadron/Signal, Warren, Mich., 1977, p. 46.

Dupuy, Trevor N., *Elusive Victory: The Arab–Israeli Wars 1947–1974*, Harper & Row, 1978, pp. 387, 390, 340, 549, 550, 559.

Encyclopedia of U.S. Air Force Aircraft and Missile Systems, U.S. Government Printing Office, pp. 223–261.

The Encyclopedia of the World's Combat Aircraft, William Gunston, Chartwell Books, Inc., New York, 1976, p. 217.

Ethell, Jeffrey, "Flying the Pucara," *Air Progress*, May 1983, p. 41.

———— and O'Leary, Michael, "The Other Side, Argentine Air War," *Air Progress*, May 1983, p. 55.

Facts On File, Volume XXV, No. 1297, pp. 313, 314.

The Falklands Campaign: The Lessons, December 1982, British Government Document, pp. 27, 31, 45.

The Falklands Conflict, Part 2, Missile Operations, *International Defense Review*.

Fricker, John, *Battle for Pakistan, The Air War of 1965*, Ian Allen, London, 1979. pp. 77, 94–96, 111, 150, 153, 164, 165, 185.

———— "The Falklands Air Claims and Losses Analyzed," *Air International*, May 1983, pp. 244, 245, 246, 249, 258.

———— "Post-Mortem on an Air War," *Air Enthusiast*, May 1972, pp. 150, 228, 229, 231, 232, 260.

———— "Thirty Seconds Over Sargodha," *Air Enthusiast*, June 1971, pp. 16, 18, 19.

Futrell, Frank R., *Aces and Aerial Victories*, Office of Air Force History, Washington, D.C., 1976, pp. 5–7, 12, 13, 19, 20–23, 35, 37, 39, 66, 85, 102, 106, 108, 109–110, 111–112, 113, 115, 170.

Goertz, Maj. Robert D., USAF, "An Analysis of Air-to-Air Missile Capability in Southeast Asia," *Air Command & Staff College Papers*, June 1968, pp. 1, 2, 14, 28, 41, 46, 58, 59, 70.

Goldman, Richard, and Rubenstein, Murray, *Shield of David*, Prentice Hall, Englewood Cliffs, N.J., 1978, pp. 80, 150–151.

Gunston, Bill, *The Illustrated Encyclopedia of the World's Rockets & Missiles*, Crescent Books, New York, 1979, pp. 188, 213.

Herzog, Chaim, *The Arab-Israeli Wars: War and Peace In The Middle East*, Random House, New York, 1982, p. 389.

———— *The War of Atonement*, Little Brown, 1975, p. 255.

Hewish, Mark, "World Missiles," *Flight International*, 29 May 1976, p. 1442.

Hotz, Robert, "Egypt Plans Modernized Air Arm," *Aviation Week & Space Technology*, Both Sides of the Suez, Special Issue, p. 30, 33, 36.

———— "Israeli Air Force Faces New Arab Arms," Both Sides of the Suez, Special Issue, p. 8.

———— "Offense, Defense Tested in 1973 War," *Aviation Week & Space Technology*, Both Sides of the Suez, Special Issue, p. 39–40, 42.

Huertas, Salvador Mafe, "South Atlantic Air War . . . The Other Side of the Coin," *Air International*, May 1983, pp. 216, 220, 221.

Hunt, David, "Recollections of the Canadair Sabre," *Air Enthusiast*, April 1972, p. 203.

"India-Pakistan Air War," *Flight International*, 16 December 1971, p. 991.

Institute for Strategic Studies, *Military Balance*, 1968–69, 1971–72, 1973–74.

———— *Strategic Survey*, 1972, 1973. Iraqi losses estimated. About 80 were estimated to have been destroyed September 1980–January 1981. "The Iran-Iraq War: The First Round," Edgar O'Ballance, *Parameters Magazine*, March 1981, pp. 54–59.

"Iraq Tank Guns Stop Missile Helicopters," *Aviation Week & Space Technology*, 24 November 1980, p. 66.

"Israeli Aircraft, Arab SAMs in Key Battle," *Aviation Week & Space Technology*, 11 October 1973, p. 14.

"The Israeli Air Force," *Air Force Magazine*, August 1976, p. 36.

Israeli Air Force Briefing to Aviation & Space Writers Association, Hatzor Air Force Base, Israel, 8 June 1978.

"The Israeli Air Force in the Yom Kippur War," *Israeli Ministry of Defense*, Publishing House, 1975, pp. 16, 48, 57, 80, 85, 86, 89, 95, 114.

"Israel and the Syrian SAMs," *Chicago Tribune*, 7 January 1983, p. 17.

"Israel to Boost Combat Aircraft Strength," *Aviation Week & Space Technology*, 14 February 1983, p. 17.

"Israel Preparing for the Next Round," *Air Enthusiast*, December 1971, pp. 344, 346, 347.

"Israel's Air Force, The Air War in the Mid East," *Born In Battle* magazine #2, Eshel Dramit, Ltd., Israel, p. 50.

"Israel's Pride of Lions," *Air International*, November 1976, pp. 220–221.

Jackson, Paul, "Strike Force South," *Air International*, April 1983, p. 170.

———— "Task Force Air Force," *Air International*, May 1983, pp. 228–230.

"Jane's All The World's Aircraft Supplement," *Air Force Magazine*, October 1976, p. 41.

Knaack, Marcelle S., *Encyclopedia of U.S. Air Force Aircraft and Missile Systems*, Office of Air Force History, Washington, D.C., 1978, pp. 130–131.

Kolcum, Edward, "Soviets' Shifting Middle East Balance," *Aviation Week & Space Technology*, 12 May 1970, p. 21.

———— "Viet Nam Lessons Helped Israel Build Mid East Air Supremacy," *Aviation Week & Space Technology*, 25 May 1970, p. 18.

Lacouture, Capt. J. E., (U.S. Navy, Ret.), "The Critical Importance of Electronics In Modern War," *Wings of Gold*, Winter, 1982, p. 44.

Lake, Julian S., and Hartmen, Richard V., "Air Electronic Warfare," *U.S. Naval Institute Proceedings*, October 1976, p. 48.

Lavelle, A. J. C., ed., *Air Power and the 1972 Spring Invasion*, U.S. Air Force SEA Monograph Series, Washington, D.C., 1976, pp. 1, 3, 4–9.

———— *Tale of Two Bridges and the Battle for Skies Over North Vietnam*, USAF SEA Monograph Series, Washington, D.C., pp. 122, 127, 135–137, 138.

Lewy, Gunther, *America In Vietnam*, Oxford University Press, New York, 1978, p. 412.

Manchester Guardian, 30 July 1981.

"Massive Resupply Narrows Israeli Margin," *Aviation Week & Space Technology*, 19 June 1967, p. 16.

Mayo, "Israeli Aircraft, Arab SAMs in Key Battle," *Aviation Week & Space Technology*, 11 October 1973, p. 14.

McCarthy, James R., and Allison, George B., *Linebacker II: A View From the Rock*, Robert E. Rayfield, ed., USAF SEA Monograph Series, Washington, D.C., pp. 110–111, 113–116, 121–123, 145–151, 153, 155.

McDonnell Douglas Report, "Feasability Study to Predict Combat Effectiveness for Selected Military Roles: Fighter Pilot Effectiveness,"

Menaul, Air Vice Marshal Stewart W. B. (Ret.), "The Falklands Campaign: A War of Yesterday?" *Strategic Review*, Fall, 1982, pp. 87–88.

"Middle East Market," *Flight International*, 3 March 1975, p. 420.

Military Aviation News, No. 124, February 1972, p. 102.

Miller, Barry, Electronic Warfare Special Report, *Aviation Week & Space Technology*; "Missile Survey," *Flight International*, 30 May 1981, p. 1640.

Momyer, William W., *Airpower in Three Wars*, U.S. Government Publication, pp. 90–91, 119, 130, 136, 178–179, 220.

Moore, Lt. Col. Brian W., "The Falklands War: The Air Defense Role," *Air Defense Artillery*, U.S. Army, Winter, 1983, p. 20.

Morison, Samuel L., "Falklands (Malvinas) Campaign: A Chronology," *U.S. Naval Institute Proceedings*, June 1983, pp. 122, 123.

Nadau, Safron, *From War To War: The Arab-Israeli Confrontation*, Pegasus Books, New York, 1969, p. 328.

Newsweek, 5 October 1965, p. 45.

New York Times, 8 April 1967, 6 June 1967, 14 February 1969, 2 July 1969, 9 July 1969, 26 July 1969, 12 Sepember 1969, 14 September 1969, 7 October 1969, 28 March 1970, 3 April 1970, 20 April 1970, 26 April 1970, 16 May 1970, 4 June 1970, 27 June 1970, 1 July 1970, 7 July 1970, 12 July 1970, 14 June 1972, 22 November 1972, 3 January 1973, 16 February 1973, 8 October 1973, 9 October 1973, 10 October 1973, 11 October 1973, 17 October 1973, 18 October 1973, 22 October 1973, 6 November 1973, 7 December 1973, 9 April 1974, 20 April 1974, 25 April 1974, 30 April 1974, 25 July 1977, 25 September 1979, 26 May 1981, 18 July 1981.

Nicolle, David, "The Holy Day Air War," *Air Enthusiast*, May 1974, pp. 242, 247, 248.

Nordeen, Lon, Conversations with B. Peled: Aviation & Space Writers Association Israeli Tour, 9 June 1978.

———— Conversations with IDF/AF Wing Commander, Hatzor AFB, Aviation and Space Writers Association Israeli Tour, 8 June 1978.

———— "Israel's Look to the Ground to Survive in the Air," *Astronautics and Aeronautics*, September 1978, pp. 13, 14.

Nutwell, Comdr. Robert M., "Postscript: The Falklands War," *U.S. Naval Institute Proceedings*, January 1983, p. 83.

O'Ballance, Edgar, *The Electronic War in the Middle East*, Anchor Books, Hamden, Conn., 1974, pp. 26, 27, 31, 71, 85, 87, 104, 109.

———— *The Third Arab-Israeli War*, Anchor Books, Hamden, Conn., 1970, pp. 50, 55, 56, 57, 58, 60–61, 62, 66, 70, 82.

———— *The Wars in Vietnam*, 1954–1973, Ian Allan Ltd., London, 1975, pp. 70, 74, 83, 167, 169–170, 177.

O'Connor, Michael, "Aces of The Yellow Star," *Air Combat*, Vol. 6, No. 5, 1978, pp. 20–22.

Owen, David Roger, "Lessons of the Iran-Iraq War," *Armada International*, p. 46.

"Pakistan Air Force Built Around MiG-19," *Aviation Week & Space Technology*, 2 December 1968, pp. 43, 45.

Palit, D. K., *Return to the Sinai*, Palit & Palit Publishers, New Delhi, India, 1974, p. 157.

Palmer, Dave R., *Summons of the Trumpet, U.S.-Vietnam in Perspective*, Presidio Press, San Rafael, Calif., 1978, pp. 248, 252.

Personal Interview by David Parsons with Lt. Comdr. Randall Cunningham, July 1979.

Pretty, R. T., ed., *Jane's Weapons Systems*, Franklin Watts, Inc., New York, 1977, p. 76.

Protto, Angel Armando, "The Electronic 'Lazarillo'," *Aeroespacio Revista Nacional Aeronautica y Espacial*.

Quandy, William B., *Soviet Policy in the 1973 War*, Rand Corporation Paper, RI864–178, May 1976, p. 24.

"Rapier's Falklands Performance Praised," *Flight International*, 25 December 1982, p. 1799.

Richards, Frank, "Guided Weapons in the Falklands," *Air Pictorial*, March 1983, p. 89.

Rikhye, Ravi, "Why India Won the 14-Day War," *Armed Forces Journal International*, April 1972, p. 41.

Roberts, Brad, "The Military Implications of the Falkland/Malvinas Islands Conflict," Congressional Research Service, The Library of Congress, 17 August 1982.

Robinson, Clarence, Jr., "Iraq, Iran Acquiring Chinese-Built Fighters," *Aviation Week & Space Technology*, 11 April 1983, p. 16.

———— "Surveillance Integration Pivotal in Israel Success," *Aviation Week & Space Technology*, 5 July 1982, p. 17.

St. Louis Post Dispatch, 31 December 1980, 10 May 1981.

"SAMs Down F-4C, Damage Three Others," *Aviation Week & Space Technology*, 2 August 1965, p. 27.

Scheina, Dr. Robert L., "The Malvinas Campaign," *U.S. Naval Institute Proceedings*, pp. 111–114.

Selected Readings in Tactics: The 1973 Middle East War, U.S. Army Command & General Staff College, RB 100–2, Vol. 1, pp. 5–13.

Sella, Amnon, "The Struggle for Air Superiority, October 1973–December 1975," *RUSI Journal*, May 1975, p. 31.

Senate Armed Services Committee Hearings FY 1974, 13–20 March 1973, pp. 4251–4265, 4299–4307,

4398–4407; 19 March 1973, pp. 4475–4497, FY 1975; 22–29 March 1974, p. 4837.

Shaheen, *The Battle of Air Forces: A Comparative Study of the PAF and IAF Successes In War*, p. 19.

——————— "The PAF at War," *Journal of the Pakistan Air Force*, May–August 1972, pp. 5, 6, 8, 9, 11.

——————— "An Unmatched Feat in the Air," *Journal of the Pakistan Air Force*, May–August 1972, p. 16.

Sharp, Ulysses S. Grant, *Strategy for Defeat*, Presidio Press, San Rafael, Calif., 1978, pp. 39, 42–43, 46, 47, 77, 103, 105–111, 160, 200, 204.

Shores, Christopher, *Fighter Aces*, Hamlyn Publishing Group, London, 1975, pp. 148, 165.

Singh, Pushpindar, *Aircraft of the Indian Air Force*, The English Book Store, New Delhi, pp. 114, 133, 143–144, 145, 150.

"The Six Day War," *Born In Battle* magazine, p. 21.

"Sixth Fleet F-14s Down Libyan Su-22s," *Aviation Week & Space Technology*, 24 August 1981, pp. 20–21.

Skyhawk, War Data, Eshel Dramit, Ltd., Israel, pp. 29–41.

Smith, Lt. David, "Royal Navy Operating Sea Harriers in the South Atlantic," *Naval Forces*, No. VI, Vol. III, 1982, pp. 75–76.

"Soviets Aim Sparks Arab Gains," *Aviation Week & Space Technology*, October 1973, p. 13.

Squire, Peter, Wing Comdr., "Falklands War From the Pilot's Seat, Bitterest Threat: AA and Small Arms," *Astronautics & Aeronautics*, May 1983, p. 99.

"Syrian SAMs Lacked Protection," *Flight International*, 21 August 1982, p. 404.

Tahtinen, Dale R., "The Arab-Israeli Military Balance Since October 1973," American Enterprise Institute for Public Policy Research, Washington, D.C., 1974.

"A Terrible Swift Sword," *Newsweek*, 21 June 1982, pp. 21–24.

Thorn, Jim, "Falklands Interview," *Australian Aviation*, December 1982, p. 60.

Time, 22 June 1981, pp. 24–38.

"To the Shores of Tripoli," *Newsweek*, 31 August 1981, pp. 14–16.

The U.S. Air Force Operations in Southeast Asia, U.S. Government Printing Office 1976, p. 71.

"U.S. Arms Used in Lebanon War Outstrip Soviets," *The Wall Street Journal*, 5 August 1982, p. 4.

Van Dyke, John M., *North Vietnam's Strategy for Survival*, Pacific Books, Palo Alto, Calif., 1972, pp. 58–64, 66, 80.

V/STOL in the Roaring Forties, British Aerospace Publication, January 1983, pp. 32–33.

Wakebridge, Charles, "Electrons Over Suez," *Ordnance Magazine*, May–June 1972, p. 475.

Walker, Bryce, *Fighting Jets: The Epic of Flight*, Time-Life, Alexandria, Va., 1983, p. 162.

Walker, Paul F., "Smart Weapons in Naval Warfare, *Scientific American*, May 1983, p. 57.

"The War in the Oil Fields," *Newsweek*, 6 October 1980, pp. 28–38.

"Weapons for the Black Box War," *Flight International*, 5 May 1979, p. 1476.

Weizman, Ezer, *On Eagles' Wings*, Macmillan & Co., New York, 1976, pp. 173–199.

Wetmore, Warren C., "Air Attacks by Israelis Leave Fiery Wake," *Aviation Week & Space Technology*, 10 July 1967.

——————— "Israelis' Air Punch Major Factor in War," *Aviation Week & Space Technology*, 3 July 1967, pp. 18–23.

——————— "Israelis Class MiG-21 As Efficient High Altitude Fighter," *Aviation Week & Space Technology*, 31 July 1967.

——————— "Israelis Display Soviet-Built Atoll Missile," *Aviation Week & Space Technology*, 24 July 1967, p. 65.

——————— "Israeli Mirage Pilot Describes MiG Kills," *Aviation Week & Space Technology*, pp. 76, 81, 17 July 1967.

——————— "Mock Dogfights Sharpened Israeli Pilots," *Aviation Week & Space Technology*, 3 July 1967, pp. 22, 24, 27.

Whetten, Lawrence, *The Canal War: Four Power Conflict in the Middle East*, MIT Press, 1974, pp. 216, 218.

——————— "June 1967–June 1971: Four Years of Canal War Reconsidered," *New Middle East*, June 1971, p. 26.

The Yom Kippur War, Insight Team of the London Sunday Times, Doubleday & Co., 1974, pp. 184–89.

Zaloga, Steven J., *Modern Soviet Armor*, Prentice Hall, 1979, pp. 81, 86.

Index